who knew?™

Deluxe Almanac

THE COMPLETE GUIDE TO THE BEST HOUSEHOLD TIPS, QUICK FIXES, AND MONEY-SAVING MIRACLES

*INCLUDES BONUS NEW INSTANT INTERNET SAVINGS SECTION

Bruce Lubin &
Jeanne Bossolina-Lubin

CASTLE POINT
PUBLISHING

Cover and interior design by Lynne Yeamans

Castle Point Publishing
58 Ninth Street
Hoboken, NJ 07030
www.castlepointpub.com

ISBN: 978-0-9883264-0-8

Printed and bound in the United States of America

10 9 8 7 6 5 4 3 2 1

Please visit us online at www.WhoKnewTips.com

Contents

» Introduction

When we began compiling household tips almost 20 years ago, we never dreamed how many people we would help. What started with, "Hey, did you know that eggs last longer when they're stored upside down?" turned into thousands of ways to save money, and it all took on a whole new meaning once times became tough. Who knew we would need the tips our grandmothers passed down more than ever before?

We've always said saving money doesn't have to be difficult, and we hope this book proves it. With a total of 20 chapters, more than 650 pages, and thousands upon thousands of tips, our most authoritative book of money-saving wisdom is guaranteed to save you time and money in every room in your home—and beyond.

As you'll see, it's easier than ever before to find the tips you need fast. Each chapter and the sections within it are in alphabetical order. You'll find the names of the sections inside each chapter on the bar going along the right page, so you can quickly flip through to find the section you need. Of course, you can always refer to the Table of Contents at the beginning of the book or the Index at the back. Find our favorite tips in the blue boxes that are throughout!

What else should you expect to find? Each chapter gives you tons of tips on the money-saving hot topic it covers. Our tips are designed to be easy to put into practice, use items you already have around your home, and save you time and money. Inside you'll find:

» AUTO Discover how to go longer between tune-ups, spend less time on ice and snow removal, and clean your car in under a half an hour.

» BAKING Learn the baking secrets you wish your grandmother had told you and find out how to make perfect cakes, cookies, and bread every time—even if that means a clever way to cover up a mistake.

» BEAUTY Did you know that the average American woman spends $86 a month on cosmetics? Shrink your beauty budget by 90 percent with our tips for making your make-up last longer and unique ways to create your own luxurious products at home.

» CLEANING Our most hated chore, cleaning is our favorite subject for finding tips that will save you time around the house. We tell you the cheapest and easiest ways to clean anything and everything, from your ceiling fan down to your floors.

» CLOTHING AND ACCESSORIES Take your wardrobe to the next level without spending a cent with our style tips, and save any outfit with our secrets to removing every stain in the universe. Also included are our jewelry-cleaning potions and favorite ways to polish your shoes!

» COOKING Our cooking chapter will make you find a place to wedge the *Who Knew? Deluxe Almanac* next to your kitchen cookbooks. Find out the easiest ways to cook whatever you're preparing, and the secrets to storing your food that will have them lasting well beyond their supposed expiration dates.

» DECORATING Are there some rooms in your home that could use a $0 make-over? You'll love our ideas for decorating on a budget and surprisingly simple tips about making rooms look bigger, your candles lasting longer, and every flower arrangement looking perfect.

» ENTERTAINING AND HOLIDAYS If it's party time, check out this chapter for ways to entertain without spending a fortune, and cool tips that will have your friends saying, "Who knew?" Also included are easy homemade gifts and tips for every holiday of the year.

» HEALTH AND WELLNESS Find out about the home-made remedies your grandparents used—as well as some modern-day must-haves—in this chapter, which covers everything from everyday aches and pains to colds, sunburns, first aid, weight loss tips, and more.

» HOME REPAIR Whether you barely know how to hammer a nail or your tool belt is the envy of all your friends, you'll love the simple solutions in our Home Repair chapter. With lots of quick tips for painting, it also includes quick fixes for tools, plumbing and drains, home improvement projects, and even five different ways to repair a scratch in your floor.

» KIDS Learn easy ways to save on baby supplies, entertain your kids without spending a lot, and solve everyday problems you encounter as a parent.

» MONEY Lower every bill you receive and get your biggest tax refund ever with these tricks that are so easy you won't believe them until you try them.

» ORGANIZATION Make controlling the chaos around your home a little easier with our no-nonsense advice for relieving clutter and making extra space in every room of your home.

» OUTDOORS Your garden will never look better with these simple ways to make your plants and lawn thrive. Also included are ways to make your winter easier and secrets to keeping your outdoor areas sparkling.

» PEST CONTROL Throw away the expensive bug sprays and repel pests inside and outside your home with these all-natural solutions.

» PETS No one said having a pet was easy! Check out this chapter for tips on caring for your pet and saving money on supplies, including our famous pet-hair removal methods!

» SHOPPING One of the easiest ways to save money is to spend less at the store. Find out the secrets to buying everything you own at a cheaper price, and cut your grocery budget in half with our couponing and supermarket-saving secrets.

» UTILITIES, SAVING ENERGY Kiss those expensive utility bills goodbye with our ingenious tips for saving energy around your home.

>> VACATIONS AND FAMILY ACTIVITIES Who said saving money couldn't be fun? Our hints for saving money on airfare and other vacation expenses will have you taking your least expensive vacation in years, and we'll give you some free things to do while you're there.

>> WEBSITES Find great deals and free stuff with our favorite websites, as well the best sites for making money online and other careers. We've also include government websites you should know about.

What are your favorite tips? Please join the Who Knew? community online at www.WhoKnewTips.com (or find us at Facebook.com/WhoKnewTips, Pinterest.com/WhoKnewTips, or Twitter.com/WhoKnewTips). We'd love to hear which of our tips have helped you save money, or about your own family favorites. And of course, if you have a question about anything you find inside the *Who Knew? Deluxe Almanac*, let us know! We're here to help.

Thriftily Yours,
Jeanne and Bruce

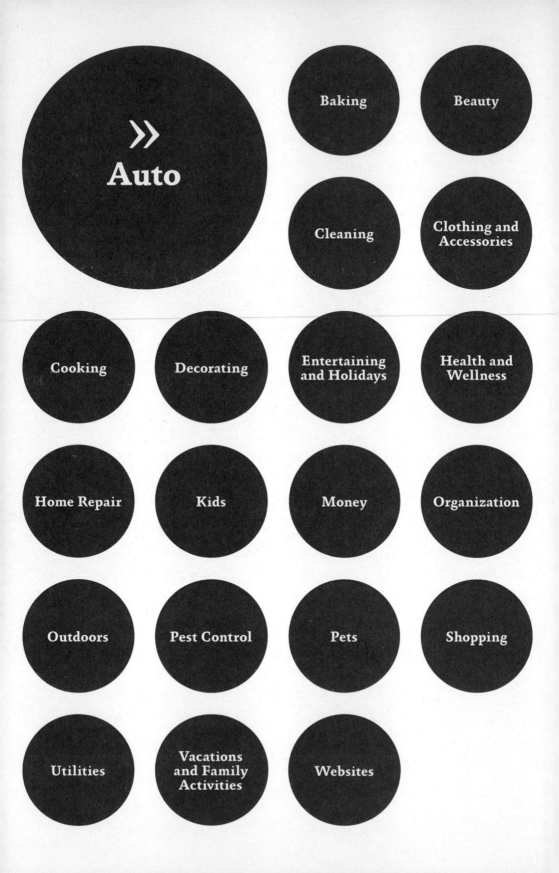

» **Auto**

Baking

Beauty

Cleaning

Clothing and Accessories

Cooking

Decorating

Entertaining and Holidays

Health and Wellness

Home Repair

Kids

Money

Organization

Outdoors

Pest Control

Pets

Shopping

Utilities

Vacations and Family Activities

Websites

» Cleaning

BODY

It's easy to remove tar from your car's exterior. Make a paste of baking soda and water, then apply it to the tar with a soft cloth. Let it dry, then rinse off with warm water.

Tree sap dripping on your car is one of the hazards of summer, but you can remove it easily with butter or margarine. Just rub the butter onto the sap with a soft cloth, and it comes right off.

After washing your car, give it a second round just like you would your head—with hair conditioner! You might think we're crazy, but applying conditioner, leaving for five minutes, and then rinsing it off will give your car a just-waxed shine. As an added bonus, it will more effectively repel water!

BUMPER

The best way to remove rust from your car's chrome bumper? Scrub the rusted area with a shiny piece of crumpled aluminum foil that has been dipped in cola.

We hate to break it to you, but John Kerry and John McCain lost their bids for the presidency. Get those old bumper stickers off and bring your car up-to-date. Rub cold cream on the stickers and wait 10 minutes. Then say goodbye to your former favorite candidate and peel the bumper stickers right off.

....

Time to get rid of an old bumper sticker? Try this: Set your blow-dryer on high and run it back and forth over the sticker until the adhesive softens. Then apply a bit of vegetable oil. Carefully lift a corner with a credit card, and peel it off.

....

You took a trip over some recently tarred roads, and now your bumper is covered in black spots. Get rid of tar with an unexpected item from your fridge— mayonnaise. Wipe on, wait five minutes, then easily wipe off both the mayo and the tar.

FRESHENING

Instead of buying a commercial freshener, repurpose a sheet of fabric softener to help sweeten the air in your car. Place sheets under the car seats, in door pockets, or in the trunk to keep your car smelling fresh.

....

There's an even better use for your car's ashtrays than spent cigarette butts. Fill them with baking soda and they'll keep your car odor-free. You won't have to resort to those annoying pine tree–shaped air fresheners. Replace the baking soda every two or three months.

GRILLE

Need a chrome polish? It's as simple as vinegar. Apply directly on chrome with a rag for a quick, simple shine.

....

Don't you hate the smashed up insects that always seem to cover your car grille in the summer? The only thing worse than looking at them is trying to scrape them off, unless you try this trick: Before screaming down the highway, use a light coating of vegetable oil or nonstick cooking spray on your grille, and the revolting bugs will wipe off easily.

INTERIOR

Got scuffs and scratches on your odometer? You can eliminate the marks on dashboard plastic by rubbing them with a bit of baby oil.

....

If your car's floor mats need to be replaced, consider going to a carpet store and finding some samples to use instead. You'll always be able to find samples that are gray or another color to match your car's interior, and best of all, they're free!

....

If you car has leather seats, regularly apply a thin layer of baby oil to the leather and let it dry. This will prevent the leather from drying out and cracking.

PREPARATION

Pricey specialty items used to clean cars are often found in big box home improvement and hardware stores. However, you'll find the same items—squee-gees, shams, and sponges—for much less in the cleaning aisle of your local grocery store.

When it's time to retire your oven mitts because they're covered in stains and burn marks, don't throw them away. Save them for use with your car. Oven mitts are great when handling hot engine parts or even as a washing mitt.

Want to know how to never have to pay for a car wash again? Make the kids do it! All you need is a bucket, a few squirts of car-washing detergent, and some sponges. Then put the kids in their swimsuits and get out the hose. Kids will love the water and suds, your car will get clean, and they'll be tired by bedtime!

TIRES

Steel-wool pads make excellent whitewall tire cleaners. It's best to use the finest steel-wool pad you can find.

To remove brake dust—that fine, black powder— from your car's tires, apply a bit of cooking spray or vegetable oil, let sit for 10 minutes, and wipe off. Then spray them again when you're done. The vegetable oil will reduce the collection of dust in the future, and you'll be able to wipe it off even more easily next time.

WINDOWS

To clean dirty windows or your car's windshield, mix a tablespoon of cornstarch with about ½ gallon of warm water, apply to the windows, and dry with a soft cloth. It's amazing how quickly the dirt is removed—and no streaking, either!

One thing that never leaves our cluttered trunk (except when we're using it) is a spray bottle filled with club soda. Club soda does wonders for getting grime, bird droppings, and bug guts off your windshield. Just spray on, wait a few minutes, and turn on the wipers.

Messy wipers are a safety hazard, and they're also pretty annoying. If your wipers are smearing the windows, wipe the blades with some rubbing alcohol.

Transparent decals may be easily removed using a solution of equal parts lukewarm water and white vinegar. Place the solution on a sponge and dampen the area thoroughly for a few minutes. If this doesn't work, saturate the decal with straight vinegar and let stand for 15 minutes.

If your windshield is covered with parking permits and inspection stickers from years gone by, you'll love this tip. Pour nail polish remover over the decals until they're soaked. Then scrape with a razor blade and they'll come off cleanly in seconds.

» Gas

FUEL EFFICIENCY

If you are waiting for longer than 30 seconds in your car, turn off the engine. You use more fuel idling after 30 seconds than you use to restart your car.

We bought a mini-van that has a luggage rack, but we find that we almost never use it unless we're on a long vacation. If that applies to you, too, then you should remove the rack until you actually need it. Driving with the rack on top increases wind drag and helps kill your gas mileage. Removing it can be a real money-saver.

—*Francesca R., Portland, OR*

Change your oil regularly and you'll have to fill up on gas less often. As oil ages, it gets thicker and harder to push through the engine, causing more energy to be used. By changing your oil regularly, you'll make sure you get the best fuel economy possible.

A clean air filter can improve your car's mileage by up to 10 percent, so make sure yours is replaced regularly. It should be changed at least every 8,000 miles, but if you live in a sandy or highly polluted area, you should change it more often. A good rule of thumb is simply to have the filter changed when you get your oil changed.

Keep your tires inflated. It's much harder for your engine to get your car to move when your tires are even a little flat. Invest in a gauge, and make sure to keep them as inflated as possible without over-inflating.

One of the easiest ways to save on gas? Stay under the speed limit. Your car will begin to lose fuel efficiency once it gets over 60 m.p.h., so go a little slower and you'll not only save, you'll be safer.

To make your car more fuel efficient, remove any excess weight from inside. Take anything heavy out of your trunk or back seat that doesn't need to be there (kids don't count). An extra 100 pounds in your car can decrease your miles per gallon by 2 percent.

When running errands, pick the best route for your fuel efficiency. Stopping and starting and going up hills will cause you to use more gas. Consider taking a route that will allow you to make fewer adjustments as you are driving, even if it takes a little longer.

Roll up your windows on the highway. Having the wind streaming through your hair might be fun, but it increases drag on the car and takes more energy to run. In this case, it's actually usually cheaper to run the AC.

To save on gas, make one long trip for all your errands rather than making several short trips. Not only will you be driving a shorter total distance, but the Department of Energy also reports that several short trips beginning from a cold start use almost twice as much energy as a single trip of the same length. In other words, keeping your engine warm means your car doesn't have to work as hard.

PAY LESS AT THE PUMP

Only 5 percent of cars actually run better on premium gas as opposed to regular. Make sure to check your owner's manual to see what it recommends.

Planning a road trip this summer? When it's time to fill up on gas, drive a little farther off the highway exit before choosing a station. The gas stations closest to the highway will often charge more per gallon than the ones located a bit off your course—you could save a few bucks by going the extra distance.

....

Before you go head to the pump, visit GasBuddy. com. Enter your zip code, and your new buddy will tell you the nearby gas stations with the lowest prices. You can also search to find the least expensive pump prices in your entire city or state. They even have cell phone apps! You'll never fill up, only to see a cheaper station on the way home, again.

....

Planning a road trip? Find out exactly how much you need to budget for gas money at FuelCostCalculator.com. Enter the make and model of your car and your starting and destination city, and AAA will calculate how much it will cost you using the Environmental Protection Agency's fuel economy ratings and its own gasoline prices report. With rising gas prices and fluctuating airfare, this is a great site to visit if you're not sure taking the car will save you money.

» Insurance

Looking for Car Insurance tips? *See* **Money chapter, Insurance**

» Maintenance

BATTERY

Epsom salts can extend the life of your car battery. Just dissolve an ounce of Epsom salts in 1½ cups warm, distilled water and fill each battery cell.

....

The corrosion around your car battery terminals can be cleaned easily with a thick solution of baking soda and water. Let it stand for 10–15 minutes before washing it off. Baking soda is a mild alkali and will neutralize the weak acid on the terminals.

....

Keeping your battery in working order by making sure corrosion doesn't build up on its terminals. Luckily, this is easy: Just pour a can of cola over the battery terminals; let it sit for a half hour, then wipe clean.

....

To prevent your car's battery from corroding, wipe down the battery posts with petroleum jelly once every couple of months.

FUEL INJECTION

You should always fill up your gas tank before it dips below a quarter of a tank. Having a sufficient amount of fuel will ensure your car's fuel injection system stays healthy.

GARAGE

If you have as much stuff stacked up in your garage as we do, you'll love this tip for making sure you don't run into it when you pull in. First, drill a hole through the middle of a tennis ball, then run a long piece of clothesline through it and knot the end so it won't pull through. Safely and successfully park your car in its ideal garage location, then tie the other end of the clothesline to the rafters of your garage so that the ball is hitting your windshield. Next time you pull in, you'll know to stop when the ball hits your windshield. No more having to slowly inch your way in!

—Bill B., Davenport, IA

If your car has leaked oil onto the floor of your garage, easily clean it up by applying some cat litter to the area (preferably the non-scoopable kind). Its super-absorbing properties will make the stain disappear in a day.

KEYS

Duct tape a spare key to the undercarriage of your car or in a wheel well and you'll never get locked out again. Make sure to do it in a location other than near the driver's door, where thieves may check.

When your car's keyless remote needs a new battery, don't head to the dealership for a replacement—depending on the kind of car you have, it can cost anywhere from $50 to $150. Instead, pry open your remote and check the size and type of battery you need. Then head to a hardware or electronics store for a much-cheaper alternative.

» Purchasing

Looking for Car Buying tips? *See* **Shopping chapter, Auto**

» Repair

BATTERY

If your car battery has died and you don't have jumper cables, don't get a headache just yet. First, try dropping a couple of aspirin tablets into the battery. The acid in the aspirin can provide it with just enough charge to get you to the nearest service station.

MECHANICS

A mechanic friend (who shall remain nameless!) once confessed to us that he does his worst work on Fridays, because he tends to rush the job to get ready for the weekend. If it can wait, take your car in on Monday, when it will get the time it deserves.

Sometimes unethical mechanics will use cheap or knockoff parts—they're a lot more prevalent than you might think—and try to pass them off as the real thing. Whenever you're having parts replaced, make sure to insist on a brand-name part and ask to see the box it came in as proof.

If you're not an automotive expert, you should be aware that small metal shavings in a transmission pan are a perfectly normal sign of usage. If a garage shows you a pan like this and uses it to pressure you into a new transmission, walk away. They're likely not being honest with you.

—JD Morse

Did you know that by law, emissions controls for your vehicle have an eight-year/80,000-mile warranty? When purchasing new parts for your car, check with the manufacturer to make sure you can't get them for free first.

When visiting a mechanic to have a part replaced, always ask for the worn or damaged part back. This way, you'll be sure it was actually replaced and that you're not getting a bum deal.

MOTORCYCLES

> **If your motorcycle is too loud (yes, there is such a thing), stick a number-3 grade steel wool pad into the muffler.**
>
> —*Jason Selway, Blacksburg, WV*

UPHOLSTERY

Oh no, your kids tore a hole in your car's seat. (OK, so it wasn't the kids, it was you.) Instead of getting an expensive upholstery replacement, use an iron-on patch instead. Hold the patch in place with a few straight pins while you iron. If you don't have a long enough extension cord to bring the iron into your car, set the iron on one setting higher than the directions on the patch recommend. When it heats up, unplug it and quickly bring it out to the car.

WINDOWS

If the seal around your car window is leaking air, making an annoying sound as you drive, patch it up with duct tape until you have the time (and money) to take it to the shop.

Never, ever ignore a chip in your windshield—get it fixed right away. A chip will often eventually grow into a crack, which will raise your costs from about $100 for a chip repair to $1,000 or more for a full windshield replacement.

» Winter Weather

FROZEN DOORS

It's hard enough having to dig out your driveway and scrape off your car after a snowstorm. Save yourself the trouble of worrying about car doors freezing closed by spraying WD-40 in the lining. Once in the beginning of the winter should do it.

If your car doors freeze shut during the frigid winter months, try this preventative measure: Rub vegetable oil on the rubber moldings around your doors. Since it's the rubber, not the metal, in your doors that freezes, lubing it with oil should do the trick.

To keep your car's door locks safe from ice during the cold winter months, place a refrigerator magnet over the lock. You can even take an old magnet (that 2008 calendar from a local realtor, perhaps) and cut it into pieces that fit perfectly.

STUCK TIRES

Before winter hits, fill a few old milk jugs with sand or kitty litter and keep them in your car's trunk. If you get stuck, sprinkle the sand on the ice to improve the tires' traction.

If your car gets stuck in an icy patch and your wheels aren't getting any traction, help free it by using your car's floor mats. Take them out and place under the tires, then drive to a safe place, retrieve the mats, and be on your way.

....

Stuck in the snow (or mud) with no way to dig yourself out? A shovel may be closer than you think. Just remove your hubcap and use it instead.

WINDOWS

If you have to leave your car outside overnight in the winter, you can still keep your windshields ice- and frost-free. Mix three parts vinegar to one part water and coat the windows with this solution. (Never pour hot water on your windshield. The glass may expand from the heat and then contract as it cools, causing the windshield to crack.)

....

If you park your car outside during winter, you can save yourself scraping and wiping time each morning by wrapping your side mirrors and windshield wipers in old plastic bags.

....

When the forecast calls for ice or snow, protect your car by placing two old bath towels across your windshield. When it's time to drive, simply pull off the towels and you're ready to go!

....

Auto

Beauty

»

Baking

Cleaning

Clothing and
Accessories

Cooking

Decorating

Entertaining
and Holidays

Health and
Wellness

Home Repair

Kids

Money

Organization

Outdoors

Pest Control

Pets

Shopping

Utilities

Vacations
and Family
Activities

Websites

» Basics

BAKING TEMPERATURE

Every time you open the oven to check on your baking goodies, you lower the temperature inside by about 50°. Open the door only when you have to; otherwise, use the oven light and look through the window!

....

If you suspect your oven's temperature doesn't match what's on the dial but you don't have an oven thermometer, try this simple test. Put a tablespoon of flour on a baking sheet and place it in a preheated oven for five minutes. If the flour turns light tan, the temperature is 250–325°. If the flour turns golden brown, the oven is 325–400°. If it turns dark brown, the oven is 400–450°. And an almost a black color means the oven is 450–525°. Figure out the disparity between what the temperature really is and what it reads, and make sure to set your oven accordingly in the future.

DRY GOODS

When baking cakes and cookies, you should always start with room temperature ingredients, never cold ones. For pastry it is just the opposite—the ingredients should be cold.

....

Did you know baking powder loses potency over time? If you can't remember when you bought yours, run a test before using it. Here's how: Put ½ teaspoon baking powder in a small bowl, then pour in ¼ cup of hot tap water. The more vigorously the baking powder bubbles, the fresher it is. (Try this test on a fresh box of baking powder so you know what to look for.) Also, when buying baking powder, be sure to check the expiration date on the box. Once opened, it will remain fresh for about a year.

> If you're not sure how old your baking soda is, test its activity level. Stir ¼ teaspoon baking soda into about 2 teaspoons of white vinegar. If it doesn't bubble vigorously, throw it out.

Not sure whether the flour in your canister is self-rising or all-purpose? Taste it. Self-rising flour is a bit salty because it contains baking powder.

Is your yeast too old? Proof it to be sure it's not ready for retirement. Dissolve a little sugar in some warm water, then sprinkle in the yeast. The mixture should begin bubbling within 5–7 minutes. If it doesn't, the yeast is too inactive to provide the leavening function, and you should throw it away.

MARSHMALLOWS

If you find an old bag of hardened marshmallows, add a slice of very fresh white bread or half an apple to the bag to soften them. Note that this is not a quick fix: You might need to leave the bag for one or two days until the marshmallows absorb the moisture.

....

Rock-hard marshmallows don't have to be thrown out. You can soften them up in a resealable plastic bag placed on top of warm water. Now go get that grill fired up!

....

In case you've always wondered where to store marshmallows, the answer is the freezer! To get them apart, just cut them with scissors dipped in very hot water.

....

It's time for s'mores, but when you take the marshmallows out of the cupboard, they're all stuck together. Separate them by adding a bit of cornstarch to the bag, then shaking vigorously. The cornstarch will absorb the moisture that's acting like glue, and they will break apart.

NUTS

The easiest way to shell pecans, walnuts, and other nuts? Freeze them first. This shrinks the nut away from the shell and makes the job a breeze. Another easy way to shell nuts is to soak them in boiling water for 15 minutes.

....

Chopping nuts in a blender? Try adding a small amount of sugar, which will keep the nut pieces from sticking together.

....

The quickest way to "chop" nuts is to place them in a sealed plastic bag, then roll over them with a rolling pin. This is also a clean, easy way to break up graham crackers or vanilla wafers to make a pie crust.

PANS

Recipes for baked goods often call for greased and floured pans, which usually involves oiling down the pan, then sprinkling flour inside and shaking until it's equally distributed. However, professional bakers generally don't use this method, which can leave flour on your baked goods or make them cook unevenly. Instead, they mix up a batch of "baker's magic," and now you can too. Mix ½ cup room temperature vegetable shortening, ½ cup vegetable oil, and ½ cup all-purpose flour. Blend the mixture well and use it to grease pans. You can refrigerate it in an airtight container for up to six months.

....

When you finish a stick of butter, don't throw away the paper wrapper. Instead, fold it in half and store it in a plastic bag. Next time you need to butter a bowl or pan, use this paper—it's easy and neat!

....

When you need to grease a baking pan, use vegetable shortening if you have it on hand. Butter has a low smoke point and burns easily, and salted butter can cause food to stick to the pan.

....

Hate that white, dusty look on your cakes after you've floured the edges of your cake pan before baking? Make it a thing of the past. Reserve a small amount of cake mix, then use that to "flour" your pans. The cake will absorb the mix, and you won't have a white mess on the outside when the cake is done.

....

Making cupcakes or muffins but don't have enough batter to fill the tin? Before sticking the pan in the oven, fill the empty cups halfway with water. This will extend the life of the tin and ensure the muffins bake evenly.

....

To easily remove muffins or rolls from a pan, set the pan on a damp kitchen towel for about 30 seconds. Repeat using a freshly moistened towel until the muffins can be eased out of the pan. Just make sure not to use your nicest towels—you can sometimes get slight scorch marks or fabric sticking.

....

Baked goods and casseroles should always be cooked at the temperature directed in the recipe, with one notable exception: If you are using a glass baking dish, reduce the specified oven temperature by 25°. Glass heats more slowly than metal, but it retains heat well; failing to lower the temperature can result in burned bottoms.

SUGAR

Here's a neat tip for those who do a lot of baking:
Fill a saltshaker with confectioners' or colored sugar for
dusting candy, cakes, and cookies. For the best results,
choose one with large holes.

If you find that the contents of your brown sugar
box have become one giant lump, wrap the box in a
ball of foil and bake in a 350° oven for five minutes.
It will be back to its old self in no time.

**Brown sugar loses moisture rather quickly and
develops lumps easily.** To soften hardened sugar, put
it in the microwave with a slice of fresh white bread or
half an apple, cover the dish tightly, and heat for 15–20
seconds; let it stand five minutes before using. The moisture from the bread or apple will produce enough steam
to soften the sugar without melting it.

Granulated sugar clumps less than brown sugar,
but it's still prone to getting lumpy. Keep this from happening by sticking a few salt-free crackers in the canister
to absorb the moisture. Replace the crackers every week.

TOPPINGS

Whipping up some cream? Heavy cream will set up faster if you add seven drops of lemon juice to each pint of cream. But you don't necessarily need heavy cream if you're making whipped cream. Light cream can be whipped to a firm, mousse-like consistency if you add 1 tablespoon unflavored gelatin dissolved in 1 tablespoon hot water for every 2 cups of cream. After whipping, refrigerate it for two hours.

Feel like going the extra mile? Grate some lemon peel and mix it with sugar in a food processor for some delicious "lemon sugar," which is perfect for the tops of cookies and other desserts, as well as the rims of cocktail glasses!

Adding a chocolate design to cakes, brownies, and other confections gives them a sophisticated touch your friends are sure to appreciate. An easy way to decorate with chocolate is to place old candy, unwrapped, in a plastic sandwich bag. Microwave for 30 seconds at a time, turning until melted. Then snip off the corner and use like a pastry bag to write words and create embellishments.

» Bread

BISCUITS

For supersoft biscuits, brush them with milk or melted unsalted butter before baking, then arrange them in a cake pan so the sides touch one another.

....

The quickest way to reheat biscuits or rolls? Sprinkle them lightly with water and wrap them in foil, then bake for five minutes in a preheated 350° oven.

....

Having a dinner party? Here's a great tip for keeping dinner rolls warm long after they've come out of the oven. When you put the rolls in the oven to bake, add a ceramic tile too. By the time the rolls are done, the tile will be (very!) hot. Place it in the basket and put your rolls on top; the tile will keep them warm. You can also use aluminum foil instead of the tile, but it won't retain the heat as long.

CRUST

We love this secret to a perfect, crispy crust, which a baker friend passed along: Put some ice cubes in a shallow pan and place in the oven with your loaf of bread. This will produce a dense steam, and as the water evaporates, the crust becomes hard and crispy. The steam also will allow the bread to rise more evenly, giving you a firm and chewy inside.

DOUGH

Whole-wheat flour absorbs water at a slower rate than other types of flour do. If you make bread with 100 percent whole-wheat flour, it will be moister if you add the flour to the water slowly and mix gently. Reserve ¼ cup of flour and knead in a tablespoon or so at a time as needed.

Want a hint of garlic without a too-garlicky taste? You can make a lightly scented garlic bread by adding 1 teaspoon garlic powder to the flour when you're making white bread.

Did you know you can freeze bread dough for later use? Let it rise once, then punch it down, wrap well, and freeze. Don't forget to label it!

Plastic wrap is perfect for covering bowls of rising dough, but if you leave the room for too long the dough will push the wrap right off, leaving it susceptible to germs and bacteria in the open air. Solve this problem by switching out the plastic wrap for a plastic shower cap—the elastic will fit perfectly over your bowl, and the plastic will stretch enough to allow for expansion.

A coffee can is the perfect container for so much more than coffee. You can also bake dough in one! Use it like you would a loaf pan, making sure to grease it first and fill only halfway if you're making bread with yeast in it.

It's not always a good idea to artificially cut the amount of time it takes your bread dough to rise (the flavor of the bread may not be as full), but if you're in a time crunch, it's nice to have a backup plan. To speed whole-wheat bread dough's rising time, add 1 tablespoon lemon juice to the dough as you are mixing it. For other breads, a little heat does wonders when it comes to cutting down on rising time. Set the dough (either in a bowl or a loaf pan) on a heating pad set on medium, or over the pilot light on a gas stove. You can also use the microwave to help speed the rising process by as much as one third. Set ½ cup hot water in the back corner of the microwave. Place the dough in a well-greased microwavable bowl and cover it with plastic wrap, then cover the plastic wrap with a damp towel. With the power level set at 10 percent, cook the dough for 6 minutes, and then let it rest for 4–5 minutes. Repeat the procedure if the dough has not doubled its size.

STALE

Bread gone stale? Simply wet your fingers and flick some water on the top and sides of the loaf. Then wrap in foil and heat in a preheated 250° oven for 10 minutes. It will taste fresh again!

....

If you really want to impress your dinner guests, make some homemade croutons for your salad. After cutting your leftover bread into cubes, fry in olive oil and a little garlic powder (not garlic salt), a pinch of Parmesan cheese, and parsley. Fry until they're brown, then let cool on paper towels. You can also cut the bread into smaller pieces, then chop in a blender or food processor to make bread crumbs (you may have to cut off the bottom crust first).

STORAGE

Looking for Bread Storage tips? *See* **Cooking chapter, Long-Lasting Food Tips**

» Cakes

BATTER

Remember the line from the nursery rhyme? "Bake me a cake as fast as you can." Those premade mixes from a box are so easy, but you can recreate the effect *and* maintain bragging rights to a homemade dessert. Measure things out a few days before you plan to bake. Store the mixes in Ziploc bags (for dry) and plastic containers (for wet), and refrigerate wet ingredients. Eggs should be added the day of. We find this trick especially great for holiday bake-offs, when we like to give tins of various cookies to neighbors and friends.

When baking a cake, try substituting two egg yolks for one whole egg. The cake will be very rich and dense, because the yolks don't hold as much air as the whites. This isn't exactly a healthy tip, but it sure tastes good!

We all know homemade cakes should not double as free weights, but what's the secret to keeping them light? A dash or two of lemon juice added to the butter and sugar mixture. That's it!

For a light, moist cake, enhance your cake flour by adding 2 tablespoons cornstarch to every cup of cake flour, then sifting them together before you add to the mix. You may be surprised by the results!

Make sure you get rid of any bubbles in your cake batter before baking. Simply hold the pan an inch or two above the counter and tap it two or three times to release any air pockets. Just be careful of your clothes, as it might spatter.

Unfortunately, part of baking is always trial and error. If your cakes "dome" when baked, one of these common mishaps may be to blame: the oven temperature was too high, your pan was too small, or the balance of liquid, egg, flour, and fat was off. Time for a new trial!

DECORATING

If you're about to show off your cake prowess by cutting up baked cakes and reassembling them in an impressing configuration, try freezing the cake first. Fresh cakes, especially those made from a mix, often crumble easily, but freezing will help your knife glide right through. Freezing detracts very little from the taste of your cake—as long as you don't frost it first.

A heart-shaped cake is easier to make than you might think. Simply divide your cake batter between one round pan and one square one. When the cakes are cool, cut the round cake in half. Turn the square cake so it looks like a diamond and set the half-rounds on the two top sides. Voilà!

Here's a great bakers' trick to make it easier to decorate the top of a cake: With a toothpick, trace the pattern, picture, or lettering before you pipe the icing. This guide will help you make fewer mistakes.

If you find icing too sweet or too rich, try this cake topping: Set a paper lace doily on the cake, then dust lightly with confectioners' sugar. Carefully lift the doily off the cake, and admire the beautiful design left behind. You can also try colored confectioners' sugar or a mixture of confectioners' sugar and cocoa powder.

ICING

Prevent flaking and cracking when making cake frosting by adding a pinch of baking soda when mixing it together.

To keep icing from hardening, just add a very small amount of white vinegar after it is whipped. You can also add a pinch of baking soda to the confectioners' sugar. This will help the icing retain some moisture, and it won't dry out as fast.

If you're making your own chocolate icing, can we come over? Also, be sure to add a teaspoon of unsalted butter to the chocolate while it is melting to improve its consistency.

....

Making a birthday cake at home is a great way to save at the bakery, but if you're not a cake-decorating genius, it never looks as good as store-bought! To give the icing on top of your cake the silky look of a profession-ally made one, ice it as usual and then blow a hair dryer over the top for a minute (yes, a hair dryer!). It will melt the icing slightly, giving it the shiny appearance you're looking for.

....

If you're having a problem keeping a layer cake together when you're icing it, stick a few bamboo skewers into the cake through both layers; remove them as you're frosting the top.

....

If you sprinkle a very thin layer of cornstarch on top of a cake before you ice it, the icing won't run down the sides.

....

You may not have time to make your own frost-ing, but you can blend store-bought frosting with a hand mixer to double the volume. This simple little trick saves money and calories!

SLICING

To keep the frosting from sticking to your knife as you cut the cake, dip your knife into a glass of hot water between each cut. It will also keep cake crumbling to a minimum.

If you've got a delicate cake that will fall apart and stick to the knife when you cut it, use dental floss—yes, dental floss—to slice it. Hold the floss tight and give it a slight sawing motion as you move it down to cut through the cake.

Your beautiful cake is perfect except for one thing—you can't get it out of the pan! Lay out a sheet of wax paper and gently turn the whole thing over. Next, put a dish towel over the pan and press it with a hot steam iron. After a few minutes the pan should be ready for liftoff.

The bad news is that your cake is stuck to the pan. The good news is that it's easy to get it out intact—you just need to heat up the bottom of the pan by submerging it in hot water. Once the pan heats back up, use a knife to easily dislodge your still-perfect cake.

STORAGE

If you need to store a cake more than a day or two, put half an apple in the container. It will provide just enough moisture to keep the cake from drying out too soon.

If you have leftover cake, you have more self-control than we do! One of the best methods of keeping the insides of a cake from drying out is to place a piece of fresh white bread next to the exposed surface. The bread can be affixed with a toothpick or a short piece of spaghetti.

Want to freeze a cake, but don't want the frosting to stick to the plastic wrap? First, put the cake in the freezer without any wrapping. Once the frosting is frozen, cover the cake with plastic wrap. The cold frosting won't stick to the wrap.

Does your cake stick to the plate? Sprinkle a thin layer of sugar on a plate before you set a cake on it. This keeps the cake from sticking, and makes the bottom delightfully crunchy.

TRANSPORTATION

Here's a new twist on transporting frosted cakes. Don't just insert toothpicks and cover in plastic—the sharp ends can puncture the wrap and create a gooey mess. Instead, attach miniature marshmallows to the toothpicks before covering. You can also use strands of spaghetti instead of toothpicks.

» Cookies

BURNING, PREVENTING

If you don't have an insulated or a thick baking sheet, here's a simple solution: Try baking the cookies on two sheets stacked one on top of the other. This will eliminate burned bottoms caused by a too-thin pan.

If you've ever burned the bottoms of your cookies when baking a number of batches, the baking sheets may be to blame. When you start with a too-hot surface, the cookies may burn. Let the baking sheets cool between batches; 2–3 minutes is usually long enough. Or you can line the baking sheets with parchment paper. When the cookies are done, simply lift them, still on the parchment, onto the cooling rack.

Cookies can go from "just right" to burned in no time. To reduce the chances of this happening, take the cookies out of the oven when they are not quite done, but don't transfer them to the cooling rack right away— let them sit on the hot pan for a minute or two to finish baking. Once you transfer them to the rack, be sure to let them fully cool before you store them; otherwise, they may become soggy.

You're covered with flour, have no idea where the kitchen table used to be, and just are about to pull your fifth blisteringly hot tray of cookies out of the oven when you realize you're out of cooling racks. Don't panic! Simply line up a bunch of butter knives in alternating directions (first with the blade toward you, then with the blade away from you), and put the baking sheet on top of them.

If you're baking cookies or pies and don't have a cooling rack, just use cardboard egg cartons. Flip over the cartons (you'll need two, spaced a little bit apart) and set the baking pan on top.

Are your cookies stuck to the baking sheet? Work some dental floss between each cookie and the sheet, and you should be able to remove them easily.

Want to know the secret to perfectly cut bar cookies? As soon as you remove your sweet creation from the oven, make a ¼-inch incision with a knife and outline your bars. Then once they've cooled, cut all the way. This will ensure that the edges of your cookies are as smooth as can be.

DOUGH

If you're having trouble rolling out cookie dough, it may be too warm; cold dough will not stick to the rolling pin. Refrigerate it for 20 minutes for the best results.

You're making cookies or another baked good, but forgot to soften the butter. Instead of the trial-and-error involved in attempting to soften (but not melt) butter in the microwave, zap the sugar instead. Mixing butter with warm sugar will soften it in a second.

—*Lindsay Herman, Cambridge, MA*

....

Our favorite part of oatmeal cookies, is—naturally—the oatmeal! Boost oatmeal flavor by toasting it lightly before adding it to the batter. Simply sprinkle the oatmeal on a baking sheet and heat it in a 300° oven for about 10 minutes. The oats should turn a golden-brown.

....

Is your cookie dough sticking to everything? It's easy to get a spoonful of cookie dough to drop onto your baking sheet if you first dip the spoon in milk.

....

Dye your cookie dough, not your hands, by dropping food coloring into a bag with the dough. Knead a bit and roll around to even out the color. You can use right away or keep in the freezer. Either way, you'll have fun, colorful cookies, and save lots of hand-cleaning time.

....

To get a sharp edge on your shaped cookies, dip the cutter in flour or warm oil occasionally during the cutting.

TEXTURE

If crisp cookies are what you're after, be sure your cookie jar has a loose-fitting lid. This allows air to circulate and evaporates any moisture.

....

To keep your cookies tasting chewy, add a half an apple or a slice of white bread to the cookie jar. This will provide just enough moisture to keep the cookies from becoming hard.

....

If your cookies typically don't brown enough, bake them on a higher rack in the oven. Other tricks are substituting a tablespoon or two of corn syrup for the sugar, using egg for the liquid, and using unbleached or bread flour in the recipe.

» Other Desserts

FROZEN TREATS

You'll never buy a box of popsicles again after you learn this easy recipe for the homemade variety. Simply pour juice into wax paper cups, then add a small plastic spoon or tongue depressor to the middle once they are half frozen. When they're completely solid, peel away the cup for an icy treat.

....

A great and healthy summer treat for kids is to cut a banana in half horizontally, put a popsicle stick in the flat end, dip it in some melted chocolate or sundae topping, and freeze it for a few hours on wax paper. Your kids will love you for these banana treats! (At least for a little while.)

One of our kid's groups sells frozen cheesecakes as a fundraiser, so we always end up with several cheesecakes in our freezer each year! If you're eating a frozen cheesecake, thaw it in the refrigerator instead of at room temperature—even though it might take a little longer, it will be much creamier.

GELATIN

If you've ever had a Jell-O salad melt at a picnic, you'll love this tip. When you add the water to any gelatin recipe in hot summer months, mix in a teaspoon of white vinegar to keep salads and desserts firm.

ICE CREAM

It's always disappointing when you remember you have one last bit of ice cream in the freezer, only to open it and find it's covered in ice crystals. To keep this from happening, simply store your ice cream container upside-down.

—*Liz Hobkirk, Waddington, NY*

Keep your ice cream cones leak-free with this simple tip: Place a miniature marshmallow or chocolate kiss in the bottom of the cone before adding the ice cream. Either can help prevent the tip of the cone from leaking—and you'll get a delicious treat at the end of the cone!

··

Here's a fun and unique way to serve ice cream next to cake. Buy a pint-sized container of your favorite ice cream, then slice right through it (cardboard and all) with a serrated knife, making ice cream "rounds" that are about 1-inch thick. Peel off the remaining cardboard, then use cookie cutters to make various shapes. Store them in your freezer between pieces of parchment paper until you're ready to serve. And if you don't use the entire pint, the top will still sit flush against your "short stack" to keep it fresh for later.

PIE

Next time you make a pie, add a little flavor to the crust by sprinkling a little ground spice or minced herbs into the flour. Use cinnamon or ginger with an apple or other dessert pie, and try finely chopped parsley with a quiche or meat pie.

··

Even if your pie's filling is near perfection, you won't win any accolades unless the crust is nice and flaky. Be sure that any liquid added to your pie crust is ice cold. In fact, anything hot that's involved with your crust will affect it—even your kitchen and equipment should be on the cool side.

··

Want to know the secret to a flaky pie crust?
We'll give you two: Add a teaspoon of vinegar to the
water, or substitute sour cream or whipping cream for
all of the water.

**You'll impress even Martha Stewart with this pie
crust tip.** After you've crimped the crust, but before you
place your work of art in the oven, go around the edge
again, this time carefully lifting the crust ever-so-slightly
from the dish so it won't stick while baking. When you
serve pieces "just like Grandma made," they'll come out in
one clean swoop rather than with insides slopped on the
plate followed by hacked-up pieces of crust.

Keep your pie crusts from getting too brown
by covering the edges of your pie with strips of
aluminum foil.

Do you want your pies to glisten like those in the
bakery? It's easy: Just beat an egg white and brush
it over the crust before baking. This works especially well for a pie that has a crust cover, like apple.

**Pies with graham cracker crusts can be difficult
to remove from the pan.** However, if you dip the bottom of the pan in warm water for 10 seconds, the pie will
come right out without any damage.

Spray a small amount of vegetable oil on your knife before cutting a pie with a cream filling. This will stop the filling from sticking to the knife.

For a unique pumpkin pie, put small marshmallows on the bottom of the pie, just above the crust. As the pie bakes, the air in the marshmallows expands and the marshmallows rise to the top.

It's always disappointing when you slice into your carefully prepared pie only to find that the bottom is soggy. If you have a problem with fruit or fruit juices soaking your pie crust and making it too wet, brush the bottom with egg white before adding the filling. This will seal the crust and solve the problem. If your fruit filling is simply too wet, thicken it up. The best thickener is 3–4 tablespoons of minute tapioca: Mix it with the sugar before adding to the fruit. Other solutions for soggy pie bottoms include prebaking the pie crust, partially cooking the filling, or brushing the crust with jelly before you fill it. When using a cream filling in a pie, sprinkle the crust with granulated sugar before adding to prevent a soggy crust.

When making a meringue, add ¼ teaspoon white vinegar for every three egg whites and watch it really fluff up.

Auto

Baking

>> **Beauty**

Cleaning

Clothing and Accessories

Cooking

Decorating

Entertaining and Holidays

Health and Wellness

Home Repair

Kids

Money

Organization

Outdoors

Pest Control

Pets

Shopping

Utilities

Vacations and Family Activities

Websites

» Bath and Shower

BATHS

You don't need expensive bath gels to get a luxurious spa tub. To make your own bubble bath, use a vegetable peeler on a sturdy bar of soap, then place the slivers in a mesh drawstring bag. Attach the bag to the tap while the water is running.

For an inexpensive, luxuriously fragrant bath oil, combine sunflower oil with crushed lavender or rose petals (or both). Let the mixture stand for a few days before using it.

You can literally bathe in your favorite perfume by making your own scented bath oil. Just add a few drops of perfume to a quart of baby oil, shake well, and add to your bath.

Have you ever noticed that oatmeal is often a main ingredient of bath products? Guess what? You have that very same oatmeal in your kitchen! Unfortunately, it's not as easy as just throwing some into a hot bath. First, grind the oatmeal in a blender or coffee grinder to expose its inner skin-soothing qualities. Then place it in a piece of cheesecloth with a few drops of your favorite scented oil. While you're running your bath, hold it under the faucet or tie it on with a bit of string. You'll have a luxurious oatmeal bath, and even a little sachet you can use as a washcloth to help exfoliate your skin.

You've finally found a few secret minutes to have a relaxing bath! Supercharge it by adding some lemon or apple juice. They're natural exfoliants, so they'll help get rid of dry skin. They'll also make the water smell wonderful!

....

Don't spend a bundle on bath salts. Instead, make your own by combining 2 cups Epsom salts and 2 drops essential oil, which can be found online and in vitamin shops, health food stores, and some drugstores. Epsom salts are made from the mineral magnesium sulfate, which draws toxins from the body, sedates the nervous system, and relaxes tired muscles.

....

To make your own bath pillow, reuse a household item no one seems to be able to get rid of: packing peanuts! Pour them into a large resealable freezer bag, then let out some of the air and seal. Place in the bath as a soft resting place for your head.

SOAP PRODUCTS

Shower gel can get expensive, so make your own from the cheapest bar soap you can find. Use a cheese grater on two bars of soap, then add to 2½ cups warm water. Add a soothing oil of your choice (baby or almond oil work well), as well as rosewater or an essential oil like eucalyptus or marjoram. Refill an empty soap dispenser and shake. (You may need to shake each time you use it.)

—*Emma Louise Haydu*

....

Don't throw out those last few slivers of soap!
Instead, cut a slice into the side of a body sponge and slip them inside. Now lather up and rinse. You'll get so many soapsuds, you probably won't need to repeat.

For a super smoothing skin exfoliant, mix a handful of Epsom salts with a tablespoon of olive oil and rub over wet skin to cleanse, exfoliate, and soften the rough spots. Rinse off well for a polished finish. If you don't have Epsom salts, use the coarsest table salt you can find.

Instead of buying expensive sea salt and other body exfoliants, get in the habit of using a loofah or soft brush each day to slough off dead skin cells and encourage new regeneration. Rubbing with a loofah or brush will also help your circulation, which will wake you up in the morning and help your skin look smoother, as better blood flow helps disperse fatty deposits.

» Face

ACNE

Sprouting pimples like they're going out of style? Try this neat trick to clear up your face. Cut a raw potato in half and rub the flat end over your face. Leave the juice on for 20 minutes before rinsing off. The starch in the potato will help dry out your oily skin.

Dab a bit of diaper rash cream on pimples: The zinc oxide in the cream will dry up oil and kill bacteria, while the moisturizers soften up your skin beautifully.

....

If a giant pimple appears while you're at work, here's a way to make it less noticeable without applying a face mask (or diaper rash cream!) at your desk: Place an ice cube on it for 30–60 seconds, then squeeze a few eye drops onto a tissue and hold it on the spot for 3 minutes. This will cause the blood vessels below your skin to contract, making the pimple less red and easing some of the irritation.

CLEANING

Overcleaning is a major cause of sensitive skin, as it strips the skin's underlying layers of natural protective properties. Make sure you use a cleanser that's right for your skin type, and don't wash your face too often—if you notice red spots or rough patches, wash less regularly or try applying a moisturizer afterward.

....

Whether you need to wake up or freshen your skin, here's the perfect 30-second skin reviver. Place a fresh hand towel under steaming hot water (not boiling—the hottest you get out of your tap is fine), then cover your entire face with it for 30 seconds. Then use the towel or a warm, wet washcloth to buff your T-zone area (chin, nose, and forehead). For a finishing touch, splash cold water all over your face to leave your pores tight and tingling.

....

Don't be tempted to use a body scrub on the delicate skin of your face. Body scrubs contain larger, rougher granules than facial exfoliants, and they'll irritate and inflame the sensitive skin on your face.

EYEBROWS

Defining your brow line with a pencil and a little plucking is a great way to open up your face and make your eyes sparkle. But how do you know where your brows should begin and end? To determine exactly where your brow should begin, imagine a vertical line or hold a make-up pencil straight alongside one nostril. Where the pencil lands by your brow is where it should begin. To work out where the brow should end, imagine a line from the outside of your nostril to the outer corner of your eye, then extend it out to your brow.

It's happened to the best of us: You look in the mirror and notice that your eyebrows are out of control. When you're in need of a fix, a little dab of petroleum jelly—or even, in a pinch, lip gloss—can help keep curly hairs in a sleek, sophisticated line. Alternatively, a little hair spray on your eyebrow brush will help smooth them into place.

EYES, PUFFY

Puffy eyes? Soak cotton pads in a solution of ½ teaspoon salt and 1 cup hot water, then apply them to your eyes and relax. Your eyes will be less swollen in 15 minutes or less.

....

To combat puffy eyes, place slices of cucumber on them. It may seem like an old wives' tale, but cucumbers have a mild anti-inflammatory action. To make your experience even more enjoyable, keep the cucumber in the fridge until you're ready to use it. The coolness will feel wonderful on your eyelids, and the cold will help further restrict blood vessels and reduce puffiness.

....

Reduce puffy or swollen eyes with a green tea compress. Dip cotton wool into the green tea, drain off excess moisture, and dab gently around the eye area. This will help tighten the skin around the eyes.

....

Fix a puffy under-eye area by rubbing egg whites on it. As the whites dry, you'll feel the skin get tighter. Leave on for a few minutes, then rinse off with cool water. You can also try applying a few slices of potato to your eyes and leaving on for 15 minutes.

....

If all else has failed in your efforts to de-puff your eyes, try frozen spoons. Put two spoons in the freezer for five minutes, then roll them slowly back and forth over your eyes until you feel them start to warm up. Make sure your skin is completely dry before you do this, or you'll be faced with an entirely new problem.

LIPS

The best remedy for chapped lips? Buy a child's toothbrush with a really soft head, dip it in petroleum jelly, and scrub the heck out of your lips. It will get rid of rough patches while moisturizing the rest.

—*Amy Forstadt, Highland Park, IL*

Get rid of dead skin on your lips with an all-natural exfoliating rub made from ingredients in your own kitchen. Mix a drop of sesame or olive oil with brown sugar, then rub the delicious mixture gently over lips to remove flaky skin. Finish by applying petroleum jelly.

MASKS

Suffering from dry skin? This homemade face mask will give you the same results as a store-bought one, and it's easy too! Mix one egg yolk with a teaspoon of honey and a teaspoon of olive oil. Leave on your face for as long as possible, then wash off. The vitamin A in the egg yolk is great for your skin!

Face masks aren't only good for your face, they're a relaxing treat. Make girls' night even more interesting by creating your own! Mix ¼ cup brown sugar with 1½ tablespoon whole or 2 percent milk. Rub into your face, then leave on for 10 minutes. The brown sugar will exfoliate while the milk will moisturize. Tastes pretty good too!

You won't believe it till you try it, but clay cat litter is actually the exact same clay that's found in some of the most expensive face masks on the market. Find cat litter labeled "100 percent all-natural clay" and mix it with water until it gets to the consistency you want. Adding a couple of drops of scented oil will also help make it seem less like you're applying cat litter to your face. Wash off the mask off after it hardens.

This face mask is perfect for sunburned or irritated skin. Combine ¼ cup full-fat yogurt with 2 tablespoons oatmeal. Mix vigorously for one minute, then apply to your face. Leave on for at least 10 minutes, then wash off with warm water.

Forget the Botox and grab the bananas instead! You can make an all-natural (and inexpensive) moisturizing face mask that's great for oily skin. Simply mash up a few bananas into a paste, then smooth onto your face and neck. (You can also use avocados, but they're much more expensive.) Let it set for about 20 minutes, then rinse with cold water. Your skin will look and feel softer.

Drinking red wine is good for the heart because it contains antioxidants such as resveratrol, which strengthens blood vessels and prevents blood clots. But red wine is also great for your skin! Add some to any hydrating face mask and the antioxidants will lend powerful anti-aging properties to the treatment.

If you skin is looking a little sallow, whip up this two-minute face-lift: Combine 1 egg yolk and 2 teaspoons lemon juice. Rub onto your face and leave for two minutes, and it will have a tightening effect that will leave your skin feeling fresh and glowing.

MOISTURIZING

In the morning, your face can look pale and puffy because of the natural nocturnal slowdown in the body. When putting on your moisturizer, take the opportunity to gently massage all the muscles in your face to waken up the lymphatic system and jump-start the circulation.

There are no oil glands in the skin directly beneath and above the eyes, which is why the skin in these areas has a tendency to get fine lines and wrinkles. Make sure to moisturize regularly around the eye to keep your skin looking fresh and young.

How do some women get that otherworldly glow? You've tried all the bronzers and sun-kissed blush powders you can find, but can't seem to achieve radiant-looking skin. One trick that works: Apply a little bit of moisturizer *after* you put on your make-up.

TEETH

Choose your lipstick color carefully! Shades of purple or blue-based pinks can help teeth look whiter, while orangey browns will make them look yellowish.

To whiten your teeth naturally (and cheaply), mash 4–5 strawberries with ½ teaspoon baking soda. Brush onto your teeth with a toothbrush and let sit for 10–15 minutes. Then rinse out and brush your teeth as usual, making sure no strawberry seeds got caught between your teeth. Repeat this process every night and you'll start to see results in 3–4 weeks.

A great way to keep your toothbrush clean is to soak it overnight, every few weeks, in a solution of equal parts of water and baking soda. Rinse well before brushing again.

TONER

Toner is a final layer of beauty product to use after cleaning your skin. It will help you get a fresh look, reduce puffiness, and tighten your pores. To make your own all-natural version, combine a quarter of a cucumber (no need to peel) with 1½ tablespoons witch hazel and 1 tablespoon water (distilled, if you have it) in a blender. Add a little lemon juice and blend until smooth (this should take only a minute). Push through a mesh tea strainer and throw out the solids. Store the toner in the fridge, and when you're ready to use it, dab on your face with a cotton pad or ball. It can be used daily and should last a few weeks. Once you try it, you'll never go back to the store-bought kind. Enjoy!

> There's no need to spend money on facial toners and astringents. Just dab lemon juice on your face with a cotton ball to tighten your pores and prevent blemishes. Use it in the morning and the scent will also help wake you up.

WRINKLE PREVENTION

To tighten a wobbly chin area, push your lips tightly together and make a wide grimace to contract your lower facial muscles. Hold for three seconds. Repeat 20 times each day.

When you're feeling too lazy to hit the gym, work out your face instead! Doing facial exercises can keep your skin looking fresh and young. Begin with this exercise for tired eyes: Simply look up and down with your eyes closed. Then move on to massaging your temples, which not only feels nice, but also helps relieve headache tension and can help prevent wrinkles. Pulling your skin from the eyebrows outward is also a good way to ward off wrinkles. Exercise your cheeks by rubbing them in circles, chewing gum, and blowing on an instrument or into a straw.

» Feet

CALLUSES

To remove hard calluses from your feet, try this old-fashioned but effective remedy: Grind a few aspirin tablets into a paste with equal parts lemon juice and water. Apply it to the calluses, then wrap your feet in a hot towel, cover them in plastic bags, and elevate for 30 minutes. When you unwrap your feet, the calluses will be soft and ready to be rubbed off with a nail file or pumice stone.

Get rid of ugly, unwanted calluses by dabbing them with chest rub, then covering them with bandages and leaving overnight. Repeat this procedure several days in a row and your calluses will disappear. Believe or not, chest rub is also good for curing toenail fungus!

FOOT BATHS

If you find you're susceptible to athlete's foot, here's a trick to keep that nasty fungus at bay. Once or twice a week, soak your feet in a hot bath mixed in with two cloves of crushed garlic. The garlic will kill athlete's foot before it starts, and you won't be afraid to walk around in sandals. To treat a case of athlete's food that has already begun, try soaking your toes in mouthwash. It may sting a little, but the fungus will be gone in just a few days.

If you need a good soak in a foot bath, here's a soothing recipe. Pour a gallon of water into whatever container you use for foot soaking, and then add 1 cup lemon juice, 1 tablespoon olive oil, and ¼ cup milk. Mix thoroughly, stick your feet in, and relax!

FRESHENING

Smelly feet? To freshen them easily, simply rub a few slices of lemon over them. This will also help prevent athlete's foot.

....

Go natural to get rid of stinky feet! Break up a few leaves of sage and spread them around inside your shoes. They'll kill the bacteria that causes foot odor. To cut down on how much you perspire in the first place, try drinking sage tea. Herbalists say it will take several weeks, but you'll see results!

....

Keep your feet smelling fresh by sprinkling a bit of cornstarch into your shoes once or twice a week. The cornstarch will absorb moisture and odors, and you won't be afraid to slip off those uncomfortable dress shoes under your desk.

MOISTURIZING

For the softest feet you've ever had, try this before-bed routine: Rub down your feet with vegetable oil, then put on some old socks. When you wake up, the oil will be gone and your feet will be supersoft.

To rejuvenate tired feet, treat them to this home spa remedy. Massage some butter into your soles, then wrap your feet in warm, moist towels and let sit for 10 minutes. When you unwrap them they may smell a little like popcorn, but they'll feel amazingly soft.

NAILS

Here's another use for those packing peanuts you never seem to be able to get rid of. The next time you're giving yourself a pedicure, insert a peanut between each pair of toes to separate them; painting your toenails will be much easier.

If you have yellow toenails, you may have a fungus problem. Get rid of this unsightly affliction by soaking your toes in mouthwash for 10–15 minutes each evening.

» Hair

BRUSHING

If you want to strengthen your hair, make sure to brush or comb it thoroughly each night. This will increase circulation in your scalp, loosen dry skin, and help moisturize your hair with your body's natural oils.

When hair is damp or wet it is much weaker and more easily damaged. Always treat wet hair carefully, and straighten out tangles with a wide-toothed comb rather than a brush, which can create split ends.

To make brushes and combs fresh again, soak them in a mixture of 1 quart hot water and 2 tablespoons baking soda for an hour. Rinse and enjoy your like-new styling tools!

CHLORINE COLORING

If you have fair hair and you're an avid swimmer, you've probably noticed the chlorine in pools can wreak havoc on the color of your hair—often turning it green! If you want your old hair color back, just dissolve a half-dozen aspirin in a bowl of warm water and rub it into your hair. Let it sit for 20 minutes before washing it out, and your hair will be good as new. Alternatively, you can rub cider vinegar into your hair *before* jumping in the pool, which helps prevent color change.

Ever heard the one about blond hair turning green in a swimming pool? We've seen it happen. Thankfully, there is a solution: our fortieth president's favorite "vegetable." Coat your hair with tomato ketchup and let it sit for a half an hour or so before you rinse it off. Then wash and condition your hair as usual. Remember to use up those packets stockpiled from fast-food places!

CONDITIONING

For a deep-conditioning hair mask, mash the meat of an avocado with 1 cup mayonnaise. Rub it into your hair and cover your head with plastic wrap or a shower cap. After 20 minutes, wash it out with your usual shampoo.

Hot summer sunshine can increase sweat production and make your scalp look and feel much greasier. To counteract this problem, try more frequent washings with a small amount of shampoo, and follow up with a much lighter conditioner than you use in the winter.

Spending a windy summer day out on the beach? Strong gusts on a sandy beach can cause as much damage to your hair as the sun, so protect your locks by applying some leave-in conditioner before you go. Choose one that contains vitamin B5, which will nourish and protect your hair.

CUTS, INEXPENSIVE

Looking for Inexpensive Haircuts? *See Shopping chapter, Cosmetics and Beauty Services*

DANDRUFF

The shiny white scales that separate from the scalp and collect on the hair and shoulders are otherwise known as dandruff. If your scalp is getting flaky, try treating it with a mixture of 2 tablespoons dried thyme and 1 cup water. Let the water boil, then add the thyme and wait five minutes. Remove from the heat and let cool, then strain out the thyme and pour the water on your hair and scalp after you've washed and rinsed it. To let it work, don't rinse it out for 12 hours—but don't worry, your hair will dry fine (and smell delicious)!

....

Aspirin may help reduce dandruff if you crush a couple of tablets and add them to your normal shampoo. Just make sure to let the shampoo sit on your hair for 1–2 minutes before washing it out.

....

To keep your scalp naturally dandruff free, use a little bit of lemon juice. Mix 2 tablespoons lemon juice with 2 cups warm water and pour over your head after you rinse out your conditioner. Let it dry in your hair and it will not only keep dandruff away, it will make you smell wonderful.

....

If you're afflicted with dandruff, try this home-grown fix: Rub 2 tablespoons of salt into your scalp before shampooing and watch those flakes become a thing of the past.

You can reduce flakes in your hair by changing your diet. Increase your intake of raw foods that are high in enzymes (fruit, vegetables, and nuts). If your dandruff still doesn't improve, try swallowing two spoonfuls of flax seed oil a day.

DRY

Suffering from dry hair? Here's a surefire way to make it moist again. Mash a banana and mix with a teaspoon of almond or olive oil. Rub the mixture into your hair and scalp, and let sit for 20 minutes. Rinse off and shampoo and condition as usual. You'll be surprised at the results!

DYEING

When dyeing clients' hair, I use this tip when they want to catch up on *Cosmo* but can't read without their glasses. Cover the arms of the glasses in foil, and none of the hair dye will get on them.

—*Sheila H., Carlisle, PA*

To remove hair dye from wooden furniture and cabinets, use this tried-and-true salon method: Wipe with a cotton ball dipped in fresh hydrogen peroxide.

—Jennifer Pilcher, Olathe, KS

....

If you have brown or dark blond hair, you can add highlights without chemicals and with hardly any cost. First, cut a lemon into quarters or eighths, then make a slit in the middle, as if you were going to put the wedge on the rim of a glass. Wash your hair as usual, and while it's still wet, place a strand of your hair in the slit, beginning at your scalp, and run the wedge down to the tips. Sit outside in direct sunlight until your hair dries, and you'll have lovely blond streaks. Repeat in one week to make the highlights even brighter.

....

Many hair products contain alcohol, which can dry out your hair and scalp. If your hair is dyed, it will also make it appear duller. Before buying a hair product, look carefully at the ingredients—and stay away from alcohol!

GREASY

Vinegar is not just for the kitchen; it gets grease out of oily hair! Simply shampoo your hair as usual, rinse, then pour ¼ cup vinegar over it and rinse again.

....

Greasy hair? Get rid of excess oil with a weekly treatment of cold peppermint tea. Simply wash your hair as usual, then pour the cooled tea over your hair. It will get rid of grease and make your hair smell fresh and minty all day long!

FRESHENING

If you run out of dry shampoo, cornstarch is a great substitute. Shake a little where your hair is parted, let it sit for a minute or two, then flip your head upside-down and massage it out.

FRIZZY

If brushing your hair makes it practically stand on end, run your brush under cold water before using it on your hair.

Try this treatment to moisturize your locks and keep frizzies at bay: Mix together 1 egg yolk and 2 tablespoons olive oil (double the recipe if you have longer hair). Rub over your hair and place a shower cap on top, then leave in for 15–30 minutes before rinsing out. You won't believe how smooth and silky your hair becomes!

LIMP

Using styling products can make your hair look limp, as shampoos don't always take care of the buildup. Every other week mix ¼ cup baking soda with enough water to create a paste. In the shower, rub the paste into your hair, rinse, and then wash and condition as usual. The baking soda takes care of all the product buildup, and there's no need to buy any expensive special shampoo.

—*Jennifer Starkey, Webster Groves, MO*

....

You may be surprised to learn that beer has practical uses other than guzzling, but it's true. One of its best perks is enlivening flat hair. Mix 3 tablespoons of your favorite brew with ½ cup warm water, and rub the solution into your hair and after shampooing. Let it sit a while before rinsing it out, and your hair will get back that lively bounce.

SHINY

Extra shiny hair starts in the shower! Finish your final rinse with a blast of the most freezing cold water you can bear. It closes the hair cuticles so that light bounces off them, resulting in super shiny locks.

....

Give your hair and scalp a treat with an organic conditioner made from honey and olive oil. Mix equal parts together and warm in the microwave. Then apply the mixture to clean, damp hair, and wrap in a warm towel for 20 minutes before washing out. Your hair will be smooth, shiny, and ultra soft.

STYLING

Many women (and some men) love having long locks, but a thick, solid curtain of glossy hair can overwhelm your face and make your skin look dull and tired. If you have long hair, make sure to cut some shorter layers from underneath to create movement around your face and let the light shine through.

Hair naturally thins out as part of the aging process, as the number of follicles capable of growing hairs gradually declines. A straight part with hair that just hangs down from it will emphasize the problem, so ask your stylist to create a style that incorporates color and texture.

For a cheap alternative to hair gel, try a light hand lotion instead. It works great to weigh down curls and frizzies, especially if you have a short cut, and costs less than half the price. Hand lotion also makes a great hair product because so many scents are available—you'll probably find one you like even more than your normal hair-care product!

For a great hair gel that doubles as a leave-in conditioner, dilute your favorite conditioner with water until it's runny, then add to a spray bottle and use in the morning when trying to tame your locks.

WASHING

It turns out that the person washing your hair at the salon is onto something! When you apply shampoo or conditioner, take a few moments to give yourself a slow fingertip scalp massage. Using gentle circular motions and a little bit of pressure on the scalp will boost blood circulation around the follicles and stimulate regrowth. Similarly, if you want to strengthen your hair, make sure to brush or comb it thoroughly each night. This will increase circulation in your scalp, loosen dry skin, and help moisturize your hair with your body's natural oils.

If your kids love to paint, they'll inevitably get some paint in their hair—or in the dog's fur! Don't fret, though—you can easily remove acrylic paint by using a cotton ball soaked in olive oil.

» Hands and Nails

CLEANING

To avoid spending money on expensive hand sanitizers, make your own at home with these ingredients: 2 cups aloe vera gel, 2 teaspoons rubbing alcohol, 4 teaspoons vegetable glycerin (available online and at health food stores), and 10 drops eucalyptus oil. Mix the ingredients well and like you would the commercially made version.

Chopping up garlic or doing other smelly kitchen chores doesn't have to leave your hands smelling bad! Just pour a few tablespoons of mouthwash into your palms and rub your hands together, and the odor will disappear. Another simple way to feed food odors off your hands is to rub them on the back of a stainless steel spoon.

This is a great tip my grandmother taught me after a grueling day of Thanksgiving cooking: To remove food stains from your hands, rub a peeled, raw potato over them. They'll come off like magic!

—*Megan O'Brien, Lovelock, NV*

To remove the fragrance of bleach (and other cleaning materials) from your hands, pour lemon juice over them and rinse.

To remove oil-based paint from your hands, rub them with a drop of vegetable or olive oil, then wash off with soap and water.

....

To remove dirt, grass, and other garden muck from your hands, add ½ teaspoon sugar to the soap lather before you wash your hands. You'll be amazed how easily the stains come off!

....

To avoid rough and flaky skin after working with garden lime, rinse your hands liberally with vinegar.

....

Kids playing in the mud? Powdered laundry detergent is an excellent cleaner for very dirty hands. It's specially formulated to get rid of grease and oil, and the powder also works as a mild abrasive.

....

We don't like to be too sappy, especially on our hands! One of the easiest ways to remove sticky tree sap from skin is to rub butter or margarine into the spots and wash with water.

....

The scent of evergreens is pure magic, no one loves the sticky sap left on your hands after collecting branches or making a wreath. Bring out the Hellmann's (or whatever mayonnaise you have on hand), and rub a small spoonful on your hands like lotion. The sap will wash right off.

....

After working on your car, clean grease and oil off your hands easily by rubbing a bit of baby oil between them, then washing as usual with soap and water.

Our kids drive us crazy by writing notes and drawing all over their hands (thankfully not answers to tests, as far as we know). The fastest way to clean them up? Green or black tea bags. Once you've brewed a cup of tea, use the wet bag to dab at ink stains.

CUTICLES

Using a cotton swab, dab a bit of vegetable or olive oil on your cuticles to keep your nail bed moisturized. You'll also be less likely to get hangnails!

To keep the cuticles of your nails supersoft, pour mayonnaise into a small bowl and submerge your fingers in it for five minutes. Keep the bowl covered in the fridge (just make sure no one uses it for sandwiches) and repeat every day.

Try this homemade cuticle cream and you'll give up the store-bought variety forever: Mix 2 tablespoons each of olive oil and petroleum jelly along with the zest of half an orange. Store in the refrigerator, and apply at bedtime for soft, lovely smelling nails.

MOISTURIZING

The skin on your hands is thin and endlessly ravaged by the elements, so keep them as dry as possible—never walk out of a restroom with wet hands. Water left on skin will evaporate, which will dry out your hands and can even cause them to turn red. If you're especially prone to dry hands, look for a cream that contains lanolin.

Once a month, cover your hands in petroleum jelly or thick hand cream, then slip them into some soft cotton gloves for the night. In the morning, your skin will have absorbed all the cream, leaving you with the smoothest, softest hands you've ever had. You can also soften your feet the same way (use socks rather than gloves, of course).

Slather on a heavy layer of hand moisturizer before painting or doing other dirty chores. It will prevent dirt and paint from seeping into your skin, making clean-up easier. White soap under your nails will help too.

Buy a small container of pure beeswax online or at a health-food store and you can make the very same luxury hand creams you always pine over (for a fraction of the cost). Just combine 1 teaspoon beeswax with 3 tablespoons water, 2 tablespoons olive oil, and 1 tablespoon vegetable shortening or shea butter. Add 2 drops essential oil for a lovely scent!

NAILS

If your manicure usually ends up getting chipped, consider buffing your nails instead of polishing them. An expensive nail buffer can bring your nails to a natural shine that is sure to get noticed. Just make sure to buff only once a week: Over-buffing weakens nails by taking away their top layer and making them more porous.

....

If dark nail polish has stained your fingernails, here's a quick fix: Plop a denture-cleaning tablet into a glass of water and soak your nails for a couple of minutes. The stain will come right off.

....

Rub a wedge of lemon on your fingernails to whiten the enamel. A perfect activity during downtime while you're baking!

....

Never paint your nails on a wooden table. Even one drop of nail polish is hard to remove, and nail polish remover will strip the varnish. Do your manicure over newspaper and you'll be sure to avoid an expensive repair bill!

....

You have just enough time to touch up your nails before you leave, but not long enough to dry them. Make your nail polish dry more quickly by spraying your final coat with cooking spray. The oil will help them dry faster, and it will moisturize your cuticles too!

....

» Make-up and Other Cosmetics

APPLYING

When putting on your make-up in the morning, always apply it in natural light, as your skin will look drastically different under the light from your bathroom bulb. Set up a magnifying mirror near a window with a good source of light, and make sure that shading is properly blended for the most natural-looking face.

Most people use far more foundation than they need—and since it's one of the most expensive types of make-up, that's money down the drain! To make sure you're using the proper amount, simply apply one dot to each of your cheeks, your forehead, and your nose, then blend thoroughly. Follow with blush and the rest of your make-up. Don't be afraid to leave some areas bare.

Summer beauty requires a lighter touch. To keep your skin tone looking fresh and even, stash your foundation and just use a tinted moisturizer with an SPF of 15 or higher to cover the occasional blemish and protect you from the sun. Lighter colors of lipstick and eye shadow will complete your summer look beautifully!

For emergency under-eye concealer, use your foundation. A good trick is to dab from the little bit on the cap, which is thicker. You can use this on blemishes too.

BRUSHES

You should wash make-up brushes and sponges regularly to rid them of dirt, oil, and bacteria—none of which you want to transfer onto your face. Lather them up with baby shampoo, massage gently, and rinse in cool water. Let them air-dry.

If you're having trouble getting your make-up brushes and sponges clean, make a simple cleaning solvent. Combine ½ cup baking soda with 2 tablespoons water and mix together. Then add the resulting paste to 1 cup water and ½ cup of fabric cleanser. Dip your brushes and sponges in the final solution, rinse clean, and reshape before allowing to air-dry.

Although we usually go with the cheapest option, it's worth investing in high-quality make-up brushes that will make application easier, faster, and more polished looking. Good brushes should have bristles that feel soft against the skin. It's important to wash them at least every three months with a mild liquid soap.

CONCEALER

Partied a little too hard over the weekend? Don't make the mistake of covering the bags under your eyes so dramatically that you draw attention to the spot by making it too light. A little bronzer applied over the concealer should even things out.

....

For emergency under-eye concealer, use your foundation. A good trick is to dab from the little bit on the cap, which is thicker. You can use this on blemishes too.

FOUNDATION AND POWDER

If you want to keep your make-up lasting longer but don't want to look too powdery, apply powder everywhere except the cheekbones, down the center of the nose, and the middle of the forehead. Those areas will still be able to reflect light and will keep a glow on the skin.

—*Samantha Hinton, Glendale, CA*

....

When applying powder or bronzer to your face, start from your jawline and work your way in. Since you have more powder on the brush where you begin, brushing the darker shade on the outside will give your face a more radiant look.

....

If a double chin is driving you nuts, use a little make-up to hide it. When applying powder or foundation to your face, use a slightly darker shade under your chin, which will make it appear to recede. Blend toward the back of the jawline to add definition. When posing for pictures, stick your chin out as much as possible to stretch out the skin in the area.

....

If you're wearing a low-cut top, use a bit of powder to give your skin an even color and smooth the appearance below your neck. A smidge of blush down your cleavage line will add a "shadow," making your bust look larger.

....

Some of the most expensive make-up is foundation and powder. Make them last longer by buying a shade darker than your natural one, then mixing it with moisturizer (for foundation), or baby powder (for powder) until it matches your normal color. You'll have more than twice as much, and you'll never be able to tell the difference!

LIPSTICK

To give the illusion of a fuller upper lip, dab a touch of pale, iridescent sheen in the center of the lips, then rub to blend in with the rest of your lipstick. This will highlight your cupid's bow (the curvy portion of your lips) by making it appear bigger.

....

To avoid getting lipstick on your teeth, after you apply, close your mouth over your finger and slowly pull it out. This will save you time and time again!

MASCARA

> When your mascara starts to clump, you don't have to toss it out! Smooth it out again by setting the tube in a teacup of near-boiling water for five minutes.

To make your lashes look fuller than ever, apply two coats of mascara every time you do your lashes. But here's the secret! Between the first and second coats, apply a thin layer of baby powder with a make-up brush. The mascara will adhere to the powder, and it will stay on your lashes longer.

—Jennifer Rivera, Indio, CA

PURCHASING

Looking for tips for Buying Make-Up? See Shopping chapter, Cosmetics and Beauty Services

REMOVING

For an inexpensive way to remove mascara, eyeliner, and shadow, try baby shampoo. It contains many of the same ingredients as eye make-up remover and works just as well, but costs a lot less. Pour a small amount on a tissue or cotton ball, rub over closed eyes, and rinse with water.

For years I've used common vegetable oil to remove my make-up. It works better than anything else (even on waterproof mascara), and it's cheap and good for your skin. Take it from someone who has worked as a mime and clown.

—*Bibi Caspari, Los Angeles, CA*

You should never leave make-up on overnight, as it can dry out your skin (and leave marks on your pillow!). One of the quickest ways to remove cosmetics is with a premoistened wipe, but skip the expensive make-up removal wipes and keep of stash of baby wipes near the sink instead. The next time you come home after a late night, rub one over your face before you hit the sack.

STORAGE

Looking for tips about Storing Your Make-Up?
See **Organization chapter, Bathroom**

 Skin

DEAD SKIN

A good way to slough off dead skin is to apply mayonnaise over dry, rough patches. Let it sit for 10 minutes, then wipe away with a washcloth dampened with warm water.

Brown spots on your skin are usually caused by dead skin cells. Slough off this skin and brighten what's underneath by rubbing lemon juice on the spot. Let it dry, then rub vigorously with a washcloth.

Brighten dull and sallow skin with a little help from your kitchen! Mix equal parts lemon juice and milk, then rub into your skin with a soft cloth and leave on for five minutes before rinsing. Thanks to these natural exfoliants, your skin will feel tingly fresh and look rejuvenated.

Rubbing a slice of pineapple or papaya onto your skin will help remove dead cells. Leave for five minutes, then rinse off with water. For a more exfoliating action, use olive oil mixed with salt.

MOISTURIZING

Soft, supple skin is as easy as using a little honey. Moisten skin with warm water, then apply honey straight from the jar. Leave for up to 30 minutes, then rinse off.

Available online and in health food and vitamin shops, horse chestnut cream can help diminish the tiny red veins that appear on your cheeks and nose as you age. Skin becomes thinner and loses some of its collagen as you get older, and horse chestnut cream improves blood circulation and can make these annoying veins disappear.

During the night, the skin rests and repairs itself after the stresses of the day, so nothing's worse than waking up to dry skin in the winter. Use a humidifier or place a damp towel over your radiator at night to replenish moisture in the air and keep your skin hydrated. This helps to humidify the air around you and reduce excessive water loss from your skin.

Make your nighttime lotion regimen even more effective: Before smoothing on your cream, take five deep breaths to boost levels of oxygen to the skin.

PERFUME

Oops! You accidentally put on way too much perfume, and you're afraid the restaurant you're dining at will smell like someone just detonated a flower-scented bomb. To make your perfume less strong, dab a cotton ball dipped in rubbing alcohol wherever you applied the scent. Your friends will thank you.

Do you find your perfume fading after a few hours? To make it last longer, rub a small amount of petroleum jelly onto your skin before you dab on your favorite scent.

PROTECTING

Don't wait until you're out in the sun to apply a protective lotion. Sunscreen needs time to work, so smooth it on about 20 minutes before you go outside, and don't be stingy—use liberal amounts and reapply after swimming or excessive sweating.

SHAVING

If your razor gets dull easily, it's probably due to rust that you can't even see. Keep rust away by storing your razor blade-down in a glass of olive oil. As a bonus, any olive oil left on the blades will help moisturize your skin!

Instead of buying expensive shaving creams or foams, try shaving with hair conditioner. (Buy the cheapest kind.) The conditioner will soften the hair and provide a layer of protection between your blade and your skin. You'll even get a closer shave!

Suffering from ingrown hairs? This all-natural solution will ease the itch and pain. Combine 1 cup sugar, the juice from half a lemon, 2 teaspoons apple cider vinegar, and ¼ cup honey. Blend together until smooth, then heat in the microwave until warm (about 15–20 seconds). Let it sit on the affected area for 20 minutes.

Auto

Baking

Beauty

Clothing and Accessories

Cooking

≫ **Cleaning**

Decorating

Entertaining and Holidays

Health and Wellness

Home Repair

Kids

Money

Organization

Outdoors

Pest Control

Pets

Shopping

Utilities

Vacations and Family Activities

Websites

» Auto

Looking for Car Cleaning tips? *See* Auto chapter, Cleaning

» Bathroom

APPLIANCES

If it's beginning to smell like fire every time you blow-dry your hair, your dryer's motor may be clogged with hair and lint. Use an old toothbrush to brush clean the back of the dryer, where it sucks in air. Now you can do your hair without someone poking their head in the bathroom to make sure everything's OK!

If your curling or straightening iron is getting a little gross from caked-on hair product and other dirt, head to the kitchen and reach for some oven cleaner. Spray it on, let it sit for an hour, then wipe it off. Then rub the iron with a damp cloth and let it dry thoroughly before you use it again.

CERAMIC

The easiest way to clean ceramic tile is with rubbing alcohol. Just pour it straight on, and mop or wipe until it dries.

To keep ceramic tile sparkling, wipe it regularly with a sponge damped with water and a splash of vinegar. Avoid soapy or oily cleaners, and never use abrasives, which will dull the finish and make glazed tiles more prone to dirt.

ENAMEL

Remove stains from enamel with a paste of baking soda and hydrogen peroxide. This will form a gentle bleach you can rub in and leave to dry, then rinse off.

Steel wool and scouring powders will scratch porcelain, so if your sink or tub is made of this fragile material, rub a freshly cut lemon around the surface to cut through grease, then rinse with running water.

FIXTURES

To clean chrome-plated fixtures in your bathroom instantly, always keep fabric softener sheets handy. Just wipe, and the chrome will sparkle.

To get the cleanest bathroom fixtures you've ever seen, apply a paste of vinegar and baking soda to stainless steel faucets, knobs, and towel bars. Lay old towels or rags on top and wait one hour, then buff off. Rinse the fixtures and then let them dry, and you'll have sparkling fixtures without a hint of water marks.

If mineral deposits have built up in your faucet, cut a lemon into quarters, then push one piece up into the faucet until it sticks. Leave for about 10 minutes, then twist the wedge out. Repeat with remaining lemon quarters until the deposits are gone.

GENERAL

Trying to clean up your bathroom fast, before guests arrive? Apply a touch of baby shampoo to a wet sponge and wipe down your sink, fixtures, tiles, and bathtub. It cuts through oily residue, and it smells good too.

If you've let the bathroom get so dirty that it now resembles a gas station restroom, turn on the hot water in the shower for 10 minutes with the door closed. The steam will loosen the buildup of mildew and mold. Then get in there and clean!

The best thing about scouring powder is its abrasive action. The worst is the harsh chemical smell. To get all the benefits without the caustic chemicals, use baking soda instead. In most instances, baking soda will work just as well as scouring powder.

If your beauty routine includes spraying your entire 'do to keep it in place, you probably have a film of hair spray on your bathroom vanity and walls. Remove it easily with a solution of two parts water and one part liquid fabric softener. Wipe on with a damp cloth, then rub off with a clean one.

You've just spent what seemed like an entire day cleaning your bathrooms. Keep them that way by applying mineral oil all over shower doors and tiled surfaces. This will delay mineral buildup and cut down on future cleaning time.

MIRRORS

Make your mirrors shine with a solution of equal parts of vinegar and water. Use old newspapers to wipe mirrors with the mix, then add extra shine by rubbing with a clean dry-erase or blackboard eraser.

Cleaning agents can leave a thin film on mirrors. Brighten them by rubbing with a cloth dampened with alcohol.

For a unique cleaner for the mirrors around your home, use aerosol air freshener. It will bring your mirrors to a glossy shine and will have people wondering where that flowery scent is coming from.

RINGS

If your shaving cream can is leaving rusty rings on the side of your tub or sink, perform this trick right after you purchase a new container: Coat the rim around the bottom of the can with clear nail polish, then let it dry. The polish will keep out water, so the can won't rust.

If your white porcelain sink or tub has rings that refuse to be removed, it's time to call in the big guns: oven cleaner. (Don't use on colored fixtures, which might get bleached out, and move your plastic shower curtain out of the way.) Simply spray oven cleaner on the affected areas, wait about an hour, and rinse off. It's that easy!

SHOWERS AND TUBS

Stay on top of mold and mildew by keeping this daily shower spray within easy reach of all family members. Mix one part vinegar with 10 parts water in an empty spray bottle and you're ready to go. Bonus: You don't have to worry about a toxic cleaner hitting the baby's bath toys.

Clogged showerhead? It's easy to remove mineral deposits from a showerhead without using harsh chemicals. Just unscrew it and submerge in white vinegar overnight, and the clogs will disappear. It you can't unscrew it, fill a small, sturdy bag with vinegar and attach to the showerhead with duct tape, or use an old toothbrush and vinegar. To clean the screen in your showerhead, wash it with water mixed with a dash of dishwashing liquid.

Removing blue-green stains from your tub that are caused by high copper content in your water can be challenging, even with the help of bleach. Try treating your shower or tub with a paste of equal parts cream of tartar and baking soda. Rub into the stains, leave for half an hour, and rinse well with water. Repeat if necessary.

Clear away shower-door soap scum effortlessly by wiping it with a used dryer sheet. It gets the job done quickly!

....

Instead of spraying down your shower every time you use it, try this solution for keeping away mildew and grime. Apply a thin layer of car wax to a completely clean shower, then buff with a dry cloth. Your cleaning job will be much easier, and you'll have to reapply the wax only once a year.

....

Need to clean those dirty glass shower doors? You can wipe them down with leftover white wine (if you haven't finished it off!). The wine contains the perfect amount of alcohol to battle soap scum and lime. Apply with a damp sponge, leave for five minutes, then rinse off. Finish by quickly buffing with a clean, dry cloth.

....

Looking for an easy mildew remover? Simply scrub the affected area with an old, damp toothbrush sprinkled with baking soda.

....

Before you throw away that old paintbrush, use it as a cleaning brush. Cut the bristles very short and use in hard-to-reach places like the corner of the tub.

....

For a free mold and mildew fighter, try vodka! It works especially well on the caulking around your tub. Just spray on, leave for 10 minutes, and wipe clean.

....

Is there anything more satisfying than nice, clean grout? A simple paste of three parts baking soda and one part water is all you need. Make a new batch each time you plan to attack the space between your tiles.

....

If you've tried milder grout cleaners and but still have black stains on your grout, it's time to break out the bleach. (Make sure to wear protective gloves and ventilate area well.) Soak some paper towels in bleach and place them around the grout. Leave for at least an hour, then remove the towels and enjoy your clean, white grout.

SHOWER CURTAINS

Help keep mildew off your shower curtain liner by soaking it in salt water for an hour or two before hanging it. The salt will help repel mildew, and your shower curtain will last longer!

....

Avoid leaving a shower curtain bunched up after use, especially in a small bathroom—the steam encourages mildew. Always pulled it closed after bathing, and if small spots of mildew do appear, dab with baking soda on a damp cloth. Wash larger areas in hot detergent, rub with lemon juice, and dry in the sun, if possible.

....

Need to remove mildew from a plastic shower curtain? Try running it through the washing machine with two large, white bath towels. Add a little bleach in with your usual detergent, and use 1 cup white vinegar in the rinse cycle to prevent future mildew growth.

....

If mildew has made your shower curtain more disgusting than you'd like to admit, first wash it in hot, soapy water. Then rub a wedge of lemon on the stains and leave the curtain out in the sun. By the time it dries, the stains will be gone.

....

If your cloth shower curtain has seen better days, wash it according to the care label, but add a cup of vinegar to the water to make it look like new. Remove as soon as the cycle is complete and hang back in position to drip-dry without any creases or wrinkles.

TOILETS

This may go against years of training your boys, but in rarely used bathrooms the lid on the toilet should always be kept up. This allows air to circulate in the bowl, which will prevent mold and mildew from forming. Also, make sure to leave toilet lids up when you go on vacation!

—*Jennifer Pilcher, Olathe, KS*

....

For a cheap and easy way to clean your toilet, use mouthwash. Just pour 1 capful into the bowl, leave for 10–15 minutes, and wipe clean with your toilet brush.

To remove hard-water deposits in your toilet bowl, pour 1 cup white vinegar into the bowl and allow it to sit for several hours or overnight before scrubbing. A fizzy denture tablet works well too!

If the caps to the bolts at the base of your toilet have cracked or gone missing, you've probably discovered that they're hard to replace. A perfectly suitable replacement? The protective caps on stick deodorants that need to be removed before you apply it for the first time. So go buy a few new sticks of deodorant, but make sure to take a look at the cap color before you buy!

When buying your first new home, you probably thought about the backyard parties and a basement rec room. Cleaning the septic tank? Not so much. Still, the time will come when you will need to do it. Add 2 teaspoons baker's yeast and 2 cups brown sugar to 4 cups warm water. Flush the mix and let sit overnight.

» Decks and Patios

Looking for tips on Cleaning Your Deck and Patio?
See Outdoors chapter, Outdoor Areas

DISHES AND DINING DUSTING ELECTRONICS AND APPLIANCES

» Dishes and Dining

BASTING BRUSHES

There's nothing like a gooey, smelly basting brush to ruin your mood. Put a stop to it today! After your usual washing routine with hot water and soap, dry it off a bit by shaking. Here's the cool part, which might remind you of your eighth-grade science class. Pour coarse salt into a cup and place the brush inside. Any remaining wetness will be absorbed by the salt, leaving the bristles as clean as can be.

CAN OPENERS

When even your can opener is superclean, you know you have mastered the art of home maintenance. Putting it in the dishwasher can lead to rust, so just churn a folded paper towel through it after each use to remove the residue, then quickly wash and rinse.

CHEESE GRATERS

**The easiest way to clean a cheese grater is to spray it
with vegetable oil before grating any cheese,** which will make it less sticky. Afterward, rub the crusty heel from a stale loaf of French bread over the dirty end, and your clean-up is finished!

> Problem: you want to break your addiction to buying pre-grated cheese in bags, but cleaning up the cheese grater is always a pain. Solution? Put the grater in the freezer or run it under cold water for several minutes before grating, and the cheese won't stick.

Clean soft cheese, garlic, or any other food from your grater by cutting a lemon in half and rubbing the pulpy side against the grater. For extra abrasion, add a little salt.

Cleaning a cheese grater will never be a problem if you grate a small piece of raw potato before trying to wash it out. An old toothbrush can also come in handy for this job.

CHINA

Antique dealers use this trick to hide hairline cracks on china plates and cups. Simmer the piece in milk for 45 minutes. Casein, a milk protein, may fill in the crack, depending on its size. If your china is old or fragile, though, this could backfire—heat can cause pieces to expand and crack.

Buff away a nick on the rim of a glass or your china with an emery board. Don't use a nail file or sandpaper; both are too coarse and will scratch the glass.

Impossible-to-remove stains on your china?
There may be hope yet. Apply a bit of nail polish remover to the spots with a soft cloth, then wash as usual. The spots should quickly fade.

CRYSTAL

Use a paste of lemon juice and baking powder to remove small stains from crystal. Treat tougher stains by placing 2 teaspoons uncooked rice inside the crystal piece, adding water, and swirling. The small amount of abrasive action from the rice will remove the stains—perfect for vases with narrow necks.

To clean your cut crystal, mix a teaspoon of baking soda with warm water, then dab it onto the crystal with a soft rag. Rinse with water, then buff with a dry, soft cloth.

CUTTING BOARDS

To quickly disinfect a plastic cutting board, wash it thoroughly, rub half a cut lemon over it, and microwave it for a minute.

To make your cutting boards look like new, vigorously rub some salt into them. You can also treat wooden cutting boards with a very light coating of mineral oil. Be careful not to overdo it, because mineral oil may affect the potency of a number of vitamins in fruits and vegetables.

Do you have a cutting board that has a lingering odor that just won't quit? Remove the smell by rubbing the board with white vinegar.

....

To remove stains on cutting boards, it's lemon to the rescue again. Pour some lemon juice on the stain and let it sit for 20 minutes, then rinse with water.

DISHWASHER

Never combine silver and stainless steel cutlery in the dishwasher, or the silver will turn black. Any contact with dishwasher detergent will also result in black spots. Remove silver cutlery from the dishwasher immediately after the cycle ends, and dry at once to avoid stains and pitting from salt residue.

....

If your plastic lids, baby spoons, and other small items in the dishwasher keep falling through the rack, place them inside a zippered mesh bag used for cleaning delicates in the washing machine.

....

If hard water in your home causes spots and stains on items that have been run through the dishwasher, add a spoonful of baking soda to your next load. Your dishes will come out spot free.

....

To get rid of mineral deposits and iron stains in your dishwasher, run it through an empty wash cycle using powdered lemonade mix instead of detergent. The citric acid in the mix will eliminate your problem.

Soap film coating your dishwasher? Run it on an empty cycle using vinegar instead of detergent. It will be sparkling clean, and your next load of dishes will be too.

GLASSES AND MUGS

If your glasses are beginning to develop a fine film because of too many trips through the dishwasher, soak them in a bath of warm vinegar for an hour. They'll emerge sparkling clean.

Who knew salt was the best way to remove lipstick from a glass? Rub a little over the stain to remove an imprint on the side of the glass, then wash as usual. Sticking lipstick-marked glasses in the dishwasher hardly ever works, because lipstick is made to resist water.

To remove coffee or tea stains from a ceramic mug or pot, gently wipe them with a lemon sprinkled with salt. The salt will act as an abrasive, while the acid will get rid of the tannins.

Get rid of really tough stains in your mugs by filling them with boiling water and adding a denture tablet. Let it sit overnight, and the stain should disappear.

If the inside of your coffee cup is stained from coffee or tea, it's not too late to make it look like new. Mix a paste of coarse salt (or baking soda) and water. Scrub the mug, then rinse it well.

HAND MIXERS

If your hand mixer isn't what it used to be thanks to jiggling beaters, hardened food in its sockets may be to blame. Take out the beaters and clean out the sockets with a toothpick or bobby pin.

HAND WASHING

If you've ever experienced the frustration of dropping and breaking a dish while washing it, you'll love this tip! Prevent losses by lining your sink with a towel or rubber mat before washing.

There's no need to buy expensive dishwashing liquid. Buy the cheapest brand you can find, then add a few tablespoons of white vinegar to the water while you're washing, and your dishes will shine. The same is true for dishwashers: Vinegar will remove spots from glass in a flash.

KNIVES

We used to throw knives in the dishwasher with everything else. Problem is, this dulls the blades, and "gunk" (scientific word for stuck-on food left from chopping onions, raw meat, and tomatoes) would still be on the sides. Luckily, there's a neat trick for cleaning knives without dulling their edges—a cork. Simply dip one in vinegar and use it to rub off the gunk, then wash by hand with a soft cloth. No scrubbing necessary!

POTS AND PANS

To remove baked-on stains from a glass casserole dish, fill it with warm water and add two tablets of Alka-Seltzer or denture cleaner. Leave for an hour and the stains will be gone.

—*Sandy Martis, Sandpoint, ID*

If the bottom of your pot or pan is a burnt-on mess, pop it in the freezer for an hour or two. The stuck food will freeze and be easier to remove.

Ammonia is a no-nonsense cleaning essential for your kitchen! To clean a really greasy pan, add a few drops into your soapsuds.

If you've ever scorched milk in a pan, you know it's almost impossible to remove the stain. However, salt can help. Dampen the pan, then sprinkle salt all over the bottom. Wait 10 minutes and scrub away the stain. The odor will be gone too!

—*Maureen Delepine, Italy*

Here's another great way to remove burnt food from pans. Sprinkle baking soda, salt, and dishwasher detergent over the crusty bits, then cover with water and boil for a half an hour. Even the toughest baked-on food will wipe off easily.

If you've given up hope of ever removing stuck-on food from your pots and pans, help is on the way—in the form of a fabric softener sheet! Just cover the stain with hot water and float a fabric softener sheet in it. Leave overnight. In the morning, the food should wipe off easily.

Cleaning up after a yummy egg breakfast? Cold water cleans egg off pans and utensils better than hot water. Hot water tends to cause the protein to bind to surfaces and harden.

The best way to clean cast iron pans is to cover any stain with a paste of cream of tartar and white vinegar. Apply liberally, let it sit, then scrub with a damp, soft cloth.

To treat rust on metal baking dishes and cookware, sprinkle powdered laundry detergent on the spot, then scour with the cut side of half a raw potato.

....

What if your nonstick pan starts sticking? For the most part, coated pots and pans are easy to keep clean, but they do stain, and over time grease and oil may build up. This will adversely affect the efficiency of the nonstick surface, so it's important to clean and reseason any stained areas. To do so, simply mix 1 cup water, 2 tablespoons baking soda, and ½ cup white vinegar in the pot, set on the stove, and boil for 10 minutes. Wash the pot as usual, then rub vegetable oil on the surface of the plastic coating to reseason it.

....

To remove coffee stains from inside of a glass coffee pot, add 1 tablespoon water, 4 teaspoons salt, and 1 cup crushed ice. Gently swirl until it's clean, then rinse thoroughly. Make sure the coffee pot is at room temperature before cleaning.

SILVER

If you didn't get it as a wedding present, you may have silver cutlery that has been passed down from generation to generation. This beautiful silverware is always a nice treat on a special occasion. But as you've probably discovered, silver will eventually tarnish if exposed to air for an extended period of time. Keep your silver shiny and beautiful by storing it in airtight containers, or wrapping in tarnish-proof cloths or papers. Never wrap silver in plastic food wrap: It will keep air away, but it can also cause stains and corrosion.

....

If your silver develops spots, dissolve a little salt in lemon juice, then dip a soft cloth into the mixture and rub it onto the cutlery. Rinse in warm water and finish by buffing to a shine with a chamois.

Rub off tarnish with toothpaste! Place some white (nongel) toothpaste on a soft cloth and use it to rub solid silver (not silver plate). Then rinse it off gently. Don't use whitening toothpaste, which can damage the surface.

To remove tarnish from the tines of a fork, coat a piece of cotton string with the toothpaste and run it between the tines.

Polishing silver is never a neat chore, but an old sock can make it easier. Slip the sock over your hand; use one side to apply the polish and the other to buff it out.

If you have large silver items that are not used with food, consider having them lacquered by a jeweler to prevent tarnishing. Candelabras, vases, and trophies are good candidates for this treatment.

Here's an easy household solution for polishing up your old heirloom silver. Combine 1 quart whole milk with 4 tablespoons lemon juice, and let your items soak in it overnight. The next day, just rinse off your silver and dry it.

You can also polish silver with aluminum foil, but not in the way you think. Line a pan with aluminum foil, add a tablespoon of salt, and fill with cold water. Then add your silverware to the mix and let it sit for a few minutes before removing and rinsing. The aluminum acts as a catalyst for ion exchange, a process that will make the tarnish transfer from your silver to the salt bath.

....

Before storing your silver, keep it tarnish free by adding in a couple of pieces of chalk wrapped in cheesecloth. The calcium carbonate in the chalk absorbs moisture from the air very slowly and prevents tarnish. For the best results, break up the chalk and expose the rough surface.

....

Some foods are particularly harsh on silver and will cause it to tarnish quickly: olives, salad dressings, vinegar, eggs, and salt are among them. Wash your silver as soon as possible after it contacts any of these items.

STEEL WOOL

You love steel wool for its abrasive cleaning power, but hate the rust stains it sometimes leaves behind. One solution is to keep your steel wool pads in an ordinary soap or sponge dish, but an even better way is to use the tray part of a terra-cotta plant pot. This is made to soak up water, so put it to work!

....

It's easy to keep your soaped steel-wool pads from rusting: Wrap them in aluminum foil and store in your freezer.

When we use scouring pads, a lot of the surface tends to get wasted, so we cut them in half before using them. They won't wear out as fast, and half the pad stays rust free. As a bonus, it's a great way to sharpen your scissors!

You have a pot that's in need of a good scrubbing, but you're out of steel wool. Simply reach for the aluminum foil! Roll it into a ball and use it (with some dishwashing liquid) to scrub off caked-on grease. This is also a great way to reuse foil before you recycle it.

STORAGE CONTAINERS

If your plastic storage containers smell like garlic, onions, or another potent food, wash them thoroughly, then stuff crumpled newspaper inside before snapping on the lids. In a few days, the odor will be gone.

To remove odors from dishes, bottles, or plastic containers, add a teaspoon of mustard to hot water and let the item soak in it for five minutes, then wash as usual.

An inexpensive way to clean smelly plastic storage containers is to wash them with hot water plus 2 tablespoons baking soda.

....

Plastic containers are perfect for keeping leftovers and sauces, but tomato sauce will often stain clear plastic. To keep this from happening, simply spray the container with nonstick cooking spray before pouring in tomato-based sauces. To remove a plastic stain, cover the area with mustard and leave overnight.

....

The easiest way to remove smells and stains from a thermos is by filling it with hot water and ½ cup baking soda, then letting it sit overnight. In the morning, just rinse well, and it should be good as new!

» Dusting

CEILING FIXTURES

To easily clean a ceiling fan, spray glass cleaner or a mixture of half vinegar and half water on the inside of a pillowcase. Put the pillowcase over one arm of the fan, then pull it off while applying gentle pressure toward the floor. The pillowcase will wipe the top of the blade clean.

....

Our kids are getting better about pitching in with housework, but this is one chore we tend not to delegate to them. (We also don't tell anyone how easy it is!) First, make sure the light switch is off. Next, lay a blanket or upside-down umbrella underneath the chandelier to catch any drips or falling pieces. Now mix ½ cup rubbing alcohol with 1½ cups water in a jar. The crystals clean themselves—all you have to do is bring the jar up to each one and dip it in, then let it air-dry. You can use a little bit of the solution on a clean cotton rag to wipe areas that can't be dipped.

CLOTHS

After you've used a piece of cheesecloth, don't toss it. Throw it into a load of laundry, then use it as a dust rag. It will trap small particles in its weave, and won't leave behind a bunch of lint.

—Fanny Lassiter

Instead of using a rag, wear a pair of old socks on your hands when dusting. It's efficient (you're using both hands) and cheap (remember, these are old socks), and you can wash and reuse them.

It's hard to get more than a few wearings out of a pair of pantyhose, but luckily there are lot of uses for them once they get runs. Save them to use as a dust rag, or use them to buff silver. We find they polish even better than regular cloth.

Many paper towels now offer rolls with "half sheets"—that is, the perforated lines are closer together. We were shocked at how much longer our paper towel roll lasted when we bought one of these brands! If your favorite paper towel doesn't offer half sheets, simply tear them in half yourself.

HARD-TO-REACH PLACES

Wrap a paper towel around the broad end of a kitchen spatula and secure with a rubber band. Use this to reach dust trapped between tubes of a radiator. Spray the paper towel with all-purpose cleaner to get rid of sticky spills and stains.

Dreading cleaning your radiator? Here's a simple way to get the job done. Hang a damp cloth or damp newspapers on the wall behind it, then use your hair dryer to blow the dust off it. The dust will stick to the wet surface behind it, and then you can simply throw away the cloth or paper.

If your spring cleaning involves getting rid of cobwebs in hard-to-reach places, here's a hint: Untangle a wire hanger, and use a rubber band to secure an old, clean sock to the end. Your arms just grew by 3 feet!

Unless your arms are 6 feet long, dusting behind radiators or under appliances can be a real drag. Try making a dusting tool by slipping a heavy-duty sock on a yardstick and securing it with a rubber band. Spray it lightly with dusting spray (we like water and a little bit of fabric softener) and you're ready to finally grab all that dust you've been avoiding.

LAMPSHADES

The trick to cleaning a pleated lampshade is finding the right tool. Stroke each pleat from top to bottom with a dry, clean paintbrush. Or use a rolling lint remover for a quicker clean. If you dust your shades with a fabric softener sheet, its static-fighting properties will keep them cleaner for longer.

KNICKKNACKS

Forget the feather duster. The easiest way to get loose dust off your knickknacks—and anywhere else in your home—is to blow it away with a hair dryer.

....

To clean dust off ceramic figurines, simply rub them with the cut side of a lemon wedge. Leave the lemon juice on for 15 minutes, then polish up with a soft, dry cloth.

» Electronics and Appliances

BATTERIES

If battery acid leaks inside the compartments of your appliances, there's no need to throw them away. Simply take few spoonfuls of baking soda and add water until it's the consistency of toothpaste. Spread it on your battery terminals, let it sit 15 minutes, and wipe clean. The acid should come off easily.

Use a pencil eraser to wipe off the metal contacts on rechargeable items such as your cordless phone and drill and they'll get a better charge. You can also use this trick for your cell phone and iPod, or between batteries and their contacts in electronics.

CDS

Unless it's cracked, skipping CDs are usually fixable. First, eliminate any dust and dirt by holding the CD under running water and rubbing with a soft, lint-free cloth to dry. To fix any scratches, rub a little white (nongel) toothpaste into the scratch, then wipe with the damp cloth to remove any excess. The toothpaste won't repair the CD entirely, but it will keep it from skipping.

COMPUTERS

If you clean the battery contacts on your laptop and cordless phone, the charge will last longer. Use the tip of a cotton swab dipped in rubbing alcohol to clean the connection points.

The easiest way to clean the gunk and dust between your computer keys is with transparent tape. Slide a 2-inch strip between the rows of your keyboard, and the adhesive will pick up any debris.

Save plastic squeeze bottles, but not for storage—they make the perfect substitute for bottles of compressed air, which are used to clean out computer keyboards, electronics, and other tiny crevices. This works especially well with squeeze bottles with small spouts, such as lemon juice dispensers. Wash them well and let them dry completely before using.

You know, of course, that dryer sheets remove static cling from your laundry—but are you aware that they remove it from just about everything else too? If you wipe down your computer screen, television—or even your hair!—with a sheet, the static cling will disappear.

» Floors and Carpets

BROOMS AND MOPS

To eliminate the trail of dust your broom leaves behind, fill a spray bottle with three parts water and one part liquid fabric softener, and spray the broom before sweeping. The spritz makes the broom strands more pliable and helps it collect dirt more efficiently.

Use an old wide-toothed comb to get the lint and hair out of your broom's bristles. Always store brooms upside-down to make sure the bristles stay straight.

There are all kinds of new products available to get your floor clean, but sometimes a simple straw broom is your best bet. Soak the broom's bristles in a bucket of warm salt water for a half an hour and then let dry. This will prolong your broom's life, and is a great way to sweep up sand!

Always clean dust mops after using them. To avoid making a dust cloud, cover a dry dust mop with a damp paper bag before you shake it out. If your mop has a removable head, put it in a large mesh lingerie bag and toss it into the washer.

You can revive porous cleaning materials, like the head of your mop, with a little salt. Fill a bucket with a mixture of ¼ cup salt and 1 quart warm water. Then soak your mops and sponges for 8–10 hours and the grunge will be gone.

If you own a mop that requires replacement cloths, substitute baby wipes instead of buying packs of those pricey cloths. Rinse off the wipes before using, and they'll get your floors just as clean. Sturdy paper towels are another solid option for ready mops—just rip small holes in the towel so the cleaning liquid sprays through.

CARPETS, GENERAL

If you've got guests coming over and need to clean your dirty carpet fast, mix a cup of ammonia with a quart of water. Use a mop to rub this solution onto the carpet, and it'll help remove the grime. You might want to test this method beforehand on an unseen area, such as underneath a chair. Do not use this mixture on wool carpets.

Finally getting around to shampooing your carpet? You don't have to remove all your furniture. Slip plastic bags over the feet of tables and chairs and secure them with rubber bands. You can clean underneath, then shift the furniture a bit and wash where its legs were. The plastic will keep the furniture from getting wet.

If you're thinking of putting in a new carpet, consider getting your old one professionally cleaned first. You'll be shocked at what a difference it makes, and you might change your mind about replacing what you have. If you still have stains that even a professional cleaning won't remove, a strategically placed rug or chair can hide them.

....

If you can't escape static electricity on your carpet, here's an easy fix. Mix 3 cups water with ½ cup liquid fabric softener, put it in a spray bottle, and apply to your carpet. Not only will the static electricity disappear, but the mixture will serve as a carpet deodorizer too.

....

If a piece of furniture has matted down a section of your carpet, you can raise up the nap with a simple trick: Let an ice cube melt into the matted area, then rub with a dry cloth.

CARPETS, STAINS

If you spill any liquid on your carpet, pour salt on the area as soon as possible and watch it absorb the liquid almost instantly. Wait until it dries, then vacuum it up. Salt tends to provide a special capillary attraction that will work for most liquids. There are a few stains that salt will actually help set, however—never sprinkle it on red wine, coffee, tea, or cola!

....

If you have kids, you've had to clean up vomit.
Baking soda can make the job a little less gross if you
sprinkle some on top as soon as possible. It will soak up
some of the mess and make the smell easier to deal with
when you have to go at it with the paper towels.

Ink stains on the carpet? Make a paste of cream of
tartar and lemon juice, and dab at the stain. Let it sit for
five minutes or so, then clean with a damp cloth.

The best way to get gum out of carpet, clothes, or
hair is with a chemical called methyl salicyclate, which
you can find in analgesic heat rubs like Bengay. Put it on
the gum, then apply heat with your hair dryer set on low.
Press a plastic sandwich bag on the gum and it should
pull away easily. Make sure to wash the area after you've
removed the gum.

What's the easiest way to remove red wine spills
from your carpet? Try applying a bit of shaving
cream (after checking that the carpet is colorfast),
and letting it sit for a minute before wiping away.
Shaving cream will also work on grease stains.

Coffee stains can be frustrating, but you can get them
out of your carpet by pouring beer on them. That's right—
just dribble a couple of sips onto the stain, and it should
vanish. Dab up the extra beer with a paper towel, and if the
coffee stain doesn't go away completely, repeat the task a
few more times. This trick works on tea stains too.

Your best bet for removing coffee stains from carpet or clothing is to rub a beaten egg yolk into the spot, leave for five minutes, then rinse with warm water.

....

Grease stains can be some of the hardest stains to remove from carpet. The big thing to remember is to not touch the stain at all—don't sop it up, wipe it, or do anything else. Instead, pour a large amount of cornstarch on top of the spot and gently stir it with your finger. Let it sit for a day, and make sure no one walks on it. The next day, use your vacuum cleaner's hose attachment (the plastic one, not the one with bristles) to suck away the cornstarch. The stain should be mostly gone, but if it's not, repeat this action until it completely disappears. You can then use the brush attachment to clear away the last remnants of cornstarch.

....

Here's how to eliminate cigarette burns in your carpet: First, cut away the burn mark. Then, cut a bit of carpet from an area that's covered by a piece of furniture (such as under a couch), and glue it carefully over the burnt spot. Finally, smack the person who dropped the ashes!

FLOORS, GENERAL

For mopping vinyl or ceramic floors, use ½ cup white vinegar added to 1 gallon warm water. It's cheap, effective, and completely nontoxic.

....

To keep your home clean during snowstorms, place the side of a large cardboard box near your door so family members can pile their filthy, slushy boots and winter gear on top of it.

RUGS

> To get the color back in your rug, take a small bucket and pour 2 cups white vinegar, 2 gallons hot water, and 2 teaspoons ammonia into it. Mix well, dip a washcloth into it, and scrub away on the carpet. Soak up any excess with a dry towel.
>
> —*Carla Renaudo*

Brighten faded rugs by rubbing them down with a rag that has been soaked in salt water, then wrung out. You can also submerge throw rugs and drapes in a solution of salt water, then wash as usual.

SCUFF MARKS

To remove scuff marks left on your floor by dark-soled shoes, rub some baking soda into the spot with a wet rag. They'll virtually disappear.

If you have black scuff marks on your linoleum of vinyl flooring, you can move them with a bit of white (nongel) toothpaste. Simply rub the toothpaste over the scuff vigorously until it disappears.

VACUUMS

Sprinkle rugs, couches, and upholstered chairs with baking soda and let it sit an hour before you vacuum. It will keep rugs cleaner and fresher over the long haul.

For a cleaner, brighter carpet, sprinkle a small amount of salt before you vacuum. The salt provides a mild abrasive cleaning action that won't hurt the fibers.

To rid your house of pet, cooking, or other smells, add a cotton ball soaked in vanilla or lavender oil to your vacuum cleaner bag. It's a great way to rid your home of an offensive odor by creating a nice scent instead.

If your vacuum hose has developed a crack and is leaking air, simply cover the crack with duct tape and keep on cleaning.

You can prevent marks on baseboards and walls when you vacuum by covering the edges of the vacuum head with masking tape.

Sprinkle some baking soda into the bag of your vacuum cleaner to keep it smelling fresh.

—*Rachel Vibbard*

....

If your disposable vacuum cleaner bag is full and you don't have replacement on hand, get out the duct tape! Remove the bag and cut a slit straight down the middle. Empty it into the garbage, then pinch the sides together at the slit and fold over. Tape the fold with a liberal amount of duct tape. The bag will hold a little less, but you'll be ready to vacuum again without having to run to the store.

» Kitchen

APPLIANCES

Microwave odors? Cut a lemon in quarters and put it in a bowl of water, then place in the microwave on high for 2 minutes. Wipe the inside with a soft cloth and any stains will lift easily.

....

To clean the smudged, greasy, food-flecked window of your microwave, use ashes from your fireplace. Rub them on into the window with a wet rag, then rinse clean.

....

How will you get the toast just right if you can't see through the toaster oven window? To clean it, mix 4 parts white vinegar with 4 parts hydrogen peroxide and 2 parts dishwashing liquid. You can wipe it down immediately with paper towels, or spray it on, let it sit for about an hour, and then wipe clean.

....

Here's the easiest way we've found to clean a countertop grill: Unplug it, then put a wet paper towel inside and close the lid for 10 minutes. The grease will be loosened up and easy to clean off.

....

To clean your electric can opener, run a piece of paper towel or wax paper through it. This will pick up the grease and most of the gunk.

....

For the best-tasting coffee, make sure to clean your coffee maker regularly. Just add several tablespoons of baking soda to your pot, fill it with water, and run it as usual. Then repeat using only water. You can also use a denture-cleaning tablet instead of baking soda.

....

Even your coffee grinder needs a good clean every now and then, and uncooked rice can do the job. Simply mill a handful of rice as you normally do to your coffee beans. The chopped rice cleans out the stuck coffee grounds and oils, and absorbs the stale odors to boot. Afterward, throw away the rice, wipe the grinder clean... and brew fresh coffee!

....

If you haven't had time to do the dishes and there's dried-on food stuck in the blades of your blender or food processor, it's baking soda to the rescue. Add 1 tablespoon baking soda along with 1 cup warm water to the bowl, put the lid on, and let it blend for 10–15 seconds. Wash as usual.

To keep your blender and mixer in top working order, be sure to lubricate all moving parts with a very light coating of mineral oil (*not* vegetable oil). Do this every three months.

COUNTERS

When you're done with an afternoon of baking, sprinkle your messy countertop with salt, and you'll be able to use a damp sponge to easily wipe away the doughy, floury mess you've left behind.

For a scratch-free cleaner that will make your countertops sparkle, apply club soda with a moist sponge.

A good all-purpose cleaner is essential to any well-run home. Keep this one on hand at all times (but out of reach of the kiddos). Start with ¼ gallon water and mix in ½ cup rubbing alcohol, a squirt of dishwashing liquid, and ¼ tablespoon ammonia (non-sudsy). Fill a spray bottle and you're ready to go.

You can remove stubborn stains from your countertop by applying a baking soda paste and rubbing with a warm, damp cloth. If the stain still remains, consider using a drop or two of bleach, but be careful—it can fade your countertop along with the stain!

If the enamel on your counter or tub has turned yellow, add a handful of salt to turpentine and rub onto the enamel, then wash as usual. Make sure to test in a small area of the counter first.

It's happened to us tons of times, and it's probably happened to you—a bag of bread is in the wrong place at the wrong time, and you end up with melted plastic all over the counter (or toaster). To remove melted plastic from metal, glass, or other plastic, first make sure the surface is cool (that is, unplug the toaster!). Then, rub the affected area with nail polish remover until the plastic scrapes off. Wipe down the surface with a damp sponge and let it dry, and you're back in business.

DISPOSALS

A quick and easy way to deodorize your in-sink garbage disposal is to grind an orange or lemon peel inside it every so often. It will get rid of grease—and smell wonderful!

Cleaning your garbage disposal is as easy as throwing a few ice cubes down your drain. Run the disposal until you no longer hear grinding, and the job is done. The cold cubes will congeal any grease in the drain, allowing your disposal to break it up.

Instead of throwing away baking soda away when it's finished its 30-day stint in your fridge, dump it down the garbage disposal with running water. It will keep your disposal fresh too!

Pour ½ cup salt down the drain of your kitchen sink with warm running water. This will freshen your drain and keep it from getting bogged down with grease.

Keep your garbage disposal running properly and odor-free with this simple once-a-month trick: Fill an ice-cube tray with white vinegar, and when frozen, grind about a dozen cubes. The ice sharpens the blades while the vinegar deodorizes the drain.

OVENS

Save a lot of clean-up time by lining the bottom rack of your oven with aluminum foil when you cook something messy. But never line the bottom of your oven with foil—this can cause a fire.

Oops, that pot in your oven boiled over, and there's a sticky mess on the bottom of your oven! To easily clean any oven spill, sprinkle salt on top as soon as possible. After a little while in a hot oven, the spill will turn to ash and you can easily clean it.

A self-cleaning oven can leave an odor after it's done its work. Eliminate the lingering smell by turning down the oven to 350° after the cleaning cycle, then placing a baking sheet lined with orange peels on the middle rack. Cook the peels for a half an hour, and not only will the oven smell fresh, but your whole kitchen will too!

A simple way to clean your oven is to place an oven-safe pot or bowl filled with water inside. Heat on 450° for 20 minutes, and steam will loosen the dirt and grease. Once your oven is cool, wipe off the condensation and the grease will come with it. When you're done, make a paste of water and baking soda and smear it on any enamel. The paste will dry into a protective layer that will absorb grease as you cook.

If you're cleaning your oven, make the job a bit easier with this solvent. Blend ¼ cup ammonia with a box of baking soda to make a soft paste. Apply this mixture to the stained, cooked-on spots inside your oven and let it sit overnight. Rinse well with regular water the next day, and your oven will look good as new.

Make your oven racks easier to clean by coating them with cleanser, placing them in a black plastic trash bag, and setting them outside in the sun. After a few hours, they'll be ready to spray off with a hose.

—Trish Mackay, Newark, DE

After you've cleaned your oven racks, coat the sides with a bit of vegetable oil. They'll slide in and out of the oven with ease.

—Claire Beevers, Essex, UK

Oven fans are magnets for grease. The simplest way to clean the resulting mess is to pop out the fan filter, then run it through your dishwasher on the top shelf.

REFRIGERATORS

There's still a use for old-fashioned correction fluid, so if you've still got it, use it as touch-up paint for white appliances, like your refrigerator. If your fridge has a ding but it's not white, try buying a small amount of touch-up paint from a car detailer.

When cleaning your refrigerator, don't use chemicals that can linger on your food and create nasty odors. After emptying the fridge, simply dissolve a cup of salt in a gallon of hot water and wipe away. Squeeze in the juice of a lemon for a nice scent.

Besides baking soda, a number of other foods are capable of removing odors. Pour a little vanilla extract into a bottle cap and set in the refrigerator to absorb odors. One of the best ways to eliminate odors from your refrigerator is to hollow out a grapefruit or orange and fill it with salt, and place in the back of the fridge. Leave it there until the salt gets completely damp, and then throw the whole thing out and replace.

....

It's time to do what you've been dreading: clean the caked-on grime that's been accumulating on top of your refrigerator. But don't worry, the job's easier than you think. Simply mix 1 tablespoon ammonia with 1 cup hot water. Apply a generous amount to the top of your fridge with a sponge or rag and let it sit for 5 minutes, then wipe away. When you're done, place an old placemat on top. When it gets gross, either replace it or throw it in the washing machine for a quick clean.

SINKS

You can quickly and easily clean your stainless steel with vodka. Place a little on a sponge or paper towel, then wipe. Your faucet, sink, and other stainless steel will soon be sparkling again, so pour yourself a little glass to celebrate!

....

Club soda is a terrific way to clean stainless steel sinks, dishwashers, ranges, and other appliances. The least expensive club soda works as well as the pricey brands; flat club soda is effective too. Add a little flour for really stubborn stains.

....

Nothing makes a kitchen look better than a shiny kitchen sink, and luckily, there's a cheap and easy method for getting one: Just use newspaper, which will get make your sink even shinier than a rag will. A tougher option is aluminum foil—crumple it up and scour with the shiny side.

For a spectacularly shiny finish on a stainless steel or aluminum sink, rub a liberal amount of baking soda in a circular motion all over its surface with a damp sponge.

For the shiniest sink you've ever seen, finish off your cleaning session by buffing the sink to a sleek shine with a touch of baby oil on a soft cloth.

For a stainless-steel sink that's been scratched, stained, and treated with every harsh chemical in the book, it might be time for a face-lift. Use chrome polish to buff it back to life.

You already know Pledge has many household uses, but did you know that one of the best ones is keeping your sink clean? If you've got a stainless-steel sink, wipe wood cleaner over it after you wash it out. If you do this at least once a month, the cleaner will keep your sink shiny.

As long as you're very careful, you can use lighter fluid to buff out rust stains on your sink! Just make sure to thoroughly wash your hands (or, better yet, wear rubber gloves) and the sink afterward.

SPONGES

There's no need to throw out your stinky, old sponges. Just soak them in cold salt water and rinse, and they're good to use again.

To quickly kill the dangerous bacteria that make a home in your kitchen sponge, wring it out, then microwave on high for 30–60 seconds. Don't nuke a dry sponge, or it might ignite.

To make your kitchen sponges and brushes last longer, wash them once a week in the utensil compartment of your dishwasher with a load of dishes. This will ward off any bacteria and mildew.

STOVES

Save on household cleaners by keeping your stove neater. How? When cooking, cover unused burners with a baking sheet or pizza pans. The pans will catch all the splatter, and they're easy to stick in the dishwasher afterward!

Forget about buying those expensive stove cleaners to get rid of cooked-on grease stains. Just wet the stains with vinegar and cover with baking soda. After watching the fun, foaming reaction, wipe with a damp sponge and buff with a dry, clean cloth.

If the hole in one of the burners of your gas-powered stove is clogged, never clean it out with a toothpick, which can break. Instead, use a straight pin or a pipe cleaner.

....

If your stove is made of stainless steel, you know how easily fingerprints appear. Clean them quickly and easily using some hand sanitizer. Just put a dab on a clean rag or paper towel, then wipe away the offending smudges.

....

Do the gas burners on your stove need a major makeover? Removing caked-on grime is easy, but it requires calling in the big guns: household ammonia. Pour ¼ cup into a large Ziploc bag, place two burners inside, and seal. Let the fumes work overnight, then rinse and rub with a rag or paper towel. Stovetop perfection!

....

If you're having trouble cleaning off the baked-on grease and grime on your range's hood or other areas around your stove, make your job easier without the help of harsh commercial cleaners. Instead, warm it up by blasting it with your hair dryer. Once it's warm, it will wipe right off with a damp cloth.

....

Car wax can be your best friend when it comes to caked-on grease and dust on your stove's hood. After cleaning it, rub approximately 2 tablespoons of car wax into the hood. The silicone in the wax will make it extra shiny while repelling future dirt.

Here's a tip to impress even your friend who has a superhuman level of household know-how: Use tea to keep gunk from sticking to your stove. Brew a pot of tea that is four times normal strength, then wipe it on your stove. The tannins in the tea will make it hard for grease and food to stick, making cleaning quick and easy.

Glass-top stoves are usually very easy to clean, but are susceptible to stuck-on stains. The trick is to make sure to remove food and grease spatters as soon as you can—if you heat up your stove again, you give them a chance to bake on, making them practically impossible to remove.

Mr. Clean Magic Erasers are one of the easiest ways to remove stuck-on food from glass-top stoves. But you don't have to spend a lot on them! These costly wonders are made from a material called melamine foam. Melamine foam has been used for decades as an insulator and sound-proofer, which means you can buy large sheets of it for less than the cost of a single box of "magic sponges." Buy some online or at a hardware store, then cut them down to size! They'll cost you less than 30¢ each.

If you have spots on your glass-top stove that you can't seem to remove, cover them with white vinegar and let sit for 10 minutes, then grab an old credit card or rewards card you rarely use. Its edge is perfect for scraping up the grime, but won't damage the stove.

We have an old dishcloth in our kitchen that we use especially for our stove. Dampen it and lay on your stove five minutes after you turn it off. By the time you're done with dinner, it will have softened any spills or spatters. All you'll have to do is just wipe them right off! Stove cleaning couldn't be easier!

—*Paula Graham, Springfield, MA*

Do you have a filthy, grease-spattered stove? Try this magic solution: Combine 4–5 spoonfuls of baking soda, ¼ cup water, and several drops of dishwashing liquid. Wipe this homemade cleanser all over your stove, and let sit for 10 minutes. Then, cut a lemon in half and rub the cut end over the cleaner. It will lift the grease and grime easily.

If you're cooking over the stove and grease splatters onto your clothes, think fast. Grab some baking soda from the cupboard and rub it into any fabric (towels, rugs, your shirt) to absorb as much grease as possible. This will make the stain harder to set, and soak up most of the grease before it works its way into the fibers.

TRASH BINS

When cleaning your kitchen garbage can, sprinkle a little scouring powder at the bottom. This will soak up any liquids if your bag leaks, and will also repel mildew and keep your bin smelling fresh.

Wash and deodorize trash cans with a solution of 1 teaspoon lemon juice mixed with 1 quart water. Sprinkling baking soda into the base of every garbage bag will also help keep odors at bay.

The next time you get a phone book you don't want, use the pages at the bottom of your trashcan. They'll sop of spills and you can simply throw them away rather than having to scrub the bottom of the can. Instead of phone book pages you can also use newspaper!

....

Here's another easy way to keep your trashcans from stinking up your home: Rip out those perfume strips from magazines and place one at the bottom of every trashcan throughout the house. Or try dryer sheets: They make your clothes smell fresh and wonderful, so they'll work miracles in stinky garbage pails too.

....

Borax is a household cleaner that you may not always have on hand, but we highly recommend picking up an inexpensive box at your local drugstore! One great use for borax is sprinkling it at the bottom of your garbage can. It will repel mildew, which can be the biggest culprit in causing trashcan odor, and it will also keep bugs away! Replace with fresh borax once every month.

....

Here's a great use for pantyhose that are too full of holes to wear again: Rip out the waistband, then stretch it around your garbage can to hold the folded-over part of the bag in place. It's like a giant, fabric rubber band that will keep your bag from slipping down into the can!

If your kitchen garbage can stinks every time you open the lid, it's time to get rid of the funk once and for all. Bring it into the bathroom and fill the bottom with a bleach-based bathroom cleaner. Let sit for a few minutes, then place it in the shower and turn on the water! Fill the can and dump it out several times, and grab your toilet brush to scrub it even further, if necessary. It's a dirty job, but somebody's got to do it!

» Jewelry

Looking for Jewelry Cleaning tips? *See Clothing and Accessories chapter, Jewelry*

» Laundry

Looking for tips about Laundry? *See Clothing and Accessories chapter, Laundry*

» Mustiness, Removing

Guests are arriving and you finally enter the guest room that's been closed off for months, only to find that the mattress smells musty even though it's perfectly dry. To solve this problem, turn the mattress and sprinkle a little baking soda on it before you make up the bed with fresh bedding. You can also sprinkle baking soda into pillow cases to freshen up pillows.

You can make your own dehumidifier for your basement or other musty areas without having to spend a lot in the process. Simply fill a coffee can with charcoal briquettes and punch a few holes in the lid. Place it in damp areas, and replace the charcoal once a month as it absorbs the humidity.

Humidifier smelling musty? Add 2 tablespoons lemon juice, and it will never smell fresher!

A great way to get rid of mustiness is with chalk. Break up a few pieces and place in a knotted sock or nylon. The chalk will absorb odors and keep enclosed areas like closets smelling fresh and clean.

» Surfaces, Other

ASHTRAYS

To make ashes slide right out of your ashtray without leaving a mess behind, clean it and coat it with a fine layer of furniture polish.

BOOKS

If you're placing some old books in storage and don't want them to acquire a musty smell, here's the solution. Place a new sheet of fabric softener inside the pages, and that battered copy of *To Kill a Mockingbird* will stay nice and fresh until you need it again. If you fail to follow this tip or if you have books that are *already* musty, just place them in a paper grocery bag with an open box of baking soda. Fold over the bag, staple it shut, and let it sit for a week or two. Your books should smell considerably better when you take them out.

Make your old, musty book smell like new with this simple trick. Sprinkle ½ inch of cat litter in the bottom of a container that has a lid, then seal the book inside for 12–24 hours. It will come out smelling like a book again.

—*Nina Harbert, Mt. Vernon, WA*

If your books stink, try this tactic for wiping out mildew. Dust mildewed pages with corn flour, French chalk, or talcum powder. Leave it inside the closed book for several days, then brush it off.

BRASS

Shining the brass hinges and knobs of your doors is easier than you think! Apply a white, nongel toothpaste (a mild abrasive) to door fittings with a soft cloth, then rub. Use a fresh cloth to wipe clean, and your brass will sparkle! To protect brass between cleanings, apply a light coating of olive or lemon oil.

To clean brass, apply white, nongel toothpaste on a soft cloth, and then rub firmly on the brass. Use a fresh cloth to wipe clean.

Here's a great cleaner for brass or aluminum. Sprinkle cream of tartar on a wedge of lemon and rub it into the surface. Let sit for 10 minutes, then rinse and buff dry. If you don't have any cream of tartar, you can also try this trick with baking soda.

Another way to clean and polish brass, make a paste of one part salt, one part flour, and one part vinegar. Rub this paste into the item using a soft cloth, then rinse with warm water and buff with a dry cloth for a glistening shine.

CHROME

What is chrome for, if not to be shiny? To bring back dull chrome fixtures, dampen them, then rub with newspaper. You can also shine them up with a paste of vinegar and cream of tartar.

If your chrome faucets are less than sparkly, try rubbing them with flour. Rinse, then buff with a soft cloth, and they'll really shine. Vinegar also works well for cleaning chrome.

COPPER

Here's an unlikely cleaning tool—ketchup. It works great on copper. Simply rub on with a soft cloth, let sit for 30–45 minutes, then rinse off with hot water and wipe dry.

We admit we kind of like the look of that green coating (patina) over copper, and it was popular as a pigment in oil paintings in the Middle Ages. But the deposit signals damage and should be removed from jewelry, antiques, coins, nameplates, and the like. Using a soft cloth but lots of elbow grease, rub a mix of equal parts baking soda and deodorized kerosene into the affected item. If it's a utensil that can take the abrasion, use fine steel wool or a toothbrush to get into tiny pieces.

One of the best cleaners for copper is a simple lemon! Cut it in half, sprinkle the cut side with salt, and rub over the surface you're cleaning. Rinse with cold water and watch it shine.

FIBERGLASS

Cleaning fiberglass is, unfortunately, an adults-only chore. Using plastic gloves in a well-ventilated room, mix together 1 cup vinegar, ½ cup baking soda, ½ cup clear ammonia, and 1 gallon warm water. Designate a sponge just for this purpose (or use a rag) and be sure the solution doesn't touch your skin when you rub it onto the fiberglass.

FIREPLACES

Looking for Fireplace Cleaning tips? *See* **Decorating chapter, Fireplaces**

FURNITURE

The best way to keep leather furniture clean is to have your children and pets stay away! But if it gets dirty, there are a few ways to tackle the problem. You can rub down treated leather with a damp cloth, and an occasional date with warm soapy water won't harm it. If you get a spot on leather furniture, try removing it by rubbing it with artists' gum—a super powerful eraser that can be found at art supply stores. If you accidentally get a liquid that badly stains on your leather, blot up as much as you can, then apply hydrogen peroxide with a cotton ball to wipe it up.

If your kid has decided to write a novel on your favorite leather chair, don't panic. Just blot the stain with milk until the ink disappears, then wipe it clean with a damp sponge.

Cornmeal absorbs grease stains on light-colored fabric or upholstery. Pour on enough to cover the soiled area and let it sit for 15–30 minutes, then vacuum. The stain will be gone!

You just bought the coffee table of your dreams, but when it was sitting in the store you didn't realize it would attract fingerprints like bees to honey. To get rid of a persistent fingerprint problem, rub down the tabletop with cornstarch. The surface will absorb the cornstarch, which will repel prints.

GLUE REMOVAL

Looking for Glue Removal tips? *See* **Home Repair chapter, Simple Solutions**

GOLF CLUBS

By now you've probably realized that we have a substitution for just about every household cleaner. But what about when your prized golf clubs get dirty? Resist the urge to spend money on fancy cleaners. Instead, dissolve a scoop of laundry detergent into a bucket of water, and soak your clubs for one minute (no longer).

PLASTICS

If you're having trouble peeling off a label or sticker without leaving a gooey mess behind, trying applying white vinegar until it's saturated. It will come right off!

....

There aren't many cleaners designed especially for plastics, but it's easy to make your own. Simply mix a quart of water with 3 tablespoons of either lemon juice or white vinegar. Pour it in a spray bottle, and you've got some plastic cleaner.

....

To get rid of duct tape residue, simply rub with vegetable or olive oil. Let it sit for 5–10 minutes, then wipe up. The residue should be much easier to scrape off with the rough side of a kitchen sponge and some warm water.

TOYS

Looking for tips on Cleaning Toys? *See* **Kids chapter, Simple Solutions**

» Walls

CRAYON MARKS

If the kids have drawn with crayons all of their bedroom walls, remove it with a bit of WD-40 spray, which works like a charm. Afterward, you'll need something to remove the grease—we like a mixture of dishwashing detergent and white vinegar. If you don't have any WD-40, dip a damp rag into baking soda and rub the mark to remove it.

HOLES

Small holes in your white wall? It's toothpaste to the rescue! Simply dab a small amount of white (non-gel) toothpaste into the hole and you'll never notice it again—or, at least, your guests won't.

PAINTED WALLS

Clean painted walls with a solution made of 1 cup white vinegar, ¼ cup club soda, and 1 quart warm water. Simply dip a rag or sponge into the solution and use to wipe down walls.

What's the easiest way to remove crayon, pencil, ink, and furniture scuffs from painted surfaces? Sprinkle baking soda on a damp sponge, rub clean, and rinse.

If your beautiful candle is staining your walls with black soot marks, don't try to simply scrub them away—that will only make more of a mess. Instead, remove those unsightly spots by sponging them with rubbing alcohol.

It seems cruel that, after spending so much of your time cleaning your home, dust still manages to get places you never thought to clean—like your ceiling. To vanquish this last bit of dirt, use a clean, dry paint roller with a long arm to dust quickly above your head.

WALLPAPER

A great way to clean wallpaper is with white bread. You can eliminate fingerprints, light stains, and even ball-point ink by simply rubbing a piece of white bread vigorously over the spot.

To eliminate grease on wallpaper without using chemical cleaning products, cover the area with a brown paper bag or kraft paper, then apply a warm iron. The paper will absorb the grease.

» Windows and Blinds

BLINDS

Is there any chore more annoying than dusting your venetian blinds? Luckily, you don't have to buy one of those "blinds cleaners." Instead, use bread crusts. Just hold a piece of crust around each slat, then run it along the length of the blinds. An old paintbrush will also do the trick, or you can use the brush attachment on your vacuum cleaner.

An easy way to clean blinds is to wrap a kitchen spatula in an old cloth and secure it with a rubber band, then dip it in rubbing alcohol or your favorite cleaner, close the blinds, and go to it!

Aluminum blinds are great for keeping out light, but they can be hard to clean! The easiest way to clean smudges off aluminum blinds is with a pencil eraser. Dust will come off with a few swipes of a fabric softener sheet.

There always seems to be one thing around your house you just haven't figured out how to clean easily. For us, it used to be the pull cords on our venetian blinds. They were grimy from years of greasy hands, but taking down the blinds always seemed liked too much work. Finally, we found a solution. Get a stepladder or something the same height as the top of the blinds (where the pull cord begins). Fill a jar with cold water and add a tablespoon of bleach. Pull your blinds up so the maximum amount of cord possible is exposed. Rest the jar on top of the ladder and soak the cord for two to three hours. When you're done, transfer the cord to a jar of water to rinse, then pat dry with some rags or towels.

··

Give mini blinds a good clean by simply throwing them in the bathtub filled with water and white vinegar or your favorite cleanser. Shake them out well and hang them up wet. There may be a few streaks once they've air-dried, but they're nearly impossible to spot.

··

Stubborn smudges and stains on your window blinds? Lay the shades on a table or countertop and rub the spots with an art-gum eraser (which can be found at art or office supply stores). It will erase the smudges away!

FROST

To keep your windows or sliding glass door from frosting over on the coldest days of winter, wash them with a mixture of 1 quart warm water and ½ cup rubbing alcohol. Now you'll be able to see clearly, even if it's too cold to actually venture outside.

··

If your windows are frosting over, dissolve 1 tablespoon salt in 1 gallon hot water and rub on the panes with a soft cloth. Then wipe away with a dry cloth. This will often keep your windows frost-free.

To create a temporary "frost" for a bathroom window, mix a solution of 1 cup beer and 4 tablespoons Epsom salts. Then paint the mixture onto the window. The paint will wash off easily.

JAMBS

Don't pull a muscle trying to shove open a stuck heavy window. Windows will open and close more easily if you occasionally rub a bar of soap across the track.

WINDOWS

Do you have streaks and lint on your windows after washing them? Instead of cleaning with paper towels, try newspaper. It's cheap, easy, and green!

We always prefer to clean our windows with something reusable, like an old rag. But if you like to go the disposable route, try coffee filters instead of paper towels. They won't leave behind any lint or paper pieces.

You don't need expensive cleaners to wash your windows! For a cheap, effective glass cleaner, fill a spray bottle with ½ teaspoon dishwashing liquid, 3 tablespoons white vinegar, and 2 cups warm water. If you're washing something that's very dirty, use more liquid soap.

Lemon juice makes an excellent glass cleaner, and will even add an extra shine. Spray it directly onto glass and rub with a soft cloth to dry. Rub newspaper over the area to get rid of any streaks.

If the sun is shining on your windows, wait until they are in the shade to wash them. When they dry too quickly, they tend to streak.

Do you feel like you can never get a window completely clean? Here's an easy tip that will help you to tell which side of the pane those godforsaken streaks are on. Simply wash your windows from top to bottom on the inside, then switch to washing side to side on the outside.

To remove the gummy remains of a label or sticker on a window or a mirror, cover it in mayonnaise and let it sit for 5–10 minutes, then gently scrape off with a putty knife.

» Wood

CLEANERS

Stale beer is a great cleanser for wooden furniture. The next time you have flat beer leftover in a can, don't dump it out. Instead, use it to dampen a soft, clean cloth, then wipe it onto your wood furniture. Dry with a dry cloth and it will shine!

There's no need to buy a special cleaner for your wood floors. Simply mix equal parts vegetable oil and white vinegar in a spray bottle, and apply. Shine with a clean cloth until the solution is gone.

GENERAL CARE

Don't keep your good wood furniture in direct sunlight, especially during the hot summer. It damages the finish and can bleach the wood.

If a piece of your wooden furniture or a wooden windowsill has gotten wet, resist the urge to dry it out with a space heater or hair dryer, as too much heat will make wood crack and warp. Instead, keep the area at room temperature and aim a fan at it.

MARKS AND STAINS

Does your wood furniture have white rings left from wet glasses? Remove them with a mixture of 2 tablespoons corn oil and enough salt to make a paste. Apply the paste to the rings and let stand for at least one hour before rubbing the area gently. If the finish on your furniture is very delicate, you can substitute baking soda for the salt (it's less abrasive).

If you have a mark on your wood furniture or floor that won't come off with furniture polish, try leaving mayonnaise on the stain for an hour, then wiping off.

If you've got kids, you probably have watermarks on your finished wood table. Use a little petroleum jelly to remove the white stains. Just rub the area with the jelly and let sit for several hours (or even overnight). Then rub again with a soft cloth—the stain should disappear.

Removing candle wax from your wood floor is easy: First soften the wax with a blow-dryer, then wipe with towel soaked in vinegar and water.

If you've just dumped nail polish on your floor or table, don't despair. You may be able to remove it with shaving cream. Using a soft cloth, rub shaving cream on the nail polish, leave for several minutes, and wipe off. Just make sure to test an inconspicuous area of the surface first, to make sure the shaving cream won't harm it.

POLISHING

For an effective alternative to wood cleaners and polishes, use baby wipes to whip your wood furniture and paneling into shape.

Preserve the beauty of wood by rubbing the surface with boiled linseed oil. Wipe away the excess with a soft cloth.

Out of furniture polish? Check the pantry! Vegetable or olive oil works wonderfully on wood furniture. A very light coat will nourish the wood and help protect the finish, but be sure to rub it in well so it doesn't leave a residue. Leftover brewed tea (at room temperature) can also be used on wood furniture.

Excess polish can build up and leave a dull finish on wooden furniture. To remove it, mix together 2 tablespoons white vinegar and 2 tablespoons water. Apply to the surface and wipe off at once. Alternatively, cornstarch will also do the trick: Sprinkle a little on the furniture and polish with a soft cloth.

SCRATCHES

Looking for tips on Repairing Wood Scratches?
See **Home Repair chapter, Woodworking**

Auto

Baking

Beauty

Cleaning

Cooking

Decorating

» Clothing and Accessories

Entertaining and Holidays

Health and Wellness

Home Repair

Kids

Money

Organization

Outdoors

Pest Control

Pets

Shopping

Utilities

Vacations and Family Activities

Websites

» Accessories

CONTACTS

Lost a contact lens and can't seem to find it anywhere? Turn off the lights and turn on a flashlight. Sweep it over the area where you lost it and the lens will reflect the light.

Nothing's worse than crawling around the floor trying to find a lost contact. If you've been looking, one-eyed, for too long, try this trick. Get an old nylon stocking and secure it over the end of your vacuum hose using a rubber band. Then run your vacuum where you think you lost the contact. The lens will stick to the stocking.

GLASSES

If you've gotten hairspray on your eyeglasses, just wipe them down with rubbing alcohol and you'll be seeing clearly again.

Most optometrists will try to sell you an expensive cleaner when you buy your glasses. Instead of buying theirs, simply use a tiny dab of white toothpaste (not a gel) on both sides of the lenses to polish them and keep them from fogging up.

What household item will cause eyeglasses or mirrors to stop fogging? Shaving cream! It's weird but true: Just rub the glass with cream, leave on for a couple of minutes, then rub off for a fog-free finish.

The next time you're digging through your pockets looking for a cloth you can clean your glasses with, try a dollar bill. Press hard and it will do the job of a glasses cloth in a pinch.

If the tiny screws of your glasses keep coming loose, add a dab of clear nail polish to the threads of the screws before screwing them back in. The polish will keep them from coming out again.

If your sunglasses have gotten completely twisted, don't throw them out. Just turn a blow-dryer on high and aim it at your frames. The heat makes the plastic arms flexible enough for you to gently bend them back to their original shape.

GLOVES

You've just come in from outside, and your snowy gloves have quickly turn into sopping wet ones. To dry them out in time for your next excursion into the winter air, pull them over the bottom of a jar, then place the jar upside down on top of a radiator or heating vent. The warm air will fill the jar and dry out your gloves in no time.

HATS

Big hat (or small head)? Make your ball cap tighter by cutting a piece of duct tape lengthwise and wrapping a few layers around the sweatband.

> Wash a baseball cap on the top rack of your dishwasher, and remove while still wet. Then, place the cap over a bowl to regain its shape, and dry it away from direct sunlight.

PANTYHOSE

Weird but true: Freezing panty hose can keep them from running. Before wearing a pair of nylons for the first time, stick them in the freezer overnight. The cold strengthens the fibers, which will keep them from running.

If your nylons seem prone to getting runs, try soaking them in salty water before you wash and wear them. Use a half a cup of salt for each quart of water, and let them soak for 30 minutes. Then launder as usual.

If you notice a run in your pantyhose, don't despair. Just place a bit of clear nail polish at either end of the run and it will keep your hose from running any further.

UMBRELLAS

Before you throw away an umbrella, see if you can fix it by sewing the fabric back onto the metal arm—easily accomplished with a simple sewing kit!

» Ironing

CLEANING

If only because they have the word "cleaner" in their name, we're always looking for ways to use pipe cleaners that don't involve crafts! Here's a good one: to clean the holes in your iron, dip a pipe cleaner in white vinegar and poke into each hole. Just make sure the iron is cool and unplugged!

....

Another way to clean your iron is to pour equal amounts of white vinegar and water into the water holder of the iron. Turn the dial to "steam" and leave it upright for five minutes. Unplug and let the iron cool down. Any loose particles should fall out when you empty the water.

....

If your iron is beginning to stick to fabrics, sprinkle some salt on a piece of waxed paper and iron it. The salt will absorb the stickiness.

....

If you've been ironing too many clothes with starch and your iron is starting to get sticky, run it over a piece of aluminum foil to clean it.

....

If you've ever had scorched, melted polyester or vinyl on your iron, you know what a mess it can be. Wait for your iron to cool, then rub the melted muck with a rag that has been dipped in nail polish remover. Scrape off the mess with a wooden spoon (or anything else made from wood—metal can scratch). Wipe with water before ironing again.

IRONING TRICKS

When ironing, vinegar can be your best friend for removing (or making) creases. Just mix one part white vinegar and one part water in a spray bottle. Spray it on your garment and then run your iron over the spot to remove even ironed-in creases! A few spritzes of this vinegar and water solution can also help remove those shiny areas on fabric that are caused by hot irons.

....

When you're done ironing, spray your half water, half white vinegar solution on collars and underarm areas to prevent yellow marks.

....

Need to clean your iron? A paste of vinegar and baking soda is the easiest way to clean the base (sole plate) of your iron. Clean your ironing board by spraying it with a vinegar and water solution and ironing it while it's still damp.

....

Covering your ironing board with shiny-side-up foil before you iron your clothes will get them unwrinkled twice as fast, saving you time and energy!

Add a drop of perfume to the water in your steam iron, then iron your shirts, underwear, lingerie—everything! You'll enjoy your favorite perfume wherever you go.

Ironing pants with pleats? Use bobby pins to keep the pleats intact and you won't have to worry about ruining them with the iron.

Keep the waistband of your slacks from curling up by ironing a strip of rug binding onto it. Problem solved!

A great way to defend the purchase of a straightening iron for your hair is to point out the contribution it will make to the household: ironing those hard-to-reach places between buttons on a blouse or dress shirt!

If you scorch a garment when ironing, cover the scorch mark with a vinegar-dampened cloth, then iron with a warm iron (not too hot). Presto! The burn is gone. For scorches on cotton garments, you can also use hydrogen peroxide or lemon juice instead. Just dab onto the scorch and leave out in the sun, which will bleach away the stain.

Nervous about ironing lace items? Don't be. Before ironing, simply dip the lace in sugar water, and your item should emerge from ironing unscathed.

....

Rescue a straw hat by placing a damp cloth between the straw and a warm iron. Rest the brim underside up on the ironing board and press, rotating the hat. For flat tops, place cardboard inside and pack with crumpled newspaper before pressing.

» Jewelry

BRACELETS

> Having trouble getting that bracelet on? Make fastening easy by attaching the bracelet to your arm with a bit of tape. Then clasp, pull the tape off, and go!

CLEANING

Baking soda is safe and effective when it comes to cleaning gold and silver jewelry. For best results, use a paste of baking soda and hydrogen peroxide, and rub gently on your jewelry. It gets rid of dirt, grime, and body oils, and leaves your gold and silver sparkling.

....

We tend to think that because gold is valuable it must be hard to clean, but the truth is it's simple. Solicit the kids' help for this one if you'd like. All they need to do is make a paste from ½ cup water and 2 teaspoons baking soda and use a soft rag to rub whatever gold piece you want clean. Then rinse with water.

....

If your silver jewelry is starting to look a little dull or needs polishing, stick it in a bowl with a few tablespoons of baking soda and a square of aluminum foil. Let it sit for about 30 minutes, then wipe clean. The aluminum acts as a catalyst for ion exchange, a process that will make the tarnish transfer from your silver to the baking soda. This is the magic of science, folks!

—*Brooke Llewellyn, Kansas City, MO*

....

Wondering how to keep your beautiful jewelry looking like the first day you wore it? Gentle dishwashing detergent and water plus a soft cloth can clean rubies, amethysts, citrines, emeralds, sapphires, and garnets. Just make sure to wash each piece separately to avoid chipping. Diamonds can be washed similarly: Fill a small pot with a cup of water, plus a teaspoon of dishwasher detergent. Add your diamonds, bring the water to a boil, then turn off the heat and let the pot sit until it cools. Once it's cool (but not before), carefully remove your jewelry and rinse.

....

Since turquoise, opals, and marcasite are porous stones, never immerse them in water. Instead, polish them with a soft, dry chamois and clean claws with a soft bristle brush.

....

Keep your beautiful amber jewelry clean by wiping with a soft cloth wrung out in warm, soapy water. Dry at once (water makes amber cloudy), and wipe with sweet almond oil to remove any grease marks.

....

Clean costume or inexpensive jewelry by dropping two Alka Seltzer tablets into a glass of water. Immerse jewelry for about five minutes and pat dry with a clean towel.

....

> The easiest way to clean emeralds, diamonds, rubies, and sapphires may be with club soda. Place your jewelry in a glass of it overnight, and they will shine like new in the morning.

....

The best way to care for a pearl (or coral) necklace is to wear it regularly—oils from your skin add a gentle luster. After wearing, wipe with a chamois to remove traces of perspiration that can damage the surface. You can also wash pearls and coral in water and very mild soap, then wipe with a soft cloth. Lay on a moist paper towel to dry.

ORGANIZING

Looking for tips on Organizing Jewelry? See Organization chapter, Jewelry

REPAIR

For annoying tangles in thin necklace chains, place on a glass surface. Add a drop of oil and use a pin to tease out the knots. Then rinse in warm water.

....

If you've ever seen condensation under your watch face, you know how frustrating it can be! Luckily, there's a solution. Simply strap the watch to a light bulb and turn it on for a few minutes. The heat from the bulb is the perfect amount to make the water disappear.

....

It sounds like something from a fairy tale, but by tapping stones on your rings you can tell if they're starting to come loose. A rattle doesn't mean you'll turn into a pumpkin by midnight, but you should go to the jeweler to get it reset.

....

If a stone has popped out of a piece of your jewelry and you were lucky enough to save it, you can easily put it back in place with a tiny dab of clear nail polish.

RINGS

If you are unable to remove a ring from your finger, run your hands under very cold water for a few seconds. The cold will make your blood vessels (and, in turn, your finger) a little bit smaller, allowing you to slip off the ring. For a really stubborn situation, go the messier route—rub baby or olive oil over the area for a little lubrication.

UPKEEP

Never wear silver jewelry in pools, because chlorine can cause pitting, small indentations in the surface. It's not a particularly good idea to wear gold jewelry in chlorinated water either, so make sure to leave your valuables at home before heading to the pool.

» Laundry

DRYING

If you find your clothes are still dripping wet when you take them out of the washing machine, put them back in and set the cycle to spin. The extra spin time will wring them out even further, and use less energy than extra time in the dryer will.

....

Add a big, dry towel to the clothes dryer when drying jeans and other bulky items. It will cut the drying time significantly.

....

Jeans are usually tight enough as it is! To minimize shrinking, wash them in cold water, dry them on medium heat for only 10 minutes, and then air dry them the rest of the way.

....

Line drying your clothes is energy efficient and great for them. Not only is air-drying less harsh, you'll love the real smell of sun-dried linens. If you don't have a clothesline, hang shirts and pants on hangers from tree limbs! Just make sure not to put brights in the sun, as they made fade.

FABRIC SOFTENER

Never buy fabric softener again! Instead, simply use white vinegar. Use the same proportions as you would for a liquid fabric softener—you'll never notice the difference.

Here's an all-natural fabric softener that is also way less expensive than the store-bought kind. Just add ¼–½ cup baking soda to the wash cycle.

Save on laundry products while you're saving the environment. Instead of buying fabric softener sheets, pick up a bottle of the liquid kind. Mix a solution of one-half fabric softener and one-half water, and put it into a spray bottle. For every laundry load, spritz onto a cloth and toss it in the dryer. A small amount (several sprays) will go a long way.

Cut your dryer sheets in half (or in quarters). You won't be able to tell the difference in your clothes, but your wallet will.

Does it seem as though your clothes get greasy stains on them in the laundry? It may not be your imagination. One cause: adding undiluted fabric softener. Remove these stains by pre-treating the fabric with a paste made of water and detergent, or use a commercial stain remover. Next time, dilute the fabric softener before you add it, or skip the stuff altogether and use vinegar instead.

FRESHENING

To remove a smoky smell from your clothes, fill your bathtub with hot water and add 1 cup white vinegar. Then just hang the clothes above the steaming water, and the smoke smell will dissipate in about a half hour. Ah, vinegar—is there anything it can't do?

Get stubborn odors left behind by cigarettes off clothes by adding a half a cup of baking soda to the wash cycle when doing your laundry.

If your clothes are extra greasy, add a can of lemon-lime soda to your washing machine along with detergent. The acid in the soda breaks down the oil in the greasy clothes, and your wash will sparkle.

Nothing stinks on your clothes like gasoline! To remove the odor, place the offending clothes in a bucket of cold water, and add a can of cola and a cup of baking soda. Soak overnight, then line dry outside if possible. If there is still any odor left, just wash as usual and it should be gone.

LEATHER AND SUEDE

If you were enjoying a nice day outside until a bird pooped on your leather jacket, don't go get your BB gun. Instead, rub a bit of petroleum jelly into the spot and let set for five minutes. It should rub right off.

....

Your emery board that you normally use on your nails can remove small stains from suede. Gently rub the file across the stain a few times to remove the mess.

....

Got a grease spot on suede? Vinegar to the rescue! Simply dip an old toothbrush in white vinegar and gently brush over the grease.

LINENS

Looking for tips on Laundering Linens? *See* **Decorating chapter, Bedding**

SORTING

Here's our tip for sock sorting the easy way: Use a mesh lingerie bag or pillowcase to launder each family member's socks separately. It's an easy way to keep them together so they'll be easier to sort later.

....

If you have a plastic laundry basket that has cracked or has a handle partially torn off, cover the rip with duct tape on both sides. It may not be pretty, but it works just as well as a new one.

STAINS

Don't let a stain "set" even if you are running out the door. Instead, spray with stain remover or soak in water and store in a resealable plastic bag until you have time to deal with it. Once a stain dries, it's much harder to remove. You should also never rub a fresh stain with a bar of soap. Many stains can set further when treated with soap.

Here's a great use for a cleaned-out plastic bottle (of the ketchup or salad dressing variety). Keep a mixture of water and laundry detergent, or your favorite stain remover, inside, and use it to quickly pre-treat stains on your clothing.

> Here's a great tip if you get those pesky yellow stains on the collars of your dress shirts. Wipe the back of your neck with an alcohol-based astringent before you get dressed in the morning. The alcohol will prevent your sweat from leaving a stain.

IRONING · JEWELRY · **LAUNDRY** · SEWING · SHOES · STYLE

Whether you're using a commercial stain remover or one of the stain remedies in this chapter, you may have to apply a stain-remover more than once for tough stains. Don't give up if it doesn't come out the first time! If all else fails, just keep the garment near your washing machine and wash it over and over (applying the stain-remover each time) until the spot is gone. Just make sure the stain is gone before you dry the fabric in the dryer. The heat from your dryer can further set the stain.

Berries

If you have berry stains on your clothes, soak them overnight in equal parts milk and white vinegar. Then launder as usual.

Blood

To get out blood stains, soak the stained area in club soda before laundering. If the blood is fresh (ouch!), make a paste of water and talcum powder, cornstarch, cornmeal, or meat tenderizer and apply it to the stain. Let it dry, and then brush it off.

Coffee

To remove coffee stains, stretch the garment over a bowl, cover the stain with salt, and pour boiling water over the stain from a height of one to two feet. (The gravity helps.) Of course, always test first that the garment can withstand hot water (unlike, say, cashmere). Repeat a couple of times if necessary, but some of the stain (especially if it's not fresh) may remain. If so, treat with your usual spray-and-wash stain remover and then launder.

Cosmetics

Dampen a stain from your make-up with water and rub gently with a white bar soap (like Dove or Ivory), then rinse well and launder.

Deodorants and Antiperspirants

When dealing with stains left by sweat and deodorant, we always turn to vinegar. Soak underarm areas in vinegar for 10 minutes before washing, and the yellow stain (and the smell) will be gone by the rinse cycle. If this doesn't work, you can also try rubbing a paste of baking soda and vinegar into the stains before washing the usual way. If the stain remains, repeat with rubbing alcohol, then launder. To prevent them in the future, coat the would-be stained area on the inside of the shirt with a spray adhesive (available at your local craft store). The adhesive will seal the fibers, so that sweat and your deodorant can't get inside—or stain the cloth. You can also try sprinkling on a little baby powder before you iron the spot.

Dirt

If your kid's been playing in the mud again, rub shampoo over the soiled area and let sit for 5 minutes before washing. For tougher stains, try pre-soaking in a mixture of one part warm water, one part ammonia, and one part laundry detergent.

Gasoline

Removing gasoline stains from clothing can be tricky. The most effective way we know of is to apply baby oil to the stain, then launder as usual. Since gasoline is an oil-based product, it takes another oil to pull out the stain and smell.

Grass

You can get rid of grass stains with toothpaste. Scrub it into the fabric with a toothbrush (naturally) before washing. The white (non-gel) kind works best.

....

Sometimes our kids get so many grass stains on their clothes, we think we should just buy them all-green outfits. To get out grass stains, try rubbing the stain with molasses or corn syrup and let stand overnight, then wash with regular dish soap by itself.

Grease

If you catch a grease stain before it dries, first remove as much of the grease as you can with baby powder or baking soda. Apply to the stain, let it sit for an hour or so, and then wipe off the powder. Then pretreat grease stains with a bit of dishwashing liquid for several minutes, and launder as usual. Liquid dish detergent is made especially to get out grease—which is why it is perfect for removing grease stains from your clothes.

Gum

Rub gum stuck on clothes with ice until the gum hardens, then carefully remove it with a dull knife before laundering. If that doesn't work, you can also try placing a piece of wax paper on the affected area, then ironing the wax paper. The gum should transfer from the cloth to the paper.

....

To remove gum stuck on fabrics, warm a cup of vinegar in the microwave. Dip an old toothbrush in the gum and brush the gum until it comes out. It saved my husband's shorts!

—*Paulette Culpepper, Hermitage, TN*

Ink

Trying to get an ink stain out? Spray ultra-stiffening hairspray on the spot, then launder as usual. Hairspray will usually remove the stain.

....

To remove ink from clothing, rub the area with a cut, raw onion, letting the onion juice soak in. Let sit for two to three hours before laundering.

Ketchup and Tomato Products

Remove excess ketchup with a dull knife, then dab with a damp, warm sponge. Apply a bit of shaving cream to the stain, and let it dry before laundering as usual.

Mustard

Hydrogen peroxide is effective at getting rid of mustard stains. After making sure the fabric is colorfast, apply a small amount to the stain and let set for several minutes before laundering.

Nail polish

Unfortunately, the only thing that can remove nail polish is nail-polish remover. If the fabric can withstand this harsh chemical, work it in from the inside of the fabric by pressing it in gently with a paper towel.

Oil

The best way to remove stains from cooking oil (olive, vegetable, canola, etc.) is with regular shampoo. Just make sure it doesn't have a built in conditioner.

Old or unknown stains

If a stain is so old that it has set, try softening it up with vegetable glycerin. Glycerin can be found in health food stores, vitamin shops, and online. Apply some to the stain and let set for an hour before laundering.

Paint

Treat a paint stain while it is still wet: latex, acrylic, and water-based paints cannot be removed once dried. While the paint is wet, rinse in warm water to flush the paint out, then launder. Oil-based paints can be removed with a solvent; your best bet will be to use one recommended on the paint can.

....

Got dried paint on your clothes? Unfortunately, it's often impossible to remove. Before you give up completely, however, try saturating the stain in one part ammonia and one part turpentine, then washing as usual.

Perspiration

A great way to remove perspiration stains from white shirts is to crush 4 aspirin tablets into ½ cup warm water, and apply to the stain. Soak for at least three hours, and launder as usual.

Rust

Remove rust stains by wetting the spots with lemon juice, then sprinkling with salt. Let the fabric stand in direct sunlight for 30–45 minutes.

Scorch marks

If you have a scorch mark on fabric, your quest to remove it begins in the kitchen. Cut the end off of an onion and grate about a fourth of it into a bowl using a cheese grater. Rub the stain with the grated onion, blotting it with as much of the onion juice as you can. Let it sit for 8–10 minutes, and if necessary, re-apply the onion juice. Once the stain is gone, launder as usual.

Shoe polish

Try applying a mixture of one part rubbing alcohol and two parts water for colored fabrics and only straight alcohol for whites for shoe polish stains. Sponge on, then launder.

Suntan lotion

You had a great time at the beach, but you accidentally got suntan lotion all over your cover-up. To remove this stubborn stain, cover with liquid dish detergent and rub in. Then turn your kitchen sink on at full blast and run under cold water.

Tar

Tar stains are tough to remove, but vinegar can help. If you've stained fabric with tar, try pouring a few drops of white vinegar on the stain and washing as usual. We've also had luck removing grass, coffee, soda, and fruit stains with vinegar.

....

Tar stain? Rub gently with kerosene until all the tar is dissolved, then wash as usual. As with all stain removers, make sure to test a small area first to be sure the fabric is colorfast.

....

If you have a tar stain on your clothes, try petroleum jelly—just rub it in until the tar is gone. The jelly itself might stain the fabric, but it's easy to remove with a spray-and-wash stain remover.

Tea

Tea and lemon are best friends—even in the laundry room. Rub a tea stain with equal parts lemon juice and water. Just make sure the mixture only gets on the stain, using a Q-tip or eyedropper if necessary.

Tobacco

If you have a tobacco stain on your clothes, we'll spare you the lecture on smoking and just tell you to moisten the stain, then rub with white bar soap (like Dove or Ivory), then rinse and launder.

IRONING JEWELRY LAUNDRY SEWING SHOES STYLE

Wine

Blot a wine stain with a mixture of one part dish-washing liquid and two parts hydrogen peroxide. If this doesn't work, apply a paste made from water and cream of tartar and let sit.

Yellowing

Weird but true: Discolored socks or other whites will return to their original color if you boil them in a pot of water with a few slices of lemon.

SWEATERS

If cuffs or necklines of woolen sweaters are stretched out of shape, dip them in hot water and dry with a blow dryer.

If your favorite cashmere or angora sweater is looking a little worn, put it in a plastic bag and place it in the freezer for half an hour. The cold causes the fibers to expand, making your sweater look new again! Who knew there was such a thing as sweater cryogenics?

When putting away your sweaters for the spring and summer months, wrap them in newspaper and tape the sides. The newspaper will keep away both moths and moisture.

If you've accidentally shrunk a sweater in the dryer, there may still be hope. Let it sit in a bucket of water with a generous amount of hair conditioner mixed in. The chemicals in the conditioner can untangle the fibers in your sweater, making them expand back to their original condition. If that doesn't work, it's time to cut up the sweater and make some new mittens!

WEAR AND TEAR

The easiest way to make your clothes last longer is to wash them less. Many of your clothes can be worn several times before you wash them, especially sweaters. Most items get more wear and tear from being in the washing machine than they do on your bodies! When you do throw in a load, make sure to turn knitted clothes and T-shirts with designs on them inside out when washing and drying.

Rotate through your bras rather than wear one for a few days in a row. You'll give the elastic time to contract and the bras will last longer. Who knew?

If your velvet dress, shawl, shirt, or pants are getting a shiny mark from too much wear, you may be able to remove it. Try lightly spraying the area with water, then rubbing against the grain with an old toothbrush.

Do you have a jacket, backpack, or tent that used to be water resistant, but has lost its effectiveness over time? Set your hair dryer to its highest setting and blow air evenly over it. The warmth will reactivate the coating on the cloth that makes it repel water.

When storing leather and suede garments, don't cover them in plastic. These materials need a little breathing space, or they'll quickly dry out.

If your black cotton items are starting to look more like they're dark blue, wash a load of only black items. But first, brew a strong pot of black coffee, then add it to the rinse cycle.

» Organization

Looking for tips on Organizing Clothes? *See* **Organization chapter, Clothing**

» Purchasing

Looking for Clothes Shopping tips? *See* **Shopping, Clothing**

» Sewing

BUTTONS

Here's a tip for the thrifty (and clever): Always remove buttons before discarding a garment. They will come in handy later!

Dab a small drop of clear nail polish on the front of a button to keep the threads in place and never lose a button again.

After rifling through your clothes for half an hour, you've finally decided on the perfect outfit to wear—but a button is loose! If you're about to lose a button and you're already halfway out the door, use a twist tie instead. Just remove the paper covering, then twist it through the holes in the button and fasten on the other side of the cloth. Just make sure to replace with real thread later!

When sewing on buttons, place a toothpick between the button and the garment. This will ensure you're not sewing it too flush with the fabric.

—*Joyce Barone, Hoboken, NJ*

Pearl buttons, whether they're real or fake, can benefit from a coating of clear nail polish. They'll never lose their shine, and it will be harder to nick them.

IRONING JEWELRY LAUNDRY SEWING SHOES STYLE

HEMMING

When you let down hems on clothes such as skirts, dresses, and pants, there is often a white mark where the fabric was turned up. Vinegar can be used to get rid of this pesky stain. First warm up your iron, and then scrub the mark with an old toothbrush dipped in white vinegar that has been diluted with small amount of water. Then press with the iron. The mark will usually come right out, but if it doesn't repeat the process until it does.

You've bought a great pair of jeans, but they're too long and you don't have time to hem them before you need to wear them. Simply fold them up and tape with duct tape. The hem will last the whole night—and maybe even through a couple of washings. This is also a great tip if you're not sure exactly where you want to hem your pants. Have a "trial run" using the duct tape, and then they're all ready to sew.

MENDING

If you're mending a hole on a sleeve or pant leg, it's easy to miss a stitch when the fabric gets all balled up. Make your job easier by rolling up a magazine and placing it inside. It will partially unroll as far as the sleeve or leg will let it, creating just enough tension to hold the fabric in place.

Do you use a thimble to sew or sort papers? If so, wet your finger before you put the thimble on. This will create suction, so the thimble stays put.

NEEDLES

To quickly thread a needle, spray the end of the thread with a bit of hair spray. It will stiffen the thread and make it much easier to get through the eye, leaving you ready to darn all those socks.

....

If your needle has grown dull, sharpen it up again by running its tip back and forth on an emery board several times.

—*Patricia S., West Plains, MO*

....

If a pin or needle will not easily penetrate thick fabric, this little household trick will make sewing a cinch: Simply stick the pin into a bar of soap to make it nice and slippery.

ORGANIZATION

Looking for tips to Organizing Sewing Supplies? *See* **Organization chapter, Clothing and Accessories**

SEWING MACHINES

There's no need to replace your sewing machine needle if it's become dull. Simply stitch through a piece of sandpaper a few times and it will be sharp again.

It's fun to work with sheer materials for curtains and lingerie, but they can be very unwieldy when you're using a sewing machine. If you sew them to paper (which you'll rip off as soon as you're done), they will stay smooth. Make sure to use needles made for lightweight fabric and fine thread.

ZIPPERS

Zipper won't budge? Try adding a tiny bit of vegetable or olive oil to the stuck teeth with a Q-tip, being careful not to get any on the fabric. This will lubricate your zipper and allow it to move more easily.

Rub a beeswax-based candle or lip gloss on a stuck zipper and the problem is solved! You can also try rubbing the zipper with the lead from a pencil.

Got a zipper that won't stay closed? Spray it lightly and carefully with hairspray after zipping up.

» Shoes

FRESHENING

Get rid of nasty shoe odors by sprinkling salt in them and leaving overnight. The salt will absorb moisture and odors.

Place a fabric softener sheet in your shoes overnight to get rid of any foul odors. This also works for hampers, gym bags, or anything else that needs a little freshening.

Here's another great tip for preventing smelly shoes. Take a couple of old socks without holes and fill them with scented cat litter. Then place them in the shoes when you're not wearing them. They'll suck up any moisture—and odor.

To keep your shoes smelling better, store them in the freezer! It sounds funny, but it's true: The cold temperature slows down the growth of microscopic funkiness-makers.

LACES

Having trouble keeping your (or your kids') shoelaces tied? Shoelaces are more likely to stay tied if you dampen them with water first.

Do you shoelaces keep getting untied? Just rub some ChapStick onto the laces and they'll stay put.

—Nikki Forshay, Colorado Springs, CO

....

If you or your children's shoelaces often come untied, you may be tying them wrong. Bows that we tie with shoelaces work by using a square knot—and you may remember the adage "right over left, left over right, that's what makes a square knot nice and tight." Unfortunately, most of us do what's easiest for our hands—and that's tying both the beginning knot and the bow "right over left." If you look down at your shoes and the loops from the bows are pointing towards you rather than laying flat across the shoes from left to right, then you aren't tying a square knot properly! To fix this, simply reverse the way that you tie the beginning knot for your bow. In other words, if you normally cross the right shoelace over the left at the beginning, switch so that you're crossing left over right. It might take your hands a while to get used to it, but your bows will stay so well you won't even need to double-knot them.

NEW

New shoes? Cobblers will stretch them out for you, but there's no need to pay their price. Do it yourself by wearing your new shoes around the house and out to run errands for a few days, and wear two pairs of thick socks with them. The extra padding will stretch out the shoes until there is plenty of room for your feet, and will also make your feet less likely to get blisters when you're ready to wear your new shoes out on the town.

—Betsy Beier, Viroqua, WI

....

To wear in new leather shoes without having to wear them around the block ten times, rub alcohol in at the heels and wear them while they're still wet. Soften them by rubbing them with olive or castor oil, which will also prevent cracking and drying.

....

Going out in new shoes? Lots of fun. Slipping as you walk past your new crush? Not so much. Use sandpaper to distress slippery leather soles and slick surfaces won't slip you up.

....

Want your white sneakers to stay white? After purchasing new white canvas sneakers, spray them with spray starch to help them resist stains. The starch will repel grease and dirt, keeping them whiter!

REPAIR

If the heels on your nicest pair of shoes broke or your shoes are starting to wear out, a shoe repair shop will be your best money-saving bet: They'll get your shoes in tip-top shape for much less than the cost of a new pair.

....

If you have a pair of espadrilles whose heels are looking ragged, patch them up with everyday brown twine you can find at the hardware store. Cut the twine into pieces that fit in the gaps and adhere with shoe glue.

SCUFF MARKS

> If you have black scuff marks on shoes, luggage, or other items, try rubbing lemon juice on them. Rubbing alcohol also works well.

Just about any scuff mark can be removed with the help of some nail polish remover. Wet a rag with some, then rub on the scuffmark lightly but quickly. You may need to give your shoes the once-over with a damp cloth afterwards.

Uh oh, your new white canvas shoes just got a big, black scuff on them. The best way to get them looking like new again is to dab a bit of liquid White-Out on the stain. You won't be able to tell the difference when looking down from above.

Are your white shoes suffering from scuff marks? Rub a little baking soda into the offending areas and the marks will practically disappear.

SHINING

For a brighter shoeshine, place a few drops of lemon juice on your shoes when you are polishing them. Lemon juice is also great for cleaning: A small amount mixed with salt will remove mold and mildew from most surfaces. The juice is just acidic enough to do the job.

Shining your leather shoes? Forget the shoe polish. First, dampen a cloth and wipe away any dirt, then put a few drops of vegetable or olive oil on a clean, soft cloth and rub into your shoes. Another way to treat scuffs is by wiping them with the cut edge of a raw potato, then buffing with a soft cloth.

To revive the beauty of leather, lightly beat two egg whites and then apply to the leather with a soft sponge. Allow the egg whites to remain on the leather for 3–5 minutes, and then wipe off with a soft cloth dampened with warm water. Dry immediately and buff off any residue.

After polishing your shoes, spray them with a bit of hairspray. People will wonder how you got them so shiny!

SLIPPERS

It's such a simple solution, you'll wonder why you didn't think of it sooner. To make your slippers waterproof and therefore safe to wear on a quick trip outdoors, simply cover the bottoms with overlapping layers of duct tape.

WINTER WEATHER

To protect your leather shoes from getting damaged and stained by too much rock salt in the winter months, coat them with hair conditioner and let it soak in. The conditioner will repel the salt, and help keep them supple.

Make your winter boots a little warmer—and make sure they're completely waterproof—by lining the bottom of the insides with duct tape. The tape will create a waterproof seal, and the shiny silver will reflect your body heat back onto your feet.

....

If your shoes or boots are stained with salt from trudging through winter streets, simply dip a cloth or an old T-shirt into white vinegar and wipe away the stain. It's that easy!

» Style

BRAS

Research has shown that 80 percent of women wear the wrong bra size. A good-fitting bra shouldn't be too tight or ride up in back, and the cups should be big enough to be supportive. At a lingerie shop or department store, ask if they offer free, professional fittings. You may be surprised to find you've been buying the wrong size your whole life.

....

One of the narrowest areas on a woman's body is across the ribs, just beneath the bustline, yet large or droopy breasts can hide this area. Make your figure look more like an hourglass by wearing a supportive, push-up style bra, which will help make the line from rib to hip look more elongated and shapely.

JACKETS

As gravity (and middle-age) takes its toll, a layer of fat may be making its way around your midsection. We'll let you decide whether to hit the gym, but when you hit the store, stay away from double-breasted jackets. Always choose single-breasted suits, as two sets of buttons make the body appear wider.

OUTFITS

The whole point of jewelry is to enhance your beauty. So if you're self-conscious about your neckline, by all means steer clear of a dramatic choker. Try bracelets and elegant headbands instead. If those daily crunches are starting to pay off, wear a flashy belt or bright scarf wrapped around just above the hips to draw attention to your slimming waistline.

You don't need to purchase a shaper and certainly not a corset to make yourself look five pounds slimmer. Try leotards, tight-fitting tank tops, leggings, and spandex running pants. The trick is to layer them underneath your nice outfit so you don't get the "Are-those-pajamas-you're-wearing?" look. You'll feel firmed up and pulled-together, at least until you catch sight of your hair.

The biggest thing people do wrong when trying to hide their weight is to buy loose-fitting clothes. The truth is, baggy clothes will just make you look bigger. Instead, find an outfit that accentuates the positives (and everybody has some positives!)—whether that's your hourglass hips, great legs, or beautiful neckline. Getting clothes that are tailored, but not tight, will not only draw attention where you want it to, but will let people know that you're still confident about your appearance—which is way sexier than losing a few pounds around your waist.

PANTS

You may scoff that low-waisted pants are for teenagers only, but they can have their benefits. Jeans and pants that sit between the hips and the waist can help hide extra weight, as higher-waisted pants clamp the middle tummy, making it appear larger and highlighting a lack of waist.

Add a little extra length to your legs by always wearing pants that cover the top of your shoes and just skim the floor.

Most of us have a little more tummy than we'd like. Luckily, you can help disguise it with the help of tailored pants. When shopping for dress pants, choose a look that has a flat front and a side zipper, which won't add any bulk to your front.

SHIRTS

If you're like us, you have a million XL T-shirts that you've gotten from various organizations and events. Unfortunately, all of them make you look like a formless blob. Fix them into something you would actually wear by getting a little creative. To make a scoop-necked shirt that's perfect to wear over bathing suits or tank tops, cut off the piece of fabric that runs along the neck hole with a pair of scissors. Try the shirt on, and cut a little at a time until it fits your style and shape. To make a fitted tank top from your XL shirt, cut off the sleeves, then slice up the sides of the shirt and stitch them back together more tightly to fit your form.

STATIC CLING

One easy way to remove static cling is to run the long part of a wire hanger over the garment. If you've suffered any skirt-stuck-to-pantyhose embarrassment, run the hanger between your skirt and the pantyhose.

Slinky skirt grabbing your pantyhose and won't let go? Solve this annoyance with an unlikely household hero: a battery! Just rub the positive end of a battery over your skirt and hose. (If this happens to you a lot, you can just keep a AAA battery in your purse!) The battery releases positively charged ions that neutralize the negative ones that cause static cling. Bada-bing, no more static cling!

If you've ever had your skirt or slip stick to your pantyhose due to static electricity, you'll love this tip. Just spritz a little hair spray on your nylons and they'll not only be free of static, they'll be less likely to run.

—*Francie J. Shor*

Auto

Baking

Beauty

Cleaning

Clothing and
Accessories

Decorating

» **Cooking**

Entertaining
and Holidays

Health and
Wellness

Home Repair

Kids

Money

Organization

Outdoors

Pest Control

Pets

Shopping

Utilities

Vacations
and Family
Activities

Websites

» Baking

Looking for tips on Baking Bread, Cookies, and Cakes? *See Baking chapter*

» Beverages

ALCOHOL

Looking for tips about Alcohol? *See Entertaining and Holidays chapter, Alcohol*

COFFEE

If you're sensitive to acidity in coffee, but love the pick-me-up in the morning, here's a way to reduce the acid level: Just add a pinch of baking soda to the drink! You can also use this tip to decrease the acidity in other high-acid drinks and foods.

Does your coffeemaker require cone-shaped filters? Save some cash by purchasing the less expensive round filters in bulk. You can buy a 500-pack for cheap, then shape the filters into cones so they fit your machine. With a few simple folds, they work just as well as the pricier alternatives.

It's 3 p.m., and with the day you've had, you're headed back for a second (or third) cup of coffee. Unfortunately, once you heat up some cold joe that's been sitting in the pot, you notice it looks thick and tastes a little bitter. Make stale coffee taste like it's just been brewed by adding a pinch of salt and a dollop of fresh water to your cup. Heat it up in the microwave, and you're ready to power through the rest of your workday.

If you love sweetened, flavored coffee, simply mix ¼ teaspoon vanilla extract or 1 teaspoon cinnamon with 1 cup sugar in a food processor until well-blended, then add a little scoop to your next cup. It's usually much cheaper than buying flavored coffees or creamers, and tastes better, too.

Flavored coffee is such a treat, but most families can barely manage to keep enough of the regular stuff stockpiled. Luckily, it's easy to add your own flavors with ingredients you have on hand. Orange peel, vanilla extract, cinnamon, allspice, or ground-up roasted nuts can all be mixed in to coffee grinds before you brew. To make 6 cups of coffee, you just need ¼ teaspoon of whatever flavor you choose. Experiment to get the proportions exactly to your liking.

If your cream or half-and-half has begun to develop an "off" odor, but you desperately need it for your coffee, try mixing in 1/8 teaspoon baking soda, which will neutralize the lactic acid that is causing the cream to sour. Before you use the cream, however, taste it to be sure the flavor is still acceptable.

Who doesn't enjoy an iced coffee on a sultry summer day? To make sure melting ice doesn't dilute your drink, make ice cubes using the small amount of coffee left at the bottom of your coffee pot each morning. Use them in your iced coffee and it will never taste watered down. This is also a great tip for iced tea!

A frothy, foamy cappuccino at home can really cheer up the family on a long, rainy afternoon (decaf for the younger crowd). But you don't need to buy an espresso machine or spend hours holding the milk up to one of those little steamers. Instead, once the milk is heated, simply beat it with a handheld mixer. You'll know it's ready when those white, luminous peaks are nicely holding themselves up. Pour into a mug, spoon the foam, and add cinnamon or chocolate powder. Voilà.

ICE CUBES

When ice cubes stay in the freezer tray more than a few days, they tend to pick up odors from foods you have stocked away. Give them a quick rinse before using them to avoid altering the flavor of your beverage.

Yes, even ice cubes can be perfected. Do yours look like they've melted and refrozen a hundred times? Make them beautiful and clear by using water that you've boiled, cooled, then poured into the tray.

If you're trying to retrieve a stubborn ice cube from the ice cube tray, here's a surefire trick. Run your finger under running water for a second, then press it to the center of the cube. The ice will stick to your finger long enough for you to transfer it into your glass.

JUICE AND SODA

Trying to break free from your soda or juice addiction? Add a couple of slices of lemon or orange (or both) to your filtered water pitcher, and try drinking that instead. Your taste buds will be satiated, and your body will thank you! If you find yourself drinking a lot of soda at work, bring the pitcher with you and place it on your desk. You'll find that you'll normally choose convenience over a run to the vending machine for your sugary fix.

> **Lost the cap to your soda bottle? Use a wine cork instead! They're usually the perfect size.**
>
> —*Maria Delakis, Shaker Heights, OH*

When you pour a warm soft drink over ice cubes, the gas escapes from the beverage at a faster rate because the ice cubes contain a greater surface area for the gas bubbles to collect on, thus releasing more of the carbon dioxide. This is the reason that warm beverages go flat rapidly (and sometimes fizz over the glass), and why warm drinks poured over ice go flat even faster. To slow down the process, add ice after you've poured the drink and the bubbles have dissipated.

The vitamin-C content of fruit juices halves after a few days in the fridge, so if you're making juice at home, it's best to drink it as soon after squeezing as possible to get the most nutrients.

TEA

Want to get more for your money when it comes to tea? Always buy the loose variety, and then use one-third of what's recommended. Just let the tea steep a little longer, and it will taste exactly the same as if you used the full amount.

Cloudiness is common in home-brewed iced tea, but it can be easily prevented. Simply let the tea cool to room temperature before refrigerating it. If the tea is still cloudy, try adding a small amount of boiling water to it until it clears up.

>> Breakfast

OATMEAL

If you're hooked on instant oatmeal packets, try this trick instead for big savings. Buy instant oats in bulk, then in a sandwich bag combine ¼ cup oats with ½ teaspoon each of sugar and cinnamon, and a pinch of salt. Pre-pack several and you're set for the week!

PANCAKES

Pancakes and other griddle treats need to be cooked at a precise temperature to turn out best. But how do you know when the cooking surface has reached the right temperature? Flick a few drops of water on the heated griddle. If the surface is 325°F (the perfect temperature for pancakes), the droplets will skitter and dance—steam causes the drops to rise, but gravity brings them back down. If the griddle is 425°F or hotter, the water drops will be propelled right off the griddle, and you should turn down the heat.

Substitute club soda for water when making pancakes, and they'll be fluffier than clouds. The air bubbles in the soda means more air in your pancakes, making them super fluffy.

Short-order cooks and chefs have a host of tricks to make the lightest pancakes. First, don't overmix the batter—you don't want the gluten in the flour to over-develop and allow the carbon dioxide that makes the little air pockets to escape. It's better to leave a couple of lumps in the batter. To further slow the development of the gluten and the leavening action, refrigerate the mixture for up to 30 minutes.

When making pancakes, always stir the batter before you pour each pancake onto the griddle. The ingredients can settle; stirring recombines them and aerates the batter.

When cooking on a griddle, you'll get better results if you clean it between each batch of pancakes or whatever you happen to be making. Do this easily with coarse salt wrapped in a piece of cheesecloth. The salt will provide a light abrasive cleaning and won't harm the surface if you're gentle.

The trick to fluffy pancakes? Make sure you flip pancakes as soon as air bubbles appear on the top, then flip them back over if necessary to finish cooking them. If you wait until the bubbles break, gas escapes, and your pancakes won't be as light or fluffy.

If you like brown-on-the-outside pancakes, add a little extra sugar to your batter. The sugar caramelizes, giving a darker color to the pancakes. Also, some people swear by adding a tablespoon of pure maple syrup (the real stuff—no imitations!) into your pancake batter.

For perfectly formed pancakes, use a meat baster to squeeze the batter onto the griddle. It gives you so much control you'll finally be able to make those animal-shaped pancakes your kids have been begging you for!

If you're a pancake lover, you can make the process painless by thoroughly rinsing out a squeezable ketchup or salad dressing bottle. Pour the batter in and squeeze, and you'll have neater, rounder, and more precise pancakes. You can even store the leftover amount in the fridge for next time.

SYRUP

Frustrated with syrup running down the sides of the bottle, making a disgusting mess? Try this trick: Rub the threads at the neck of the bottle with a small amount of vegetable oil. The oil will prevent the syrup from running and the cap from sticking next time you open it. This also works for molasses and honey containers.

....

Out of maple syrup and still want to make waffles this morning? Try this delicious substitute. Combine $1/3$ cup butter, $1/3$ cup sugar, and half a can of frozen orange juice concentrate in a saucepan. Cook over medium heat, stirring constantly, until the sugar has dissolved and the mixture is syrupy.

WAFFLES

Here's a trick to keep waffles from sticking to the waffle iron: Beat a teaspoon of white wine into the batter. You'll never taste the wine, but it will keep the batter from adhering to the hot surface.

....

For a quick and healthy breakfast, make waffles ahead of time, then freeze them. When you or your family is ready to eat, pop them in the toaster to re-heat. Making waffles from scratch, rather than buying them in the frozen foods section, will save you money. You can also easily do this with French toast!

....

For a different type of toast, lightly butter a slice of bread on both sides and cook it in a waffle iron. Your kids will love it!

» Dairy

BUTTER

Whenever I need soft butter and all I have are hard, refrigerated sticks, I simply shave off the needed amount with a vegetable peeler. In a matter of seconds, the butter shavings will be soft.

—*Grace Carrick, Arlington, VA*

BUTTERMILK

Next time you need buttermilk in a recipe, don't go buy a whole carton that you'll later throw away half-full. Instead, make an easy buttermilk substitute by adding a tablespoon of vinegar to a cup of milk and letting it stand for five minutes to thicken.

CHEESE

Here's a chef's secret for keeping a grater clean so you can use it repeatedly without washing: Simply grate the softest items first, then grate the firmer ones.

One of the easiest ways to cut soft cheeses like feta and goat cheese? Use dental floss! Hold the floss tight and give it a slight sawing motion as you move it down to cut through the cheese.

To quickly and easily "grate" Feta or other soft cheeses, just push the cheese through a colander with a potato masher.

Always bring cheese to room temperature for one hour before serving it. Even if the cheese melts a little, the flavor will be much better.

Believe it or not, cheese with a little mold on it is still perfectly safe to eat once you remove the offending areas. The easiest way to do this is to take a knife, dip it in vinegar, and slice the mold off.

The rinds of hard cheeses like Parmesan are great flavor enhancers for soups. Add a 3-inch square to your next pot of soup, and when you're serving the soup, break up the delicious, softened rind and include a little of it in each bowl. It's completely edible.

CURDLING

If you've added too much citrus to dairy and caused it to curdle, add an ice cube to the mix and you'll be back in business in no time. The cold will actually reverse the curdling process.

—*Charles Strohm, Calgary, AB*

To keep milk from curdling, stir in a pinch of baking soda before you heat it.

» Desserts

Looking for Dessert tips? *See Baking chapter,* **Other Desserts**

» Eggs

DEVILED

When it comes to picnics, nothing is more impressive than a perfect deviled egg. To keep yolks centered when boiling eggs for deviled eggs, stir the water while they are cooking.

Deviled eggs wobbling on the platter? Cut a thin slice off two sides of the egg before you halve it lengthwise. This will give each egg half a flat base.

Here's a method for making deviled eggs that's so simple you'll want to make them for every picnic. After hard-boiling eggs, slice them open and place their yolks in a resealable plastic bag. After mashing them up through the bag, add the mayonnaise and the rest of the ingredients. Mash some more to blend, then cut off the corner of the bag and use like a pastry bag to easily dispense the mixture into egg halves.

FRYING

When frying an egg, the butter or margarine should be very hot before the eggs are added—a drop of water should sizzle when added to the melted butter. However, the heat should be reduced just before the eggs hit the pan. Cook the eggs over low heat until the whites are completely set.

Want to get that perfect white film over the yolks of your eggs? Add a couple drops of water and cover the pan just before the eggs are done.

HARD-BOILING

Who doesn't love a hard-boiled egg? Great for snacks or a light lunch, these tasty treats are easy to prepare—especially if you add a teaspoon of vinegar and a tablespoon of salt to the boiling water. The salt will make them easier to peel, and the vinegar keeps them from cracking while they're in the pot.

Another way to prevent boiled eggs from cracking is by using lemon. Just cut a lemon in half, then rub the cut side on the shells before cooking them.

If an egg does crack while it's boiling, it's easy to fix. Just remove it from the water and, while it is still wet, pour a generous amount of salt over the crack. Let the egg stand for 20 seconds, then put it back into the boiling water.

....

To remove the shell from a hard-boiled egg in one piece, exert gentle pressure while rolling it around on the counter, then insert a teaspoon between the shell and the egg white and rotate it.

....

Always cool a hard-boiled egg before you try to slice it; it will slice more easily and won't fall apart. Your best implement if you don't have an egg slicer? Dental floss! Just hold taut and slice through the egg.

....

Using your hard-boiled eggs for egg salad? The fastest way to chop eggs is to peel them, place them in a bowl, and run a pizza cutter through them several times.

....

It's easy to tell whether an egg has been hard-boiled: Spin it. If it wobbles, it's raw—the yolk sloshes from one end of the egg to the other. Hard-cooked eggs spin evenly, because the yolk is held in place by the cooked egg white. Reduce your risk of spinning an egg right off the counter by adding a drop or two of food coloring to the water when you boil them. It will dye the shells so you can tell the difference between the two kinds.

OMELETS

To make a great omelet, be sure the eggs are at room temperature (take them out of the fridge 30 minutes beforehand). Cold eggs are too stiff to make a fluffy omelet.

....

For a super fluffy omelet, add ½ teaspoon baking soda for every three eggs. Also, try adding a drop or two of water instead of milk. The water increases the volume of the eggs at least three times more than the milk does. The coagulated proteins hold in the liquid, resulting in a moist omelet.

....

The best omelet you will ever eat has mustard in it. Just add ¼ teaspoon fancy mustard for each egg, and mix in when scrambling. The mustard will add a hint of mysteriously delicious flavor to the eggs, as well as making them the perfect consistency.

—*Aggie Bossolina, Jupiter, FL*

POACHING

The fresher the egg, the better it is for poaching. The white will be firmer and will help to keep the yolk from breaking. Salt, lemon juice, and vinegar will make egg whites coagulate faster. Add a dash of one of these ingredients to the water before poaching eggs to help them keep their shape.

SEPARATING

Even if you don't have an egg separator, it's easy to divide an egg's yolk and white. Place the smallest funnel you have over a container, then gently crack the egg into it. The white will slide into the container; the yolk will stay behind.

....

Believe it or not, you can save egg yolks for later use. If you have used egg whites in a recipe and want to save the yolks, slide them into a bowl of water, cover with plastic wrap, and store in the refrigerator for a day or two. It beats throwing them out!

....

When beating egg whites for a recipe, remove all traces of yolk from the bowl with a Q-tip or the edge of a paper towel before trying to beat the whites. The slightest trace of yolk will prevent the whites from rising properly, as will any trace of fat on the beaters or bowl.

....

When you're going to beat egg whites for a recipe, let the eggs sit at room temperature for 30 minutes before using them. The egg whites will then beat to a greater volume.

....

If your recipe requires eggs but you don't want the calories of egg yolk, use the egg white mixed with a teaspoon of olive oil instead. This gives a better consistency than using the whites on their own, which can make the mixture too light, plus you'll reap extra health benefits.

» Fruit

APPLES

> If apples are dry or bland, slice them and put them in a dish, and then pour cold apple juice over them and refrigerate for 30 minutes. OK, so it's kind of a cheat, but it will ensure picky eaters get their nutrients!

If you have a bunch of apples that are going to go bad soon, here's how you can use them up quickly: Cut them into wedges or smaller chunks, dump them in a saucepan, and sauté them in butter over medium heat. When that's finished, sprinkle a half sugar/half cinnamon mixture on top, and you've got a yummy treat that the kids will love. You can even use them as the start of a homemade apple pie!

AVOCADOS

This trick is for adults only: To easily remove an avocado pit, thrust the blade of a sharp knife into the pit, twist slightly, and the pit will come right out.

If you bought a whole bunch of avocados for your guacamole and one or two are still not ripe enough to use, try this tip—which isn't ideal, but will do the trick. Prick the skin of the unripe avocado in several places, then microwave it on high for 40–70 seconds, flipping it over halfway through. This won't ripen the avocado, but it will soften it enough that you'll be able to mash it with ripe avocados and your guests won't notice the difference.

You may look good with a tan, but your guacamole sure doesn't! To keep the avocados from oxidizing (which causes the brown color), cut the avocados with a silver or stainless steel knife, and leave the pit in the dip (until serving). Sprinkle lemon juice on the surface of the dip, and cover tightly with plastic wrap until you're ready to eat.

CHERRIES

For a quick and easy way to pit cherries, use a pastry bag tip. Just set the tip on a cutting board with the jagged edge pointed up, then firmly press the cherry down on top of it. Be careful not to cut your fingers!

GRAPEFRUIT

It's surprising, but true: A small amount of salt will make a grapefruit taste sweeter.

MANGOES

If you slice open a mango and it tastes too acidic, place it in warm (not hot) water for ten minutes. This will speed up the process of its starches turning into sugars, and it will be sweet in no time! Just make sure not to leave it in the water for more than ten minutes, as it might begin to shrivel.

MELONS

To keep melons from getting moldy as they ripen, rub the exterior peel with a teaspoonful of full-strength vinegar every few days.

RAISINS

Sad-looking raisins? To plump them up to perfection, place them a small baking dish with a little water, cover, and bake in a preheated 325°F oven for 6–8 minutes. Or, pour boiling water over the raisins and let them stand for 10–15 minutes.

Raisins and other dried fruits won't stick to your knife (or anything) if you first soak them in cold water for 10 minutes.

RIPENING

Fruit normally gives off ethylene gas, which hastens ripening. Some fruits give off more gas than others and ripen faster. Other fruits are picked before they are ripe and need a bit of help. If an unripe fruit is placed in a brown paper bag, the ethylene gas it gives off does not dissipate into the air but is trapped and concentrated, causing the fruit to ripen faster. To get it to ripen even more quickly, add a ripe apple—one of those ethylene-rich fruits.

SALADS

Even though the taste isn't affected, it's still disappointing to unveil your fruit salad only to discover a thin layer of brown oxidation all over the fruit. A common method for keeping cut fruit looking fresh is to add a bit of lemon juice. However, an even more effective method is to fill a spray bottle with water and a few dissolved vitamin C tablets (usually available in the vitamin and nutritional supplement section of your drug store). Spray this mixture on the cut fruit and not only will you stop the oxidation, you'll be getting added vitamins!

STRAWBERRIES

Hate the waste of lopping off strawberry stems with a knife but like to serve the delicious summer treats ready-to-eat? Try this: after washing, push the stems out from the bottom up using a plastic straw.

» Grilling

Looking for Grilling tips? *See Entertaining and Holidays chapter, Barbecues and Picnics*

» Long-Lasting Food Tips

BEVERAGES

Unlike other kinds of coffee beans, fresh-roasted coffee beans should not be stored in airtight containers. Fresh-roasted beans are usually packed in bags that are not airtight, allowing the carbon monoxide formed during the roasting process to escape. If the carbon monoxide doesn't escape, the coffee will have a poor taste.

To make the bubbles in your soda last longer, decrease the amount of air that the carbon dioxide (which causes the fizz) has to escape into. This is easily accomplished by squeezing in the sides of the bottle after you pour a glass.

BREAD

Bread stays fresh for a longer time if you place it in an airtight bag with a stalk of celery. If you are going to freeze a loaf of bread, make sure you include a paper towel in the package to absorb moisture. This will keep the bread from becoming mushy when thawed.

If you find that your bread often goes stale before you use it, slice it and store in the freezer. Separate out slices and let them sit for about five minutes at room temperature to defrost, or stick them directly in the toaster. Frozen bread is also great to use for grilled cheese sandwiches—it's much easier to butter, and it will defrost as it cooks in the pan.

CONDIMENTS

It's frustrating to have to throw out condiments like sour cream, mayo, yogurt, and mustard because you didn't use the entire container before it went bad. However, you can easily combat this by changing containers as you use up the item. Using a smaller container exposes the condiment to less air—and fewer bacteria. The trick, of course, is making sure you successfully transfer every bit of mayo possible from the jar to the tiny Tupperware. We usually do our container downsizing right before we're about to use the condiment on something. That way, we can scrape out what we don't transfer for our sandwiches.

DAIRY

It's better to store milk on an inside shelf toward the back of the refrigerator, not on the door. Why? All dairy products are very perishable. The optimal refrigeration temperature is actually just over 32°F; however, few refrigerators are ever set at or hold that low a temperature. Most home refrigerators remain around 40°F, and the temperature rises every time the door is opened. Store cheese near the bottom of the refrigerator, where temperature fluctuations are minimal.

....

Adding a teaspoon of baking soda or a pinch of salt to a carton of milk will keep it fresh for a week or so past its expiration date.

....

When you know your milk is going to go bad before you can use up the rest of it, separate it out into a few resealable containers and put them in your freezer. That's right, milk can be frozen! If you use skim milk, it can be thawed and drunk later, and you'll never be able to tell the difference in taste. For other varieties of milk, after thawing, use for sauces or baking. This is a great strategy for when you find milk at a deep discount. Buy as much as you can and freeze for later!

....

Inside the fridge, margarine and butter quickly absorb odors from other foods. Make sure you always keep them tightly sealed to keep them at their best quality.

Cheese will stay mold-free longer if placed in a sealed plastic container with a tight-fitting lid. Add three or four sugar cubes, which will attract any mold if some does form.

> To keep cheese fresh and moist, wrap it in a cloth dampened in white vinegar and put it in an airtight container.

Before you store semi-hard cheeses like Cheddar, Swiss, or Gruyère, rub the cut edges with a little bit of butter. You'll never notice the taste difference, and the cheese will be less likely to dry out or become moldy.

Because of its high water content, cottage cheese doesn't last as long as other food products in the refrigerator. To extend its life, store it in the container upside down.

Believe it or not, you can successfully freeze many varieties of cheese without them losing their taste or texture. Cut into small blocks, place in sealed plastic bags, and then keep in the freezer for when you need them. Cheese varieties that can be successfully frozen are Brick, Cheddar, Camembert, Edam, Gouda, Mozzarella, Muenster, Parmesan, Port du

Salut, Swiss, Provolone, Mozzarella, and Romano. Small cheeses, such as Camembert, can even be frozen in their original packages. When removed from the freezer, cheese should be put in the refrigerator and used as soon as possible after thawing.

....

To help sour cream last longer, add white vinegar right after you open it (1 teaspoon for a small container and 2 tablespoons for a large container). You won't notice the taste, and the sour cream won't go bad as quickly.

EGGS

To avoid the absorption of refrigerator odors, always store eggs in their original carton on an inside shelf of the refrigerator. Before you put away the carton, though, turn each egg upside down. Storing eggs with the tapered end down maximizes the distance between the yolk and the air pocket, which may contain bacteria. The yolk is more perishable than the white, and even though it is more or less centered in the egg, the yolk can shift slightly and will move away from possible contamination.

....

For eggs that last practically forever, separate them into whites and yolks, then freeze them separately in a lightly oiled ice-cube tray. When frozen, pop them out and store in separate Ziploc bags in the freezer. These frozen eggs are perfect for baking, and will last longer since they're separated. Egg-cellent!

MEAT AND SEAFOOD

Store cooked foods above uncooked meat in your fridge. This minimizes the risk of food poisoning caused by drips from uncooked meat and other foods. Wrap any food with strong odors and avoid storing it close to dairy foods, which can become easily tainted. And throw away that slimy lettuce at the back of the vegetable drawer!

Is chicken on sale this week? Stock up and use your freezer! For meal-size portions, store it in double freezer bags. For whole chickens, remove their original packaging and store them in freezer bags. Whole birds last up to a year; pieces last up to eight months.

When storing a cooked roast in the fridge, place it back into its own juices whenever possible. When reheating sliced meat, place it in a casserole dish with lettuce leaves between each of the slices. The lettuce provides just the right amount of moisture to keep the slices from drying out.

When freezing burgers or chops, put sheets of parchment paper between each item before storing in freezer bags. The paper makes it easy to remove the meat when it's time to cook. As an alternative to parchment paper, repurpose coffee can lids.

—*Caren C., Red Bank, SC*

Seafood is responsible for a lot of food poisoning, but it's perfectly safe and very healthy if handled correctly. If you can't use the fish immediately, remove it from its original wrapping and rinse in cold water. Wrap it loosely in plastic wrap, store in the coldest part of the refrigerator, and use within two days. Store ready-to-eat fish such as smoked mackerel separately from raw fish.

PASTA AND RICE

Never use quick-cooking rice in a dish that will be frozen, as it becomes mushy when reheated. Use regular or long-grain rice instead.

Rice can be stored in fridge for a longer amount of time if you store a slice of toast on top of it. The toast will absorb excess moisture and keep the rice fluffy and fresh.

PRODUCE

If you've ever had a debate with a roommate or spouse about which produce should be refrigerated and which shouldn't, you're not alone. Refrigerating your produce can help it last longer, but not all produce does well in the cooler temperature. The majority of fruits and vegetables handle cold fairly well, but naturally enough, the exceptions are tropical fruits, whose cells are just not used to the cold. Bananas will suffer cell damage and release a skin-browning chemical, avocados don't ripen when stored below 45°F, and citrus fruit will develop brown-spotted skin. These fruits, as well as squash, tomatoes, cucumbers, melons, bell peppers, and pineapples, are best stored at 50°F—so keep them out of the fridge. Most other vegetables, including lettuce, carrots, and cabbage, will do better in your refrigerator. Potatoes, however, should be stored outside of the fridge and away from light.

....

If possible, store fruits and vegetables in separate drawers in your fridge. Even when chilled, fruits give off ethylene gas that shortens the shelf life of vegetables (and other fruit) by causing them to ripen more quickly.

....

It is always a good idea to line the crisper bins of your refrigerator with newspaper or a few paper towels to absorb excess moisture. Mold spores love moisture, but the paper will keep it away.

....

Wrap all produce loosely; air circulation around fruits and vegetables reduces spoilage. A sealed perforated plastic bag is ideal—but instead of buying them at the market, make your own by simply poking several holes in an ordinary sandwich or freezer bag.

....

Never wrap foods that contain natural acids—like tomatoes, lemons, or onions—in aluminum foil. The combination of the foil and the acid in the foods produces a chemical reaction, which affects the taste of the food.

Fruits

The moisture content of fresh berries is high, so make sure to dry them thoroughly before you stick them in the fridge, or wait until you're ready to eat them before you wash them. Otherwise, they can easily rot.

Never throw out overripe bananas! Stick them in the freezer once they get completely brown, and you can still use them later for banana bread and other baking projects.

Blueberries and cranberries are two more foods that are easy to buy when in abundance and freeze for later. Place them in a single layer on a cookie sheet and stick the sheet in the freezer. Once they're frozen, you can transfer them to a resealable plastic bag and save. Frozen berries are great in smoothies and pies and perfect for eating cold!

The best way to keep your grapes lasting longer? Keep them unwashed and attached to their stems until you're ready to eat them. This will ensure they don't become waterlogged and susceptible to bacteria.

It's easy to keep your avocado from turning brown after you've cut it: Just squeeze a little lemon juice on the cut end, cover in plastic wrap, and store in the refrigerator. It should keep for another four days.

If you have a bunch of lemons that are about to go bad, just freeze them! First cut in slices, then freeze on a baking sheet or in between pieces of wax paper. They're perfect for adding to glasses of water.

Raisins will last for several months at room temperature if they are wrapped tightly in plastic or stored in a plastic bag. They will last even longer (up to a year) if you place the plastic bag in the refrigerator.

For the best storage, keep tomatoes stem-side down in a cool place. Try to keep them from touching, but if they are still attached to the stem, it's best to leave them that way.

Place unripe tomatoes in a brown paper bag and leave them on your counter—they'll ripen in a day or two. If they're ripe already, store them in a cool place (around 55°F) and they'll keep for five days. In order to keep its membranes intact, you should never refrigerate a tomato!

Vegetables

If you've purchased vegetables with leafy tops, such as beets or carrots, remove the green tops before you store them in the fridge. The greens will leach moisture from the root or bulb and shorten the vegetable's shelf life.

....

To make sure iceberg lettuce lasts as long as possible, you should remove the innermost core before you store it. An easy (and admittedly fun) way to do this is to hit the lettuce against a hard surface and then twist the core out.

....

Always store corn in a cool, dry location, and keep the ears separated in order to prevent them from becoming moldy. As it warms up, the sugar in corn converts to starch very quickly, so eat as soon as possible for the sweetest corn.

....

Did you know you could freeze corn on the cob? After shucking the corn, boil it for five minutes, then plunge it into ice water and pat dry. Pack in a freezer bag before freezing. To cook, place the frozen corn in boiling water for 10–15 minutes.

....

When storing a cucumber, keep it away from apples and tomatoes, which will shorten its life. Cucumbers stay fresh for up to a week, when the water content starts to drop.

....

When using only part of a red, green, or yellow pepper, cut it from the bottom or the sides, leaving the seeds attached, and it will remain moist for longer. You can put the rest in a resealable plastic bag and use it up to 3–4 days later.

If you eat pimientos, make sure to cover them in vinegar before storing them in the fridge. They'll last much longer!

The best way to store mushrooms in the fridge? Leave them in their original container, uncovered except for a single layer of cheesecloth on top.

The sugar content of yellow onions makes them spoil quickly if they are stored closely together— who knew? The solution is to store your onions in an old (clean) pair of pantyhose, making knots in the legs so the onions can't touch. It might look a little weird, but it works!

If you need only half an onion, use the bottom (root) half first, because the top half will store longer in the refrigerator (it won't sprout).

You've chopped up half an onion and you'd like to save the rest for later. Make sure the onion lasts longer in your fridge by rubbing the cut end with butter, then wrapping in plastic wrap.

Potatoes hate onions...at least until they're cooked together. Onions should never be stored with potatoes because moisture from the onions can cause potatoes to sprout. Onions also release gases that will alter the flavor of a potato.

If you store fresh ginger with potatoes it will help keep them fresh longer. Half an apple stored with potatoes will stop them from sprouting by absorbing moisture before the potato does.

To make asparagus last longer in the refrigerator, place the stem ends in a container of water, or wrap them in a wet paper towel and put in a plastic bag. Like flowers, the asparagus will continue "drinking" the water and stay fresh until they're ready to use.

Keep celery lasting even longer in your refrigerator by wrapping it in aluminum foil!

Shriveled mushrooms? No problem. They can still be sliced or chopped and used in cooking. You won't be able to tell the difference!

To freeze mushrooms, wipe them off with a damp paper towel and slice them. Then sauté them in a small amount of butter of olive oil until they are almost done. Remove from the heat, allow them to cool, then place them in an airtight plastic bag in the freezer. They should keep for up to 10–12 months!

REFRIGERATING AND FREEZING

When refrigerating leftovers, make sure to cover them to retain moisture and prevent them from picking up odors from other foods in your fridge. A large pot of food like soup or stew should be divided into small portions and put in shallow containers before being refrigerated. A large cut of meat or whole poultry should be divided into smaller pieces for refrigerating as well.

Do your refrigerator's crisper drawers have those little levers that allow you to adjust the humidity of each bin? We had no idea what we should be putting them on until we finally read the manual (go figure). Vegetables require higher humidity conditions while fruits and cheese require lower humidity conditions. So go adjust those controls now!

For best results, thaw frozen foods in the refrigerator before cooking. However, When there is not enough time to thaw frozen foods, or you're simply in a hurry, raw or cooked meat, poultry, or casseroles can be cooked or reheated from their frozen state. Just be sure to remember that it will take approximately one and a half times as long to cook.

You can freeze almost any food. The exceptions? Food still in a can, eggs in their shells, and food with a high water content like mayonnaise, cream sauce, and lettuce. Raw meat and poultry maintain their quality longer than their cooked counterparts because moisture is lost during cooking.

During a summer power outage, nothing's worse than hoping the food in your freezer won't go bad. If there is a power outage, the freezer fails, or if the freezer door has been left ajar by mistake, your food may still be safe to use if ice crystals remain. If the freezer has failed and a repairman is on the way, or it appears the power will be on soon, don't open the freezer door. A freezer full of food will usually keep about 2 days if the door is kept shut; a half-full freezer will last about a day. If your freezer is not full, quickly group packages together so they will retain the cold more effectively. Separate meat and poultry items from other foods so if they begin to thaw, their juices won't drip onto other foods. To determine the safety of foods once the power is back on, check their condition and temperature. If food is partly frozen, still has ice crystals, or is as cold as if it were in a refrigerator (40 °F), it is safe to refreeze or use.

....

Freezer burn does not make food unsafe to eat, merely dry and discolored in spots. It appears as grayish-brown leathery spots and is caused by air coming in contact with the surface of the food. Cut freezer-burned portions away either before or after cooking the food. Heavily freezer-burned foods may have to be discarded for quality reasons.

SPICES AND SEASONINGS

Do your dried herbs and spices lose some of their zest after sitting on your spice rack for years? Spices and dried herbs keep their flavor better if stored in a cupboard away from heat, light, and moisture, all of which impair flavor, change color, and shorten life. Make them last longer by putting half into a sealed, airtight container when you purchase them. Label the container and keep it in your dark cabinet, or better yet, your freezer. When the spice on-hand loses its aroma, replace it with some from your stash, and you'll never have to be irritated about throwing away an entire container of mustard seed or marjoram again.

Fresh herbs are a wonderful addition to any dinner, but let's face it: They go bad quickly and they're hard to freeze. To keep herbs fresh longer, loosely wrap them in a damp paper towel, store in a plastic bag, and keep in the vegetable crisper of the refrigerator. If you have more fresh herbs than you can use, hang them upside down to dry.

> Fresh herbs like parsley and cilantro will last for at least a couple of weeks if you store them in a jar. Just clip the stems of the herbs, and place them in a jar with water in it, like you would with flowers. Cover loosely with a plastic bag and refrigerate.

Don't throw away fresh herbs if you've got more on hand than you need. Just rinse the leaves, air dry, and place (on a single layer) on a plate with a paper towel. Then microwave them in 30-second intervals until they're crunchy (which can take up to four minutes). If you store them in an airtight container, they'll last for a year!

Enjoy fresh herbs from your garden all year round (or preserve expensive herbs before they go bad) with this tip: Just chop clean leaves, pat dry, and freeze in ice cube trays with enough water to cover the leaves. Then pop into dishes for a fresh, summery taste.

Both cayenne pepper and paprika are affected by light and heat, and have a shorter shelf life than just about anything else on your spice rack. In fact, take them off your spice rack and store them both in the refrigerator for a longer life.

Keep raw ginger in a sealed plastic bag in the freezer, and it will last pretty much forever. Best of all, you don't need to defrost it before you grate it into stir-fries, sauces, or whatever else you're making.

Store brown sugar in the freezer and lumps will be a thing of the past!

—*Chelsea Boettcher*

Do you love pimentos? To make sure they last virtually forever, cover what remains in the jar with vinegar, and keep in the fridge.

» Meat

BACON

Always rinse bacon under cold water before frying—it will reduce the amount the bacon shrinks when you cook it.

To keep bacon from splattering, soak it in ice-cold water for 2–4 minutes, and then dry it well with paper towels before frying it. Or try sprinkling the bacon with a bit of flour before cooking it.

If you're cooking less than a full package of bacon, how do you store the extra slices? Just roll each slice into a tight cylinder, place in an airtight plastic bag, and freeze. Simply thaw and unroll when you're ready to cook!

BEEF

There are few kitchen disasters more disheartening than burning a roast. But there's help! If you burn or scorch a roast, remove it from the pan and cover it with a towel dampened with hot water for about five minutes, which will stop the cooking. Then remove or scrape off any burnt areas with a sharp knife, and put the roast back in the oven to reheat if necessary.

Let a roast stand at room temperature for about 15 minutes before you carve it. This gives the juices time to be reabsorbed and distribute evenly. When you cook a roast, the juices tend to be forced to the center as those near the surface are evaporated by the heat. Resting the roast also allows the meat to firm up a bit, making it easier to carve into thinner slices.

Always use a shallow pot for cooking roasts. It will allow air to circulate more efficiently. Elevating the meat by cooking it atop celery ribs, carrot sticks, thick onion slices also helps get the air underneath the meat (and gives it a great flavor!).

When cooking steak, it's good to know that the internal temperature of a rare steak is 135°F, medium-rare is 145°F, medium is 160°F, and well done is 170°F. However, an experienced chef rarely whips out a meat thermometer. Meat has a certain resiliency at different temperatures, and the chef can just press the steak with a finger to tell whether the meat is rare, medium-rare, medium, medium-well, or well done. As meat cooks it loses water, and the more it cooks, the firmer it becomes. Try pressing on your steaks to get a sense for how they feel at different stages of doneness, and you'll never need to cut them open to find out again.

BREADING

Don't spend money on store-bought bread crumbs. Set aside a special jar and pour in the crumbs from the bottom of cracker or low-sugar cereal boxes. Also add crumbs from leftover garlic bread and a few dried herbs, and soon you'll have seasoned bread crumbs! The great thing is that homemade bread crumbs are even better than store-bought, since their uneven texture helps make them stick.

....

Always refrigerate chicken breasts after breading, but before cooking. The coating will adhere better that way. Also, try adding a teaspoon of baking powder to your batter, and use club soda instead of water for a delicate texture.

....

When breading chicken cutlets, make sure you don't bread your fingers, too: Use one hand for wet ingredients and the other for the breadcrumbs.

....

Breaded cutlets are less appealing when the breadcrumbs have all dropped off in the oven. One extra step is all you need. After coating with crumbs, let the cutlets dry on a rack for ten minutes, *then* cook.

....

Keeping breading on foods can be a challenge, but here are a couple of tricks to try (other than using superglue, which we don't recommend). First, make sure that the food to be breaded is very dry. As for your eggs, make sure they're at room temperature, and beat them lightly.

BURGERS AND MEATBALLS

Here's a simple tip: If you wet your hands with cold water before shaping hamburger patties or meatballs, the mixture won't stick to your fingers.

> When making meatballs, meatloaf, or hamburger patties, try adding ½ cup cottage cheese for every pound of ground meat. Not only does it add flavor and protein, but it will stretch your recipe to serve a few more people.

The secret to juicy burgers is simple. Just let them sit, covered, at room temperature for an hour before you cook them. This is safe to do as long as it isn't too hot (over 80°F) where they will be resting.

When you refrigerate cooked beef, its fat oxidizes quickly, which will often give day-old burgers an "off" taste. If you know you'll be eating tonight's meal tomorrow as well, discourage fat oxidization by not cooking the beef in iron or aluminum pots and pans, and not salting the meat until you are ready to eat it.

Want the fastest way to make meatballs? Well, here it is! Shape the meat mixture into a log and then cut off slices, which then roll easily into balls.

COOKING QUICK TIPS

If you've ever defrosted meat or fish in the microwave, you probably know that the "defrost" or low power settings are your best bets for ensuring that the outer edges of the food don't cook before the middle can defrost. But here's something you might not know: Arranging loose pieces of meat in a single layer with thickest parts or largest pieces toward the outside will also ensure more even defrosting.

Want to cook once and eat twice? Next time you're preparing boneless, skinless chicken breasts, make a few extra, then toss the cooked chicken in a freezer bag with some Caesar dressing, and refrigerate. Tomorrow night, warm them in the microwave, toss over salad greens, shave a little Parmesan cheese on top, and dinner is ready!

All meat (except organ meat and ground beef) should stand at room temperature for a few minutes before cooking. This allows it to brown more evenly, cook faster, remain juicier, and stick less when frying.

Cutting meat into bite-sized pieces for dishes like pastas and stir-fries is easier when it's half frozen. Place fresh meat in the freezer for two hours before you start dinner. Or, place frozen meat in the microwave and cook on the defrost setting for about five minutes (turning once if you don't have a turntable). Your knife will glide right through!

Before sautéing meats, sprinkle a tiny amount of sugar on the surface of the meat. The sugar will react with the juices and then caramelize, causing a deeper browning as well as a tastier result.

Add salt to the pan when you're cooking greasy foods like bacon, and the grease will be less likely to pop out of the pan and burn your hand.

If you're broiling steaks or chops, put a few slices of stale bread in the bottom of the broiler pan to absorb fat drippings. This will eliminate smoking fat, and it should also reduce any danger of a grease fire.

HAM

A little salt in ham is a good thing, but if your ham slices are too salty, place them in a dish of low-fat milk for 20 minutes before heating, then rinse them off in cold water and dry them with paper towels. The ham won't pick up the taste of the milk, but will taste much less salty.

To make your ham less salty, pour a can of ginger ale over it, then rub the meat with salt at least an hour before baking it. This will cause the saltwater in the meat to come to the surface, which will reduce the saltiness of the ham. There's no need to rinse the ham before cooking!

MARINADES

Vinegar helps tenderize the tough protein fibers in meats, so using it in marinades and braising liquids makes your dishes even more succulent. Simply add some garlic and your favorite spices to balsamic or wine vinegar and you've got a marvelous marinade!

The last bits of tomato sauce, ketchup, salsa, or chutney left in their bottles and jars are great to use in marinades. Simply add some vinegar and oil to the bottle and shake. The liquid will pour out easily. Now add a little onion, garlic, and spices, and you have a marinade!

—*Lupe Velasquez*

Marinate the meat for your chili in beer. It's a great tenderizer for tough, inexpensive cuts of beef, and it will add great flavor. All you ne ed to do is soak the meat for an hour before cooking, or marinate it overnight in the refrigerator.

POULTRY

Poultry must be thoroughly cleaned inside and out before cooking. If you detect a slight "off" odor when you open the package, rinse the bird under cool water, then submerge in a solution of water plus 1 tablespoon lemon juice or vinegar and 1 teaspoon salt per cup of water. Then refrigerate 1–4 hours before cooking.

The best way to thaw turkey is on a shallow baking sheet in the refrigerator, in its original packaging, allowing 24 hours for every five pounds of bird. But if it's Thanksgiving morning and you've forgotten to stick the bird in the fridge, the fastest, safest method of thawing frozen poultry fast is to place it—still wrapped in plastic—in a bowl (or bucket) of cold water. Check the water regularly and change it as the water warms up—you should never use hot water for large pieces of meat, as it will promote bacterial growth.

For the most tender poultry you've ever eaten, try submerging the chicken or turkey in buttermilk and refrigerating for two to three hours before cooking.

Try basting your bird with a small amount of white zinfandel or vermouth—it will help crisp the skin, and the alcohol imparts a brown color and glaze to the outside of the meat. Or, brush the skin with reduced-sodium soy sauce during the last 30 minutes of cooking to produce a beautiful burnished color.

If your roasted chicken or turkey tends to be too dry, try stuffing a whole apple inside the bird before roasting. (Just toss the apple afterward.) You can also line the bottom of the pan with lemon and onion slices. They'll give the bird a lovely flavor and make sure it stays moist.

Once poultry has finished cooking, it should be allowed to rest for about 20 minutes (but not more than 40 minutes) before carving. As with other roasts, this standing time allows the proteins in the meat to reabsorb the juices, so they stay in the meat rather than spilling onto the cutting board.

SAUSAGES

Keep sausages from splitting when cooking them by piercing the skin in one or two places while they are cooking. Rolling them in flour before cooking will reduce shrinkage.

STEWS

Cooking a lamb or beef stew? Try this secret ingredient: Add a few tablespoons of black coffee and your stew will have a nice dark color and a rich taste. This tip also works well for gravies.

An easy method of thickening stews, soups, or creamed vegetables is to add a small amount of quick-cooking oats, a grated potato, or some instant mashed potatoes. Never add flour directly, as it will clump. But if you're a particularly prepared cook, you can combine a stick of melted butter with ½ cup flour, then place it in a covered bowl in the refrigerator and let it harden. Then when you want a thickener, simply add some of this special mixture. It melts easily and will thicken without lumps.

STOCK

When carving a chicken or turkey, it's easy to make a stock at the same time. Place all unused parts in a pot with celery and onion (using the skins of the onion will give the stock a nice, rich color), then heat up to boiling. Reduce the heat and simmer while you make dinner. Then turn off and skim the fat when cooled. Stock can be used for gravies, made into soup (naturally), and used to flavor rice, potatoes, and tomato sauce. This free and easy seasoning would have cost you up to $5 for a quart at the grocery store!

One mistake people frequently make when preparing stock is to place soup bones in the water after it has come to a boil. This tends to seal the bones and prevent all the flavor and nutrients from being released into the stock! The bones should be added to the cold water when the pot is first placed on the stove to allow the maximum release of flavors, nutrients, and especially the gelatinous thickening agents that add body to the stock.

To easily freeze the delicious stock you've just made into smaller portions, line a drinking glass with a resealable plastic bag. Pour the stock into the glass until it's about three-quarters full, then seal the bag and lay flat on a baking pan. Repeat until you've used up all your stock, laying the bags on top of one another. Once they're frozen, you can move them anywhere in the freezer that there's room.

Make your own bouillon cubes by freezing left-over chicken broth in ice-cube trays. Once frozen, the cubes can be stored in the freezer in resealable plastic bags until needed. They are easily defrosted in the microwave—or just toss them into a soup or sauce, and they'll melt quickly.

TENDERIZING

Here's a simple tip to make your meat more tender. When it's ready to slice, make sure to cut it against the grain (look for slight lines on the surface).

To tenderize tough meat without store-bought tenderizer, use baking soda. Just rub baking soda all over the meat, refrigerate for a few hours, and rinse well before cooking. For extra tenderizing, cover the meat with slices of kiwi.

Wine corks (the natural kind, not plastic) contain a chemical that, when heated, will help tenderize beef stew. Just throw in 3 or 4 corks while cooking your stew, and don't tell anyone your secret!

The tannic acid in strong black tea can tenderize meat in a stew, as well as reduce the cooking time. Just add ½ cup strong tea to the stew when you add the other liquid. It will also give your stew a great brown color.

Do you tend to buy those tougher, bargain-priced meats at your local supermarket? If so, you can tenderize them without spending extra money on powdered tenderizer. Just let your meat soak in a can's worth of beer for at least an hour, and that should do the job.

When roasting a pork loin, cook it with the fat-side down for the first 20 minutes, which will cause the fat to begin to liquefy. Then turn the roast over for the balance of the cooking time, and the fat will baste the meat.

» Microwaving

BREAD AND TORTILLAS

For soft and warm rolls, place them on a microwave-safe plate and microwave on high for 30–60 seconds for 5 rolls.

It's easy to soften tortillas in the microwave. Just place four 6- to 7-inch tortillas between two white paper towels and microwave on high for 20–30 seconds.

DAIRY

If you have a pint of ice cream that threatens to break your ice cream scoop, uncover the container and place it in the microwave for 15 seconds on high, or until softened.

Want to melt or soften butter or margarine in the microwave? Here's how: Place in a microwave-safe container and microwave on high. A whole stick will take 45–60 seconds, while 2 tablespoons will take 35–45 seconds. To soften butter, heat on low (10% power) until softened, about 45–60 seconds for 1 stick.

Microwaving is probably the easiest way to soften cream cheese. For 8 ounces, remove from package and heat uncovered in a microwave-safe container for 30–60 seconds, or until softened.

Chocolate is easy to melt in the microwave. For 1 cup of chocolate pieces, microwave on high, uncovered, for 1½–2½ minutes.

DEFROSTING

When defrosting food in the microwave, make sure to remove it from its packaging first. Never use foam trays or plastic wraps (unless they're marked at microwave-safe), because they're not heat stable at high temperatures, and melting or warping may cause harmful chemicals to migrate into your food.

Cover any food you're defrosting in the microwave with microwave-safe plastic wrap, lids, or upside-down saucers. This will hold in moisture and provide safe, even heating.

After thawing food in a microwave, always cook it immediately. Because the food has become warm, it will attract bacteria, but won't be hot enough to kill it. Cooking it immediately minimizes this risk.

EVEN COOKING

If you're not careful, microwaves can sometimes cook food unevenly and leave cold spots—which are not only unappetizing, but can harbor harmful bacteria. Therefore, it's important to cook your food evenly. If you don't have a turntable in your microwave, make sure to stop the microwave and turn the dish a quarter-turn halfway through cooking time.

....

When cooking food in the microwave, arrange food items evenly in a covered dish and add some liquid if you're worried about the food drying out. The moist heat that is created will help destroy harmful bacteria and ensure uniform cooking. Cooking bags also provide safe, even cooking.

....

Heating up some leftovers? Food will continue to cook after being taking out of the microwave, so always allow some "standing time" before eating. More standing time is required for dense food like meat and poultry.

....

When cooking something in the microwave, make sure you leave enough room, or it may not cook evenly. There should be at least 3 inches of clearance in the microwave above whatever you're cooking, and 2–3 inches of space on all sides.

MEAT AND SEAFOOD

Cooking ground beef in the microwave is a great way to quickly cook it while keeping it tender. To do so, just place 1 pound in a microwave-safe casserole dish and cook, covered, on HIGH until no longer pink, for 3–5 minutes. Stir to break up meat once or twice throughout cooking time. Let sit for 2 minutes after cooking, and drain. If you have an old, microwave-safe colander, you can also place the meat in the colander and then the colander in a microwave-safe dish. The colander will drain the fat off the meat as it cooks, but it may stain.

When cooking hamburgers or meatballs in the microwave, place in a covered container and flip halfway through cooking, then allow to sit for a few minutes and use a food thermometer to check that the internal temperature is 160°.

Make cooking giblets for gravy or stuffing super easy by doing it in the microwave. Place the neck, gizzard and heart in a 2-quart casserole dish with 3 cups of water or broth. Cover with a lid or plastic wrap with holes. Microwave on medium (50% power) for 35 minutes. Add liver, re-cover and microwave on medium for 10 an additional minutes. Once cooked, the liver will become crumbly and the heart and gizzard will soften and become easy to chop. Cooked giblets should have a firm texture.

When microwaving unequal size pieces of steak, chicken, or fish in the microwave, arrange in a casserole dish so that the thick parts are toward the outside of dish and thin parts are in the center. If there are any very thin parts, overlap them with each other. Anything thicker than 2 inches should be sliced in half lengthwise before cooking, to make them thinner. In general, add ½ cup water or broth and cover before microwaving. Check every couple of minutes and turn if you don't have a turntable in your microwave.

To cook bacon in the microwave, place white paper towels on a white paper plate and top with a single layer of bacon. Microwave on high for 1½–2 minutes for 2 slices on bacon or 4–5 minutes for 6 slices. Bacon will continue to cook after being remove from microwave.

NUTS

Did you know that you can toast nuts in the microwave? To toast 1 cup of nutse, place in a microwave-safe container and microwave on HIGH until toasted, stirring after the first and second minutes, then every 30 seconds during cook time. Allow 2–3 minutes for almonds, 3–4 minutes for pecans, and 3½–5 minutes for peanuts or walnuts. Crack open whole nuts to test for doneness, and at the first signs of beginning to toast, spread on paper towels to cool. Let sit for 15 minutes.

SAFE CONTAINERS FOR MICROWAVING

Use only cookware that is specially manufactured for use in the microwave oven. Check the label on glass, ceramics, and plastics to make sure they say "microwave safe." Don't heat anything in a container that has any metal in or on it, as it can damage your microwave. This includes plates with a gold or metal trim, metal twist-ties, and take-out containers with a metal handle. Dishes made of heatproof glass (such as Pyrex and Anchor Hocking brands) or glass-ceramic (such as CorningWare) should all be OK, as are reusable plastic containers like GladWare and most Tupperware.

Because of the possibility of harmful additives, plastic storage containers that aren't made specifically to go into the microwave should never be used to heat your food. These include margarine tubs, take-out containers, whipped topping bowls, and other one-time use containers. These plastics can warp or melt, possibly causing harmful chemicals to migrate into your food.

When microwaving foods, paper products like paper plates, towels, napkins, and bags are safe to use inside, but for optimal safety, you should stick to white, unprinted materials. Microwave-safe plastic wraps, wax paper, cooking bags, and parchment paper should also be safe to use. However, you shouldn't let plastic wrap touch foods while microwaving, and you should punch a few holes in it to allow a vent for steam to escape. Never use thin plastic storage bags, brown paper or plastic grocery bags, newspaper, Styrofoam containers, or any plastic that has ever melted in the microwave oven.

As long as they don't contain metal, baskets (straw and wood) are great for quick warm-ups of rolls, bread, or tortillas. Line the basket with napkins to absorb moisture.

If a container isn't labeled safe for microwave use, but you think it might be, you can test it before using to make sure it's microwave-safe. Here's how to do it: Put 1 cup tap water in a container you know is microwave-safe and place it in the microwave along with (but not touching) the container to be tested. Microwave on high for 1 minute. If the container in question feels warm or hot, it's not microwave safe, and you shouldn't use it.

Conventional wisdom is that you should never use aluminum foil in the microwave, but that isn't always true—it can be safe to use small amounts of aluminum foil in a microwave oven. Using small bits of foil can be especially helpful when you want to "shield" a certain area of the food you're cooking, like poultry drumsticks and wings, to prevent overcooking. The microwaves that are penetrating your food can't pass through metal, so you should never cover food in aluminum foil—make sure at least three-quarters of the food is uncovered. Not only will your food not get cooked, but something completely encased in foil can damage your microwave. If you are going to use foil in the microwave, use new, smooth foil only (wrinkled foil can cause sparks); and don't place the foil closer than 1 inch from the oven walls. Shape the foil smoothly to the food so no edges stick out, and if your microwave has a metal rack of turntable, don't let the foil touch it. When wrapping food in aluminum foil, it doesn't matter which side of the foil (shiny or dull) is facing out.

» Pasta and Rice

OVERCOOKED

If you forgot about your simmering pot of pasta on the stove, and your noodles are now limp and mushy, try this trick. First run them under the coldest water possible—this will stop the cooking process immediately, and make the starch inside them contract. If you're making a dish with tomato sauce, heat them back up directly in the sauce, as the acid will help them hold up even better.

If you burned the rice, fear not! It's white bread to the rescue. Get rid of the scorched taste by placing a slice of fresh white bread on top of the rice while it's still hot, and covering it for a few minutes.

PREPARING

Keep pots of pasta or rice from boiling over by adding a tablespoon of butter to the water when you add the pasta or rice.

Here's a trick that will keep freshly cooked pasta warmer longer. Place a large mixing bowl underneath your colander as you drain the pasta. The hot water will fill the bowl and heat it up. Once the bowl is warm, dump out the water and put the pasta in the bowl instead. Then cover the bowl, and take your time as you finish cooking the rest of your meal.

Ordering in Chinese always left us with leftover rice, but it never tasted quite right when we reheated it. I finally perfected (OK, stumbled upon) the perfect microwaving method. Place the rice in its original container or in a microwave-safe bowl. Cover it, then microwave for one minute on medium (50 percent) heat. Stir, then re-cover and heat for another minute on high. Let sit for one minute more and you'll have perfect rice.

—*Brian Shelby, Brooklyn, NY*

STICKINESS, DECREASING

If your pasta or rice sticks together when you cook it, next time add a teaspoon of lemon juice to the water when boiling. Your sticky problem will be gone! The lemon juice will also help naturally fluff up the rice.

Preparing pasta? If you put a few drops of vinegar into the water as it boils, the starch will be reduced, making the pasta less sticky. This also works with rice: for every cup of uncooked rice, add a splash of vinegar.

If your pasta came out too sticky, let it cool, then sauté it with enough olive oil to lightly coat each noodle. Make sure to stir or toss while reheating.

If you like dry, fluffy rice, try this trick as soon as the rice is done cooking: Wrap the lid with a cotton dishtowel and set it on the pot for about 15 minutes. The cloth will absorb the steam.

» Purchasing Food

Looking for tips on Purchasing Groceries? *See* Shopping chapter, Groceries

» Seafood

CLAMS

The most effective way to get rid of sand and grit from clams is to soak them in water with a bit of cornmeal stirred in. It irritates the clams, and they expel the sand while trying to eliminate the cornmeal.

COOKING QUICK TIPS

Pining for fresh fish but stuck with frozen? Try this: Cover the frozen fish in milk until it thaws, then cook. It will taste fresher and your family will never know it was frozen.

If you're grilling or broiling thick fish steaks, marinate them for 15 minutes in lemon or lime juice before cooking. The acid from the juice "cooks" the fish a bit, cutting down on the time it needs to stay on the heat—so your steaks are less likely to dry out.

For added crunch with fewer calories, use cornflakes instead of breadcrumbs to coat fish fillets. Not only do cornflakes contain fewer calories than breadcrumbs, they are less absorbent and give a lighter covering, so the fish will soak up less oil.

Our favorite way to prepare fish is also super quick and tasty. Wrap your fillets individually in foil, adding a bit of chopped onion, salt and pepper, and a sprig of dill. Bake for 30 minutes in a 350°F oven, then unwrap for a tender, flavorful fish.

To steam fish fillets in the microwave, place them in a shallow microwavable dish (a glass pie plate is ideal) with the thinner parts overlapping at the center of the dish. Sprinkle with lemon juice or herbs, if you like, season with salt and pepper, then cover the dish with plastic wrap (making sure it doesn't touch the fish) and cook for 3 minutes per pound. If your microwave doesn't have a turntable, rotate the dish about halfway through the cooking time.

....

To test fish for doneness, insert a thin-bladed knife into the flesh at the thickest part. If it's done, it will be just barely translucent in the center. Even though it might look not quite done, the fish will continue to cook after you remove it from the heat, so make sure not to overcook it.

....

If you're cooking fish and it comes out too dry, brush it with a mixture of equal parts melted butter and lemon juice and some dried or fresh herbs. The butter will help make it moister, while the lemon juice will help it hold together and cause your diners to salivate—perhaps making them less likely to notice your cooking error.

FRYING

When frying fish, be sure the surface of the fish is dry before putting it in the oil. Moisture can cool the oil down and make the fish cook less evenly.

....

> To keep fish to keep from sticking to your skillet while you're frying it, toss a handful of salt in the pan before the fish.

LOBSTER

If you love the taste of lobster but hate cooking it because you're bothered by the lobster's movements, you're not alone. Luckily, we can help with the "squee" factor: Just put the lobsters in the freezer for 10 minutes before cooking. The cold will dull their senses and the amount they move will be significantly decreased.

....

It might sound crazy, but the taste, texture, and color of microwaved lobster is far superior to boiled or steamed, and microwaving produces an evenly cooked, tender lobster. Unfortunately, you can only cook one lobster at a time, so put your oven on the lowest heat and use it to keep already-cooked lobsters warm until your entire meal is done. To cook a lobster, place it in a large, microwavable plastic bag with ¼ cup water, and knot the bag loosely. A 1½ pound lobster should take five to six minutes on high, providing you have a 600–700 watt microwave. If you have a lower wattage oven, allow about eight minutes. To be sure the lobster is fully cooked, separate the tail from the body. The tail meat should be creamy white, not translucent. (Unfortunately, even when microwaved, the lobster must still be cooked live because of the enzymatic breakdown that occurs immediately upon its death.) Serve your lobsters with some melted garlic butter and try not to laugh when people ask your secret!

ODOR ELIMINATION

Before handling fish, rub your hands with lemon juice and you won't smell of fish for the rest of the day! After frying fish, put a little white vinegar into the frying pan to help get rid of the odor on the surface.

When frying up fish in a pan, add a dollop of peanut butter. It won't affect the taste of the fish, but it will affect the odor—peanut butter contains a chemical that absorbs that stinky fish odor, so your whole house doesn't have to.

—*Marlena Kahn, Steubenville, OH*

SCALING

If you're gutsy enough to scale your own fish, we salute you! Make it easier to get the scales off by rubbing the flesh with vinegar five minutes before scaling.

SHRIMP

For the most tender shrimp, cool them down before cooking. Place fresh shrimp in the freezer for 10–15 minutes, or set them in a bowl of ice water for about 5 minutes.

» Snacks

CHIPS

It's 2 a.m.—do you know where your potato chips are? Yes, but unfortunately, they've been there way too long. Microwaving, which turns bread to mush, has the opposite effect on potato chips. Just give them a whirl for 30 seconds on a glass plate. Be careful when you bring them out: they may need to cool down a bit before you can eat them.

....

Instead of buying those clips for fastening cereal and chip bags, simply buy a box of large binder clips from an office supply store. They're the exact same thing at less than half the cost.

FRENCH FRIES

For the greatest French fries, soak cut potatoes in ice-cold water in the refrigerator for an hour; this will harden them so that they absorb less fat. Dry them thoroughly, then fry them twice. First cook them for 6–7 minutes, drain them well, and then sprinkle them lightly with flour or cornstarch (this step makes them extra crispy and crunchy). Then fry them again for 1–2 minutes, until they are golden brown.

PIZZA

The best way to heat up leftover pizza is in the toaster oven, but if you don't have a toaster oven you don't need to endure the soggy crust that results from microwaving yesterday's slice. Just place the piece in a covered skillet and heat over medium-low heat until warm.

POPCORN

Are your popcorn kernels too pooped to pop? It's probably because they have lost too much moisture, but they can be revived. Soak the kernels in water for five minutes, then dry them off and try again. Or freeze them overnight and pop them when frozen.

If you're serving popcorn to the kids but don't want to wash a bunch of bowls afterwards, consider using coffee filters as disposable bowls.

If you've ever burned popcorn in your microwave, you know that it stinks, and the smell permeates the entire household. Make it smell fresh again by stuffing the microwave with crumpled newspaper—leaving the microwave off, of course! After a few hours have gone by, remove the paper. If the smell is still there, dissolve 2–3 teaspoons in a bowl of water, and heat on high in the microwave for five minutes.

We love hot-pressed sandwiches! And we were tempted to buy an expensive sandwich press to make ours at home until we learned this ingenious trick. Simply fry the sandwich in a pan as you would a grilled cheese, but place a piece of foil on top and weigh down the entire sandwich by pressing a kettle full of water on top.

» Spices and Seasonings

COOKING QUICK TIPS

Crushing dried herbs before using them will boost their flavor, as will soaking them for a few seconds in hot water. This also works well for older spices that have lost their flavor.

....

Don't have a mortar and pestle? A great way to mix and crush spices is to place them in a pan and press then with the bottom of a smaller pan. A dedicated coffee grinder works well, too.

....

Want to wake up the flavor of dried herbs before using them in a recipe? Just toast them in a pan for a minute or two, and their flavors will be revived.

....

If you're cooking with herbs that will need to be removed before eating, make them easy to remove by putting them all in a tea infuser before you add them to your dish.

—*Sandi Govac*

GARLIC

If your head of garlic sprouts, it's still perfectly good to eat. Some of the flavor will go into the sprouts— chop them off and add to salads for a delicious treat!

....

Garlic is one of our favorite seasonings, and we find it's much better fresh than in powdered form. If you love fresh garlic too, make the cloves easier to peel by putting in the microwave for about eight seconds.

—*Jennifer Nelson, Philo, CA*

....

Mincing garlic can be a sticky mess, but won't be if you drizzle the garlic with a few drops of olive oil beforehand. The oil will prevent the garlic from sticking on your hands or the knife.

....

If you have added too much garlic to your soup or stew, add a small quantity of parsley and simmer for about 10 minutes.

GINGER

Want to know the easiest way to peel ginger? Use a spoon! Turn the spoon so that it's facing the ginger, then simply press and scrape away its skin. You won't believe how easy it is!

....

If you're preparing a recipe that calls for crushed ginger, don't bother getting out your knife. Simply peel the ginger and put it through a garlic press.

LEMONS AND ZEST

Don't discard the rinds of limes, lemons, oranges, or other citrus. Grate them, then store in tightly covered glass jars in the fridge. They make excellent flavorings for cakes and can be sprinkled over chicken and fish as well.

....

To easily extract juice from a lemon, first roll it on the counter under your hand. Heat it in the microwave for 10 seconds, then insert a toothpick. You'll be surprised how easily the juice dribbles out.

SALT

Have you ever had to throw out a batch of soup because you accidentally oversalted it? Not anymore! Potatoes contain starch, which absorbs salt, so all you need to do is peel a raw potato or two and toss it in the soup. Let the pot simmer for about 15 minutes before removing the potato, and your soup will be almost as good as new.

When your salt gets sticky in high humidity, keep it flowing freely by adding some raw rice to the shaker. Rice absorbs moisture and lasts for a long time.

You love your antique rooster-shaped salt shaker, but every time you shake it over something, way too much salt empties out. Easily fix this problem by painting over a few of the holes with clear nail polish.

SWEETENERS

In spiced recipes like muffins and biscuits, try reducing the amount of sugar in your recipes by half and doubling the cinnamon. Not only will the cinnamon taste help retain sweetness with the fewest calories possible, it has also been shown to help control blood sugar levels.

There's nothing more sweetly delicious than real honey, but we find it often gets thick and full of crystals after a little while in the cabinet. To get it back to its former consistency, simply place the open container in the microwave, then microwave on high for 10 seconds and stir. Continue microwaving in 10 second increments and stirring until it's back to its lovely, spreadable self.

» Tools, Preparation, and Safety

COOKBOOKS

A well-worn cookbook is a good sign, but company shouldn't be able to guess your favorite recipes just by inspecting the splatters. So here is yet another use for one of the million plastic bags taking over your pantry: Use one to cover the binding and pages surrounding the recipe you are using. Then to keep the book open and the pages clean, just place it under a glass pie plate—unless you're making pie, of course!

Oops! You just spilled something on your favorite cookbook. Don't despair. Simply blot the page with a paper towel and then insert a piece of waxed paper on the page before closing the book. The pages won't stick together.

Making dinner and need something to mark your page in the cookbook? Try using a single strand of raw spaghetti!

—*Cindy Beck*

COOKING PREP

To use the fewest cooking utensils possible, first measure out all the dry ingredients, then the wet ingredients. This way, you can reuse the measuring spoons or cups, and only have to wash them once.

....

If you like to channel surf while cooking, place your remote control in a resealable plastic bag or plastic wrap. The buttons will still be visible, and the control will stay clean.

....

Professional cooks keep small plastic bags nearby in case both hands are covered with dough or food and they need to answer the telephone. Or, you could put your hands in plastic bags *before* mixing meatloaf or kneading dough.

....

Sprinkle a little baking soda into each of your latex kitchen gloves and they'll stick less when you're putting them on and taking them off.

....

Your potholders don't have to look stained and dirty. Wash them frequently, and after each wash, spray them with starch. Spray starch repels grease, so your potholders will stay unblemished.

....

Before measuring a sticky liquid like honey, coat the inside of the measuring cup with vegetable oil or non-stick cooking spray. The liquid will pour out easily. You can also run the measuring cup under hot water.

To lessen your clean-up time when using a food processor, protect the lid by first covering the bowl of food with a piece of plastic wrap. The lid will stay clean and you can toss the plastic wrap in the trash when you're finished.

When you've used all the ketchup in a plastic squeeze bottle, throw the cap in the dishwasher to remove the caked-on ketchup. Keep it, along with other condiment bottle tops, handy in the kitchen. When your current bottle top gets all mucked-up, simply switch it out with a clean top and throw the dirty one in the dishwasher.

JAR OPENERS

You've seen those nifty, colorful jar openers in cool houseware shops, but you might not realize you've got a bunch of tools that are just as effective lying around your garage or basement. Using an X-Acto knife, slice open an old tennis ball and you've got two handy openers—set, point, match. Now pass the olives.

An easy way to open a tight jar lid is to cover the top in plastic wrap to create a firm grip. Rubber kitchen gloves or rubber bands work well, too. If the jar lid still won't budge, set it in a bowl with a little hot tap water for a few minutes, and then try again. Or smack the bottom of the jar squarely with the flat of your palm, then immediately try the lid again. This will send an air bubble to the top of the jar to hopefully help your cause. *Still* stuck? Try this solution with a puncture-type can opener: Carefully work the pointed tip under the lid and gently loosen the cap. This should release enough pressure to allow you to open the jar.

KNIVES AND CUTTING BOARDS

You've finally saved up enough to buy a brand new knife set (or, better yet, are compiling a gift registry). So which knives should you get? The three basic knives everyone should own are a chef's knife, for chopping and slicing; a paring knife, for deseeding and other small jobs; and a boning knife, for meat and poultry. Additional knives you may want to have are a serrated knife for slicing bread, a cleaver, a fish-filleting knife, and a pair of kitchen scissors.

If your knife is rusty, it's time to chop some onions. Believe or not, onions will remove rust from metal objects. Plunge the knife into the biggest onion you can find, let it sit for a few seconds, then pull it out. Repeat this process until the rust has dissolved, then wash as usual and dry.

Cutting boards that slip around on the counter are an obvious no-no, yet it's amazing how often we turn cutting a watermelon into an extreme sport in our house. We finally figured out that all that extra shelf liner in the pantry *could* in fact come in handy one day. We simply cut it to the right size to use as a placemat for the board, and it never slipped again.

How do you keep your cutting board from sliding around when you're trying to chop? It's easy—just lightly dampen a kitchen towel, place it on your counter, and put the board on top. It won't move again!

Studies continue regarding the safety of plastic cutting boards versus wood ones. Most cooks have their favorite, and many use both. No matter which kind you prefer, reserve one cutting board only for raw meats, poultry, and fish; use other cutting boards for prepping vegetables, cheeses, and cooked meats. It will ensure your veggies stay free from bacteria. Many cooks also only use plastic cutting boards for meat, since they can be safely washed in the dishwasher at high temperatures.

Avoid setting hot pans on wood cutting boards or butcher-block countertops. Bacteria love heat, and the hot pan may serve to activate them or draw them to the surface f the wood.

PAPER TOWELS

Many paper towels now offer rolls with "half sheets"—that is, the perforated lines are closer together. We were shocked at how much longer our paper towel roll lasted when we bought one of these brands! And if your favorite brand doesn't offer half sheets, you can simply tear them in half yourself, of course!

When preparing a recipe that requires you to drain something you've just cooked on several layers of paper towels to absorb the grease, use this trick to waste fewer paper towels. Lay down several sheets of old newspaper, then place a single layer of paper towels on top.

POTS AND PANS

You shouldn't need a ruler in the kitchen. Yet when a recipe gives you cooking times for five different pan sizes, you wish you knew the actual measurements of your baking pans. And now you will. All you have to do is use nail polish to mark the dimensions on the bottom of each pan. Then put that ruler back in the home office where it belongs.

To keep a pot from boiling over, stick a toothpick between the lid and the pot. Other tricks include placing a wooden spoon across the top of the uncovered pot or rubbing butter around the inside lip of the pot.

When cooking on a gas stove, the flame should extend no farther than two-thirds up the pan. (If it does, opt for a bigger pan.) Never leave an empty pan on a hot stove for more than a couple of minutes, and keep an eye out for shiny rainbow-colored marks on the pan. These are signs that you've been cooking at too high a heat.

....

If you lose the knob to a pot lid, don't throw out the pot! Place a screw into the hole, with the thread side up, then attach a cork to it.

....

The handles on pots and pans can get very hot, hence the invention of potholders. If your pans have hollow handles, however, you can place some aluminum foil inside to keep them cool. It seems counterintuitive, but the foil blocks heat from traveling up from the burner. Don't tell anyone how you did it. Use your bare hands. Impress your friends!

....

Have you ever left a covered pot on the stove only to find that the lid is stuck on? If this happens to you, just try setting the pot over moderate heat for a minute or two. Why? When you cook a food in a covered pot, the air inside the pot increases in pressure, raising the lid ever so slightly so heated air can escape. When you turn off the heat, the air pressure decreases along with the temperature and may become lower than the air pressure outside. This decrease in pressure, along with the water from the steam, creates a vacuum around the lid and seals it tight. The longer the lid is left on, the tighter the seal. Turning the heat back on will increase the air pressure in the pot, loosening the lid's seal.

QUICK SUBSTITUTIONS

Have you ever seen those bowl scrapers in kitchen stores that sell for $3 to $10? These circular, plastic tools are easy to make at home. Simply take the lid of a round take-out container, cut it in half, then remove the rim. Instant savings!

Who needs a martini shaker? Instead of buying this expensive bar tool, simply use a stainless steel thermos with a screw-in lid. If there's no way to close the sipping hole on the top, cover it with your thumb while you shake!

If your plastic bags are not resealable, you can seal them yourself with this quick trick: Fold a small piece of aluminum foil over the end you'd like to seal, and iron it so both ends of the foil close over the plastic. This will ensure that the plastic doesn't melt.

Instead of purchasing a handheld juicer (also known as a reamer) for fruit, simply use one blade from a hand mixer instead. Halve the fruit and twist the blade into it for easy juicing.

You might know that "trussing" means tying the wings and legs of a bird down for more even cooking. But do you know which is the best string to use for trussing? Dental floss! Not only does it come in a small container, it's usually easy to get for free at your dentist's office. It's also very strong and won't burn in high heat.

Toasting nuts is often an essential (and delicious) recipe step. Toast them in a popcorn air popper! Just add ¼ cup nuts, plug in the popper for 60 seconds, and your nuts will be a perfect golden brown.

Pizza cutters can be used for a lot more than just pizza. Use your pizza cutter to quickly slice tortillas, sandwiches, pancakes, omelets, brownies, and even stale bread to make croutons.

Hardware and home improvement stores have lots of ceramic tiles that can be adapted as mix 'n' match trivets. Choose from a variety of designs and colors to add unique accents to your table setting. Protect tables and other surfaces by affixing felt corners (peel and stick) underneath each tile.

If you grind the average pepper mill 10 times, you'll have ¼ teaspoon pepper. Figure out how many grinds your pepper mill takes to make a teaspoon and you won't have to measure every time a recipe calls for black pepper.

At our house, all of our wooden mixing spoons have a rubber band wrapped tightly around the top of the handle. Why? Because they keep the spoons from falling into whatever you're stirring. Wrap some rubber bands around your spoons and you can safely rest the spoon on the side of the bowl without it slipping.

....

An easy way to protect your dining room table is to purchase table pads that go underneath your tablecloth. But since they usually have to be custom-made, they can cost a bundle. For a large, rectangular table, use a twin-size mattress pad instead. It's not as nice, but it will do the job.

....

Yes, there's a utensil specifically designed for pulling corn out of boiling water (tongs). But if you can't find them and the corn is ready, a potato masher does the trick quite nicely with a tiny bit of balance. And our 11-year-old says airlifting the cobs this way is great practice for the crane machine filled with toys at the arcade!

....

If you have aluminum foil in your kitchen, you don't need a funnel. Simply fold a sheet of foil in half width-wise and roll into the shape of a funnel.

....

When you started preparing the recipe, you didn't realize its contents would double in size! If you run out of space in your bowl, and you're in a pinch, simply line your entire kitchen sink with foil and throw your ingredients in there. Then serve in smaller containers.

....

Never pay for aerosol cooking sprays. Instead, buy a giant jug of vegetable oil and add it to a clean spray bottle as needed. It's the same thing and will cost a fraction of the price.

Your supermarket has only canned whole tomatoes, and you need chopped! Don't take out each tomato and make a mess on your cutting board. Instead, simply insert a clean pair of scissors into the can and snip.

SAFETY

If there's a grease fire in a pan, cover the pan immediately with a lid. You'll cut off the oxygen supply and the fire will go out. Baking soda is one of the best fire extinguishers. Because it creates carbon dioxide, it will prevent oxygen from feeding the flames. Always keep an open box next to the stove to dump onto grease fires—and never use water!

Water should never, ever be thrown on a grease fire, because it will only spread. If there's a fire caused by grease or oil in your kitchen, throw salt on it until it is extinguished. The salt will absorb the liquid causing the flames.

Microwave doors may become misaligned, especially if you pull down on them when opening them. When the doors don't close properly, the oven can leak radiation, making your food take longer to cook.

You reach to get a glass out of a stack of glasses, only to realize they're stuck together. Reach into the cabinet again to get some vegetable oil, then pour a bit down the side of the glasses to unstick them without the risk of breaking them.

....

The next time you find two drinking glasses stuck together, try this: Fill the top glass with ice water and then place the bottom one in a few inches of hot tap water in the sink. It should only take a few seconds for them to come unstuck.

SLOW COOKERS

Many people question whether a Crock-Pot is safe for cooking foods, or if it's a breeding ground for bacteria because it cooks at low temperatures. Most slow cookers have settings that range from 170–280° F, and most bacteria die at 140°F, so you should be safe. However, to minimize the risk of food poisoning, don't attempt to cook frozen or partially thawed foods, and don't use the cooker to reheat leftovers. (Uncooked foods at refrigerator temperature are safe to use.) Cook only cut-up pieces of meat—not whole roasts or poultry—to allow the heat to penetrate fully. Finally, make sure that the cooker is at least half to two-thirds full or the food may not absorb enough heat to kill any bacteria.

....

Want to make perfect slow cooker creations every time? The secret is steam. Make sure to cover the food with enough liquid to generate sufficient steam. When possible, cook on the highest setting for the first hour, then reduce it to low if necessary.

» Vegetables

BEANS

You don't have to avoid baked beans because you fear they'll make you gassy. Instead, just add a dash or two of baking soda to the beans when they're cooking, and their gas-producing properties will be dramatically reduced.

CAULIFLOWER

Love the taste of cauliflower but don't like that "off" look it sometimes gets when you boil it? Just add a small amount of lemon juice to the water to keep cauliflower white during cooking.

CELERY

Don't throw away celery leaves—while they don't work well with dips, they still have a wonderful flavor. When chopping celery, set the leaves aside on a paper plate, let them dry, and throw them in stuffing, salads, and soups for great extra flavor.

....

For the most part, celery is easy to cook—the pectin in its cells breaks down easily in water. However, celery strings, which are made of cellulose, are virtually indestructible and won't break down at all under normal cooking conditions. Even the body has a difficult time breaking the strings down, and many people can't digest them at all. Remove the strings before preparing celery with this simple trick: Once you remove a stalk from the bunch, place it curved-side up on the counter or a cutting board, then grab hold of the very bottom (white part) of the stalk and quickly bend it up. It will crack off the bottom of the celery, but the strings will still be attached. Now all you need to do is simply pull this piece up toward the leaves, pulling as many strings with it as you can.

COOKING QUICK TIPS

Save at the store by going canned—all recipes except for salads can be made with canned vegetables instead of the fresh ones. As long as you check the ingredients to make sure sugar hasn't been added, any vegetable in a can will taste nearly indistinguishable from a fresh one you cooked yourself, especially if it's going into sauces or casseroles.

....

If you're microwaving vegetables to eat with dinner, here's an easy way to do it: Place them in a gallon- or quart-sized Ziploc bag and cut a ½-inch slit on the side, about an inch from the top. Microwave them for 2–3 minutes on high, and they'll come out perfectly every time!

....

When you scrape out the last of the margarine from the tub, don't throw the container away just yet. Throw some vegetables into the tub, microwave it for a few seconds, and voilà!—instant yummy veggies.

....

Baking stuffed bell peppers or tomatoes in a well-greased muffin tin will help them to hold their shape—and make sure they don't tip over when you take them out of the oven.

....

Cooking Thanksgiving dinner and your vegetables turned to mush? Simply add some herbs along with tomato sauce or cream. Then top with cheese and/or bread crumbs and stick in the oven for 30 minutes. Your family is sure to be impressed with your new recipe for "vegetables gratin"!

....

If your kids don't like vegetables, you'll love this clever way of getting more nutrients into them. If you have too many vegetables to use before they go bad, puree them in a blender with a little bit of lemon juice, then freeze. Defrost and add to sauces, soups, stews, enchiladas, and more—your kids won't be able to taste the difference! The key is to make sure you don't dramatically alter the color of the dish you're serving. So if you're making a white sauce, for instance, try a puree of cauliflower and summer squash. Tomato-based sauces can usually handle one part "green puree" for every four parts tomato sauce. So grind up that broccoli and spinach and get going!

CORN

The easiest way to husk corn is to cut off both ends, then roll the corn on your counter for a moment. The husk will then peel right off!

—*Sona Gajiwala, Chicago, IL*

Never add salt to the water when boiling corn; table salt contains traces of calcium, which will toughen the kernels. Instead, add a little milk to the cooking water, which will bring out the sweetness of the corn.

There are many uses for an old toothbrush—you probably already use one to clean small spaces. Our favorite second-life for an old toothbrush, however, has to be in the kitchen. Use an old toothbrush to quickly and easy remove the silk from a fresh ear of corn.

GREENS

To wash spinach, Swiss chard, or any other leafy vegetable, fill a large bowl with cold water and add a teaspoon of baking soda. Move the vegetables around in the water, soaking them for three minutes, then rinse. All the dirt will fall to the bottom of the bowl and you'll have clean greens.

If you're having a hard time trying to get the last pieces of grit off of leafy vegetables or herbs, add a pinch of two of salt to the water.

You've left the lettuce in the crisper for a few days, and now it's too wilted to use for a salad. Perk up any green (including herbs like cilantro) by submerging it in a bowl of ice-cold water (and 1 tablespoon lemon juice if it's especially wilted). Let sit for 5–10 minutes and it will be as good as fresh.

Kale, cabbage, and collard greens are delicious to eat, but can sometimes smell stinky when they're being prepared. Make sure not to overcook them—that's what makes them release odors. Also try placing a few unshelled pecans in the saucepan while cooking, which will help absorb any scents.

Don't throw away the outer leaves from a head of lettuce! They come in handy when you need to cover foods in the microwave. You won't have to use up a paper towel, and the leaves will keep your food moist.

....

When cooking spinach, always do it in an uncovered pot. The steam that builds up when a pot is covered causes the plant's volatile acids to condense on the lid and fall back into the water. Keeping the lid off will make sure your spinach keeps its lovely green color.

GRILLING

Looking for tips on Grilling Vegetables? *See* **Entertaining and Holidays chapter, Barbecues and Picnics**

MUSHROOMS

Mushrooms can be kept white and firm during sautéing if you add ¼ teaspoon lemon juice for every 2 tablespoons butter or olive oil.

ONIONS

Rinse the bitterness away! Rinsing chopped red onions in cold water will help ease their sharp taste.

....

Do you become a blubbering mess when you chop onions? Keep the tears away by leaving your onions in your refrigerator's crisper drawer. At the colder temperature, they'll release less of the chemical that makes you cry.

PEPPERS

A great way to save money on peppers is to grow your own! Peppers are perennials and can be grown year-round in two- to five-gallon containers of potting soil. Just bring the plants in when the nights drop below 50°F, and let them live indoors until the nights are consistently above that temperature.

POTATOES

Did you know that wrapping a potato in foil won't actually make it bake faster? Rubbing it lightly with vegetable oil, however, will.

Halve the oven-time needed for baked potatoes by placing each medium-sized potato in a muffin tin on its end. Turn over after 10 minutes, and they'll be ready in a half-hour or less.

Never pour cold milk into cooked potatoes. It will change the taste of the starch, giving it an unpleasant flavor, not unlike cardboard. The milk should be warmed in a pan (preferably with a small amount of garlic or chives for flavor) before being added.

If you're watching your weight but love mashed potatoes, cut out the milk and the butter (or just some of it). Instead, save some of the cooking water from the potatoes and use that instead. Season with freshly ground black pepper and a bit of lemon juice for a no-added-fat mash that is flavorful and goes fantastically well with roast chicken.

Want super-fluffy mashed potatoes? Add a pinch or two of baking powder, powdered milk, or even instant potatoes for extra fluff. (Never put baking soda in potatoes! It will turn them black.)

If your mashed potatoes sometimes end up a little gluey, it may be because you overmixed them. When potatoes are mashed, their cell walls rupture, releasing an excess of starch and resulting in the gluey texture. Potatoes should be mashed with a vertical motion, not stirred, to minimize the damage that occurs by crushing the cells on the side of the bowl.

Skip the last-minute panic on major holidays and mash the potatoes first thing in the morning. Transfer them to a slow cooker while you move onto the stuffing and string beans and let them cool, wiping off condensation on the lid with a dishtowel. Two hours before you're ready to serve the meal, turn on the slow cooker. You won't have to give the potatoes another thought until the guests are seated and it's time to serve the meal.

—*Sue Pratt, Jasper, GA*

You've managed to talk your kids into helping you with tonight's scalloped potatoes, but now the potatoes are peeled long before you need them! To keep peeled potatoes from discoloring, place them in a bowl of cold water with a few drops of white vinegar, then refrigerate. Drain before cooking and add a small amount of sugar to the cooking water to revive some of the lost flavor.

SALADS

It's so much easier to prepare food a day ahead for a dinner party—but what to do about the salad? Making the salad before guests arrive usually leads to a soggy mess, but here's a tip to allow you to make the salad in advance without it going soft. Gather lettuce and any of the following ingredients: broccoli, cabbage, carrots, cauliflower, celery, cucumbers, onions, peppers, and radishes. Chop them up and place them in a large bowl. Then completely cover all your ingredients with water and keep the bowl in the refrigerator until you need it. On the day of the party, drain the ingredients in a colander, and spin in a salad spinner. Finally, add tomatoes, croutons, and any other toppings.

For the crispiest salad, prepare it in a metal bowl and then place it in the freezer for one minute before serving.

Avoid wet, limp salads by placing an inverted saucer in the bottom of the salad bowl before you throw in all your veggies. The excess water that is left after washing the vegetables and greens will drain under the saucer and leave the greens high and dry.

It's a beautiful, fresh, colorful salad until—no! Close the floodgates! Someone overdressed it and now it's barely edible. To keep this from ever happening again, titrate your vinaigrette with a baby sippy cup. Mix inside the cup, shake (covering the opening), and scatter over the salad with its perfectly sized spout.

To cut calories, make vinaigrette salad dressings from milder vinegars like balsamic, champagne, fruit, or rice wine vinegar. They're less pungent, so you can use a higher ratio of vinegar to oil.

Too much dressing can ruin your salad, so if you accidentally add too much, just add more croutons or crunched up tortilla chips. These salad toppings will soak up the excess.

TOMATOES

Some people are unable to eat spaghetti sauces and other tomato-based foods because of their high acid content. Cooking chopped carrots with tomato dishes will reduce the acidity without affecting the taste.

To bring already-picked tomatoes from green to red, place them in a closed paper bag with an apple. The apple gives off ethylene gas, which speeds up ripening.

Need to quickly peel tomatoes for a recipe? The easiest way is to place them in a pot of boiling water for a minute. The skins will practically fall off.

If your tomatoes have started to shrivel, don't despair! Simply dip them in cold water, then sprinkle a bit of salt over them and leave them for several hours or overnight. They'll be firm to the touch the next day.

Auto

Baking

Beauty

Cleaning

Clothing and Accessories

Cooking

》》 **Decorating**

Entertaining and Holidays

Health and Wellness

Home Repair

Kids

Money

Organization

Outdoors

Pest Control

Pets

Shopping

Utilities

Vacations and Family Activities

Websites

» Accents

DECORATING SHORTCUTS

A pair of wine bottles, either full or empty, makes great bookends for your shelf—especially if there are cookbooks on it!

....

Fill a large, glass bowl with citrus fruit for a bright centerpiece that's especially good for the dining room table. Use whatever is on sale—lemons, limes, oranges, or a mixture.

....

We hate throwing out *anything* at our house. Even plastic from the dry cleaners is turned into trash bags by tying a knot by the hanger hole. They're great for showing off pretty wastebaskets because they're clear!

....

To make a ceiling look higher, all you need to do is change the lighting. Floor lamps that have the shade below the light bulb—like halogens—reflect the light onto the ceiling, which will make it look farther away.

....

If you have the interior decorating bug, but don't have much to spend on home accents, here's an easy way to add ambience: use Christmas lights. Great over a doorway, winding up a large houseplant, along a counter, or out on your patio, you'll be surprised how many compliments you'll get for this simple technique. Especially great to implement in January, when all the holiday decorations are half off!

....

You can easily create an attractive tabletop display by color-coordinating. Gather whatever objects you have that are the same color, and they'll catch the eye more easily. If you have more than one space to fill, create different displays using different colors for each.

....

If you have a room whose decor seems disorganized or mishmash, place a dark brown or black piece of furniture, like a table, in the center. The darker item will attract the eye and focus people's attention.

....

For something new and interesting to decorate your coffee table with, why not coffee table books? Choose a few of the most interesting ones from your collection (including this one, of course) and leave them out for visitors to peruse. If you really want to go the extra mile, you can also select a couple of random, heavy doodads to use as bookends.

....

Your local dollar store can be a boon for home decorating, even if you're not using the items for the purpose they were intended. A cheap, small plate can become a candleholder, while a teacup or bowl can be used as a pot for indoor plants.

—*Carol Ann Laplante, Omak, WA*

DIY DECORATIONS

For an easy decorating project, gloss colorful autumn leaves. The whole family can collect them together and spread them out on newspaper inside. To gloss, combine equal parts milk and water and paint over the leaves or brush over with a clean rag. When the leaves are dry, use them to adorn indoor plants, fill a vase with them for an eye-catching centerpiece, spread them out on the mantle, or place them underneath candles to catch the drips.

For a sunny room that gets a lot of light, try this neat decorating trick: Fill clear bottles with water and add food coloring, then place in the window sill. The sun will filter through them, casting brightly colored shades and shapes reminiscent of stained glass around the room.

Have some beautiful clear jars, but don't know what to do with them? Try putting photos inside! Add marbles, rocks, colored sand, or other decoration at the bottom, then bend the photo ever-so-slightly so it fits the curve of the jar.

To turn an old picture frame into a lovely tray for your vanity, take out the glass and pry off the arm that allows it to sit on a shelf. Reinforce what is now the bottom of the tray with a piece of cardboard and a nice fabric of your choosing.

An easy way to add custom knick-knacks to your home is to buy clock mechanisms from your hardware store. These do-it-yourself clocks are just the hands and the motor, and allow you to add them to household items, turning them into clocks. Add them to tins, plates, photos with a cardboard backing, or just about anything else in your home. All it takes is a little creativity!

» Bedding and Other Linens

COMFORTERS

If you love the look of lace, add some to your bedroom or guest room with this inexpensive trick. Buy a rectangular lace tablecloth that is 70-by-90 inches, and you can place it directly on top of your existing comforter. You'll have friends asking how you could afford to dress up your bed with lace!

Even the sewing-challenged can manage to make a cover for their comforter using two sheets sewn together. Mix and match patterns if you'd like. Ours has a flannel sheet on one side, which makes it extra cozy. Don't forget to leave one side open (with a few buttons intact) so you can remove the cover for washing.

DOILIES

Even if you hand-wash it, lace can get easily tangled and torn when cleaning. To prevent this from happening, safety-pin the lace to a sheet or smaller cloth. Wash gently as usual, then unpin when dry.

If you own a lace tablecloth or doily that is beginning to turn yellow, let it soak in a bucket of sour milk for a few hours to return it to its former brilliant white. Just make sure to hand-wash it in mild detergent afterward!

DUST RUFFLES

A dust ruffle is one item that can safely be consigned to the "things you really don't need" category—unless you're trying to hide everything you've stored under the bed. Make your own with a sheet or tablecloth. Only the sides of the bed that show need to have something hanging down over them. A more streamlined option is simply to cover the box spring with a fitted sheet.

Have a dust ruffle for a double bed buy your mattress is twin? Just bunch the ruffle up o whatever side of the bed touches the wall, and safety-pin it to the box spring to keep it in place. No one will ever know!

HEADBOARDS

To perk up your bedroom with a splash of color, get crafty with a DIY faux-headboard. Find a colorful sheet that complements the décor of your room; any fabric will work, so consider cotton, linen, velvet, and even fur! First, consider the width of your bed; a headboard should be slightly wider than your mattress. Then decide what style of headboard you like best, and cut your fabric to the right size and shape. Either wrap your fabric around a foam base and hang it on the wall, or hang it up on its own.

MATTRESSES

To keep your mattress from sagging, it's a good idea to reverse it once a month. If it dips in the middle, place a few folded sheets under the center to even it out.

ORGANIZATION

Looking for ways to Organize Linens? *See* **Organization chapter, Clutter, Relieving**

PILLOWS

If your tights, knee-highs, or other nylon items have holes that can't be solved with the old clear nail polish trick, use them as extra stuffing in sagging throw pillows.

Here's an easy way to start your spring-cleaning: begin with your bed pillows. To make them fluffy and fresh, just place them in the clothes dryer with fabric softener and two clean tennis balls for a few minutes.

RUGS

If you're finding it hard to keep a floor rug in one place, buy some self-adhesive Velcro strips. Attach to the floor and the to the corners of the rug and your skidding problems will be over for good! This also works great for keeping cushions on chairs.

—*Robert Lepovetsky, Camp Hill, PA*

If your braided rug is coming undone, it's not a goner yet. Try repairing it by using a hot glue gun. Just lay down some newspaper, then carefully apply a small amount of glue in between the braids. Press them back together again and hold for a few seconds for the glue to dry.

SHEETS

Want to know the quickest way to a perfectly made bed every time? Stitch a small x in the center of your flat sheet and blankets, then line them up with the center of the headboard. Presto!

—*Stefanie Pole*

Though we like wrinkle-free linens as much as the next person, we simply don't have the time to iron bed sheets like our mothers used to. Still, there are a few things you can do to stop wrinkles before they start. Believe it or not, drying your sheets in the dryer can actually increase and set wrinkles. Instead, fold the sheet into quarters or eighths, snapping it and smoothing it out after each fold. Then place the last fold over a clothesline. The fabric is so light, it will easily dry, with only a few wrinkles still intact.

White sheets can turn yellow for any number of reasons—detergents, plastic storage containers, the oils in your skin, or simply old age. To whiten old linens, soak them for eight hours in a large stainless steel pot of boiling water with ¼ cup dishwasher detergent. Rinse and wash as usual. The whitening powers of the dishwasher soap will restore the brightness to your whites.

> Make yellow sheets white again by soaking them in a tub with warm water along with a cup of salt and a cup of baking soda. Rinse well and dry.
>
> —*Anna Zaia, Baltimore, MD*

Salt is a miracle worker when it comes to removing linen stains; and if you use scented salts in your laundry, you'll get the extra bonus of lovely-smelling sheets. Add ¼ cup scented bath salts during your washing machine's rinse cycle. Not only will your sheets smell great, but the salt acts like a starch to keep them extra crisp. Just make sure to use bath salts that do not contain dyes.

Before using your woolen or cotton blankets when the weather turns cold, wash them in the gentle cycle with 2½ cups white vinegar. It will leave them fluffy and soft as new.

—*Laura Jean Mucha, Cranford, NJ*

On sticky summer nights, cool down by sprinkling a little baby powder between your sheets before retiring for the night.

SHOWER CURTAINS

Want to add a little style to your bathroom? Replace old, boring shower curtain rings with pretty ribbon that matches your curtain. Just run it through the grommets and tie a bow on top of the rod.

TABLECLOTHS

If you spill wine on a tablecloth, blot up as much as you can as soon as you can with a cloth, then sponge with cool water. Wash immediately. If the fabric is not machine washable, cover the stain with a small cloth dampened with a solution of detergent, water, and vinegar, then rinse. Get the cloth to the drycleaner as soon as you can.

If you can't get a coffee or tea stain out of a white tablecloth, there is one last solution. Soak the tablecloth in a bucket of strong coffee or tea (depending on the type of stain) for two hours. You won't get the stain out, but you will dye your linen a lovely earth tone!

WINDOW TREATMENTS

Who knew your windows will appear larger—and will let a little more light into the room—if you just raise the curtain rod a few inches? You'll be surprised how much difference this makes.

Here's the thing about drapes: They're expensive, and a cheaper option is usually available. If you can sew, simply buy a nice, heavy piece of fabric, hem the sides and bottom, and cut Xs instead of holes on top. Run ribbon through the Xs and hang on a rod! Another less-expensive option is a fabric shower curtain. The holes are already there, so just cut to size. Hem the bottom for a more finished look.

When slipping curtains over a metal rod, first place a plastic freezer or sandwich bag over the metal end. This will help you avoid snagging the curtains so they go on easily.

> The easiest way to freshen draperies is to place them in your dryer with a damp towel, on the delicate cycle, for one half hour. For extra freshness, hang them outside afterward if the weather allows.

Need to wash your sheer curtains but hate the thought of ironing them afterwards? Simply dissolve a packet of clear gelatin in the final rinse when laundering, and hang them up damp afterwards. The gelatin will remove almost all the wrinkles.

» Candles

DRIPS, PREVENTING

To keep candles from dripping, soak them in a strong salt-water solution after purchasing. To make sure your salt water is as strong as possible, heat up some water and add salt until it won't dissolve anymore—then you'll know the water is completely saturated. Leave your candles in this solution for two hours, then remove and dry.

Store your candles in the freezer. Once you light them, they'll go hours before they start dripping.

HOLDERS

To prevent wax from sticking to a candleholder, rub a thin coat of olive oil on the base of the holder before lighting the candle. If your holder already has some wax buildup, mix olive oil with dish soap to clean it out.

Most taper candles are too large to fit into standard candlesticks, so you'll have to do a little work to ensure your candle fits securely. (Do not light the candle and melt wax into the base—this is messy and dangerous!) First, try placing the candle base under hot water; this softens the wax and allows it to mold to its new surroundings. If this doesn't do the trick, whittle down the wax around the base of the candle with a paring knife, checking the fit as you go. Stop when you get it narrow enough to fit the holder. Apply wax adhesive (or some sticky tack) around the base of the candle, and place it in the candlestick.

Do your candles slide around in their holders like a kid wearing his dad's pants? Wrap the bottom with tape to get the right fit.

To keep votive candles from sticking to their holders after a night of wax run-off, add a little sand or water to the bottom of the holder before you light the candle. This will keep the wax from making a mess at the bottom.

After your jar candles burn out, they can be cleaned out and re-used for any number of things—including other candles. One way to clean a candle jar is by setting your oven to 200 degrees, melting the leftover wax, and then pouring it out. An even better way, though, is to put it in the freezer for an hour and then pry out the frozen block of wax. It should pop right out.

If you have a favorite candle you might wince each time you go to light it, knowing it will eventually be gone. Yet letting it sit unused on the shelf seems like bad feng shui. As a compromise, try this: Let your favorite candle be a candleholder. When there's a big enough hole worn down the middle, put another, smaller candle inside and light that one. Votive candles work well for inside and can be easily replaced when they burn down.

SIMPLE SOLUTIONS

Looking for a container to store long, tapered candles in? Now you have one: the tubes that Pringles potato crisps come in. It even has a lid!

....

If you like decorating your home with candles, buy them on clearance at after-holiday sales. There's nothing wrong with burning a pumpkin-scented candle in spring or a Christmas-scented one in January. If that feels weird, though, just stash the seasonal scents in the closet until next year's holidays come around.

....

Here's another great use for used, clear 2-liter bottles. Cut off the top and bottom, then place the middle portion over candles that you're using outside. The plastic will act as a shield to keep wind away and the fire lit.

....

To light hard-to-reach wicks at the bottom of jar candles, use an uncooked strand of spaghetti. Light the end of it, then use it like a fireplace match.

....

Rub a bit of oil on candlesticks before inserting candles and they'll be easy to remove. Any dripped wax will also peel off with ease.

WAX REMOVERS

Removing candle wax from your floor is easy if you soften the wax first with a blow dryer, then peel it off. Wipe any excess with a paper towel, and then clean with a mixture of half white vinegar and half water.

....

Accidentally dripped candle wax on a tablecloth? Remove it by rubbing with an ice cube and then scraping with a dull knife. Then wash on the hottest heat possible.

....

Nothing is more disheartening than discovering hot wax has just dripped onto your sofa or tablecloth. But there may be a way to fix it. Place a brown paper bag on top of the wax, then iron the bag with an iron set on medium heat. The wax should transfer to the bag, and you can peel it right up.

....

If you've just removed your candlesticks from the cupboard for a party and they're covered in wax, try this handy trick: just stick them in the freezer for a couple of hours. The wax will harden and chip right off.

» Fireplaces

CLEANING

Cleaning out a fireplace is easy when you line the bottom with aluminum foil. Just wait for the ashes to cool, fold up the foil, and lay a fresh layer out.

Before cleaning the ashes from your fireplace, sprinkle some damp coffee grounds over them. They'll weigh the ashes down and keep dust to a minimum.

If you've been burning a lot of fires this winter, get your brick fireplace nice and clean in the spring with a simple household solution. Take 3 cups vinegar, 3 cups ammonia, and 3 cups borax, mix the ingredients thoroughly, and scrub the bricks clean. This will work for any bricks inside or outside your home.

Try an old masonry trick to brighten up soot-stained brick. Mix a can of cola with 3½ fluid ounces all-purpose household cleaner and 3½ quarts water in a bucket. Sponge onto sooty brick and leave for 15 minutes. Loosen the soot by scrubbing with a stiff-bristled brush. Sponge with clean water. For a stronger solution, add more cola.

If you throw some salt in your fireplace every now and then, soot will be easier to clean from your chimney. It will also make your fire burn a cool yellow color!

FIREWOOD AND KINDLING

The best thing to use as kindling in your fireplace isn't newspaper (or printed out emails from your ex). It's lemon peels! Lemon (and orange) peels smell delicious when they burn, and they contain oils that not only make them burn longer, but help ignite the wood around them. Finally, they produce less creosote than paper, which will help keep your chimney clean.

Instead of throwing away lint you've cleaned out of your dryer's screen, use it as kindling for your fireplace. It lights quickly and can be stuffed places paper can't.

Cardboard egg cartons are great to use when starting fires (in your fireplace or outside). Fill them with bits of wood and pieces of paper that would be too small to use on their own, like receipts. You can also fill an egg carton with charcoal and use it to start your barbecue grill.

Instead of buying an expensive container to hold firewood and kindling next to your fireplace, use a ceramic flower pot instead. They're cheap and easy to find in tons of different designs.

—*Lamar Wallace, Shiprock, NV*

You're ready to go to bed, but the fire you started a few hours ago is still awake, glowing with its last few embers. Instead of making a mess with water, throw some salt over anything that's still burning. It will snuff out the flame and you'll end up with less soot than if you let it smolder.

» Flowers

ARRANGING

When arranging flowers, use transparent tape across the mouth of the vase in a grid to make an invisible guide. Then stick stems into the individual holes created by the tape. Not only will it be easier to decide where to put each flower, but they'll stay more upright with the tape to lean against.

Ever have the problem of a beautiful bouquet spreading out too much in the vase? It ends up looking rather sad and scrawny, but here's a simple fix: use a hair elastic to hold stems together.

Daffodils are one of our favorite flowers. Just remember not to mix them with other flowers when making an arrangement, as daffodils produce a toxin that kills other flowers!

> Got some nice flowers whose stems are too short for the vase you want to put them in? Take a clear plastic straw and cut a segment off, then slide it over the bottom of the flower stem. Your floral display will now stand tall!

If you've perfectly arranged a vase of flowers that's filled to the brim, water it without disturbing your design by filling a turkey baster with water, then slipping it between the stems.

ARTIFICIAL

To revitalize artificial flowers, forget about using expensive cleaners. Just pour salt or rice into a paper or plastic bag, place the flowers inside petal-side-down, and shake vigorously. The salt or rice will attract the dust, leaving your flowers looking as good as the real thing!

To clean silk flowers, try blowing off the dust with a hairdryer set on cool.

Make a holding place for your fake flowers using salt. Fill your vase with salt and add just enough cold water to get the salt wet, but not submerge it. Then stick the stems of your artificial flowers inside. The salt and water mixture will turn hard, keeping your flowers exactly where you want them. When you're ready to take the flowers out, fill the vase with warm water until the salt starts to dissolve.

BLOOMS

If you've tried cutting their stems at an angle and changing their water but the flowers in your vase just won't bloom, try a hair dryer. Put a diffuser on it and set it to low, then point it at your bouquet and slowly sweep it back and forth for five minutes. The warmth simulates the sun, which may get your shy flowers to open up.

LONG-LASTING TIPS

Florists sometimes cut flowers in the open air, which allows air into the stems and prevents the flowers from absorbing all the water they need. To ensure that your store-bought flowers stay fresh longer, submerge the stems in hot water, and trim an inch off the ends. Always cut on a diagonal to expose the most surface area to the water.

....

My mother used to make flower arrangements with the flowers from our garden. She told me to always crush the stems of roses at the ends to encourage absorption of water. With tulips, she would make a series of small holes down the length of their stems with a pin instead. To this day people always ask me how I keep my flowers lasting so long!

—*Wendy Lundgren, North Platte, NE*

If you're cutting flowers from your garden, do it first thing in the morning. Flowers have more moisture then and will last longer if cut early in the day.

Who doesn't love a bouquet of flowers displayed in a vase? Unfortunately, it's not always easy to keep your display looking fresh and beautiful. To prevent flowers from wilting, gently spray the undersides of petals and leaves with a little bit of hairspray. It really works!

To prolong the life of your flower bouquet, simply replace their water each day, rinsing off the bottom of their stems as you do. This will discourage the growth of bacteria while making sure they get the nutrients they need.

You may have heard the old household tip about extending the life of your cut flowers by adding a penny to the bottom of the vase. However, today's pennies aren't made with enough copper to effectively work as a fungicide. Pennies made before 1981 do, however, so if you find one make sure to keep it for your flowers.

FURNITURE | HOUSEPLANTS | WALL HANGINGS

Florists do it, so why not you? If you have room in your refrigerator, place your entire vase of flowers inside when you go to bed each night. The cooler temperature will preserve your flowers when you're not awake to enjoy them.

> To prolong the life of cut flowers without using commercial plant food, add 2 tablespoons vinegar and 1 teaspoon sugar to the water.
>
> —*Kim Brickman*

Ever experienced that "unfresh" smell when taking your flowers out of the vase? To keep your cut flowers smelling fresh and lasting longer, make sure you remove any of the stem leaves that will be underwater in your vase. If left underwater, leaves rot quickly. A drop or two of bleach can keep flowers alive for longer. This always struck us as odd, until we stopped to think that you use bleach to kill bacteria, viruses, and "germs" in general. Why not flower germs? You can also add aspirin and a little sugar; or even vodka (yes, vodka!). These ingredients will keep your flowers disease-free.

To easily transport cut flowers, slip a balloon over the faucet and fill it with some water, then pull the opening over the stems of your flowers and secure with a rubber band. It's an unmessy way to let them have a drink in transit.

VASES

When you're serving breakfast in bed, don't despair if you can't find a vase for that elegant touch of fresh flowers. Grab a toothbrush holder, which gives a mod look and holds the flowers up quite nicely.

Just because there's a crack in your grandmother's old vase doesn't mean you can't use it for fresh flowers anymore. Just line it with one of those clear plastic bags you get in the produce section of your grocery store, and your problem is solved. It makes for simple cleaning as well! Just dump the water out, then throw away the bag with the dead flowers in it.

Fresh flowers and greenery make beautiful holiday decorations, but where do you put them? All you need are some empty wine or other bottles (like beer or juice bottles), old newspaper, and spray paint. Place the bottles outside on the newspaper, spray paint them gold, silver, or the holiday color of your choice, and let them dry. Voilà!—unique vases that will have your guests guessing as to where you purchased them.

> Don't put a beautiful bouquet of flowers in a cloudy vase! To make it shine like new, just pour a little white vinegar and uncooked rice inside, swish it around, and watch the clouds disappear.

FURNITURE | HOUSEPLANTS | WALL HANGINGS

Even eggshells have a great use before you throw them away: getting rid of rings on hard-to-clean places in vases. Fill the vase mostly full with warm water, then add a drop of dishwashing liquid and the eggshells. They'll act as an abrasive to scrub off the stains.

....

Effervescent tablets like Alka-Seltzer aren't just good for curing hangovers—dissolve a tablet in warm water at the base of a vase to remove stains and leave it shiny-new.

....

Do you have leftover vases from flowers that are long gone? Ask your local florist (not at the grocery store) if they'd be willing to give you a bouquet of flowers in return for several clean vases! They will probably take you up on it.

» Furniture

COVERS

When washing a slipcover for a couch or chair, put it back on your furniture while the cover is still damp. Not only will the slipcover be easier to get on, but it won't need to be ironed. It will help keep them from shrinking, too!

MOVING

Slice old corks into thin disks, then glue them to the feet of your heavy furniture. It's a great way to protect your floors, and makes moving the furniture a bit easier.

You've probably seen those little cushions with the sticky material on the back that can be placed on the bottom of furniture or the backs of picture frames to keep them from scratching. Rather than spending the money for these expensive items, buy cushions for corns and bunions instead! As long as they aren't medicated, they're the exact same thing, and usually much cheaper.

Moving a large appliance or piece of furniture? Make your job easier by first placing carpet scraps (carpet-side down) under each corner—or do the same with flattened, waxy milk cartons. Either way, the piece of furniture will slide easily along your floor. If you're moving something in the kitchen (like a refrigerator), try squirting liquid dish detergent all over the floor. Watch your step, because it will be very slippery! So slippery, in fact, that your large appliance will just glide to the other side of the room.

PURCHASING

Looking for tips on Shopping for furniture? *See* **Shopping chapter, Household Items**

REPURPOSING

If your country kitchen is running out of room, consider a dresser. Even though you're used to bureaus being only for bedrooms, it can be a valuable addition to a kitchen for storing napkins, utensils, and more. Repaint the dresser in colors to match your kitchen and you'll have guests asking where you got your newest piece of kitchen furniture.

If your furniture is weathered or out of style, that's not necessarily a reason to replace it. There are plenty of ways to spruce up old dressers, chairs, and tables. Everybody loves quilts, so why not drape one over that old chair that needs re-upholstering? You can also try using colorful fabrics on the fronts of nightstand and dresser drawers. Just get some scrap cloth from your last project or from a fabric store, and attach it to the dresser drawers with a staple gun. To have even more fun with it, we like to paint part of the piece and color-coordinate it with the cloth we're using.

If your cabinets are getting old and worn, you can revive them just by replacing the knobs and handles. A good variety should be available inexpensively at your local hardware store. They'll make your kitchen or bathroom look brand new!

You've probably noticed this at the restaurants you frequent, but it's becoming more and more acceptable nowadays—even hip—to eat your meals on vintage, mismatched chairs. Instead of spending a fortune on a dining-room set, go for the mismatched look and hunt for your chairs at thrift shops and used furniture stores.

» Houseplants

CHOOSING

Purify the air in the your without an air filter by buying potted plants that naturally clean your air. Some good choices are rubber trees, corn plants, bamboo palm, ficus, mums, gerbera daisies, English ivy, peace lily, and philodendrons.

Always buy houseplants in the spring, when you'll find a better selection and prices that are 20–60 percent cheaper.

FEEDING AND CARE

To keep mud from spattering when you water plants in window boxes, top the soil with a half-inch layer of gravel. Do the same for outdoor plants to prevent mud bombs during heavy rainfalls.

When watering houseplants, always use lukewarm water. Cold water may chill their roots.

No matter how long you've had your houseplant, it's still hard to tell exactly how much water it needs. Our son loves performing this test to see when a plant has had enough to drink. (It's just like sticking a fork in a pan of brownies to see if they're done.) Poke a pencil into the dirt and pull it back out. Clean means it's time to water. Soil on the pencil means the plant is okay for now.

. . . .

If you host a big party at your house, don't throw away all the beer from those half-empty bottles. Instead, pour it into a bucket, let it sit for a day or two until the beer gets flat, then pour into your potted plants. The nutrients from the beer will give the plants an extra boost. Wait a minute, wasn't this in *Little Shop of Horrors*?

. . . .

Your houseplants need nourishment, particularly in the dead of winter when the sunlight is limited, yet there's no need to buy expensive plant food. Just remember to save the water in which you boil potatoes or pasta, let it cool, and use it to water your plants. They love the starchy water.

. . . .

If you have an aquarium, save the water each time you change it and use it to water your houseplants. The fishy water contains nitrogen, potassium, and phosphorus—all three function as natural fertilizers for plants. You'll be amazed at the results.

. . . .

Forget expensive food for your houseplants. Just feed them flat club soda periodically and they should thrive. The minerals in club soda are beneficial to plants.

Don't spend money on a watering can unless it's for decorating purposes—it's much easier to make your own. Simply wash out an old 1-gallon milk jug, then poke or drill very small holes below the spout on the side opposite the handle. Fill it with water, screw the top back on, and you have a homemade device to water your plants!

PLANTING

If you are going to re-pot a plant, place a small coffee filter on the bottom of the new pot to keep the soil from leaking out the drainage holes. Not a coffee drinker? Try a paper towel or napkin instead.

Use dryer lint to prevent dirt from falling out of your potted houseplants when you water them: Place some dryer lint in the pots so it covers the holes. The water will drain out, but the dirt will stay in!

Packing peanuts will take several decades to decompose, so you can make better use of them than throwing them away. Place them at the bottom of flowerpots before covering with soil and planting flowers and other plants. They'll keep the pot well-drained and much lighter than if you had used rocks.

If you have any doubt that tea really is a panacea,
here's one more amazing use for it: nurturing your
plants and keeping them moist. Place a lining of tea
bags along the bottom of a plant container, then pot
and water as usual.

POTS

Although fancy pots may look pretty, the best kind
of container to grow plants in is an unglazed clay pot. It's
porous, which allows the soil to breathe, and the hole at
the bottom makes it difficult to over-water. Be wary of
both plastic pots and decorative glazed clay pots.

....

**Sure you can stick with plain flowerpots for your
potted foliage,** but here are some ideas for days when
you're feeling more inspired: pretty watering cans, an
old mailbox, a leather boot, crockery from a second-hand
shop, a broken teakettle, a dresser drawer. If you use them
outside, all you'll need are holes in the bottom (cut or drill
as appropriate), and you might want to add some stones to
the bottom as well.

....

Never place a clay pot on wooden furniture, unless you use a coaster. Clay is porous, so water will seep
through and possibly damage the wood finish.

....

**Remove the stains in clay and plastic flowerpots
with vinegar.** Just fill the kitchen sink with two-thirds
water and one-third vinegar, and soak the pots. In an hour,
they'll be good as new! Make sure to wash with soap and
water before re-using.

REVIVING

If your houseplants aren't getting enough sun,
maximize the amount of light they *are* getting by placing
them on top of a table covered in foil (shiny side up). The
foil will reflect the light, and your plants will thank you.

Give dying indoor plants a second chance with this
odd little treatment. Let three empty eggshells sit
overnight in a couple of cups of water. (Multiply
the amounts as needed.) Then use the eggshell water the next day when it's time to water the plants.

**To get rid of bugs that are harming your house-
plant,** place the entire plant (pot and all) in a clear,
plastic dry cleaning bag. Throw several mothballs in
with it, and tie a knot at the top. The sun will still get
through, but the bugs will die after a week in seclusion
with the mothballs.

If you have a fern that's seen better days, water
it with lukewarm salt water and that'll help it recover.
If your fern is plagued by worms, that problem is easily
solved, too. Just stick half a dozen unlit matches into the
soil, coated end facing down. The sulfur content in the
matches will keep the worms away.

If your houseplants are dusty, gently wipe the leaves with a soft cloth and a damp sponge. If you want your plants' leaves to *really* shine, rub them (gently!) with a cotton ball dipped in either mayonnaise, diluted mineral oil, or a solution of half baking soda and half water. Wipe off any excess with a soft cloth.

Easily dust your houseplant by rubbing the inside of a banana peel on each leaf. Not only will it remove dust, but it will leave the leaves even shinier than before.

Stale milk will do a great job of cleaning plant leaves. The protein in milk called "casein" has a mild cleansing effect on the plant cell walls.

Want your houseplant leaves to shine the way they did in the nursery where you bought them? It's easy, even if you don't have time to spray them every day with a light mist. Instead, mix ¼ cup baking soda with ½ gallon cold water and use to clean each leaf with a soft rag. (Fuzzy leaves are better left *au natural*.)

» Parties

Looking for tips about Party Decorations? *See Entertaining and Holidays chapter, Parties*

» Wall Hangings

DECORATING IDEAS

Do you have an old, dusty picture hanging in a place of prominence on your wall? Has it finally worn out its welcome? If so, replacing it with a large mirror can help brighten and reinvigorate your room.

....

Looking for a fun and vintage-themed decoration for your kitchen? Try framing seed packets! Dig through whatever is available at your gardening store, then carefully slit the top to let the seeds loose. Center the empty pack on a matte or solid-color background, then glue with rubber cement or white glue. Frame, then hang on the wall for a perfectly themed picture.

....

If you've got lots of bare wall space that you need to fill, there's a way to fill it cheaply and attractively. Buy a pile of cheap frames at the store, and then head to your nearest used bookstore to find a discounted art or photography book on a subject that interests you. When you find an image you like, use a box opener or X-Acto knife to cut the image out of the book cleanly. (Instead of a book, you can also use your favorite wall calendar from a year gone by.) If all the images you use come from the same book, the pages will all be the same size, which will enable you to arrange the frames in a cohesive way on the wall.

....

Hanging any image you'd like on your wall is as easy as a color printer and some internet-searching know-how. To find images that won't be too small or fuzzy when you print them out, go to Images.Google.com and click on "Advanced Image Search." Enter the subject of your desired picture (for example, "moon") in the box labeled "Related to any of the words" and select "Large" next to "Size." Even "large" images won't be poster-sized, but they'll still have enough pixels per inch to make sure they're not blurry when you print them out.

....

For beautiful art at cheap prices, try the gift shop of an art museum. They sell a wide variety of prints from their collection (and sometimes famous works as well) available in several different styles. Our favorite gift shop buy, however, is art postcards. Buy some cheap, black plastic frames, pop your postcards inside, and you have a lovely mini art display for your wall.

....

For fun wall decorations for kids' rooms or a family room, frame movie posters from your family's favorite movies. Try asking at video stores or movie theaters to see if you can have their posters when they are done with them. Often, they'll just give them to you for free. If you're looking for an older movie, you can also find them inexpensively on the internet. Just type in the name of the movie and the word "poster" into Google or another search engine. Another inexpensive decoration option is buying old magazines and hanging vintage ads and photo spreads in frames.

....

Here's a great decorating idea for a child's room: make a magnetic chalkboard out of the wall! This can be easily accomplished by purchasing a can of magnetic paint and a can of chalkboard paint, both of which should be available at your local hardware store and will run you about $15–$25 apiece. Mark off the area that you're going to paint with masking tape, and remember that it can be any shape or size. Then paint several layers of the magnetic paint, waiting for each layer to dry before adding another layer on top of it. Finally, paint on a layer of the chalkboard paint and let it sit for 2–3 days. With the help of some magnets, you'll be able to hang your child's artwork on the wall, and she'll be able to doodle to her heart's delight.

HANGING

A terrific way to hang posters in your kid's room without leaving holes or stains is with white, non-gel toothpaste. Just put a generous drop on the back of each corner, press to the wall, and watch it stick.

To hang lightweight artwork that's not in a heavy frame, there's no need to buy picture wire. Dental floss will do the trick.

If you have a picture frame that won't stop tilting, simply stick a bit of something sticky behind one of the corners. Two options are "sticky tack," which can be found at office supply stores, and mounting putty, which can be purchased in hardware stores.

—*Tamara Joseph, Saginaw, MI*

....

When a picture refuses to hang straight, wrap clear adhesive tape around the center of the wire to prevent it from slipping sideways.

....

To get rid of the guesswork that comes with putting a nail in the wall to hang a picture, try this easy trick. Place a dab of toothpaste on the back of the frame on the hook or string (whatever will touch the nail). Then hold the frame up to the wall, position it carefully, and press it against the wall. The toothpaste will leave a mark that you can hammer a nail through, then wipe away.

....

Instead of spending tons of money on impressive, expensive frames, give your photos a personal touch. Buy the cheap frames at the store and re-paint them yourself. Not only will they look almost as good as the expensive kind, but you can customize them to perfectly match your home decor.

....

To make a fun display for your favorite photos, hang twine in a corner and place clothespins on it like a clothesline. Then clip photos, artwork, or your children's drawings up to show off.

Auto

Baking

Beauty

Cleaning

Clothing and Accessories

Cooking

Decorating

Health and Wellness

Home Repair

>> Entertaining and Holidays

Kids

Money

Organization

Outdoors

Pest Control

Pets

Shopping

Utilities

Vacations and Family Activities

Websites

» Alcohol

CHAMPAGNE

Champagne lost its fizz? Place a raisin in the glass and the last bits of carbon dioxide that remain will cling to the raisin, then be released again as bubbles. You can also try throwing a few raisins into the bottle before you make the final pour.

For a snazzy party treat especially good for New Year's, add some color and sweetness to champagne. First color some granulated sugar by adding a few drops of food coloring to it. Then wet the rim of each champagne glass and press into the sugar to give it a sweet, colorful rim—perfect for guests who find champagne a little too dry.

ICE

If you run out of ice at a party, you're in trouble! But how do you know how much to buy? Use this simple metric. If you're serving mostly cocktails, the average person at a party will go through 10–15 cubes. When you buy ice cubes in a bag, you will get about 10 cubes per pound.

To keep ice cubes from melting at a party, put them in a bowl, and then set that bowl in a larger one filled with dry ice.

If you're serving punch at a party, pour some of it into ice cube trays and freeze. This way, you can keep the punch nice and cold without diluting it. This also works well with wine, iced tea, or any number of other beverages. If you want to get really exotic, mint leaves are a great thing to make ice cubes out of—just fill the ice tray with water like normal and then stuff the leaves so that they rest below the surface.

Drinking punch that's half water is never fun, but ice cubes can melt so quickly when left out in a bowl. One of the easiest ways to keep a large punch bowl cold is to make larger ice cubes, as it will take one giant ice cube much longer to melt than many little ones. To make a long-lasting, large cube, fill a rinsed-out milk or juice carton half-full with water. Then peel off the cardboard when it's time to use.

It's nice to keep an ice bucket next to your drinks on the table, but once the ice melts you're left with a few cubes soaking in a puddle of water. To fix this problem, place a colander on the top of your ice bucket and fill it with the ice. Water will drip through the bottom, and the ice will be easier to grab with some tongs.

—*Cynthia Ferris*

If you're having a party and have run out of space to cool beverages, don't go buy a Styrofoam cooler. Instead, fill your washing machine with ice and store bottles and cans inside. The lid will keep everything cool, and once the ice melts you can simply run the rinse cycle to get rid of the all the water.

SERVING

We love anything that gives us more time to talk to our company and cuts down on hosting duties during a party. One simple way to hand out drinks—use muffin trays instead of flat trays. You can easily carry two dozen glasses without breaking a sweat and even younger family members will be able to help.

....

Keep a handle on whose drink is whose by pressing window decals onto the sides of glassware. This is a perfect trick for a party that takes place around a holiday, when you can use festive decals that are easy to find at party stores.

....

Having a party? Instead of buying "wine rings," which go around the base of wine glasses to mark whose drink is whose, simply have a dry-erase marker on-hand and have guests write their names (or a funny message) right on their glass.

WINE

Uh oh, you were uncorking a bottle of wine, and didn't do a very good job. You're not above drinking wine that has a little cork floating in it, but you definitely don't want to serve it to guests! Simply hold a coffee filter over a carafe and pour. It will filter out the cork pieces and your reputation will be saved...for now.

Red wines that are more than eight years old tend to develop sediment. It's harmless, but it doesn't always look too nice. Get rid of sediment, and any bits of cork, by pouring your wine through a coffee filter and into a decanter before you serve it.

Wondering what to do with leftover wine (besides drinking it, of course)? Keep it fresh by putting whatever is left in a small container such as a jam jar. This limits the amount of air the wine is put in contact with, keeping it fresh. Incidentally, that is the same thing those expensive "wine vacuum sealers" do!

Here's a neat trick to get rid of the tiny bit of wine at the end of the bottle. Freeze leftover wine in ice cube trays, then store the cubes in a freezer bag. Use them in wine coolers and any dish that calls for wine.

» Barbecues and Picnics

BEVERAGES AND COOLERS

Because salt lowers the freezing point of water, your beverages will cool more quickly if you use salt in your cooler. Simply layer ice with salt, throw in the bottles and cans, and wait for them to chill.

To keep your cooler fresh and odor free, throw in 10–15 charcoal briquettes, close the top, and leave it overnight. In the morning, clean the cooler with soapy water, and it will smell like new.

Before stashing away your cooler for the winter, stuff it with a few balls of newspaper. The newspaper will absorb any lingering odors, so it won't be a mildewy nightmare when you open it back up in the spring.

The best way to chill beer or soda rapidly is to fill a cooler with layers of water, ice, and salt, then plunge the beers inside. In about 20 minutes or less, the beer will be ice cold! Even if the ice water is warmer than your freezer, it absorbs the warmth from the bottles or cans more rapidly and more efficiently than the cold air of the freezer does. Just remember that premium lagers should be served between 42°F and 48°F and ales between 44°F and 52°F, so don't let them get too cold.

. . . .

If you want to keep your wine (or other beverage) cool on hot summer days, use frozen grapes instead of ice cubes. They'll keep the drink cold and they won't dilute it or change the taste as they thaw. Just make sure you wash them before freezing!

CLEANING AND PREP

When the next three-day weekend rolls around, make sure your outdoor grill is prepped for the first barbecue of the season. Clean the grates by placing them in the tub and covering with very hot water and one cup each ammonia and dishwasher detergent. Cover with old fabric softener sheets and soak overnight. The next day, don your rubber gloves, scrub away, and watch the grease dissolve.

. . . .

A great way to clean your barbecue grill is with wet newspaper. After cooking, just place it on a warm grill for one hour with the lid closed. You'll be amazed how easily the grime comes off!

. . . .

Save on expensive grill cleaners by simply using WD-40 instead. Get rid of charred food stuck to the grill by removing it from the barbeque and spraying it with the oil. Let sit for five to ten minutes, then wipe off and clean with soap and water.

. . . .

When you're done grilling, place a large piece of aluminum foil over the entire top of your grill, then put the top back on and let it sit for 10–15 minutes. The caked-on mess from the burgers and hot dogs will turn to ash.

Six-packs are a must-have at a barbecue—and not just for the beer. Turn an old six-pack container into a holder and carrier for condiments like ketchup, mustard, and relish. You can even stick napkins and plastic utensils inside. To make it extra strong (and waterproof), wrap in duct tape!

You're hosting a backyard barbecue that's turned into an evening affair. Unfortunately, your outdoor accent lights aren't bright enough, but you don't want to have to turn on the glaring light by your door. Instead, fold pieces of aluminum foil in half (shiny side out) and wrap like a bowl around the bottom of the light, then attach with a few pieces of electrical tape. The foil will reflect the light in a nice, shimmering pattern.

Nothing gets the summertime party going faster than firing up the backyard grill. Just make sure you keep all that smoked and grilled meat coming—it's unforgivable to run out of fuel before the last kebab is bobbed. Even without a gas gauge, there is a way to figure out how much fuel you have left. Here's what to do a day or two *before* the flip-flopped masses are set to arrive. Boil water, then pour it down the side of the tank. Place your hand on the side: the cool part has propane inside, the warm part is empty.

Store charcoal briquettes in airtight plastic bags—they absorb moisture very easily and won't be as easy to light if exposed to air.

COOKING QUICK TIPS

Always leave 30 percent of your grill empty when cooking. Next time a flare up occurs, it's easy to move your dinner out of harm's way and prevent charring.

Spraying your grill with a bit of vegetable oil before you start grilling will make cleaning ever easier, and your grill even hotter (which will put those cool "grill marks" on your meat and veggies). For the easiest clean-up, coat the grill with vegetable (or canola) oil before starting the fire, then wipe it with a wet rag shortly after you are through. Never spray the oil on the grill after the fire has started—it may cause a flare-up.

Always use tongs when turning meat on the grill. When a fork pierces the meat, it releases some of its juices, making it dry out more quickly. Keep tongs in a mug near your grill!

When the coals start to die down on your grill, don't squirt them with more lighter fluid, which not only costs money, but can leave your food tasting bad (not to mention, burn the hair off your arm). Instead, blow a hair dryer on the base of the coals. The hairdryer acts as a pair of bellows, and your fire will be going again in no time.

To get your grill even hotter (making sure the bar marks on your steak are extra impressive), cover it with a large sheet of foil for 10 minutes before cooking. This will keep the heat from escaping.

If you're grilling a steak on a closed barbecue, here's a neat trick to impress your friends. Open a can of beer and place it on the hottest part of the grill. It will boil and keep the meat moist, while adding flavor, too.

If you plan on grilling fish, be sure to purchase steaks that are at least 1-inch thick. Fish dries out very quickly on the grill, so the thicker it is the better. The skin should be left on fillets while grilling and removed after they are cooked.

Grilling fish is always a drag because the skin inevitably gets stuck to the grate—particularly when cooking salmon. Avoid this by placing a few thin slices on lemon or lime on the grill, and then the fish on top. Not only will your clean-up be easier, but the citrus flavor will taste great with the seafood.

If you have two small wire racks, you can easily cook a fish (and impress your friends) on your outdoor grill. First, find toaster-oven or cooling wracks and some fireproof wire. Oil the racks, then put the fish between them and tie the racks together. Grill the fish on one side, then flip your newly constructed basket with large tongs or a spatula. This makeshift cage will keep delicate fish from breaking apart.

PICNICS

If you're looking for a platter for devilled eggs, brownies, or other picnic items, here's a great makeshift platter idea: Cover a piece of corrugated cardboard with aluminum foil (dull side up), then use it instead! It's easy to use and easy to throw away or recycle when you're finished!

....

When going on a picnic, bring a roll of duct tape. Use the tape to tape the sides of the tablecloth to the picnic table, and you won't have to worry about it blowing away.

....

Linoleum or vinyl floor tiles are excellent for covering picnic tabletops. You can also use linoleum on kitchen shelves, instead of contact paper. It will last longer and is easier to keep clean.

....

To win the war against ants at your picnic, place the picnic table's legs in old coffee cans filled with water. The ants won't be able to climb up the table, and your food will stay safe.

....

Include some sprigs of fresh mint in your picnic basket when eating al fresco. Bees and wasps don't like mint, so add some to your plate to keep it stinger-free.

SEASONING

To help reduce smoke and improve the flavor of food on your grill, use an onion! Cut a red onion in half, pierce it with a fork, and dip in water. Then use the onion half to wipe down the grill rack.

To get the most out of that grilled flavor everyone loves so much, add a few sprigs of your favorite herbs, such as rosemary, thyme, and savory, directly to the top of the charcoal as you grill. It will infuse whatever you're cooking with mouthwatering flavor.

Remember that barbecue sauces contain sugar, and high heat can burn the sugar as well as some of the spices in the sauce. Never apply the sauce until about five minutes before your meat is fully cooked. Another secret is to use low heat and leave the meat on the grill for a longer period.

Make applying barbecue sauce easier with one of those disposable sport water bottles with a squirt top. Store your sauce inside and squeeze while cooking as needed. Keep in the fridge when not in use.

VEGETABLES

Using wooden skewers for your veggies on the grill? Make sure to soak them first. If you don't soak them they may burn, imparting an unwanted taste to your vegetables.

Cooking up some corn? Impress your guests by barbecuing fresh corn to perfection this way: Before grilling, peel all but the innermost layer of husk from the corn, and trim the excess silks as well. Place on the grill and as soon as the husk darkens enough that the outline of the kernels are visible through it, remove the corn. It will be perfectly cooked and have a wonderful, smoky flavor.

If you're serving bread with your barbecue, use a slice to easily butter your corn. Spread a generous amount of butter onto the bread, then gently wrap it around your corn. Twist the cob until the butter has gotten into every crack, then enjoy perfectly buttered corn and bread with melted butter.

» Gifts

CARDS

Show your friends you care and save money by making your own cards to send for birthdays or other occasions. Look through old magazines for funny photos (or shots of your friend's celebrity crush) to use for the front. Or for something more complicated, visit Card-Making-World.com for ideas and free backgrounds and embellishments to download.

If you're sending a get-well card to a friend in the hospital, but aren't sure how long she'll be there, try this: Put the hospital's address on front of the envelope, and your friend's address as the return address. That way, you're certain she'll get the card—at the hospital or once she returns home. (Just don't tell the post office!)

Mailing a card and want to do something creative for that extra-special touch? Visit your local coin and stamp dealer to find unique, vintage postage sold at face value or less. Many dealers sell old yet valid stamps that aren't worth much to collectors, so you're likely to find a bargain on cool, old-fashioned postage.

GIFT IDEAS

Here's a wonderful, one-of-a-kind gift for a bridal shower: Buy a blank hardcover book, add dividers, and create a family cookbook. Just ask the bride and groom's families to provide their favorite treasured recipes.

Looking for an easy, heartfelt (but inexpensive) holiday gift? How about a personalized calendar of your children's artwork? Pick up free calendars distributed by local companies, then paste drawings or paintings from the past year on top of each month's image. Your kids will feel proud of their work, and their grandparent, uncle, or godparent will love their new calendar.

Clippings from a houseplant make great (and free!) housewarming presents. Cut your plant at the "knuckle" (or joint) section of the stem, then place in a cup of water until it grows roots. To present it, wrap the bottom in a wet paper towel and place in a plastic bag, tying it up with ribbon. Or plant in an old mug!

Soaps never seem to lose their appeal as holiday gifts. They're useful and don't add clutter to people's houses (something we're always trying to avoid in ours). You can make your own by grating white, unscented soap it into a bowl with warm water. For color, add a few drops of food coloring appropriate for the holiday. Next, a drop or two of an essential oil (lavender or rose are lovely) then knead like pizza dough and make into little balls. As an alternative, use candy molds for fun shapes. Leave them to dry on wax paper for a day or so.

For the couple who has everything, why not show them how much they've already had? A tour of places they used to live (or go to school or work) is a personal and moving way to celebrate a special day. For an anniversary, find out where they met, where they had their first date, and where they got married. You can start out narrating, but be prepared for the recipients to take over. They'll likely enjoy telling stories as much as anything else you can give them.

—*Marge Lenkel, Laguna Beach, CA*

Mailing books, CDs, or DVDs as presents? The cheapest way to get them there is to take your package to the post office and ask for it to be sent "media mail." Though it will take a little longer to get there, this low rate—reserved for mailing "media"—will save you a lot of money, especially if your package is heavy.

If you're sending flowers for a special occasion, skip the national delivery services and web sites. Instead, find a flower shop that is local to the recipient and call them directly. Most national services simply charge you a fee, then contact these very same stores themselves.

Say "no" to styrofoam popcorn! Instead, save your old egg cartons for the holiday season—they'll come in handy when packing up gifts to mail. Cut them up and use the pieces as packing material. It's cheap and environmentally friendly. Those plastic grocery bags that have been piling up are also great for filling boxes.

When packing up those holiday presents, make sure nothing rattles in the box and the lid closes firmly (without being easily depressed into the box). This will ensure your presents arrive safely, even if heavier boxes are stacked on top (plus, the post office won't insure your package if it sounds like it contains loose items!). To help fill out the space in a big box, use Ziploc bags. Seal them all the way, then open them up just enough to fit a straw through. Blow through the straw to inflate them, then reseal—a homemade air pillow!

WRAPPING

Turn your gift packaging into part of the gift itself. For a bridal shower, wrap your gift with a pretty bath, kitchen, or tea towel. Write a recipe onto the gift tag, or use a recipe card *for* the tag, and tie a bow with a beautiful ribbon and a kitchen utensil, such as salad tongs, inserted inside.

Use pages from the past year's calendar (photo-side up, obviously) to wrap smaller gifts—two taped together are great for books or DVD sets at Christmastime.

Copied sheet music makes for unique and festive wrapping paper. At your local library it should be easy to enough to find books of whatever music suits your friend (classical, show tunes, rock music, etc.). Make a copy on colored paper if you can, and be sure the title of the piece shows when you fold it over the gift.

Instead of doling out cash for fancy bows to decorate gifts, use your actual dollars to *make* the bows. Fold a dollar bill (or more, if you're a high roller) accordion-style and affix with a ribbon over a wrapped gift. As a variation, give a nod to Chinese New Year by putting two dollars inside a traditional red envelope and taping it to the top of a gift for good luck.

....

Do you have collections of paper napkins that are "too pretty to use"? Then use them in a way that takes advantage of their design—as wrapping paper for little gifts or candy bars.

....

For personalized (and inexpensive) wrapping paper, have your kids draw on some taped-together printer paper and use it to wrap gifts that are "from them."

....

Quickest buzz kill when wrapping presents: trying to reuse tired out, wrinkled tissue paper and hoping the recipient won't take it personally. Turns out you can iron used tissue paper on low to get it to look "like new"! Amazing.

....

After everyone's done opening their presents, don't forget to save bigger sheets of paper, bows, and pretty cards (to use for next year's gift tags). We keep our stash in one of those giant popcorn tins with a Christmas design from years ago!

» Holidays

CHRISTMAS ACTIVITIES

Count down the days till Christmas with this fun family activity: Pull together all your holiday-themed books and wrap them as individual gifts. Let your children open one gift per night, and read the book together; save "The Night Before Christmas" for the 24th. The pre-holiday festivities might keep your kids satiated enough to lay off the presents under the tree until Christmas!

....

We like to add a little more excitement and surprise to the holidays by labeling our kids' gifts with colorful stickers rather than gift tags. The stickers are color-coded for each recipient, and we don't reveal the code until gift-opening time on Christmas Day. It's a clever, fun, and inexpensive way to keep the kids guessing.

....

If opening presents is going to take drastically less time than usual this year, fill the gap by starting some new Christmas traditions. Make a popcorn string for the tree, cut out sugar cookies with different-colored sugars for decoration, or try this game to make gift-opening take longer (it's a favorite at our gatherings): Find as many holiday present rejects as you have people playing—all those candles with scents you can't stand, weird gifts from office gift exchanges, or your silliest finds from the dollar bin at Target. Wrap each one and have each guest pick a gift. Go around the room clockwise, starting with the youngest person. Before opening their gift, guests can decide to trade with someone else (even if that person's gift has been unwrapped). After one round of gift opening, have one more round of trades, with players deciding if they want to keep their current gift or switch with someone else. You'll be surprised which gifts people actually like, and get a laugh at the expense of the person left with the worst one.

....

For a holiday treat, carve the nuts out of walnut shells split in half and place fortunes or little prizes inside. Glue back together and decorate with sparkle paint. When the shells are dry, collect them in a basket for a unique centerpiece and fun activity one dark night of the advent. Pass around the table after dinner and let family members take turns reaching for a walnut and cracking it open to find out what's hidden inside.

....

These are a favorite Christmas tradition in our house. We cut paper towel tubes into three pieces and then load them up with candy, little toys, and tissue paper crowns. Then we use wrapping paper to cover the tubes completely, leaving extra paper on each end that we tie up with ribbon. Everyone gets a popper with his or her place setting for Christmas dinner. Our kids love to show guests how to yank from the sides, so that the poppers actually pop!

CHRISTMAS, DECORATING

Used wisely, a little holiday ribbon can go a long way. Wrap it around just about anything—a vase, throw pillow, lamp shade, curtain, pillar candle, and the list goes on—to create a festive atmosphere at little or no cost.

If you want your home to look super-Christmassy, scan your living room for brightly colored objects that aren't red or green, and move them to invisible or inconspicuous locations for the season. Without the other colors to distract people's eyes, your red and green Christmas decorations will stand out even more.

When pruning your trees and bushes in the spring or summer, make sure to save some branches for later use. Then spray paint them red, white, silver, or gold and you have an instant Christmas decoration! Place them in planters of flowers that are dead for the winter, and add lights or ornaments for extra flair.

We love the look of a pine wreaths and garlands, but hate it when needles get all over the floor. To keep the needles from falling, spritz your holiday greenery with hairspray right after you purchase it. The hair spray will keep the needles moist and where they belong.

If you're getting tired of that old drab-looking Christmas wreath, don't get rid of it—just spruce it up a little. Use a glue gun to attach some pinecones from your yard onto it, or buy some cheap doo-dads at your local crafts store and do the same. You'll get a brand-new wreath for a fraction of the cost.

Making a popcorn garland for the holidays? Use dental floss! It's stronger than regular string, and less likely to break when you wrap it around the tree.

> You can easily dust your Christmas wreath with "snow" by using salt. Go outside in the backyard with a large paper grocery bag and half a cup of salt. Pour the salt in the bag, place the wreath inside, and fold the bag closed. Then shake gently for 20 seconds and your wreath will look as good as new.

Eventually, you do have to give in and take down the Christmas tree, but before it goes out the door, pull off a few handfuls of needles that you can keep as simple potpourri. Little cloth bags are readily available in craft stores, or you can make your own out of old nylons. Just cut a scrap into a square, place the needles inside, bundle up, and tie with a ribbon. There's no reason not to enjoy that woodland scent all year long.

Put those unused holiday ornaments to good use by using them for an inexpensive centerpiece. Simply pick your favorites and put them in a clear punch bowl, and add tinsel or pine sprigs around the base. It works great with those solid-colored orbs we always seem to have so many of!

If you want your windows to look like they've been touched with frost this holiday season, just mix 1 tablespoon Epsom salts with 1 cup beer, then brush onto the window with a small paintbrush. When you're ready to remove the frost, just wash it off with ammonia and water.

Pinecones are a family favorite during Christmastime, whether they're hanging on the tree or from a stocking, or simply radiating their delicious piney fragrance. But sometimes they're just too sticky to handle. To remove some of that sticky sap, place the pinecones in the oven at 300 degrees for 10 minutes.

Poinsettia plants are gifts that keep on giving, if *you* give *them* a little extra care. After the last of the Christmas decorations are packed away, bring your poinsettia plants down to the basement (or elsewhere) where it's cool and dark. Then keep them like prisoners, giving them very little water, until they're almost dried out but not quite. Toward the end up April, bring the plants back out, trim them down about halfway, and give them lots of water and sun. You'll be amazed at how well they re-bloom.

When nights are warm enough for just a sweater, we sometimes plant them outside in a sunny spot to enjoy from the deck all summer long. Then back inside in the fall, where they still get full sun and lots of water.

CHRISTMAS TREES

Don't waste your money on an expensive tree skirt this Christmas. Instead, look for a small, round table cloth from a department store—they usually have a big selection and they're inexpensive, too. Cut a round opening in the center for the tree stand, and a straight line to one edge. Place the opening in the back of the tree and you're done.

Instead of buying a stand for your Christmas tree, simply fill a bucket with sand. You can still water it, and you won't have to deal with the hassle of re-adjusting the stand so the tree isn't crooked.

If you have trouble getting a watering can to reach underneath the lowest bows of your Christmas tree, throw several ice cubes into the base each day to easily keep it watered.

—*Fran Kaiser, Shalimar, FL*

We've been known to keep our Christmas tree up until well into January, and with this little trick, you can enjoy the holidays a little longer too. Add a small amount of sugar or Pine-Sol to the water to extend the life of your tree.

Did you know that one strand of traditional Christmas lights running five hours a day for 30 days can add up to $10 to your electricity bill? This Christmas, make sure you use LED lights, which will only run you 12¢ for the same amount of time. LED lights also last much longer!

When you take down your Christmas tree, always wrap the lights around the outside of a cardboard tube (try the tube from a roll of paper towels) and secure with masking tape. They'll be easy to unwind next year, and you'll never have another nightmarish day of untangling all the lights while the kids wait to decorate the tree.

When it's time to bring down the tree and lights, take great care with the more delicate ornaments. Slip them into old socks or nylons; for extra safety, then place them in disposable plastic cups before storing. Old egg cartons are another ultra-safe (and eco-friendly) way to store bulbs and glass trinkets.

The best container we've found for storing Christmas ornaments is an empty case of wine or liquor (no comment on how we came across this!). Keep the cardboard dividers inside, and you have a handy place to ball up your ornaments with newspaper and keep them safe until next year. These boxes are also great for storing rolled-up artwork and posters.

Keep an eye out during the year for cool drink coasters that are served at bars. These cardboard circles and squares are great for ornaments and gift tags. Simply punch a hole through the top, insert a ribbon, and hang!

....

Still have film canisters? It's easy to turn them into little Christmas treasure boxes. Any scraps from the arts and crafts table (glitter, sequins, bits of wrapping paper, mini buttons) can be applied with a hot glue gun to decorate the outside. Fill with little candies or toys from the five and dime store. Miniatures have a certain holiday magic and kids never seem to grow tired of them. To make into hanging ornaments, simply knot a ribbon into a loop and glue to the top.

—*Rachel Federman*

....

The holidays have been over for weeks, but you've been dreading the removal of your Christmas tree, which has been shedding pine needles pretty much ever since you bought it. To get a dead tree out of your house without too much mess behind you, find the biggest, strongest garbage bag you can. Open it up so you can see the bottom, then place on the floor next to your tree. Once you free the tree from its stand, place the trunk squarely in the middle of the bag, then work your way around the tree, pulling the bag up as far as you can over its branches. (This is often easiest as a two-person job, with one person holding the tree and one person moving the bag.) Even if you can't get the bag all the way over your tree, you can still hold the bag in place while you carry the tree out to the curb. By the time you get there, there will be a huge pile of needles at the bottom of the bag that never made it onto your carpet.

EASTER

Never, ever pay for egg dye! Simply mix ½ cup boiling water with ½ teaspoon white vinegar, and add food coloring until you get a hue you like. For a striped egg even the Easter Bunny would be proud of, wrap tape around the egg before dipping. Once the egg dries, remove the tape, tape over the colored parts, and dip again in a different color. You can also use stickers in the shapes of hearts, stars, and letters.

....

It's easy to make natural Easter egg dyes. Just add colorful ingredients to the water while you boil your eggs. Use grass for green, onionskins for yellow and deep orange, and beets for pink. If you plan to eat the eggs, be sure to use plants that haven't been fertilized or treated with pesticides or other chemicals.

....

You might think only older kids can dye Easter Eggs, but we started our boys off when they were still in diapers. Give your little helpers a plastic container filled with food coloring, water, and a little vinegar. Let them drop the hard-boiled egg in, help them seal it closed, and tell them to "Shake, shake, shake." Pure magic.

....

Instead of packing away those plastic Easter eggs for once-a-year use (or tossing them out all together), you can keep using them throughout the year. For instance, instead of putting snacks in Ziploc bags in your child's sack lunch, put the snacks inside the eggs. They can be filled with M&Ms, Skittles, Cheerios, Goldfish crackers, and a variety of other things.

—*Hadley Moore, West Hartford, CT*

FOURTH OF JULY

It's Fourth of July and time to bust out the legal explosives. Kids love to hold sparklers, but make sure their hands are safe by sticking the sparkler in Play-Doh inside its container, which is the perfect size for the kids to wrap their patriotic hands around.

HALLOWEEN

Adding stretchy cobwebs to the doorjambs and corners of your home is a great way to add Halloween flair to the entire house. Instead of buying the ones packaged as spider webs, though, simply go to a craft store and buy a bag of fiberfill. It's the exact same stuff, and a 16-ounce bag of fiberfill is less than half the cost. You can usually find bags of plastic spider rings for super-cheap at party supply or superstores—add them to the webs and on tables around your house for more atmosphere, and encourage your guests to take them home!

Getting dry ice to put at the bottom of the punch bowl is a bit difficult, so to make your punch seem haunted quickly and easily, freeze grapes to use as ice cubes. Once they're frozen, peel off the skin and they'll look like creepy eyeballs.

A problem we used to have every Halloween was that our pumpkins got soft and mushy soon after they were carved. It turns out that this happens because air comes in contact with the inside flesh, allowing bacteria to grow. So to solve the problem of every jack-o-lantern looking like an old man, we now spray the inside of the hollowed-out pumpkin with an antiseptic spray, which slows down the bacterial growth and increases the time it takes for the pumpkin to deteriorate. Just make sure no one eats a pumpkin that has been sprayed! You can also try using WD-40 spray instead.

Duct tape may be the best aide for a last-minute Halloween costume. Make a robot or the Tin Man using a brown paper bag or box as a mask. Cover it, as well as a shirt and old pair of jeans, with duct tape, then send your kid out for some much-deserved candy.

HOLIDAYS, GENERAL

Flora-lovers don't need fancy arrangements to celebrate every holiday with style. Start your own tradition of dying white carnations whatever color is fitting for the occasion. Various shades of red and pink for Valentine's Day, green for St. Patrick's Day, a combination of red, white, and blue for July Fourth, orange and black for Halloween, and so on. It's also fun to do favorite colors for birthdays. All you need to do is add a bit of food coloring to your flowers' vase with some warm water. Half the fun watching the flower take on the new color as it sucks up the water, so make sure the kids don't miss out.

Whoever had the idea for the first Christmas tree must have retired young. Why not spread the wealth and decorate an indoor tree you already have for other holidays? Our kids love to hang eggshell ornaments and tie pastel ribbons on the dracena in our kitchen at Easter. And when they were younger, we used to arrange their stuffed bunnies, ducks, and lambs on a blanket spread out on the floor underneath the tree. For Valentine's Day, a simple afternoon project of making and hanging paper hearts cut out of last year's Valentines (hole-punch the top and tie a ribbon) can become a family tradition.

With holidays, always make sure to stock up a year ahead of time! We always hit up stores after each holiday to check out what kind of deals we can get on decorations or gifts for the following year. Also keep in mind that many stores start discounting holiday items a week before the holiday—so if you're willing to wait until the last minute, you can save big.

THANKSGIVING

Give hyper kids something to do *and* decorate your table at the same time this Thanksgiving by sending them out into the yard to find the last remaining yellow, red, and orange leaves. Make sure they're not visibly dirty, then arrange them along the middle of the table in lieu of a runner. We love this activity because it's good for kids of any age, and the older ones can help the younger ones.

The day after thanksgiving is Black Friday—the craziest shopping day of the year. Before you head out to the mall, hit up FatWallet.com first. They keep track of each store's Black Friday deals, so you can keep an eye out for promised bargains and make a plan of attack for your day of shopping.

VALENTINE'S DAY

Instead of worrying all day about how to make the perfect romantic dinner for your Valentine, try breakfast in bed and get a whole day's worth of credit for it. A flower, a chocolate, and a heart shaped placemat are all you need to make eggs, toast, and a fruit bowl look especially festive.

....

Sometimes, showing your sweetheart you love them is as easy as telling them so. Write a quick love message on a post-it note and leave it where your lover will see it first thing in the morning, like on the bathroom mirror. For something more special, compose a letter where you tell your valentine just how much you care, and hand-write it for that personal touch.

....

If you don't really have a way with words, steal them from the pros! At Poets.org, you'll not only find tons of classic and contemporary love poems, you can include one in an e-card to send to loved ones. To make it more romantic, however, try printing out a poem to read aloud on Valentine's Day, or pasting it inside a home-made card.

» Parties

DECORATING AND DISPLAYS

Here's a great way to display dip on your table.
Cut off the top of a bell pepper, then hollow it out and
spoon your dip inside. You can also use a sturdy bread
like pumpernickel as a hollowed-out dip container. Put
spinach dip inside, then cut the bread you removed into
large cubes and use for dipping. Your guests will love it!

For a fun display on your buffet table, hollow out a
melon, orange, or grapefruit and fill it with cut-up fruits
(and maybe even some miniature marshmallows). For a
more attractive holder, you can scallop the edges or cut it
in the shape of a basket.

To keep meat or cheese hors d'oeuvres moist, cover
them with a damp paper towel, then cover loosely
with plastic wrap. Many fillings (as well as bread)
dry out very quickly, but with this tip, you can
make these simple appetizers first and have them
ready on the table when guests arrive.

Here's an original idea for a cheap New Year's Eve decoration: gather all the devices you use to tell time—stopwatches, alarm clocks, calendars, pocket planners, even the little hourglasses from board games—and place them on a tray next to the champagne bowl. Tell all your guests to set their alarms for midnight and do the same with the items you've collected.

KIDS'

Your daughter's party is about to start, and you just realized you don't have a plastic tablecloth on which to serve the cake. Don't worry, your dining room table isn't ruined yet. Just use the mat from your Twister game. It's covered with colorful dots, and food wipes right off.

Life Savers are an excellent accent for your child's birthday cake. Not only do kids enjoy sucking on them, but they are perfect for holding candles! Use the regular size (not the jumbo kind that come individually wrapped in bags), put them on top of the cake, and then insert the candle in the middle. The candy will hold the candle straighter and is easily disposed of if wax drips on it.

Having a birthday party for your child? Consider serving cupcakes instead of one large cake, which will eliminate the need for forks and paper plates—and save you money.

If your children's birthday parties are putting a hurt on your budget, there's a simple solution—have the party during the week instead of on a weekend. Sure, everyone wants a weekend party, and that's why restaurants and other popular birthday locales charge a lot more for Saturday and Sunday events. They'll be only too happy to accommodate your request for a weekday party, and it might even be easier for you, too—just offer to pick up your child's playmates from school that afternoon and have them picked up from the party later. Your child will have just as much fun as they would at a weekend party, maybe even more, since it's a rare weekday treat. A great, but rarely utilized, location for a summer party is your local minor league baseball park. Tickets are cheap, kids will love interacting with the mascot, and there's no need to stay the whole game—five innings or so should suffice. The team might even offer you discounted group tickets and flash your child's name on the scoreboard.

When it comes to piñatas, the spoils go to the bullies, but not if you separate the candies and prizes into Ziploc bags for each guest before stuffing them inside the paper-mâché animal. The kids will still get a rush of excitement when the piñata drops, but the game won't dissolve into an "Are we having fun yet?" moment when they start fighting over Tootsie Rolls and Milky Ways.

Here's a cheap and easy game for a kids' party that's become a birthday tradition our kids always ask for. Before the party, gather up enough party favors for each child who will be playing, then add a "special" party favor for just one child. Put the favors in a box and wrap it with an old scrap of wrapping paper, newspaper, or construction paper. Then wrap it again. And again, and again, and again.... After you've wrapped the box 6–12 times (depending on how many guests you're expecting), you're ready to play. Sit the children in a circle and start up some music. While the music plays, the children pass the present around to their right. When the music stops, the kid holding the present gets to unwrap a layer of wrapping paper. The game continues until the last child unwraps the present, and discovers the special prize for herself and the ones for everyone else.

PARTY PREP

If you're hosting a party that requires you to hire someone like a clown, face painter, or bartender, head to your local college first. There, you'll find hundreds of young people who will do the job for a lot less than a pro. Put up an ad near the cafeteria, and stop by the careers office to see if they have an online "bulletin board."

If you're mailing out invitations, stick them in the mailbox on Wednesday, so that they'll arrive on Friday or Saturday. People respond more quickly to mail received on the weekend—so you'll get your headcount finalized sooner!

Wondering how much food to make for your big soiree? Wonder no longer. At a cocktail party (no dinner served), 10–12 bite-sized portions per person is a good bet. If you're also serving a meal, figure on 4–5 bites per guest. For dip, figure 2 tablespoons per person (plus veggies or crackers for dipping), and for cheese, get 4 ounces for each person.

A party is about the people, not how much you spend on it. Before you throw a huge bash, write out your priorities in terms of what you think is most important to spend your money on (for example, the least on decorations and the most on food). Then figure out how much you're willing to spend on the highest item on your list, and work your way down. Friends always ask, "Can I bring anything?" and you shouldn't be afraid of asking your good friends to bring a dessert or appetizer. And don't forget—potlucks and picnics are cheap and always popular.

This simple trick offers peace-of-mind when several folding tables are placed together to form a bigger table. Use cleaned-out coffee cans as holders for adjoining legs from different tables and rest assured that your grandmother's hand-blown glass punch bowl is safe.

During parties, our giant TV suddenly becomes a dead spot in the room (when normally it's the center of attention!). Pop a movie into the DVD player and let it run on mute. Play a scary movie if it's a Halloween party, or a Christmas classic if it's a holiday party. Or play movies from your teenage years or favorites amongst your group of friends. And if it's your birthday, of course, it's your pick! Once you've picked your theme, pile the rest of your DVDs that fit it on top of the player and change the movie throughout the night.

....

Having a Super Bowl party? Consider having two TVs—one of which is reserved for the hardcore fans only. A lot of people will come to the party just looking to socialize (and maybe watch the halftime show), so let them watch away from the football freaks, who will want to be able to catch every moment of pig-skinned glory.

PHOTOS

When taking photos at night, sometimes the flash from your camera can leave an ugly glare on people's faces (making sure they'll never let you post the pics online!). Get rid of glare by taping a tiny piece of white coffee filter over the flash. The scene will still light up, but won't be as harsh.

Auto

Baking

Beauty

Cleaning

Clothing and
Accessories

Cooking

Decorating

Entertaining
and Holidays

>> **Health and
Wellness**

Home Repair

Kids

Money

Organization

Outdoors

Pest Control

Pets

Shopping

Utilities

Vacations
and Family
Activities

Websites

» Body

BITES AND STINGS

Looking for tips on treating Bites and Stings?
See **Pest Control chapter, Bites and Stings**

BRUISES

Bananas to the rescue! A simple way to help bruises fade fast is with a banana peel. Just apply a piece of banana peel, flesh side down, to the bruise, cover with a bandage, and leave on overnight. By the morning, the bruise will have faded.

White vinegar will also help heal bruises. Soak a cotton ball in vinegar, then apply it to the bruise for an hour. It will reduce the blueness of the bruise and speed up the healing process.

BURNS

Soothe burns with an unlikely hero from your medicine cabinet: your toothpaste! If you've sustained a minor burn, cover it with white, non-gel toothpaste to ease the pain and help it heal. Simply dab a small amount onto affected areas and leave overnight.

CANKER SORES

Hydrogen peroxide may help reduce and relieve canker sores. Simply mix one part peroxide with one part water, then dab on any affected areas several times a day or swish around in your mouth for as long as possible.

....

If you have a canker sore, hold a damp tea bag over the area. Tea bags are filled with healthful tannins. Cool the tea bag for even more relief.

CORNS

To get rid of corns, soak a Band-Aid in apple cider vinegar, and apply it to the corn for a day or two. You can also try soaking your feet in a shallow pan of warm water with half a cup of vinegar. Either way, finish by rubbing the corn with a clean pumice stone.

RASHES

An effective and natural way to any kind of rash on your skin is by adding a cup of baking soda to a warm bath. This also works with diaper rash.

To ease the itching of a rash caused by poison ivy, soak the affected area in a strong salt bath. Make sure the water is warm to fully get the itch out.

SUNBURNS

You had a great day on the beach, but now your back is burned to a crisp. To help ease the pain of a sunburn, rub vinegar on the affected area with a cotton ball or soft cloth. You may smell a bit like salad dressing, but your skin will immediately feel cooler.

Lots of people swear by aloe lotion for treating sunburns, but green tea is a cheaper option and just as effective. Use a cooled, tea-soaked washcloth as a compress on your tender skin. (Some people say topically applied green tea may even protect against skin cancer.) This is also a great way to ease a sunburned scalp. After washing and rinsing your hair as usual, pour the cooled tea over your scalp. Your poor skin will thank you!

Nothing's worse than a bad sunburn. The good news is you don't need an expensive lotion to soothe your burnt skin. Just cut an apple in half, remove the core, and rub over the affected area for 3–4 minutes. Apples will keep your skin from blistering or peeling.

WARTS

It's long been stated as fact—then disputed—that duct tape can help cure warts. It may seem strange, but medical studies have concluded that when patients cover their warts with duct tape every day for a month, 85 percent of them will see a reduction in the wart. That's compared to only a 60 percent reduction in patients who used cryotherapy (having the wart frozen off by a dermatologist). It's hard to believe, but many people swear by the treatment! Our opinion? Especially if you don't have health insurance, it's worth a shot.

» Colds, Allergies, and Congestion

ALLERGIES

If you have a pollen allergy, try to keep sneeze-inducing allergens out of your home. Take a shower immediately after doing any yard work to get rid of pollens you may have carried in on your hair and skin, and throw your clothes in the laundry basket. Animals can carry in pollen, too. After taking your dog for a walk or letting your cat out, wipe him or her down with a wet rag or baby wipe. Showering at night can also reduce pollen on your hair and skin and help you sleep better.

If your eyes are itchy, try this quick fix to cut down on your misery: Rub a small amount of baby shampoo on your eyelids. It should reduce your symptoms dramatically.

If you find yourself getting headaches or sinus trouble more often than you used to, it might be that your home's ducts simply need a good cleaning. Whenever air conditioning or heating is on, tiny particles that have accumulated inside the ducts blow out, too, including mold, mouse droppings, and plain old dust. If you have severe allergies, a professional duct cleaning may be just what the doctor ordered.

COLDS

If you have a cold that's been hanging around forever, try this remedy to rid yourself of congestion once and for all. Get a pair of cotton socks damp, but not dripping, with cold water. You can even put them in the freezer for a couple minutes to make them extra cold. Put them on, and then put a pair of dry wool socks on over them. Go to bed immediately. As you sleep, the heat from your upper body will be drawn down to your feet, allowing the inflammation to reduce. You'll also be stunned to find that your feet are warm and dry by morning.

Steam is a wonderful household remedy for colds, especially with some aromatherapy oils mixed in. Try pouring hot water into a bowl and breathing in as you lean over it. Stick your tongue out as you do it—this will open the throat and allow more steam through, preventing membranes from drying out. Aromatherapy oils especially known to alleviate the symptoms of congestion include black pepper, eucalyptus, hyssop, pine, and sweet thyme.

....

Stuffy nose? Don't spend money on decongestant— head to your fridge instead. Cut the "root" end of two scallions and carefully insert the white ends into your nose (being cautious not to shove them too high!). You may look silly, but your nose will start to clear in a couple of minutes.

Ayurveda is a practice of natural medicine that's been used in India since around 1500 BC. Try this cold remedy that's been passed down through the ages: At the very first sign of a cold, mix 1 teaspoon water with 1 teaspoon raw honey and ½ teaspoon turmeric. Eat it several times a day until symptoms disappear.

EARS

If your children are prone to swimmer's ear, a bacterial infection of the ear canal, take this precaution when they've been in the pool: Dab a solution of one part vinegar and five parts warm water into each ear three times a day. The vinegar will ward off bacteria and keep your kids' ears pain-free.

....

Oil found in raw onion is antimicrobial, which makes onions great cures for upper respiratory ailments. If you have a minor earache, onion may help. Slice a fresh onion and heat it in the microwave on high for one minute. Wrap it in cheesecloth or another thin cloth so that it doesn't burn your skin, and then hold it against the ailing ear for 20–30 minutes. See a doctor if the pain gets worse or continues for longer than 24 hours.

SORE THROATS

Everyone hates a sore throat, so here's the best remedy we know: Fill a shot glass with honey, then warm it in the microwave for about 10 seconds on high. Stir in ¼ teaspoon cinnamon, then drink. Repeat this delicious method for a few days and it will help your poor, aching throat.

....

Aspirin does more than just relieve headaches! If you have a sore throat, dissolve two non-coated tablets in a glass of water and gargle. Just be sure to note that this only works with aspirin—don't try it with other pain relievers like ibuprofen.

....

To cure a sore throat in a day or two, mix equal parts vinegar and honey and take one tablespoonful every two hours.

—*Ruth Leibenguth*

....

Relieve your sore throat with a time-tested home remedy. Slice off two-thirds of a lemon and place it on a shish kebab skewer or barbecue fork. Set your gas stove to high and roast the lemon over the open flame until the peel acquires a golden brown color. (This works on electric stoves, too, although not quite as well.) Let the lemon cool off for a moment, then squeeze the juice into a small cup. Add one teaspoon of honey, mix well, and swallow.

Sore throat? Here's another lemon remedy: Gargle with one part lemon juice and one part warm water. Lemon helps fight bacteria and soothes your throat.

» Daily Cures

ARTHRITIS

If you suffer from arthritis, try this trick to make it easier to open jars and perform other daily tasks. Take a medium-sized binder clip and push back the wings with your thumb and index finger. Hold for 5–10 seconds, then move on to each finger of each hand. Do this a few times a day and it should help your grip.

Believe it or not, you can help relieve arthritis pain with oatmeal. Just mix 2 cups oatmeal with 1 cup water, warm the mixture in the microwave, and apply to the affected area.

BACK PAIN

If you find sitting at your desk is causing lower back pain, try slightly elevating your feet. And old phone book is perfect for the job.

If you're a man who suffers from back pain, your wallet may be to blame. Sitting on a bulky wallet can cause your spine to become misaligned and your muscles to compensate. Try carrying your wallet in a front pocket (where it's also safer from pick-pockets), or make sure it's as thin as possible.

If you have chronic back pain—especially associated with arthritis—or other sore muscles, try adding yellow mustard to a hot bath. Add a few tablespoons for mild pain, and up to a whole eight-ounce bottle if the pain is severe. The bathwater may look strange, but your aching back will thank you.

BREATH

You don't need expensive mouthwashes to get better breath. Simply gargle with a mixture of 1 cup water, ½ teaspoon baking soda, and ½ teaspoon salt. This combo will knock out any germs that are causing your bad breath.

To freshen your breath, try sucking on a coffee bean. It's much cheaper than a breath mint, and tastes great to us coffee addicts!

....

Bad breath? Eat some yogurt! The "good" bacteria in yogurt has been found to be effective in targeting the odor-causing bacteria in your mouth. Make sure you go for the plain kind, no sugar. Breath mints and sprays mask the odor but they don't help the underlying problem—eating yogurt does.

EXERCISING

Exercise the easy way! Oftentimes, surveying the latest home exercise equipment or worrying about which gym to join are just excuses to put off actually getting in shape. Start exercising *today* by using your stairs (if you have them) and cans of food as hand weights. You can march in place anywhere, do squats while waiting for the pasta to cook, and rotate your arms while talking on the phone with a headset. If you do have some equipment, but want access to more, try circuit training with a neighbor— you have a bike and treadmill, she has a weight machine and rower. Trade every other day. Even without any machines you can create your own little circuit, setting up stations to do sit-ups, push-ups, jumping jacks, and even a few yoga poses if you're feeling adventurous.

....

If you have teenage boys, odds are they'll sign up for a sport at some point that requires them to do minor strength conditioning at home. If you can't afford a set of weights, just take some empty plastic milk jugs and fill them with dry beans. The result won't be perfect, but it'll be good enough to fake it.

If you find you're often stiff after exercising, you probably just need more water. Dehydration is a major cause of post-exercise muscle soreness. Drinking water regularly while you work out should keep water levels high enough to combat pain.

HEADACHES

Many headaches are caused by dehydration. Before you reach for the pain reliever, try drinking two or three glasses of water or an energy drink like Gatorade. You may find you're back to normal in no time.

If your tend to get headaches in the late mornings, late afternoons, and after a long nap, they might be due to low blood sugar, also known as hypoglycemia. These headaches can be helped by eating foods that release sugar slowly, such as bananas, whole grains, and oats.

An old-fashioned and effective way to treat head-aches is to cut a lime in half and rub it on your fore-head. In a few minutes, the throbbing should subside.

Party too hard last night? Just spread a little honey on your favorite crackers. The honey provides your body with the essential sodium, potassium, and fructose it needs after a raucous night out!

Less-than-perfect eyesight can trigger head-aches because the muscles around the eyes squeeze in order to focus. If your headaches come on after reading or working at a computer, make sure you give your eyes a rest every 15 minutes by focusing on a distant object for at least a minute. You may also want to get your eyes examined to see if you need glasses.

HICCUPS

When "Boo!", drinking upside down, and holding your breath don't work, try this to get rid of your hiccups. Insert a Q-tip into your mouth and gently dab the back of the throat under the soft palate. You're trying to hit the uvula, which requires good aim, a diagram, or both! If this doesn't work, try putting sugar under the tongue and letting it dissolve, or swallowing a tablespoon of lemon juice.

INSOMNIA

If you're having trouble sleeping, try this salty tip: At bedtime, drink a glass of water, then let a pinch of salt dissolve on your tongue, making sure it doesn't touch the roof of your mouth. Studies have shown that the combination of salt and water can induce a deep sleep.

....

The herb valerian has been used in traditional sleep remedies for hundreds of years. Sometimes called "valerian root," it relieves anxiety and aids the induction of sleep in a natural and nonaddictive way.

NAUSEA

Ginger root, taken as a powder or in tea, works directly in the gastrointestinal tract by interfering with the feedback mechanisms that send sickness messages to the brain. Take some when you're feeling nauseated to help alleviate your symptoms.

....

Nothing's worse than a bad bout of nausea. Try this simple trick to help relieve your discomfort: Drink a little ginger ale, then chew a handful of crushed ice, and finally sniff a piece of black-and-white newspaper. It may seem like an old wives' tale, but it works!

....

If you get nauseated every time you ride in a car, boat, or train, take some lemon wedges with you. Suck on them as you ride to relieve nausea. You can also try sucking on a piece of ginger or drinking ginger tea.

NECK PAIN

Been leaning over your work too long? Try this to help a hurting neck. Inhale and raise your shoulders up to your ears, pulling them as high as they will go. Then let go with an "ahhh" and drop them slowly back down. Repeat several times to release muscle tension.

STOMACH ACHES

Feeling bloated? It could just be trapped gas. Encourage it to move by gently stroking from your right hip up towards your ribs, then across the bottom of your ribcage and down towards your left hip. Repeat several times.

If you've got an upset stomach due to indigestion or a hangover, try drinking a glass of club soda with a dash of bitters. It should help ease your pain.

STRESS BUSTERS

Don't spend your money on an aromatherapy pillow! Instead, add uncooked, long-grain rice to a sock and tie it shut. Whenever you need a little heat after a long day, stick it in the microwave on high for 1–2 minutes, and you'll have soothing warmth. To add a little scent to the pillow, put a few drops of your favorite essential oil into the rice.

You'll love the feeling of this simple routine that will help boost your immune and circulatory systems and even relieve stress. Toward the end of your shower, turn it up as hot as you can stand it and allow it to warm your body for three minutes. Then turn it down so the water is cool, and let it run over your body for 30–60 seconds. Repeat as many times as you like, ending on cold. When you get out of the shower, rub yourself vigorously with a towel to encourage circulation. Do not continue the contrasting temperatures, however, if you feel dizzy, nauseated, or excessively chilled.

Many people hold stress in the area between their eyebrows, and in time, vertical stress lines will develop here. When you feel your brow knit together with concentration or stress, take a moment to pinch the muscle there, working from the center of the brow along the brow-line in each direction with a thumb and bent forefinger. Not only will it make you feel better, it will prevent wrinkles, too!

Playing with or petting your pet is known to reduce blood pressure, improve your mood, and reduce stress. It been proven to work with all kinds of pets: dogs, cats, hamsters—every type but dust bunnies.

....

The right essential oils can help to relieve tension and stress. Try lavender, chamomile, geranium, spearmint, or peppermint. Add these delicious-smelling oils to your bath water for a relaxing soak, or inhale them by placing a few drops on a cotton pad.

....

It's official—children have known it for years, but scientists now admit that eating ice cream can actually make you feel better. Eating a spoonful of ice cream lights up the same pleasure center in the brain as winning money!

TEETH

Serve hard cheeses like Romano and aged Cheddar as an after-dinner snack. They'll help scrub your teeth of acids found in other foods, and the calcium inside helps make teeth stronger.

....

Here's an effective method for cleaning dentures that works just as well as the expensive tablets: Soak them overnight in a solution of 1 part white vinegar and 1 part water. The acidity of the vinegar fights tartar buildup and removes stains.

WEIGHT LOSS

When a baking recipe calls for vegetable oil, try substituting half of the oil with applesauce. It's an easy way to reduce the fat content in your food.

It's hard to resist taking something from the bread basket when you're out to eat. But if you're looking to lose weight (or just maintain it), choose a hard roll, a piece of French or Italian bread, a wafer, pita bread, or melba toast. These don't have as much butter or sugar as soft rolls, breadsticks, biscuits, croissants, and muffins.

Lose weight without lifting a pound! Derived from the plant *Capsicum annuum*, cayenne pepper has been reported to not only make you lose weight by elevating body temperature, but also to improve circulation and to lower cholesterol. As it's a mild stimulant, it can also be added to hot water with lemon juice as an alternative to coffee.

There are two ways to eliminate the craving for sweets (without hitting the fridge). One way is to place a small amount of salt on your tongue and let it slowly dissolve. The second: Mix about a teaspoon of baking soda into a glass of warm water, then rinse your mouth out and spit (don't swallow). The salt or baking soda tends to stimulate the production of saliva, which eliminates your sweet craving.

Trying to lose weight but keep craving something sweet? Keep a bunch of grapes in your fridge and grab a handful when the hunger hits. Grapes release sugar quickly, so they are great for satisfying your sweet tooth. If you don't feel like the grapes are hitting the spot, wait 10 minutes and see how you feel before reaching for the candy!

If you're a chocolate junkie but are trying to lose weight, you may be interested to hear that your favorite food may actually *help* you take off the pounds. Chocolate increases serotonin levels, so it can help lessen depression, stress, and other reasons why you may find yourself wanting to consume more food. The trick? You can only eat 1.4 ounces per day, preferably in the morning. (But hey, that's better than nothing!) Doctors recommend 70 percent dark chocolate for the biggest weight-loss effects.

The easiest way to stay under your diet's daily calorie limit? Snack all day on low-calorie foods like carrot sticks. You won't feel the need to eat, but you won't be consuming too many calories.

—*Faye Baxter*

» First Aid

BANDAGES

You put a Band-Aid on your finger to cover up a scratch, but you still have to go through your day full of hand-washing, child-bathing, and dishes-doing. To keep the bandage dry while you work, cover it with a non-inflated balloon—any color will do!

You just got a nasty cut on your hand, but don't have anything to clean it out with before you put the bandage on. Luckily, there's something in your medicine cabinet that you may not have thought of—mouthwash. The alcohol-based formula for mouthwash was originally used as an antiseptic during surgeries, so it will definitely work for your cut, too.

COMPRESSES

In an emergency, a one-liter plastic soda bottle can make an excellent hot-water bottle. Just make sure that you wrap it in a hand towel before placing it against your skin.

If you're a vodka drinker, you're well aware that it doesn't solidify in the freezer. For this reason, it's also a great tool for making your own homemade gel ice pack to use on aches or injuries. Just pour two cups of water, one-third cup of Smirnoff (or any brand of vodka), and a few drops of green or yellow food coloring (so everyone will know not to eat the contents) into a heavy-duty Ziploc freezer bag. Put it in the freezer for a while, and you've got an instant ice pack. If you don't keep vodka around, you can simulate the same effect with liquid dishwasher detergent. (If you do use detergent, though, make absolutely certain to label the bag so nobody ingests it.)

NOSEBLEEDS

White vinegar stops nosebleeds. Just dampen a cotton ball and plug the nostril. The acetic acid in the vinegar cauterizes the wound. Who knew?

SPLINTER REMOVAL

Got a splinter you can't get out? Try soaking the area in vegetable oil for several minutes. It should soften your skin enough to allow you to ease the splinter out.

The easiest way to remove a splinter? Just put a drop of white glue over the offending piece of wood in your finger, let it dry, and then peel off the dried glue. The splinter will stick to the glue and come right out.

If you get a splinter, a little duct tape does the trick to get it out. Cut off a piece and gently press it to the affected area.

» Painting

BRUSHES

We'll usually tell you to go for the cheapest option, but when it comes to paint brushes, quality matters. To make sure you're buying a high-quality brush, look at the tips of the bristles. If they have a lot of split-ends, they'll spread paint more evenly.

The fastest way we've found to clean a paintbrush is in a solution of ½ cup liquid fabric softener and 1 gallon of warm water. Stick the brush in a bucket of this solution, then swirl it vigorously for 20 seconds.

Even if you clean your paintbrush thoroughly, the bristles are likely to be stiff after they dry. Keep them soft and flexible with ordinary hair conditioner. Just add a tablespoon of conditioner to a pint of warm water, and after cleaning the brush, dip it in the solution for a few minutes.

Old, crusty paintbrushes put a cramp in our paint projects. To soften those bristles, we soak them in full-strength white vinegar and then clean them with a comb. To prevent brushes from hardening in the first place, rub a few drops of vegetable oil into the bristles after using and cleaning.

PAINT, APPLYING

Quicken your interior paint jobs by mixing a quart of semigloss latex paint into a gallon of flat latex paint. The finish won't shine more than it would with straight flat paint, but the paint will glide on and cover much more easily.

Did you know that enamel paint spreads more smoothly when it's warm? To get it up to a higher temperature, place it in a warm bath before you use it.

To catch drips while you paint, try this makeshift drip cup: Cut a tennis ball in half and slice a thin slot in the bottom bowl of one half. Then slide your brush handle through the slot so the bristles stick out of the open side. A small paper plate or cup works, too.

Lumpy paint? No problem. Use the lid of the paint can as a stencil to cut a circle out of a screen that will fit perfectly inside the container. Push down with a stir stick as far as it will go so the lumps will be out of the way at the bottom.

Before stirring paint, place a few old marbles in the can. They'll stir the paint so well you should just be able to give it a good shake to remix before its next use. To make shaking and storing even easier, first empty the paint into a plastic jug with a funnel.

Maybe we're just messy painters, but when we paint a room, we find that the interior rim around the paint can is never big enough to catch the paint that has slopped over the edge—eventually it fills up and runs down the side of the can. To solve this problem, we make several holes in the bottom of the rim with a small nail and hammer. Now the paint drips back into the can rather than running down the side.

Another way to make painting neater is to wrap a wide rubber band around your open paint can from top to bottom. The rubber band will run right over the opening of the can, and you can use it to wipe the excess paint from your brush instead of using the edge of the can. Then when you're done painting, wrap the band around the paint can the other way, at the exact level that the paint is at inside. That way, you won't have to open the can to see how much paint is left.

When painting steps, paint every other one as you work your way down. When those are dry, go back and paint the rest. This way, you'll still be able to use the stairs while your paint is drying (as long as you're careful!).

You've been painting baseboards for what seems like hours, thanks to the constant bending over and moving around. Make the job easier on yourself (and your back!) by borrowing your kid's skateboard. It makes a great bench on wheels!

PAINT, LEFTOVER

If you've got leftover paint, you can prevent it from drying up with this crafty maneuver: Blow up a balloon until it's about the size of the remaining space in the can. Then put it inside the can and close the lid. This will reduce the amount of air in the can, thus prolonging the paint's freshness.

Want to know an easy way store leftover paint in the can? First, place a piece of plastic wrap under the paint can's lid, make certain the lid is on tight, and turn the can over. The paint is exposed to less oxygen this way and will last much, much longer.

Keep paint in half-used cans from developing a film on top. Before you close the can for storage, place the lid of the can on top of aluminum foil or wax paper and trace around it. Cut out the circle, then drop it gently into the can so it covers the paint. When you open the container later, just take out the foil and you won't have any messy dried paint bits to worry about.

PAINT, REMOVAL

Accidentally paint the edge of your windowpane while doing some remodeling? Hot vinegar can be used to remove paint from glass. Just microwave a cup of vinegar until hot (about 1–2 minutes), then dip a cloth in it and wipe the offending paint away.

You've just painted your window trim and got a big glob of "country yellow" on the glass pane. But there's no need to use a dangerous razor blade to remove the paint that spilled on the glass. Instead, remove the paint safely and easily with a pencil eraser. If the paint has dried, or is old, dab on some nail polish remover, wait a minute, then erase.

If you've spilled paint on your carpet, stop cursing and head to the kitchen. Mix together 1 tablespoon vinegar, 1 tablespoon dishwashing liquid, and 1 quart warm water. Douse the area with this mixture and try rubbing it away. If that doesn't work, wait for the paint to dry and snip off the areas that have paint on it—your carpet's "hair cut" will be less noticeable than a giant paint stain.

It's hard not to get paint all over yourself when painting a room. An old household trick is to wipe turpentine on your hands to get latex paint off, but there's a much less smelly way! Simply rub your hands with olive oil, let sit a couple of seconds, then rub off with a damp, soapy sponge. Not only will the olive oil remove the paint, but it's great for your skin, too! For enamel or oil-based paint, rub your hands with floor paste wax, and then wash with soap and water.

PAINTING PREP

When painting your house, it's always a good idea to keep track of paint colors—you may need them to match future paint jobs or to help you coordinate other items in the house. Create swatches by dipping a 3-by-5-inch index card into your paint can and writing down the details.

....

If you've tried saving your paint swatches in the past and can never find them when you need them, try this simple trick: Write the name and type of paint you used for each room under the light switch plate. That way, you'll know where the info is when you need it.

....

Your friend has some leftover paint, but you're not sure what it will look like when it dries. To find out, try this simple trick: Paint a piece of glass (a microscope slide works well, if you have one), then look at the color from the non-painted side. It will reflect what the dried color will look like.

....

When painting walls and ceilings white, it's best to add several drops of black paint into each can of white. Why? The paint will cover with fewer coats, and be more reflective. Many experts say it will also cause the paint to yellow less quickly.

....

Before you begin that big painting project, cover doorknobs, drawer pulls, and any other small object you're worried about catching spills with aluminum foil. The foil easily molds to any shape and comes off when you're done.

....

Painting doors? Avoid getting paint on the hinges by coating them lightly with petroleum jelly before you start. It's easier to protect the rounded corners than when using painter's tape, and it wipes right off!

ROLLERS AND TRAYS

If you want to avoid cleaning a paint roller (for now), wrap it in foil or a plastic bag and place it in the refrigerator. The covering will keep the roller moist and usable for a few days, so you can finish where you left off later.

....

Looking to add some character to a room by painting stripes on the wall? Make it easy by first adding "stripes" to your paint roller. Run masking tape around it in several places to mat down the roller. When you paint, the masking tape won't touch the wall and will leave clearly defined stripes behind.

....

There's no need to spend your money on disposable paint liners for your roller pan. It's just as easy to line the pan with aluminum foil—and a lot cheaper, too.

....

The easiest way to clean a paint tray after you're done rolling on paint is never to get it dirty in the first place! Instead of using plastic wrap or foil, put the paint tray in a plastic bag and pour the paint on top. Once you're done, simply turn the bag inside out and throw away.

WALLPAPER

Putting up new wallpaper? Here's a great trick to quickly and easily get rid of the old stuff. First, score the paper with a utility knife by cutting slashes through several parts of the paper. Then, dab on a mixture of half water and half liquid fabric softener. Leave on for 10–15 minutes, then watch your old wallpaper peel right off.

—*Lora Boudinot, Woodridge, IL*

If grease is still visible on the wall after removing wallpaper, apply a coat of clear varnish to the spots. The grease won't soak through to the new wallpaper.

Take your wallpaper out of its roll a few days before you hang it and re-roll it the opposite way. It will make it flatter and easier to hang.

Hanging wallpaper? Get help from a paint roller. First, try using a paint roller instead of a sponge to apply paste for a more even consistency. You can also use a clean, dry paint roller to smooth out the wallpaper afterward. You'll get more coverage per stroke.

If your wallpaper needs a fix-up in a small area, don't use scissors to cut off the replacement piece. Instead, tear it off with your hands. The ragged edge of the new piece will blend in better than a straight edge.

You've just finished a big wallpaper job and have at least a half a roll left. Use your scraps to decorate accessories in the room. Cover the fronts of drawers or cabinets, even the backs of chairs! Wallpaper can also be used to cover notebooks, pencil cases, and other office supplies.

» Safety

FALL PREVENTION

Most stepladders are perfectly safe, of course, but if you want to amp up the nonskid surface of the rungs, there's an easy way to do it. Just paint the steps of the ladder and, before they dry, sprinkle fine-grained sand on top. The sand will stick to the steps and create a sandpaper-like surface.

Here's another use for old coffee cans: If you're using a ladder on soft ground, set each of the legs inside an empty can. The cans will help keep the ladder steady as you climb it.

Those nonslip bath strips aren't just good for preventing you from slipping in the tub. Available at any hardware store, they can provide traction for anything that slips you up, whether it's the stairs to your attic or a tiled floor.

If you've ever accidentally skipped the last step of your basement stairs and fallen flat on your face, you'll take us up on this tip immediately. Paint the last step a bright white. Even if your basement is pitch black and your arms are full, you still won't miss it.

GLASS SHATTERING

You've just shattered a vase or glass, and there are shards of glass everywhere. Don't panic. Put on some shoes, keep kids and pets away from the area, and then head for your newspaper bin. Wet several sheets of newsprint (usually an entire section will do) and use them to wipe up the mess. First pick up any big pieces, then wipe the newspaper on the floor. The small pieces will stick to the wet paper, making sure you get every last piece. If you get any ink streaks on the floor, just clean them up with a bit of warm water or vinegar.

If you shatter something made out of glass on your floor, try out this crafty tip. Dampen a piece of white bread, and dab it on the glass fragments. It's much more effective than using a broom.

If a shattered light bulb needs replacing, don't try unscrewing it with your bare hands, since there are almost always shards of glass left behind. Instead, make sure the lamp is unplugged, then put on some dish gloves and use a wadded-up piece of newspaper.

To remove a broken light bulb from the socket, first turn off the electricity or unplug the lamp, and then push half of a raw potato or small apple into the broken bulb's base. Turn it to unscrew the base. Just don't eat it afterward!

» Simple Solutions

CAULK

When caulking the edges of your bathtub, keep in mind that the caulking will often expand and crack the first time you fill the tub with hot water. To combat this, fill the tub with water *first*, then caulk away.

Caulking can be tricky business—it's hard to get perfect lines, but if you try smoothing them down with you finger, it sticks, creating an even uglier sight. When you need to smooth down caulk, try using an ice cube instead. The cold will help set the line, and it won't stick to the ice.

CHAIRS

A chair's caning can loosen and begin to droop.
If you let it go long enough, you might even fall through
the seat and hurt your bum (not to mention your ego).
But, no fear! You can tighten it easily and cheaply. Apply
very hot water to the underside, then dry the chair in
direct sunlight.

CONTAINERS

**If tubes of glue, caulk, and other home repair
necessities are cluttering up your workbench,**
hang them from the wall with nails. Create holes that
the tubes can hang from by wrapping a piece of duct
tape from front to back on the bottom (non-dispensing
end) of the tube. Leave an extra ½-inch flap of tape at
the end that doesn't touch the tube and just folds onto
itself. Then poke a hole through this part and you'll
have a handy hanging hole. Wrap another piece of tape
around the tube the other way to reinforce the tape
you've already applied.

If you lose the tiny cap to your glue or caulk tube,
stick a screw in there instead! We actually prefer
ong screws to caps, because they'll clean out the
narrow area in the tube and make sure the glue or
caulk doesn't harden between uses.

DRAINS AND PIPES

Most people know the old science fair project of mixing vinegar and baking soda to cause a chemical reaction worthy of a model volcano, but not many know that this powerful combination is also a great drain cleaner. Baking soda and vinegar break down fatty acids from grease, food, and soap build-up into simpler substances that can be more easily flushed down the drain. Here's how to do it: Pour 2 ounces baking soda and 5 ounces vinegar into your drain. Cover with a towel or dishrag while the solution fizzes. Wait 5–10 minutes, then flush the drain with very hot water. Repeat until your drain is clear.

Not only is drain cleaner expensive, it can weaken your pipes. Instead of using Drano to unclog a slow-moving drain, use a gel dishwasher detergent like Cascade. Pour the detergent into the drain and chase it with boiling water.

Don't wait until your drain gets clogged before you flush out grime, grease, and hair. Perform monthly maintenance with the help of a little yeast. Pour two packets of dry yeast and a pinch of salt down the drain, then follow with very hot water. Wait half an hour, then flush again with hot water. The yeast reproduces and expands, which breaks up stubborn grime and hair clogs and saves you from calling the plumber.

Add a little petroleum jelly to the rim of your rubber plunger. It helps achieve great suction, so the disgusting job ahead is a little bit easier.

If your water pipes are banging and pounding, you may be able to get rid of the noise without paying for a plumber to visit. First, turn off your main water valve, which is usually located near the water meter. Turn on all your water faucets, set them to cold, and let them drain until dry. Then close them again. Turn your main valve back on, then turn each faucet back on as well. After making spitting and coughing noises for a few moments, they should now flow freely with no noise coming from the pipes.

Instead of using expensive Teflon tape to prevent leaking between pipes and other parts that screw together, just use dental floss. Wrap the floss around the item's threads, and you'll have a tight connection.

If you're planning a big remodel of your home but don't want to spend a bundle, try to keep major plumbing appliances like toilets and kitchen sinks where they are. These types of improvements can cost around $1,000 apiece and could be a major portion of your renovation budget.

DRAWERS, STUCK

If you've been fussing with a drawer that won't open, it's probably expanded due to humidity. Dry it out with a hair dryer set on low heat, or place a work lamp with a 60-watt bulb inside and leave for 30 minutes. The drawer will contract, and you'll be able to move it easily again.

....

Have a drawer that keeps sticking? Rub its runners or anywhere it seems to be sticking with a bar of soap or a candle. This should grease it up enough to get it moving again.

ELECTRONICS AND APPLIANCES

If "brrrring!!" isn't enough to wake you up anymore, maybe it's time to make your alarm even louder. Place it on a cookie tin lid, metal tray, or ceramic tile. The material will amplify the sound, creating a "BRRRRING!!" you can't ignore.

....

If the picture on your television isn't crystal clear, it may be caused by interference. Place a sheet of aluminum foil between any electronics (like your DVD player, cable box, or TV) that are stacked on top of each other and those wavy lines will be history.

....

Here's a trick that could save you hundreds: If your cell phone gets wet, first take the battery out and dry it with a paper towel. Then bury the phone and the battery in a bowl of uncooked rice for 24 hours. The rice will draw the rest of the water out of the phone, and hopefully it will be back in business again.

If an electric plug on an appliance fits too snugly and is difficult to pull out, rub its prongs with a soft lead pencil, and it will move in and out more easily.

Did your washing machine just break down, and you're not sure if it's still under warranty? Do you need to replace a part in your dishwasher, but don't know what its specifications are? Want to buy a microwave and not sure what you should be looking for? Appliance411.com is here to help. They have purchasing information (including rebates), FAQs about appliances big and small, and best yet, online manuals and warranty information for just about any model of any appliance. If you're looking for help with any machine in your home, go here first.

FAUCETS

If the handles of your sink shriek when you turn them, try this simple fix. Unscrew the handles and rub petroleum jelly on all the threads. The jelly will keep them lubricated and (hopefully) squeak-free.

If you have a shower that has a detachable showerhead, use duct tape to repair any holes when the connecting arm inevitably begins to leak. That was easy, huh?

FLOORS

Back when our kids were still tiny, this trick was a lifesaver. There's nothing worse than finally getting a grouchy baby to sleep and tip-toeing out of the room only to have the wooden floor in the hallway creak like the second coming. Shake talcum powder over the cracks and rub in with an old rag, and you can escape in silence!

If that squeak in your floor is about to drive you crazy, you may be able to repair it yourself. Most squeaks are caused not by the floorboards themselves, but by the support beams that hold up your floor, called joists. If a joist gets too dry, it will shrink, causing the boards under your floor to rub against them rather than being held flush. To fix a squeak, first find the joist closest to it using a stud finder or a nail. Joists are usually located 16 inches apart and run lengthwise from the front to the back of your house. Once you find the joist, drill a number 8 wood screw through the floor into it. This should fix your problem.

If there's a small hole in your vinyl floor, here's how to patch it up without anyone noticing the spot. Find a tile that is the same color, or better yet, one that you've saved for a replacement. Make some vinyl shavings from the tile using a cheese grater, then mix them with a small amount of clear nail polish. Dab the nail polish mixture into the hole and let dry. Voilà! Your floor is like new again.

If your vinyl flooring is coming up, put it back where it belongs! Lay a sheet of foil on top (shiny side down), then run a hot iron over it several times until you feel the glue on the bottom of the tile starting to melt again. Place something heavy, like a stack of books, on top and leave it overnight to set.

GLUE

You're trying to make a repair in a drawer or somewhere else with a tight corner, and you keep dripping glue that's nearly impossible to wipe up. Solve your problem by flattening a drinking straw, then folding it in half. The *v* shape is perfect for getting into tiny corners and crevices.

Broke a dish? Sand poured into the bottom of a little tray (Tupperware will do) can come in handy to hold broken china while you line the edge with glue and stick the other piece (also lined with glue) on top. Leave the repaired cup balanced on its side to dry so the break won't have to fight gravity before the glue takes hold.

> To remove glue residue from almost any surface, pour some vegetable oil on a rag and rub vigorously. The oil will neutralize the glue's bonds.

If your gluing project gets a little messy, use WD-40 to lift off dried glue spots. Wipe clean, and get back to arts and crafts.

Superglue's claim to fame is that it sticks to everything—and is impossible to get off. But if you accidentally get some on your work project or even your fingers, there is one substance that can get you out of your "bind." Soak the corner of a soft cloth or paper towel in nail polish remover, then hold it on the area until the glue dissolves. Be aware, however, that nail polish remover will eat away at varnish and other finishes.

HINGES

Who needs WD-40 when you have vegetable oil?
Simply rub it on squeaky hinges with a cloth, letting the oil run down the sides of each hinge. Or just spritz non-stick cooking spray right on them.

....

Squeaky door hinges can be fixed with a pencil.
Just rub the point over the hinge. Pencils contain graphite, which is an effective lubricant. Rubbing a pencil over the ridges of a stubborn house key will also help it slide into the lock more easily.

....

If your door won't stop squeaking, and you're sick of constantly reapplying WD-40, try this trick. Take the door off its hinges, then rub the hinges all over with a candle. The wax will stick and prevent the hinge components from rubbing against each other, which causes that annoying sound.

OUTDOOR PROJECTS

If you want your fences to last, it's important to keep the posts safe from rot, pests, and mold. It's true the ingredients for this fence-post protector sound like they're meant for a witches' brew, but it really does work like magic! Mix together pulverized charcoal and boiled linseed oil to get a paint-like consistency, then simply paint the substance onto the bottom of each post. Best of all, it's a one-time project that will last a lifetime! Spend a Saturday on it, and you'll definitely deserve that beer!

....

If one of your roof's shingles has fallen off, you can make a temporary replacement using duct tape. Cut a ¼-inch thick piece of plywood to match the same size as the missing shingle. Then wrap it in duct tape (you will need several strips), and wedge it in place. Use extra duct tape to keep it there, if necessary.

Never pay to have your gutters cleaned again! To easily keep falling leaves from clogging them up, place a Slinky (yes, the child's toy) in your gutters. Stretch it out, then fasten the ends to your gutters with binder clips. The coil will allow water to get through, but keep leaves out.

If your curbside trashcan has a crack, the easiest way to repair it is to slap some duct tape over it on both sides. Duct tape can withstand the rigors of the outdoors, and it's not like you're really worried about your can looking nice, anyway.

STUDS, FINDING

Looking for a stud and don't have a stud finder? Use an electric razor instead. Most razors will change slightly in tone when going over a stud in the wall.

If you're looking for a stud without a stud finder, this measurement will help: Studs are normally 16 inches apart, so measure 17 inches from a corner to find your first stud, then keep measuring down the wall. Alternatively, you can use a compass. Walk along the wall pointing a compass toward it. When the needle moves, that's where you will find a stud.

WALLS

Before driving a nail into a plaster wall, place a small piece of tape over the spot you're working on. This simple prep step will prevent cracking in the plaster.

....

To make a putty for quick patches, combine a tablespoon of salt with a tablespoon of cornstarch. Mix them together with just enough water to make a paste. Apply while still wet.

....

Before spackling small holes in your wall caused by nails, first cut a Q-tip in half and insert in the hole, stick end first. Then spackle as you normally would. The Q-tip will completely fill the hole and ensure you won't have to go back for a second pass.

....

Filling and sanding every hole in the wall before you paint can be enough of a pain, but sometimes it's hard to find every crack, hole, and imperfection. Make your job easier by turning off the lights in a room, then slowly running a flashlight over the entire surface of the wall. The light will cast different shadows in these areas, making them easier to see than they would have been in the daylight.

....

If you have a crack in your ceiling, but you can't quite afford to re-plaster yet, you can fake it with some readily available household supplies. Take one part white glue and one part baking soda, mix them together thoroughly, and then dab the paste onto the crack using your fingers, a Q-tip, or similar object. If your ceiling isn't white, you can try mixing different food colorings into the paste until you get exactly the right shade.

›› Tools

HAMMERS

How many times have you hit your fingers while hammering in a nail? Next time you're hanging pictures, put the nail between the tines of a fork before hammering. Your fingers will thank you, and your kids won't have to hear you swear.

QUICK SUBSTITUTIONS

If you need to measure something and don't have a ruler, grab a dollar bill instead. A dollar is exactly six and a quarter inches long.

If the screwdriver, hammer, or other tool that you're using is hard to grip, wrap duct tape around the handle until it more easily fits your hand.

Before you toss out that set of old Venetian blinds, cut out a dozen of the blinds to use as straight edges. They're great for home projects, because if you get any paint, varnish, or other material on them, you can just throw them away. We especially like them in lieu of using tape to make sure paint stops at the ceiling, because it's easier than trying to tape a straight line.

RUST

To remove rust from nuts, bolts, screws, nails, hinges, or any other objects you might have in your toolbox, place them in a container and cover with vinegar. Seal the container, shake it, and let it stand overnight. Dry the objects to prevent corrosion.

To remove that pesky rusted nut or bolt, put a few drops of ammonia or hydrogen peroxide on it, and wait 30 minutes. If you're out of both, try a little bit of cola instead.

When you buy a rust remover, what you're really paying for is phosphoric acid. However, phosphoric acid can also be found in something you probably have around the house—cola. Dip screws or anything else that needs de-rusting into cola and leave for several minutes. Then scrub away the black substance that remains and repeat if necessary.

Prevent your tools from rusting now and avoid the annoying rust-removal process later. Place a few mothballs, a piece of chalk, or a piece of charcoal in your toolbox—all three eliminate moisture and fight rusting before it begins.

If you're trying to keep something free of rust, here's a solution you can make. Combine two cups petroleum jelly and a half a cup of lanolin in a microwave-safe bowl, and heat the mixture until it melts together. Stir frequently, and make sure to apply to the rust-prone item while the mixture is still warm. Remember, don't wipe it off; allow the paste to dry on the item.

SCISSORS

If your household scissors are getting dull, sharpen them back up by cutting through several layers of aluminum foil at one time. It's that easy!

Rehabilitate a pair of old scissors with these simple tips. First, remove any rust by applying a paste of salt and lemon juice, leaving for 15 minutes, and then rubbing thoroughly with a dry cloth. Then, sharpen the scissors by cutting a piece of steel wool 10–15 times.

SCREWDRIVERS

If you're using a flat-head screwdriver and are having trouble keeping the screw on the end, try rubbing each side of the screwdriver with a piece of chalk. The chalk will increase the friction and give you a tighter hold.

—Jim Dwyer, Gettysburg, SD

....

If you're having trouble with your screws falling off your screwdriver as you're trying to get them into the wall, first poke the screw through a piece of plastic wrap. Hold on to the wrap while you're screwing, then pull it away when you're finished.

....

If a hole in your wall (or whatever else you're working on) is too stripped to hold a screw, dab some glue on a tiny piece of steel wool (which can be cut with scissors) and stuff it into the hole. Once the glue dries, you can screw in your screw without a problem.

—Jian Liu, Charlotte, NC

SOLDERING IRONS

If you regularly use a soldering iron, place several pieces of steel wool in an old coffee can. When you're done soldering, you can easily place the iron tip-down in the can to make sure you don't burn your work area.

TAPE

If you use tape a lot near your workbench, make the search for rolls a thing of the past. Attach a toilet paper holder or a wall-mounted paper towel holder to the wall, and you have a great storage spot for tape rolls.

Nothing's more irritating than trying to find the end of a roll of packaging tape. So after you tear off a piece, stick a toothpick to the tape at the end of the roll. It will make it easy to find and easy to lift.

Duct tape is so sturdy that you can use it as a rope by twisting it around itself. Use as a backup for clotheslines, leashes, tying twine, or anything else you would normally use rope for.

≫ Woodworking

HOLES

If you're painting old woodwork and need to patch small holes, fill them with flour and then paint. They will harden and not be noticeable.

If you need to repair a hole in a piece of wood, add a small amount of instant coffee to the Spackle. The coffee tints the paste to camouflage the patched-up spot.

SANDING

Sanding wood and want to know if it's completely smooth? Slip an old nylon stocking over your hand and run it over the wood. If there's a rough spot, the nylon will snag.

....

Your bedroom door has expanded, and realigning the hinges didn't work. Instead of taking the entire door down to sand the bottom, try this trick instead. Place enough newspaper under the door until it can just barely close on top of it. Then tape a piece of coarse sandpaper on top of the newspaper, and open and close the door until it glides over the floor without a noise.

SAWING

Need a sawhorse? Don't worry; it isn't time to cash in on that favor from a handy neighbor just yet. Instead, turn a sturdy ladder on its side. It works almost as well.

....

When cutting plywood, first reinforce where you plan on cutting with a strip of duct tape. The tape will keep the wood from splitting as you saw, and then you can peel the tape right off.

....

Whether you keep saws in the workshop, tool shed, or basement, make sure to protect yourself and others from those dangerous blades. Use a split piece of old garden hose to cover them whenever they're not in use.

SCRATCHES AND DENTS

For tiny scratches in your wooden table or floor, rub vegetable or canola oil into the surface. The oil will darken the area and help it blend in.

....

If you notice a scratch, try this crafty (and delicious!) solution. Find a nut that matches the color of the wood; the most common types for this purpose are pecans, walnuts, and hazelnuts. Rub the scratched area gently with the broken edges of the nuts—using the insides, not the shells. When you're all done, enjoy a snack break.

....

Repair scratches in your wood furniture with shoe polish. A crayon also works. Just find a color that's a close match to the wood, then rub the crayon or polish into the scratch. Wipe off any excess wax with a credit card edge, then buff with a cotton cloth.

....

> **To fix tiny furniture scratches, use eyeliner in a matching color to fill in the hole.**
>
> —*Margie Parker, Tampa, FL*

....

If you've scratched your floor while doing some home repairs, it's time to ask your kid for help. No, really! Go to his box of a million different-colored crayons, and pick the one that most closely matches the color of your floor. Cut off half the crayon and place it in an old take-out container (or something else you won't mind getting crayon all over). Melt the crayon in the micro-wave, then spread the hot wax into the crack. Wax your floor and it will look like new.

As long as the wood hasn't broken apart under-neath, you may be able to fix dents in wooden floors or furniture. Here's how: Run a rag under warm water and wring it out, then place it on top of the dent. Apply an iron set on medium heat to the rag until the rag dries out. Repeat this process until your dent is gone.

STAINING

When staining a piece of furniture, make sure to choose your varnish carefully. Oil-based stains are easier to apply, but harder to clean up if you make a mistake. Water-based stains are nontoxic and more forgiving, but won't give you as smooth of a finish.

If you allow wood to "weather" before you apply a stain, the stain will last years longer. It's a case where patience pays off. Let wood sit for several months before putting on the varnish.

Stir varnish thoroughly from the bottom of the can, but *don't* stir vigorously. Stirring can create air bubbles, which can ruin a smooth finish. If you notice air bubbles, brush them out while the varnish is still wet. If it's already dry, gently buff them with very fine steel wool.

Auto

Baking

Beauty

Cleaning

Clothing and
Accessories

Cooking

Decorating

Entertaining
and Holidays

Health and
Wellness

Home Repair

>> Kids

Money

Organization

Outdoors

Pest Control

Pets

Shopping

Utilities

Vacations
and Family
Activities

Websites

» Babies

BOTTLES AND FEEDING

We're a little embarrassed to admit this, but when our boys were young we had the perfect holder for extra bottles for the babysitter: an old six-pack container. If you don't think it's funny to have "Heineken" written on the side, cover with contact paper, wrapping paper, or stickers. Your baby won't know the difference, and you'll make sure to leave with as many bottles as you came with.

....

To easily wash bottle caps, nipples, and rings in the dishwasher, simply use a plastic basket that strawberries and other berries come in. Secure it to your dishwasher rack with clothespins, twist ties, or rubber bands, and the small pieces won't fall through the cracks.

....

Baking soda is a gift to anyone who is feeding an infant. Keep some on hand, and if (and when) your baby spits up, sprinkle baking soda on the spot to neutralize odors and absorb the spill before it sets.

DIAPERS

If you get a nasty whiff every time you open the diaper pail, drop a few charcoal briquettes under the pail's liner. You'll be amazed at what you don't smell.

....

If you use cloth diapers, soak them before you wash them in a mixture of 1 cup white vinegar for every 9 quarts water. It will balance out the pH, neutralizing urine and keeping the diapers from staining. Vinegar is also said to help prevent diaper rash.

....

When you purchase new cloth diapers, make sure to wash them 8–10 times before using. This will not only increase their absorbency by puffing the fabric up a bit, but it will make sure all the chemicals used in their production and packaging have been washed out.

WIPES

If you have a baby, you know that one costly item that's impossible to use less of is baby wipes. When we had babies, we saved hundreds per year by making our own diaper wipes! They are easy to make and can be kept in an old baby wipes container, a plastic storage bin with a lid, or a resealable plastic bag. Here's how to do it: combine 2 tablespoons each of baby oil and baby shampoo (or baby wash) with 2 cups boiled and cooled water and one or two drops of your favorite essential oil for scent (optional). Remove the cardboard roll from a package of paper towels, then cut the entire roll in half (you can also tear off sheets by hand and stack them in a pile). Put some of the liquid mixture at the bottom of your container, then place the half-roll in the container. Pour the rest of the liquid over your paper towels and voilà—homemade baby wipes! Let the wipes sit for about an hour to absorb all the liquid, and your baby will never know the difference.

» Homemade Diversions

ACTION FIGURE ADD-ONS

Make an old action figure fun again by creating a mini parachute. First, cut out a square from a plastic sandwich bag. Poke a hole in each corner, then thread a foot-long piece of dental floss through the hole, tying a knot at the end so the floss can't be pulled back through. Once you've threaded a piece of floss through each hole, tie their other ends around the arms or—dare we say it— the neck of the figurine. Now you're ready to launch.

....

Cutting down new blinds to the appropriate size? Take the ladder-shaped strings that hold them together and give them to your older kids. You'll quickly find that action figures and small dolls always have a use for ladders.

BATHTIME

If you're looking for a cheap and practical toy for kids, thoroughly wash old ketchup, salad dressing, and shampoo bottles and let the kids use them to play in the swimming pool or bathtub. They're also a good way to wash shampoo out of hair at bath time.

....

For more fun at bath time, take all those little plastic toys your kids have gotten from vending machines and goody bags, and place one or two in each hole of a muffin tin. Then fill the tin with water and freeze. When it's time for a bath, pop one out and throw it in the tub. Your toddler will love watching it melt in their hands and then having a toy to play with.

CRAFTS

Art project? Make mixing paint easy by using a piece of cardboard covered in aluminum foil as your artist's palette. You can even cut the cardboard in the shape of a palette first.

> **An old plastic, cylindrical dispenser for baby or disinfectant wipes is perfect for holding your child's chunky markers. (Cut to size if necessary.)**

When it's finally time to replace your shower curtain liner, keep the old one and use it for a drop cloth while painting or doing art projects.

If your child has lots of little crayon pieces left over, turn them into a fun craft project that will give you some more use out of them! First, remove the paper, then place the pieces in a muffin tin. Heat at 250° until the crayons are melted (about 10–20 minutes), then remove from the oven and let cool. Your child will love the new, enormous crayons with unpredictable colors!

For a fun craft project, have your children make paper lunch bags into puppets. All you have to do is turn the bag upside down, then draw a face on what would be the bottom of the bag. Draw the mouth so that it's half on the bottom, half on the bag itself—that way, when someone puts a hand inside, the "mouth" can be opened and closed. Give your kids extras from your sewing box such as trim, fabric scraps, and buttons to embellish the puppets.

If your kids need glitter in an emergency (and who hasn't had a glitter emergency?), you can make your own at home. Just take a cup of salt, add 10–15 drops of your favorite food coloring, and mix it thoroughly. Microwave on high for 2–3 minutes, then spread it out on a sheet of nonstick foil or wax paper to dry. If you don't use it all right away, make sure to store it in an airtight container.

Keep your kids busy and encourage their creativity with homemade finger paints: Start by mixing two cups cold water with ¼ cup cornstarch, then boil until the liquid is as thick as, um, finger paints. Pour into small containers, swirl in some food coloring, and watch them create their masterpieces (just keep those colorful fingers away from walls!).

Get creative with watercolors and candles—but perhaps not in the way you think. Give your child a white candle and have her draw a picture on a piece of paper with it. Add watercolors and the invisible drawing appears! This is an especially good activity for two kids. Let them write "secret messages" to each other, then exchange the papers, apply some watercolors, and see what happens.

DOUGH AND CLAY

Don't spend money on store-bought Play-Doh; make your own at home instead with the following ingredients: 2 cups flour, 2 cups water, 1 cup salt, 2 tablespoons vegetable oil, 1 tablespoon cream of tartar, and the food coloring of your choice. Combine the ingredients in a large saucepan and stir continuously over medium heat until a solid ball forms. Remove it from the heat, knead it until all the lumps are out, and you should end up with a finished product nearly identical to the real thing. Make sure to store it in a completely airtight container; you might even want to dab a few drops of water on the underside of the lid before sealing it.

Make a Play-Doh substitute for your kids with an unlikely ingredient: dryer lint! First save up 3 cups of dryer lint, then stick it into a pot with 2 cups water, 1 cup flour, 6–10 drops food coloring, and ½ teaspoon vegetable or canola oil. Cook, stirring constantly, over low heat until the mixture is smooth. Then pour onto a sheet of wax paper to cool.

When they were younger, our kids loved making ceramic objects out of clay. Best of all, the clay is easy to make at home. Thoroughly mix the following ingredients in a bowl: 4 cups flour, 1⅓ cups salt, ¾ cup white glue, 1⅓ teaspoons lemon juice, and 1⅓ cups water. When you've got it all mixed together, you should end up with a pliable clay that can be either sculpted into different shapes or sliced with cookie cutters. When your kids are done molding the clay, let the creations sit over-night, allowing them to harden and air-dry. Then they can apply paint and/or glaze.

MUSICAL INSTRUMENTS

Short of shaking vitamin bottles, this might be the easiest instrument a human can make. Put dry beans between two paper plates, then tape the plates together. Decorate with markers, crayons, sequins, or anything else you have on hand. Your kids will love creating rhythms with their new toys.

If you or your child plays guitar (or has a toy uku-lele) there's no need to buy a pick! Instead, use the plastic fasteners found on bread bags. They work just as well, and they're free!

OUTDOOR FUN

Instead of throwing away an old dustpan (even a cracked one), wash it thoroughly and throw it in with your kid's sandbox toys. It makes a great scoop.

If your kids have tired of that expensive play-ground set you bought them, make the slide even more fun by giving them each a large piece of wax paper. If they sit on the paper as they're going down the slide, they'll move much faster, and they'll never call it boring again (or at least not for a few weeks).

Here's a quick, homemade toy that will keep your boys busy for hours, if not days: Take a large piece of corrugated cardboard and cut it in the shape of a sword (use two pieces and tape them together, if necessary). Wrap the handle with electrical tape and the "blade" with duct tape. Your kids can practice their fencing skills against each other, and since they're playing with cardboard, you won't have to worry about them getting hurt.

....

Warm weather is bubble season for kids who want some outdoor fun. Here's an inexpensive homemade solution for bubble greatness: Mix 1 tablespoon glycerin with 2 tablespoons powdered laundry detergent in 1 cup warm water. (Glycerin, often called "vegetable glycerin," can be found online and at many health-food and vitamin shops.) Any unpainted piece of metal wire (like a hanger) can be turned into a bubble wand: Just shape one end of the wire into a circle. Blowing into the mixture with a straw will make smaller bubbles float into the air. For colored bubbles, add food coloring.

TODDLERS

Here's a free, soft toy for your wee one: an old sock! Stuff it with old pantyhose, fiberfill, or even more old socks, then sew it shut to make a soft ball. Sure, it might not look as impressive as the $10 ones you'd buy at a toy store, but your baby won't know the difference!

....

If your young child likes building toys but you don't want to pay for expensive blocks, buy plastic cups in several different colors and use those instead. They're extremely cheap and just as fun to knock down!

>> Parties

Looking for Kids' Party tips? *See* **Entertaining and Holidays chapter, Parties**

>> School

LUNCHES

When packing a sack lunch for your child, place a juice box in the freezer the night before and add it to the lunch bag while still frozen the next morning. It'll help keep the lunch cool, and as an extra bonus, the juice will be nice and cold when your child finally gets around to drinking it at lunchtime.

—*Adriana Smith, Youngstown, OH*

If your kids complain that the sandwiches you make in the morning are mushy by lunchtime, put the mayonnaise (or any condiment) in a resealable plastic bag, and stick it in the lunch box. This way, the kids can season their own sandwiches at lunchtime by turning the bag inside out and rubbing it on the bread.

....

Make school-day mornings a little less crazy by preparing a few days' worth of the kids' sandwiches at the same time (without condiments), then freezing them. Each morning, just toss the pre-made sandwich in their lunch boxes, add a small container or plastic bag with the condiments, and by lunchtime, the bread will have thawed and become soft and fresh-tasting.

....

Kid's lunchbox starting to smell funky? Freshen it up with bread and vinegar! Just moisten a slice of bread with white vinegar and let it sit in the closed lunchbox overnight. In the morning, any bad odors should be gone.

SUPPLIES

To waterproof something you've written with marker on your child's school supplies (or even on a package you're sending), rub over the writing with a white candle. The wax will repel water, but you'll still be able to see through it.

....

If your child tears his backpack, there's no need to buy a new one. Just thread some floss onto a needle with a large eye, and use that to sew up the hole. It's sturdier than regular thread and will hold up well.

If your kids are like ours, they have all kinds of problems keeping their school supplies organized. You can help remedy this by taking a heavy-duty Ziploc freezer bag, punching holes in it so that it fits in their three-ring school binder, and filling it with pencils, erasers, and other easily misplaced items.

Our kids, like many, are incorrigible procrastinators when it comes to schoolwork. When they need index cards at a moment's notice, however, a late-night trip to the store is unnecessary. Simply take an ordinary paper plate and measure out a 3-by-5-inch or 4-by-6-inch rectangle. Cut it out and use the first card as a stencil for the rest. —*Nathaniel M.*

TEACHERS

It can be a struggle to find the right gifts for teachers, and yet it's not hard when you think of something that will enhance their classrooms. Here are some ideas: books, magazine subscriptions, educational games, posters of material they teach (the solar system or animal kingdom, for example), art supplies, easy-to-care-for plants, and gift certificates to bookstores. Many teachers use their own money for classroom supplies, so this kind of gift will be especially appreciated.

This school season, consider replacing your kids' flimsy backpacks with a sturdier (and cooler) alternative: military backpacks. These bags are built to last in the battlefields, so they'll certainly stand up throughout the wear and tear of the school year. You can find them in any Army/Navy surplus store.

» Simple Solutions

CHILD PROOFING

> Use a shower curtain ring to keep a toddler out of your cabinets. Just run the ring through two handles that are close by and latch.
> —*Randy Rodriguez, Waxahachie, TX*

If you've got kids who never seem to know when enough is enough, add water to your hand soap. Your hands will get just as clean, but the soap will last longer! You can also buy foaming soap dispensers, which are good for keeping the amount of soap you use to a minimum.

If you need to accident-proof your child's mattress, and you don't have a waterproof mattress cover, just lay overlapping sheets of foil on top of your mattress, then cover with a couple of old towels and then the rest of your sheets. Now onto the harder task: coming up with a potty-training strategy!

CLOTHING AND ACCESSORIES

When your kids' socks finally need to be thrown away (or turned into rags) because of holes, rips, or stains, make sure to keep their mates. Since you probably bought them in a pack, it's only a matter of time before another one just like it bites the dust. And if you end up with mismatching socks, your kids can still wear them around the house or to bed.

—*Debra R. Young*

If you or your child's shoelace breaks, use a ribbon as a replacement. It often looks better than the original!

—*Francie J. Shor*

If your child refuses to wear gloves or mittens, don't give him the opportunity to take them off once he goes outside to play. Duct tape the cuffs of the gloves to the cuffs of his coat!

There's nothing kids love more than temporary tattoos—until they decide they hate them. To easily remove a temp tat before it rubs off itself, dab some cold cream on the area, then wipe it off with a washcloth.

EATING AND DRINKING

Sneak some calcium into your kids' food by adding powdered milk to their meals. It'll be inconspicuous to them in dishes such as mashed potatoes, meatballs, and peanut butter sandwiches (mixed in with the peanut butter).

If your child never wants to eat his vegetables at dinnertime, try putting out a plate of raw veggies like carrots, celery, and broccoli right before dinner. Since he'll be hungry (and probably pestering you in the kitchen), it will be more likely that he'll succumb to this healthy snack.

—Terry Gallo, Breeding, KY

Keep messy melting Popsicles from getting all over your kids' hands (and the floor) by poking the stick-end of the Popsicle through a coffee filter before you hand it over. The filter will act like a bowl, catching any drips.

You can reduce your children's calorie and sugar intake by diluting their apple and orange juice with a bit of water. When you open a new bottle, empty a quarter of the juice into a pitcher, then fill the original juice bottle back to the brim with water. It'll still taste delicious, but the kids will get less of a sugar rush, and the juice will last longer to boot.

—Rosemary Deibler, Harrodsburg, KY

Make your own version of sippy cups using the real glassware you already have. If your glasses are slippery, put a wide rubber band around them so children can get a better grip.

....

If you're one of those super-parents who don't let their kids eat sugary cereal, have you thought about using it as a reward? Kids not used to having a morning sugar fix normally like sugary cereal brands as much as they like candy, so why not use it instead? That way, when kids are getting a sugary treat for being good, they'll at least getting it from a food that is also enriched with vitamins. And if you want to wean your children off the sugary stuff in the morning, this might be a good way to start!

....

It's a legendary kid problem: chewing gum stuck in the hair. Before you chop off a chunk of your kid's hair or attempt to shampoo it out, give this old trick a shot. Massage a small amount of smooth peanut butter into the gum-stuck section of the hair. Yep, it really works: The oils in the peanut butter counteract the stickiness of the gum. If you're out of peanut butter, try mayonnaise or salad dressing.

ORGANIZED ACTIVITIES

Organized activities for your kids are great, but the expense of enrolling them can take a toll. Instead of paying for a pricey arts and crafts class, for example, simply search online for the necessary information and hold the "class" yourself. In lieu of signing up for swimming lessons, just take your kids to a relative's pool or a public pool. Spending money on beginner-level instruction is often a waste, but if your child shows an aptitude for a certain activity or sport, *then* you can spend money on more advanced lessons. If you have to cut down on activities or sports they're already involved in, ask your children if there are any they don't really like. You might find they're just playing soccer, for instance, because their friends are on the team.

The best time to sign up your kids for camp is right after camp has ended. Many camps allow you to pay in advance for the next summer and save 5–10 percent. Ask at your camp as you're picking your kids up this year!

SAFETY AND FIRST AID

It's often a battle to get a sick child to take medicine he can't stand the taste of. To make things a little easier, have him suck on a Popsicle for a few minutes before taking the medicine. The Popsicle will not only act as an incentive, it will numb his taste buds a bit, making the medicine easier to swallow.

Nothing strikes fear in the hearts of parents like the words "lice outbreak." The harsh chemicals that are used to fight lice are almost as bad as the lice themselves. Luckily, there is a cheaper, more natural alternative. Cover your child's head (or yours, if the little buggers have gotten you!) with a thick conditioner like Pantene Pro V. Put on a Disney movie to keep your kid busy, then get a fine-toothed metal comb. Dip the comb into rubbing alcohol and comb through the hair, staying close to the scalp. Between each swipe, wipe the comb on a white paper towel to make sure you're getting the lice. Dip the comb in the alcohol again and keep going. Cover the hair with baking soda, and then repeat the process with the alcohol and the comb. Wash hair thoroughly when finished, and repeat this procedure each day for a week or until the lice are gone.

Before removing a bandage from your child's skin, douse the area with baby oil. The baby oil will soak into the bandage and make it easy to remove without hurting her.

If you know you're going to a crowded place, make sure to dress your children in bright colors so you can easily spot them. To make them stick out even more, buy each kid a cheap helium balloon and tie it around their wrists. Kids love balloons, and so will you when you realize you can see them from a mile away at the mall.

You've just bought your kids a new swing set, and you're peering out the window just waiting for one of them to fall off. Fear no more! Place carpet remnants or free carpet samples from a local store underneath the swings. They'll kill the grass underneath, but your kids would have done that anyway.

STROLLERS

If your stroller has become unbalanced thanks to the hundreds of shopping bags you have hanging from the handles, use arm and ankle weights that are used for exercise to more evenly distribute the weight. Attach the weights (with come with Velcro) to the bars of the stroller right above its front wheels. Now when your child jumps out, you won't end up with your bags all over the sidewalk.

—Donna Inklovich, Calumet City, IL

TANTRUMS

When I'm taking trips with my children, I always bring along a bottle of bubbles. If (and when) a tantrum hits, I take out the bubbles and start blowing. This distracts them enough so that they calm down and I can actually speak to them! By handling over the wand and letting them help, I not only reward them for stopping the screaming, but it allows them to take deep breaths and become even more relaxed.

—Mary Bowers, Salt Lake City, UT

TOYS

When you notice your kids getting bored with a toy (and they always do), don't buy them a new one. Instead, stash the old toy away in a bag or box. Once you have several toys, swap with a friend for toys her kids have gotten sick of. Not only will you save money, you'll avoid the clutter that comes with continually purchasing new playthings for your kids.

If your kids love video games, try to buy games that can be played over and over (such as puzzle games) rather than ones that aren't fun once you "win" them—you'll go a lot longer before you start hearing requests to buy a new game! When you finally do cave, make sure to buy used games whenever possible.

Before you buy your kid that bike he's been begging for, make sure it's the proper size. When sitting on the seat with hands on the handlebar, your child should be able to place the balls of both feet on the ground. He should also be able to straddle the center bar standing up with an inch or so clearance. Make sure to buy a bike that is adjustable past this point, so you don't have to buy another one when he quickly outgrows it.

To clean stuffed animals, just place them in a cloth bag or pillowcase, add baking soda or cornmeal, and shake. The dirt will transfer to the powder.

An oft-used deck of cards can get sticky and grimy from the oils on our hands. De-grease the cards by placing them in a plastic bag with a few blasts of baby powder. Give it a good shake before dealing the first hand.

....

Almost all soft rubber balls, including tennis balls, can be brought back to life by spending a night in the oven with only the pilot light on. The heat causes the air inside the ball to expand. Just be sure to remove the balls before you turn the oven on!

....

The sound of Ping-Pong balls being paddled all over the basement is worth every minute if it's keeping your kids busy! Unfortunately, when the kids finally emerge from downstairs, you notice that the balls are filled with dents. To get the balls round again, fill a jar to the brim with warm water, then place the balls inside and close the lid so that they're submerged. In twenty minutes or less, the water's pressure will make them pop back into place.

....

If you have an electronic toy whose batteries are loose due to a missing spring, don't throw it away or pay to get it fixed. Simply ball up a small amount of aluminum foil and put it in the spring's place. The aluminum will conduct electricity in lieu of the spring.

Auto

Baking

Beauty

Cleaning

Clothing and Accessories

Cooking

Decorating

Entertaining and Holidays

Health and Wellness

Home Repair

Kids

>> **Money**

Organization

Outdoors

Pest Control

Pets

Shopping

Utilities

Vacations and Family Activities

Websites

» Banking and Investments

CHECKING AND SAVINGS

It may be a pain, but if you're getting socked with fees for your checking or savings accounts, it's time to switch banks. You should never have to pay monthly service charges, and many banks are now even offering cash for opening a new account. Make sure to visit several banks in your area and ask about their fees, interest rates, opening bonuses, and other perks like free checking.

Don't be fooled by a sneaky bank! Many banks are desperate for your money these days, and like to offer free stuff. Don't take their advertisements at face value, and make sure to read the fine print carefully. One major bank recently touted, "Access to over 35,000 free ATMs! Never pay a fee again!" The fine print? Their offer is just a link to AllPoint-Network.com, where you can, in fact, get access to 35,000 free ATMs—without joining anything at all!

Tired of all the fees and high interest rates at your bank? Consider joining a credit union instead. CUs are not-for-profit, member-owned institutions, thus allowing them to be more beneficial for every account holder—not just the ultra-wealthy ones. To find one in your area and determine if it's right for you, visit NCUA. gov and select "Credit union data."

INVESTMENTS

Unlike 401(k) plans and traditional IRAs, there is no age at which you must begin to distribute money from your Roth IRA. As a result, Roth IRAs are great for young investors, as well as an excellent tool to pass along wealth to your children or grandchildren. Unlike with a plain-vanilla IRA, you contribute to a Roth IRA after you pay taxes on it. Then, once you reach retirement, you won't owe any taxes on withdrawals. Strange as it may sound, one of our advisors suggested thinking of yourself as a farmer: "It's like paying tax on a seed and getting the harvest for free."

If you're interested in saving for your child's education, a "529" savings plan is probably your best bet. Here's why: First, these state-sponsored investment accounts allow parents and grandparents to invest large sums of money (often $300,000 or more per beneficiary). Moreover, just as with a 401(k), money invested in a 529 is allowed to grow and compound tax-free! That offers parents a huge advantage over traditional brokerage accounts, whose gains, dividends, and interest income all are taxed along the way. Finally, 529s are advantageous from a financial-aid standpoint, because none of the money held in a 529 is considered the student's asset when calculating aid eligibility.

With IRAs, 401(k)s, stocks, and other invest-ments, it's hard to keep everything straight. It's easier, however, if you join Kiplinger's Portfolio Tracker, where you can track all your investments for free. When it comes time to file your taxes, you'll thank us! Just go to Kiplinger.com/portfolio and click on the "First time users click here" tab.

—*Greg Chu, Fayetteville, NC*

....

Want to trade your stock commission-free? Head over to WellsFargo.com/jump/investments/freetradeson-line to check out Wells Fargo's online trading program. If your cumulative account balance is $25,000 or more (in-cluding your Wells Fargo checking and savings accounts, certificates of deposit, IRAs, and brokerage accounts), you'll receive 100 commission-free online trades per year. Check it out before you pay for a trade.

» Bills

CELL PHONE

If you find yourself under-using your mobile minutes each month, consider canceling your current plan when your contract runs out and paying as you go instead. With pay-as-you-go phones, you pay an amount of money up front instead of getting a bill each month. Most plans will charge you 5–10¢ a minute, and offer discounts if you put a large amount of money—usually $100—on the phone. The good news is that you can also send and receive text (and sometimes picture) messages, and even surf the web on some phones. The bad news is that the minutes usually expire after a certain amount of time. Pay-as-you-go phones are great for phones that you pretty much only use in an emergency, and for giving to teens so that you can make sure they don't overspend. Ask at a cell phone or electronics store about pay-as-you-go phones and promotions.

Looking to change your cell phone plan but aren't sure how much you're going to have to pay to get out of your contract? Head over to CellTradeUSA. com, which will tell you how much it will cost to cancel. The site also allows you to transfer your contract to another CellTrade user, if your cell company allows it.

It's easy to track how many minutes of cell phone time you've used. Most cell phone companies allow you to track your minutes via their website. You can also sign up with a service like OverMyMinutes.com, which will send you a text message when you approach your monthly limit.

When purchasing a cell phone, never sign up for insurance or a warranty—and if you're paying a monthly fee for insurance, cancel it immediately. The insurance plan of many cellular providers has a deductible of up to $50 that you are responsible for paying, and the phone you'll usually receive as a replacement will be an already-outdated model from last year. The cost of taking your chances and buying a cheap replacement if necessary is much less than what your cellular company is offering you.

....

If your cell phone company charges you data fees, make sure you only do high-data tasks while connected to a wi-fi network. This includes streaming music and videos and downloading apps, music, podcasts, or any other content. Also keep an eye on any apps that may be using your location data in the background, as this will use up data. When surfing the web while on the go, mobile-optimized webpages will use less data than others, because they're stripped of the movies and advertisements that also make them load slowly. Finally, make sure your email on your phone is set to manually download, as your phone constantly checking for new emails can waste a lot of data minutes.

INTERNET AND CABLE

Do you and your neighbors both use wireless internet? A great way to save is to go-in on an internet plan together. If you already have a plan, ask a neighbor you trust if they'd like to pay you for half the cost if you give them the password to your network. Especially if you live in an apartment building, you should be able to use the wireless internet hub you currently own, but if your homes are particularly far apart you may need to extend your network with a second hub or router.

....

You can save money by disconnecting your cable TV service during the times of year that you don't need it. Going on a long vacation? Have a summer ahead filled with time-consuming activities? Just get rid of the cable during the time you won't be using it, and who knows, you might even be offered an enticing deal when it's time to re-subscribe!

LOWERING YOUR BILLS

It sounds too simple to be true, but you can often just ask credit card companies, utilities, landlords, and others to waive late fees. If you're a longtime customer with a good history, companies will often re-credit your account, especially if it was your first offense.

At LowerMyBills.com, you'll find a way to reduce just about any bill. Whether you're looking to refinance your home, consolidate your credit card debt, or just lower your phone bill, this site will give you the tools you need to compare different companies and calculate your costs. You can also sign up for an email newsletter filled with tips and deals.

PAYMENTS, MAKING

Is there anything more annoying than late fees on credit cards and other bills? Say goodbye to late fees forever by setting up an automatic debit from your checking account. You can usually set up automatic debit by calling the company the account is with or visiting their website.

Here's an easy solution if you keep getting socked with late fees, or neglect to pay more than the minimum on your credit cards because the payment is always due at the same time as your rent. Ask your credit card company to change the date your payment is due. It might take a few months to kick in, but you'll be able to pay down the card more easily during the part of the month that isn't as much of a crunch.

When paying bills by mail, always put them in a post office or street mailbox instead of the mailbox on your front door. A thief could get to your mail before the mailman, and the information provided on your check or bill could lead to identity theft.

PHONE, HOME

Are you sure you know what's on your phone bill? Phone companies are notorious for automatically enrolling you in a calling package filled with services you never use. Make sure to check your phone bills for extra charges such as voicemail, three-way calling, and call forwarding. If you don't use these services, cancel them to save! If you use your cell phone more than your home phone, you might want to consider stripping your landline down to the bare minimum or canceling your service outright.

When making international phone calls, never dial directly. Instead, buy an international phone card at your local convenience store. Most specialize in a particular country or continent, and will allow you to talk for only pennies a minute. You can also go to AITelephone.com, which works pretty much the same way, but gives you the option of prepaying online or being sent a bill.

Although households with no landline use an average of 332 more minutes per month on their cell phones than those with a landline, they still spend an average of $33 less per month on phone service. Consider going cell-phone-only in your household. If you don't like losing that phone number you've had for so many years, you should also know that the FCC mandates that phone companies allow you to "port" your home phone number to a cell phone when you're first signing up for service.

UTILITIES

If you're lucky enough to live in an area that has more than one company providing phone, cable, or other utilities, use this to your advantage by lowering your payment amount—without having to switch companies! Find out what your company's competitors are charging by calling them or visiting WhiteFence.com, then call and ask for your rates to be lowered. If the first person you talk to says no, don't be discouraged and don't be afraid to ask to speak to a supervisor. If you call between 9 a.m. and 5 p.m. you'll be more likely to get an experienced supervisor on the phone who's willing to bargain.

Is there a fuel co-op in your area? A fuel co-op is an organization that negotiates lower rates for your heating gas by buying in bulk. Even though you normally have to pay a membership fee, you can save big bucks on your heating bill by joining a fuel co-op, and you often don't even need to change from your current gas company. Most co-ops will offer you discounts if you're a senior citizen or are on a fixed income. To find one in your region simply type "fuel co-op" and your geographic location (e.g., "New Jersey") into Google or another search engine.

» Budgeting and Debt

BUDGETING TOOLS

Trying to get a handle on budgeting? Check out FrugalMom.net/blog/?p=364, which will not only walk you through how to better budget your money, but will also give you free, downloadable forms like a spending tracker to help get you started.

As Veruca Salt said in *Willy Wonka and the Chocolate Factory*, "I want it, and I want it now!" It's hard to break ourselves of using credit to buy high-ticket items when we want them, rather than saving up before we spend. But making a wish list can help. Whenever you get the urge to buy something, write it down, but don't buy it. Every few months, read through your list. Do you still want that leopard-print Snuggie, ultimate pet stroller, or personalized yoga mat? Chances are, you're willing to let most of them go. It's amazing how fast "I absolutely have to have this" turns into "That's so last year."

COLLECTION AGENCIES

Nothing feels worse than having collection agencies calling you to try to collect on a debt. If you have old debt, it's time to stop feeling bad about it and confront the collection agencies or credit card companies head-on, especially since you're harming your credit score each day you don't. What you may be surprised to know is that most collection agencies will settle for 40 to 60 percent of the total amount you owe, and they will be willing to set up a payment plan with you. The more quickly you can pay it off, the better deal they will be willing to give you, but make sure you only agree to pay as much as you think you can each month—never commit to more than you can pay and risk being unable to make payments.

....

If you're having problems with a collection agency, you should know that in local and state courts in many areas, lawsuits from collection and credit card agencies have been overturned. If you are being asked to pay more than 60 percent of the debt, the agency has been unable to show you proof that you owe the debt, or you otherwise feel like you're getting a raw deal, don't be afraid to go to court with the collection agency. Not only do you deserve to go in front of a neutral arbitrator, it will it make the other party more likely to settle (because they won't want to pay lawyer's fees). However, it is vitally important that you stay apprised of court dates and show up to every one of them. If you don't appear to make your case, the judge will have no choice but to side with the collection agency.

DEBT

If you're having trouble paying down your debt, try making a chart or graph of what you want to accomplish. Place it somewhere you'll see if often, and update it as you send in checks. Being able to track your progress will help keep you motivated!

—*Linda Everett*

If you feel like you're in over your head with your debt, or if you simply want some answers about the most efficient way to pay it off and manage a budget, there is free counseling available to you. These one-on-one sessions are offered by organizations across the country who want to help people who are struggling with money problems. They also often offer consolidation loans and debt management programs. To find an agency that will work with you in person, over the phone, online, or via mail, call the National Foundation for Credit Counseling at 1-800-388-2227. This organization makes sure its members are accredited, not-for-profit, and generally on the level.

SAVING

To help you save on a monthly basis, make it easier to contribute to your savings account. Banks allow you to set up recurring transfers, so set one up for each time you get paid. Putting even $50 into your savings account each time you get a paycheck will quickly add up, and you'll be glad you have it on a rainy day or when vacation time rolls around.

....

If you get a bump in salary, the smartest thing you can do with it is put a higher proportion of your salary into your savings account. For instance, if you get a 4 percent raise, add 1 percent to your household budget and set aside the other 3 percent for your retirement account. You won't have to cut back to save more, and you'll thank yourself later!

ENTERTAINMENT COSTS

The point of making a budget isn't getting rid of your entertainment spending, it's just prioritizing what you like to spend your money on. Decide what your favorite activities are (as a family, couple, and by yourself or with friends). Then make sure you save enough to spend on the things you really enjoy. For instance, you may decide you'd like to give up going to the movies a few times a month so you can go to a concert. Or you might prefer to spend your money on a nice dinner rather than a couple of trips to the bar.

....

You're trying to keep your socializing budget under control, but your friends are constantly inviting you on expensive outings you can't afford! Instead of having to turn down invitations, take the initiative and be first to invite everyone out. This way, you can decide the place—something more in your price range. Better yet, host a potluck or movie night at your home.

» Credit

CREDIT CARDS, BALANCES

If you owe lots of money to one credit card and not-so-much to one with a lower interest rate, ask your credit card company if you can do a balance transfer. You may incur a fee, but you often end up saving in the end, and many cards offer them for free during the first year of your agreement. If you have two cards from the same company, ask if the card with the better deal allows "credit reallocation," which would let you transfer not only the balance from the other card but its credit limit as well, without even submitting you for another credit check.

....

If you are a homeowner with a significant balance of high-interest credit card debt, and substantial equity in your home, you can save big on interest expense by consolidating your credit cards with a home equity loan, while also making the interest expense deductible on your tax return. Caution: Only do this if you are willing to cut up the credit cards at the same time! Assuming it wasn't a medical or severe emergency that brought about the high balances, your inability to manage them is what got you in trouble. If you consolidate and go back to your old ways, then all you've done is turn unsecured credit card debt into secured debt (i.e., now the bank can take your house!). If you've learned your lesson about credit card spending and what to pay less in interest, consider taking out a home equity loan to pay off the cards, then cancel the accounts.

....

If you want to reduce the annual percentage rate on your credit card, ask and you shall receive! It sounds too simple to be true, but one of the first things you should do when attempting to reduce your debt is call up your credit card company and ask them to reduce your interest rate or annual percentage rate (APR). If you have had the card for a while and have routinely made payments on time, the company is usually happy to take this piece-of-cake step to keep your business.

....

Credit card interest is calculated based on your average daily balance over the month, which means you can reduce your charges by making more payments. Instead of paying, say, $300 at the end of the month, split that up into two $150 payments. That way, your average daily balance will be lower, and therefore your finance charges will be, too.

CREDIT CARDS, CHOOSING

If you're in the market for a new credit card, the first site you should visit is CardTrak.com, where you can find hundreds of cards sorted by types of rewards, your credit history, and their brand. When choosing the one that's right for you, make sure to consider the perks the card offers. If you fly a lot, cards with air-mile programs can save you hundreds. Other cards offer insurance on purchases or car rentals. Figure out how much you think these extras will save you, and take this into consideration when you pick a card.

Take an extra-careful look at credit cards offered by gas companies—most have a higher interest rate than average credit cards. Before you sign up, make sure to ask about their fraud protection, which is usually pretty weak. You may be better off using a "regular" credit card that offers rebates on gas purchases. Two good choices are the Discover platinum gas card and the Chase cash plus card.

Always read the terms of a credit card agreement before you sign up for the card. The fine print may be boring, but you owe it to yourself to make sure you're not getting a bum deal. Highlight any passages you don't understand, and find out what they mean by asking a lawyer or accountant; or simply look the phrase up in an internet search engine. Some agreements will try to scam you—one recent ploy is for companies to buy up your bad debt, then trick you into signing up for a card that already has the bad debt tacked onto the balance. (If this happens to you, you should insist on getting documents that prove that you are accountable for that debt or the interest, so don't agree to anything until you speak with that lawyer or accountant). Be especially careful if the offer seems too good to be true.

CREDIT SCORE

Did you know that legally, you are entitled to one free credit report per year? However, many credit report sites will make you pay to see your score, or charge you a membership or "credit monitoring" fee. Visit CreditKarma.com for a free, no-strings-attached estimation of your credit score. Then go to AnnualCreditReport.com (the only truly free credit report site) to see how they came up with that score, and to make sure there no errors on your report.

When offered financing by a store you are purchasing a big-ticket item from, think carefully before you accept. If they basically give you a store credit card with a spending limit that matches the price of the item, this credit card will pop up on your credit report as being opened and immediately maxed out. Obviously, this isn't good news for your credit score.

To improve your credit score, get rid of credit cards you rarely use. Even if you don't carry balances on these cards, one of the things that can lower your credit rating is the amount of available credit you have. Call the number on the back of the cards and cancel them!

If you are listed as a secondary cardholder for an account of someone who's racked up a lot of debt on the card, this can negatively impact your credit rating. If it isn't necessary for you to be on this credit card account, call the company and get your name taken off.

» Insurance

AUTO

When your auto insurance renewal comes in the mail, don't just write a check and send it in. Review your policy and make sure it's still the type of coverage you need as your vehicle ages year after year. When it gets to the point where your collision coverage premiums (plus the deductible) are almost the same as the value of the car itself, drop that portion of the coverage—you're only flushing money down the toilet.

You can save hundreds each year on your auto insurance by raising your deductible. If have more than one type of insurance with the same carrier, you may also qualify for bundled discounts. It's not in your insurance company's best interests to keep you informed about the lowest rates, so make sure you call them and ask.

Been involved in a car accident? The best thing to do is to leave the vehicles where they are and call the police. Whether anyone is ticketed or not, your insurance company will usually require you to complete a police report, which will help them decide which party is to blame. But if the damage is minor and you either don't have time to call the police or have to move your car out of traffic, you should document what happened. Use your cell phone's camera to take as many pictures possible of the accident, so you can prove what happened later.

HEALTH

Those of us lucky enough to have health insurance love having to pay less for health care—as long as the system works. If (OK, *when*) you have problems with your health insurance reimbursing you for a claim, it's important to stay organized. Take notes when you are disputing a claim, and refer to them when you call the company. The representative will be more likely to take you seriously if you can state the dates you spoke to someone, what the claim or reference number is, and the amount it was for. Also make sure to have the date the service was performed and the date the claim was submitted on-hand.

....

Having trouble getting paid for a health insurance claim? If you have a group plan, see if you can get the administrator of the plan (usually in your HR department) to help you complain to the company. Someone who may be in charge of switching plans will have more pull than you do.

PROPERTY

Did you know that most homeowners' insurance policies will deduct 3–5 percent of your cost for adding simple security features such as a smoke alarm or dead bolts? You can often save a lot more if you're willing to install a more sophisticated security system. These systems can get expensive, but the savings (not to mention the security) may be worth it. Before you choose one, make sure to call your insurance company to see what kind of system they recommend. You may also to be able to save if you are 65 or over.

....

A big factor in how much you're charged for homeowners insurance is where you live. So if there have been improvements to your neighborhood or subdivision, such as storm drains being installed or a fire hazard being cleared away, make sure to alert your insurance company and see if they will lower your rates.

≫ Medical Expenses

DOCTORS

If you need medical treatment but can't afford a doctor, consider a walk-in clinic. Walk-in retail clinics can be found in many drug and even department stores. You'll see a nurse or nurse practitioner and may get everything you need, with the convenience of the pharmacy on-site. Besides the quick service and low cost, you'll appreciate the extended evening and weekend hours. Remember these clinics are meant for minor illnesses and injuries such as colds and flus, sprained muscles, pinkeye, burns, and ear infections. If your situation goes beyond the scope of the clinic, you'll be advised to see a doctor.

—*Samantha Chumley*

DENTAL CARE

Many companies don't offer dental insurance, but you can join a plan on your own for discounts ranging from 10–60 percent off. Check out DentalPlans.com or call 1-888-632-5353 to find a plan and dentist in your neighborhood. Certain plans may be used in combination with dental insurance you already have.

....

Did you know that the first Friday in February each year is Give Kids a Smile Day? Dentists around the country provide free check-ups and cleanings to kids on this day, so if you schedule your kids' 6-month check-ups in February and August, that's one less cleaning you have to pay for! Visit the American Dental Association's website at GiveKidsASmile.ADA. org for more information.

....

It's true: you can get that root canal you've been putting off and keep your retirement account. Find a dental school in your area to visit for regular cleanings and check-ups, and you'll save big. Be prepared, however, for crowded waiting rooms, long visits, and less privacy. Still, you'll get the care you need at a fraction of the cost.

PRESCRIPTIONS

Before you re-order a prescription, find out if your insurance provider offers a pharmacy-by-mail service. Though it's not as easy as going to your local pharmacy, you can save up to 30 percent on some medicines.

—*Emme Boutin-Robertson, Cambridge, MA*

....

If you don't have a prescription plan, or if your prescription plan has denied you coverage for an expensive medication, you may be able to get it for free or at a deep discount. NeedyMeds.com will tell you how to get the medicine you need from the government, private outreach programs, and even the pharmaceutical companies themselves. Just simply find the name of your medication in the "Brand name" or "Generics" list and see if you qualify! You should never be without the prescriptions you need.

» Taxes

DEDUCTIONS

Recently bought a home? To get your home mortgage loan, you may have paid all sorts of charges not labeled as interest, like origination fees, maximum loan charges, and premium charges. If any of these charges were solely for the use of the money and not for a specific service (like an appraisal), then good news—they're considered prepaid interest and can be deducted. Check your closing statement.

If you think you may qualify for interest deduction from your home equity loan, it's important to know that it is not unlimited. You can generally deduct interest you pay on the first $100,000 of a home equity loan. After that, it depends. If the home equity loan was used to improve your first or second home—or to purchase a second home—you can probably take the deduction on an amount up to $1 million or the value of the home. IRS Publication 936 Section 2 contains more detail. If you use the alternative minimum tax (AMT) on your 1040, your home equity loan deductions will only help you if you used the money for home improvements.

Here's a strategy tip if you have a college-age child and the ability to invest in real estate. Buy a house, condo, or apartment building near your child's college campus, and have your child (and hopefully a roommate) pay you rent. Hire your child to maintain and manage the property. The salary you pay your kid will be a tax deductible rental expense, just like property taxes, mortgage interest, repairs, depreciation, and other operating deductions that landlords are entitled to. Meanwhile, your student will pay income tax on the salary at their lower tax rates. The benefits are huge: Your child has housing and a job, you shifted income to your child at a lower tax rate, and you have a tax-advantaged investment that is being watched over by somebody you can (hopefully) trust.

If you have an old car you want to get rid of, donating it to charity can seem like a great idea. It's an easy thing to do and it gives you a charitable deduction. The problem is that many people in recent years had the same idea, and too many of them abused the tax rules by grossly inflating the value of their old junker, sometimes claiming a deduction for thousands on a bomb that the charity ultimately sold for less than $100. So the IRS tightened up these regulations recently. Now, if you donate a car and claim a deduction greater than $500, your deduction is limited to the amount that the charity receives when it actually sells the car. The charity must provide you with an IRS Form 1098-C (Contributions of Motor Vehicles, Boats, and Airplanes), which documents the sale price, and must be attached to your return. To learn more, see IRS Publication 4303: A Donor's Guide to Vehicle Donations.

When you're job searching, it's important to keep track of your job search expenses, because these costs may be a tax deduction when you file your income taxes. You don't have to be out of work to have some of your costs qualify as a deductible expense, but only expenses that exceed 2 percent of your income count. If you've been looking for a job in the same line of work you're currently in, many of your expenses—like phone calls, the costs of preparing and copying your resume, traveling to interviews, and career counseling—are deductible, even if you do not get a new job. However, you usually cannot deduct these expenses if you're looking for a job in a new occupation, there was a long period of unemployment between the ending of your last job and your looking for a new one, or if you are looking for a job for the first time.

Do you work from home? Welcome to a giant tax break. Generally, in order to claim a business deduction for your home, you must use part of your home exclusively and regularly as a principal place of business, or as a place to meet or deal with patients, clients, or customers in the normal course of your business. The amount you can deduct depends on the percentage of your home that you used for business. For example, if you are self-employed and use 10 percent of the square footage of your house as your office, then you can only deduct 10 percent of your rent or mortgage. Different rules apply for claiming the home office deduction if you are not self-employed. For example, your working from home must be for the convenience of your employer. There are also special rules for qualified daycare providers and for persons storing business inventory or product samples. For more information, see IRS Publication 587: Business Use of Your Home.

Even if you don't work from home, there may be many work expenses you can deduct on your taxes. As long as your company didn't reimburse you for them, some allowable deductions include dues to professional societies and unions, tools and supplies used in your work, work clothes and uniforms (only if required and not suitable for everyday use), and education costs and relate directly to your work.

If you itemize your deductions, you can deduct medical and dental expenses for you and your family (if an elderly parent is your dependent, this can really add up!). The bad news is that you can only deduct the amount of these expenses that exceeds 7.5 percent of your adjusted gross income (AGI). This hefty limitation on the deduction makes it useless for many taxpayers, but if you've had surgery or lots of medical procedures this year, you probably qualify. If possible, you also may want to hold off on elective surgery or expensive dental procedures until you can do them all in the same year and qualify for the deduction. Things you can deduct include any costs not covered by your insurance and associated with medical procedures, check-ups, or tests; insurance premiums; prescription and over-the-counter medications; eyeglasses and contacts; dental supplies (including toothbrushes!); medical supplies like bandages and even aloe vera gel; ambulance or other transportation costs to the hospital, doctor's office, and programs like AA; costs to get to and attend a medical conference on an illness or condition suffered by you, your spouse, or a dependent; the cost of renovating your home to accommodate a disability (like a wheelchair ramp); and lodging to receive outpatient care at a hospital or clinic ($50 per night, or $100 per night if you're accompanying your sick child). To learn more, see IRS Publication 502: Medical and Dental Expenses.

....

If you happen to find yourself in the lucky position of having net gambling winnings near the end of the year, maybe it's a good time to treat yourself to a gambling vacation. Net winnings are taxable (and can only be offset by gambling losses), but net loses are deductible. So if you lose on your trip, you'll be able to write it off. And if you happen to win on vacation, well just consider it your lucky year.

FILING

It may seem crazy to pay your taxes before they're due, but it may be worth it. State income taxes paid are an itemized tax deduction on your federal return. Many people can benefit by paying their state income taxes before year end in order to maximize their deductions for federal taxes. Be careful, though, as this strategy can possibly throw you into AMT (alternative minimum tax). If you plan on prepaying a substantial amount of state tax, consult with a tax advisor to make sure this strategy will work for you.

....

It's 4:00 p.m. on April 15, and you're probably not going to be meeting that filing deadline. Luckily, you can get an automatic six month extension from the IRS. Just submit Form 4868 (Application for Automatic Extension of Time to File U.S. Individual Income Tax Return) or request an extension online at IRS.gov. An extension will give you extra time to get your paperwork to the IRS, but it doesn't extend the time you have to pay any tax due. You'll also owe interest on any amount not paid by the April deadline, plus a late payment charge if it amount already withheld doesn't cover at least 90 percent of your total tax.

....

Free File, a form of e-filing your taxes, is a free federal tax preparation and electronic filing program that you can access at IRS.gov. By visiting their site, you can fill out forms and electronically "sign" them, print them out for your records, and then submit your taxes through the computer. People who e-file normally receive tax refunds sooner, so this is a great system to check out.

REFUNDS

Never sign up for a "refund anticipation loan" from an accountant. While it would be nice to get your hard-earned money back in your pocket as quickly as possible, these short-term loans can cost you big—in some cases, the fees on an anticipation loan are the equivalent of over 200% APR! Instead, file electronically and request direct deposit, and you should expect your refund in as little as two weeks. Those few weeks could save you a few hundred dollars in fees that you would have otherwise spent on a refund anticipation loan. Credit cards are never a good fix, but if you really need the money fast, most credit cards will give you better terms than an anticipation loan.

....

Getting a refund? You can now receive it in the form of US bonds instead. These bonds are a great investment because you don't have to pay any federal income taxes on the interest earned on them until you cash them in. This tax deferral feature is automatic, so you don't have to do anything to get it, and this interest is not subject to state or local tax. An added bonus is that you may not have to pay any federal tax on the interest if you use the money from these bonds to pay for higher education expenses for yourself or someone else.

....

Whether you didn't file because you had too little income, or you didn't file a return for a year that you would have gotten a refund, you can still get that money from the government. As long as it's within 3 years, you can file that return and get your money. Just search for that year's 1040, 1040A, or 1040EZ form on the IRS's website, IRS.gov. There is no penalty assessed by the IRS for filing a late return qualifying for a refund.

....

Did your tax refund never show up? You can check the status of any check that was supposed to have been sent in the last 12 months by clicking on "Where's My Refund?" at the IRS.gov site. If the check was undeliverable, you can even update your address.

....

What should you do if you accidentally entered the wrong banking information on your tax return? If you've just mailed it in, call the IRS immediately at 1-800-829-1040 and ask that the IRS convert the refund to a paper check. Otherwise, the IRS will assume that the information you put in the direct deposit area is correct and will initiate the direct deposit in as little as eight days. If you don't catch them and the money has been deposited, there is probably no recourse through the IRS. Instead, you'll need to deal with the bank directly. If you entered the wrong routing number, go to RoutingNumbers.org to find the bank where the money was deposited by looking up he routing number you accidentally entered on your return. Otherwise, the money was routed to your own bank, just the wrong account. Next comes the tricky part. You'll have to call the bank and persuade them to send the refund back to the IRS. Ask to speak to the ACH manager, explain the situation, and hope for the best. Then call the IRS (1-800-829-1040) and explain the error and that the bank will be sending back the refund. The good news is that you'll always triple-check the info from now on!

Auto

Baking

Beauty

Cleaning

Clothing and Accessories

Cooking

Decorating

Entertaining and Holidays

Health and Wellness

Home Repair

Kids

Money

» **Organization**

Outdoors

Pest Control

Pets

Shopping

Utilities

Vacations and Family Activities

Websites

» Bathroom

BATH AND SHOWER

Transfer your shampoo, conditioner, and body wash into pump bottles. Your products will not only be easier to dispense, but you'll make sure not to use too much. One pump is all you should need!

—*Alexis Raizen-Rubenstein*

....

Instead of letting your soap sit in standing water on your soap dish, put it in a mesh bag (like the kind you would get a bunch of onions in) and tie it to your faucet or an in-shower towel rod. The water will run right through.

....

When you purchase a new bar of soap, take it out of its box or wrapper and place it in your linen closet. The exposure to the air will harden the soap slightly, which will help it last longer. Meanwhile, it will freshen your closet while it's waiting to be used in the shower.

STORAGE

Many forms of make-up are sensitive to the sun due to their preservatives. Keep your make-up away from the window to ensure it lasts as long as possible.

....

Perfume is very volatile—the fragrance breaks down rapidly when exposed to heat and air. If you're not going to use the entire bottle within 30 days, store it in the refrigerator to extend its life.

Store all your medications in a cool, dry spot in your home, such as a linen closet or kitchen cabinet. Contrary to popular belief, medications do *not* belong in a bathroom medicine cabinet, where the heat and humidity will cause them to go bad more quickly.

The refrigerator is the perfect place to store hydrogen peroxide—the colder temperature will help it stay active for a longer period. Nail polish is another chemical that likes the cold. It will last longer if you keep it in the refrigerator, but bring it up to room temperature before your manicure.

If you have a metal medicine cabinet, mount a magnet inside it, and you'll be able to place nail clippers, tweezers, safety pins, or other handy items at your fingertips. And if your cabinet is not made of metal, just glue the magnet inside.

Those three-tiered baskets that you usually find holding fruit in the kitchen are also perfect for bathrooms. Store brushes, hair gel, Band-Aids, or whatever else is taking up too much space in your medicine cabinet. If placed out of reach of your kids, it's also a great place to store shaving supplies.

» Clothing and Accessories

ACCESSORIES, OTHER

Stop hunting around the house every time you need a hair band! Get a toilet paper tube and wrap the bands around it. Keep it in your bathroom or on your dresser and you'll never be without a ponytail holder again.

—Jackie Bavel, Manahawkin, NJ

Here's a handy storage tip: Hanging purses to store them puts stress on the handles. You'll do better keeping them on shelves or in one big bag so they'll last longer.

Got new curtain rings (or took our advice to change them out with ribbon)? Use the old ones to organize your coat closet. Hammer a nail into the wall, then hang a couple of curtain rings on it. They can be used to grasp items like gloves and hats, or you can run a scarf through one.

Don't throw away the little *z*-shaped hooks that come with dress socks—use them as tie holders! Slip them onto a hanger, and they are perfect for hanging the tie that accompanies that particular suit.

Is pantyhose overrunning your sock drawer?
Place each pair in its own resealable sandwich bag.
Write any pertinent information (like the size, or
whether or not it's control top) on the outside. If
they're still taking up too much space, place them in a
plastic storage bin under your dresser or somewhere else
out of the way.

CLOTHES

In need of some new hangers? Try your local department store. When making a purchase, let the sales
clerk know that you'd like to take the hangers too. If you
notice any empty hangers lying around the register area,
ask for those as well—it couldn't hurt!

Hang your blazers and suit jackets properly to save
yourself trips to the cleaners for pressing. If you
use wooden hangers, turn them so the curve is facing you when you slip the jacket or blazer around
the shoulders. The hanger will be backward, and
this method will keep the jacket's shoulders nice,
tight, and wrinkle free.

JEWELRY

This organizational tip is also a great bedroom decoration. Buy a bulletin board and lots of sturdy pushpins, then use them to hang your bracelets, necklaces, rings, and hook earrings. With all your jewelry on display, you'll be able to more quickly decide what you want to wear, and it won't be a tangled mess. You'll also get a chance to look at beautiful pieces that may not make it into your regular rotation.

—*Devorah Klein, Silver Spring, MD*

It's great to organize necklaces by hanging them—all except pearls. These gems are strung on a delicate silk thread that can't sustain the weight. Who knew?

Here's an easy way to keep your earrings together: Thread the posts through old buttons, and then attach the backs.

Don't throw away the cork when you finish a bottle of wine. Repurpose it! Cork is a perfect material for storing and toting stud earrings. Cut the cork into thin slices, then poke the earrings through, put the backs back on, and toss them into your toiletry bag when traveling.

You don't have to buy a jewelry organizer to keep your necklaces untangled. Just cut plastic straws in half, thread your necklaces through, and fasten the clasps.

SEWING AND YARN

If you use a sewing machine often, mount a small bulletin board on the wall next to it. Then fill it with pushpins or straight pins. That way when you've got your hands full, you can use the pins to hang extra thread, buttons, bobbins, and other miscellany until you need it.

....

You've lost the wick of an old candle, and you were never really crazy about the scent anyway. Turn your old candle into a pincushion by simply sticking pins in the top or the sides. The wax will even help them slide more easily into cloth.

....

Doing some knitting? Keep yarn from getting tangled, especially if you're working with two strands at a time, by running the ends of the rolls through straws. If you pull the yarn through straws as you knit, they'll straighten out each strand.

—*Missy Miller, Loveland, CO*

....

Yarn can get out of control fast (especially if you have cats), so keep each ball of yarn in a dispenser made from an appropriately sized soda bottle (cleaned-out, of course). Cut a hole in the bottom big enough to slip the yarn through, then place your skein inside and pull the string out through the bottle opening.

....

If you're working with a ball of yarn or twine that keeps getting tangled, find two baskets and overturn one to make a cage. Place the ball inside and run the end of the string through a hole in the basket. The ball will be caught inside while the string unspools freely.

SHOES AND SKATES

Keep your boots looking their best by storing them with empty wine or soda bottles inside. They'll stay upright and maintain their shape.

Old garden hose finally kick the bucket? Before you throw it away, cut two portions that are each about a foot long, then cut a slit in them. They'll make perfect covers for the blades of ice skates.

» Clutter, Relieving

AROUND THE HOUSE

It's often hard to keep track of your household scissors, cell phone, remote control...and the list goes on! Find these commonly lost items more quickly by slapping a piece of reflective tape on each of them. The shimmering surface will pop out at you, even from between couch cushions.

If you're always searching for the remote control, pick one designated place for it and try to always return it to that spot when you're done watching television. You can, for example, keep it on the same end table, or attach self-adhesive Velcro to it and to your TV and affix it there. If you have two (or three, or four, or five) remotes, keep them together in a small basket by your favorite chair.

....

Rather than purchase a bulletin board or whiteboard for your home, write messages to your family members on the mirror in your bathroom with dry-erase markers. The bathroom gets heavy foot traffic, so it's a great place to keep notes and reminders for everyone in your family.

....

If you live in an urban area, you probably get a take-out menu stuck under your door every day. To get rid of the clutter caused by having menus stacked up in a drawer, on a table, or practically all over your house, pick a storage method and stick to it. We use a sturdy, waterproof pocket folder for our menus, but you can also use a magazine holder, an inbox, or an old cardboard box with the flaps cut off. If you have a three-hole punch handy, you can even store them in a three-ring binder. Whatever you decide, go through your menus first and get rid of any duplicates. Also throw away any menus that serve similar food to a restaurant you order from regularly— once you find your favorite Chinese joint in the area, you're unlikely to order from the mediocre one the next neighborhood over. Make sure to tell your family where your menus now reside, and the next time someone says, "Time for take-out," dinner really will be a breeze.

....

Glue one side of a sturdy clothespin to the inside of cabinet doors, the front of your washing machine, and elsewhere around your home. Hanging clothespins are great for holding plastic shopping bags, and plastic shopping bags are great for holding trash, clean rags, cleaning supplies, and more.

—Katie N., Philadelphia, PA

Magnetic strips made to hold knives in your kitchen are useful in many other ways as well. Use them to hold keys, nail clippers and other bathroom must-haves, office supplies, even family photos with a magnet.

CORDS

Don't throw away empty toilet paper or paper towel rolls! Use them to store the millions of cords running behind your entertainment center. The rolls keep the cords untangled, and if you also write which appliances the cords belong to on the roll, you just might be the most organized person in your neighborhood.

If the cables in your office are a tangled mess of computer, printer, and internet cords, keep them tidy by running them through an old, coiled telephone cord. The coils will keep everything together neatly.

From blow-dryers to blenders to electric shavers, most small electrical appliances have cords that can get a little unwieldy. Keep them neat and out of the way with ponytail holders or rubber bands, or fold up detachable cords and store them in paper towel tubes. This works well for storing Christmas tree lights, too.

DRAWERS

Is your dresser drawer starting to look like someone ransacked it? Egg cartons and plastic ice cube trays make great organizational tools for jewelry, cuff links, and other trinkets, and they'll easily fit inside your drawer.

It's true: even your junk drawer needs organizing. Make it simple by using baby food jars. They're perfect for storing screws, rubber bands, thumbtacks, matches, sugar packets, loose change, and anything else that finds its way inside.

If your bathroom drawers are a jumbled mess, invest in an inexpensive plastic silverware tray. It's a great way to organize the little things you've got rattling around in there.

A nonskid rug pad is a terrific liner for your kitchen or office drawers. The tacky surface prevents utensils, paper clips, thumbtacks—anything!—from slipping around.

Keep bureau drawers under control by using shoeboxes to separate underwear, socks, tights, and whatever else gets quickly stuffed in there when company comes.

LINENS

Our closets are kind of a mess, but we manage never to misplace part of a sheet set. That's because after washing and folding the pieces, we put the whole set right inside one of the pillowcases, which is a convenient way to make sure everything stays in one place.

....

Easily keep your cloth napkins and other matching linens together when you store them by using binder clips to keep like kinds together. You'll never have to dig through the closet looking for a lost place setting again.

....

Clean laundry loses its fresh scent quickly when sitting in stuffy drawers and closets. To keep your clothes, lingerie, and linens smelling freshly washed all the time, place fabric softener sheets in your dresser drawers.

MAIL

With such a busy family, it's hard to control the clutter in our house. So we try to prevent the clutter before it starts: We keep a small, inconspicuous trashcan near our usual mail-opening spot. That way, we can easily toss junk mail into the garbage without setting it on a table.

....

Sick of getting a million credit card offers every time you open your mail box? You can opt out for free by calling 1-888-567-8688 or by visiting OptOutPrescreen. com. Signing up will eliminate all of those "pre-approved" offers from taking up space in your mailbox and your trashcan. While you're at it, visit DMAChoice.org to remove yourself from even more companies' mailing lists.

....

If you're like us, you receive free address labels in the mail from time to time. Put them to good use by labeling notebooks, items your kids take to school or camp, and anything else you'd like to personalize.

PLASTIC BAGS

Instead of trashing cardboard tubes from paper towels or toilet paper, create a cozy storage container for all those plastic grocery bags. Stuff the plastic bags inside, one by one, until the tubes are full. Then you can tie several tubes together with a rubber band and store them in a drawer or on a closet shelf.

....

An empty tissue box is great for holding plastic shopping bags that are waiting for their chance at a second life. As you place each bag in the box, make sure its handles are poking up through the hole. Then thread each new bag through the previous bag's handles. That way, when you pull a bag out of the box, the next one will pop right up.

....

Move your bed sheets and linens from the hallway linen closet to a top shelf in your bedroom closet. That way, they'll be closer to where they're actually used, and if you fold them properly, they won't take up much room. The major bonus? You've now freed up a valuable hallway closet to store something else.

If your living room sofa has a skirt that reaches the floor, you have storage space you didn't even know about. The space underneath the sofa is a great place to store a bin of wrapping paper and accessories, old photo albums, and other skinny items you reach for often.

Here's a quick and ingenious way to make a cover that will hide objects underneath the sink or a small table. Take an old pillowcase or two and cut through the seams on the top, bottom, and unopened side. Then run a ribbon or piece of elastic through the hemmed portion on the end where you formerly would have stuffed a pillow. Wrap the ribbon around the tabletop or the base of the sink—you may need to string more than one pillowcase on to get full coverage. Tack or tape the string to the wall or the back of the table, then stuff all your power cords, cleaning supplies, or anything else you want out-of-sight underneath!

You're in desperate need of more closet space, but you can't afford a fancy armoire. Here's what to do: Find two old doors at a yard sale or scrap yard. Paint or decorate them how you please, then hinge them together. Place the doors in the corner of the room at a 90-degree angle to each other so that you make a "box." Use one as the door of your new closet, and the other to hang shelves and attach a bar to. (Drill into the wall or bolt to the floor for more stability—just don't tell your landlord we put you up to it!) Suspend a clothesline between them for additional hanging. It may not be fancy, but we bet your friends will be impressed!

STORAGE

Don't discard that partitioned wine or liquor carton! Instead, cut the top off and keep it in the garage for storage of sporting goods, fishing poles, and other sundries.

Instead of throwing away the boxes that powdered laundry detergent comes in, we keep them to store household items. We have one in the garage for tools, one for my wife's sewing supplies, and we also give them to the kids for toys. They're perfect because they're easy to carry and lined with water-proof wax. Just make sure to rinse them out first!

—*Eggbert Joliet, Toronto, ON*

Use an old egg carton to sort small items like nails, screws, and nuts. It can even be used for earrings!

....

The containers to Tic Tacs and other breath mints are perfect for storing tiny items like pins, needles, buttons, beads, and nails. Plus, they'll still smell minty fresh when you open them!

....

Clear plastic storage bins may be God's gift to organization. If you feel like your house is constantly cluttered, go to your nearest organizational store, superstore, or even dollar store, and stock up immediately. But before you go, take a look around your house to find empty areas for some covert storage. Buy long, flat bins for under the couch and you can store board games, video games, and DVDs. Buy tall, stackable ones for keeping items in a closet. And buy whatever fits best under your bed to maximize this perfect space for storing off-season clothes. Make sure to keep at least one in easy reach—we have one that's simply for all the *stuff* we find in our living room that needs to be put back elsewhere in the house.

....

One of our favorite organizational tools is a hanging shoe organizer. These canvas contraptions are made to allow you to store your shoes on the back of a door, but their individualized compartments make them perfect for storing anything. Keep one in the bathroom for bobby pins, make-up, and lotion; one in your kitchen for spices; and one in the TV room for rarely used remotes and video game controllers. We also keep one in each of our children's rooms, so that when we yell, "Clean up your room!" they have a handy place to stow toy cars, action figures, and the million other little things that find their way onto their floors.

The school year is over, and you need a place to store the kids' artwork and diplomas. Try rolling them tightly in paper towel tubes so they won't crease, then label the outside, so you know what's what. The tubes can also be used to store marriage certificates and other important documents.

Batteries will last longer if they're stored in the refrigerator. To boost their energy, place them in the sun for a day before you use them.

VALUABLES

Instead of leaving your valuables in obvious where burglars can find them, like a jewelry box, here's an ingenious hiding place: Wash out an old mayonnaise jar and paint the inside of it white. Let the paint dry and then place your money, jewelry, and other items inside. Store it in the back of your fridge, and it'll still be there even if you're burglarized.

Keep your valuables from burglars without buying a safe. Simply keep them somewhere where they would never find them. One great idea is to buy a container of tennis balls, then cut a slice in one or two of the balls. Store your jewelry or other valuables inside the hollow space and they'll never be found!

>> Coupons

Looking for tips for Organizing Your Coupons? *See* **Shopping chapter, Coupons**

>> Kitchen

CABINETS

Avoid slamming kitchen cabinets by putting homemade silencers on them. Just save the cork from your next bottle of wine, slice it into skinny pieces, and glue them onto each inside corner of your cabinet. Problem solved!

....

Are plastic lids taking over your kitchen? We feel your pain and can offer a solution: Store a dish drainer in your cabinet, and file the lids on their sides in size order. You'll find the lid you need in seconds, and your kitchen will be much more organized.

....

Forget buying one more specialty-organizing device and instead use the time to actually organize. A dish rack or V-rack (meant for roasting) both make great devices for sorting pan lids in the cabinet. Act now and do away with banging and rummaging for good. Simply reach for the lid you need!

....

Stacking fine china? Insert paper plates between the real plates before stacking to prevent scratches.

....

To prevent glasses from becoming dusty, place them upside down on shelves. Arrange in order of size so they are easier to find and also to avoid breakages.

COUNTERS

When you're preparing a big meal and need more counter space, try this clever quick fix: Simply open a drawer in your kitchen and cover it with a heavy-duty cutting board. Voilà! Just don't keep anything too heavy or put pressure on it.

....

Consider keeping a clean powder puff in your flour container. It's a great way to dust flour onto rolling pins or pastry boards. And remember, always store your flour in the freezer to prevent any sort of bug infestation.

....

Put all those vases you get with flower bouquets to good use. Use them on your kitchen counter to store gadgets, large utensils, or anything else that is clogging up your drawers.

....

Under-the-shelf cup holders are a clever, super-efficient way to save space in your kitchen. You can buy a slip-on cup holder for less than $10, no tools required. You'll save tons of shelf space for plates and bowls, while your cups, mugs, glasses, and cooking utensils stay out of the way.

....

A great tip if you've ever said, "Where's my ring?": Screw a small hook into the wall near your kitchen sink. It will make a handy place to store your rings while you're doing the dishes.

—*Tawnya Crawford*

....

The switch for our garbage disposal is right next to the one for an overhead light, and I used to always flick the disposal switch when I just wanted more light in the room. It's bad for the disposal to run without any water running, not to mention the fact it would always startle me half to death! To get rid of this problem, I finally found a very simple solution. I put a dot of red nail polish on the disposal switch. No more accidental grinding!

—*June Panella, Phoenix, AZ*

....

Make cooking a little more like a kindergarten paint session to save yourself some time! Just keep a jar with warm soapy water on your counter and place whatever knife or other utensil you're working with in it when you're done with that part of the recipe. When you need it again, you don't have to stop what you're doing to wash it. A quick rinse will do. Then again, one of us (not naming names) saves time by just reusing dirty utensils for the rest of the night.

PANTRIES

Keep packets of sauces and gravies in one easy-to-manage spot in your pantry—we suggest using an empty child's shoebox! Stand the envelopes upright in the box, so the labels are easy to read, and the shoebox should fit perfectly on a shelf in your pantry.

Save cabinet space by reusing an empty six-pack container to store aluminum foil, plastic wrap, waxed paper, and other boxes of wrap on your counter. A magazine holder is also great for the less-slender boxes of plastic bags.

REFRIGERATORS AND FREEZERS

If your kids are like ours, they tend to grab whatever snacks are most easily accessible in the fridge. We've solved that problem and encouraged healthier eating by keeping a sandwich basket right in front, containing all the ingredients necessary for a quick meal—deli meats, cheese, condiments, and so on.

Keep plastic wrap from clinging to itself when you're trying to dispense it by storing it in the refrigerator. The colder temperature will keep it from sticking.

If your ice cube trays stick to the bottom of the shelf, try placing a piece of waxed paper underneath the tray. Freezing temperatures do not affect waxed paper.

....

Store your rolling pin in the freezer. It's much easier to roll out pastry dough and piecrusts with a frozen rolling pin.

» Office

MEMENTOS

If you discover a couple of photos stuck together, don't lose hope! They can be unstuck. Place them in the freezer for half an hour, then gently pry them apart with a butter knife. You can also slowly unstick them with a hairdryer set on low.

....

If your photographs are stuck to each other or to a glass frame, the solution is steam. Use a steamer, a steam iron set on its highest setting, or a pan of boiling water to get steam as close as you can between the photo and whatever its stuck to (being careful not to burn yourself). As the photo gets warmer and wetter, it should become easy to peel away. Lay out to dry, then flatten with a fat book if it has curled.

....

To preserve special newspaper clippings, dissolve a Milk of Magnesia tablet in a shallow pan with a quart of club soda. Soak the paper for an hour, then let it lay flat to dry. Afterward, it's best to keep the paper under plastic in a photo album.

PASSWORDS AND PINS

Here's a question we often get asked: "Where's a safe place to keep PINs for bank and credit cards?" The answer isn't so much *where* as *how*: hide them inside a fake phone number. For example, if your PIN is 1234 (and hopefully, it isn't!), scribble 347-1234 on the inside of your day planner or somewhere else accessible. Would-be thieves won't know it's the number they're looking for.

In these modern times, everyone is registered for more websites than they can count, making it next to impossible to remember all of one's usernames and passwords. Instead of forgetting these all the time, just create a computer document listing all your logins and passwords, and place it on your desktop. Whenever you sign up for a new site, it'll take about 10 seconds to add the new login to the document.

> If you can never remember your computer passwords, consider trying out RoboForm.com. This neat site keeps track of your passwords on one encrypted site, then enters them when you're at sites that require passwords.

SUPPLIES, SAVING ON

For a pocket folder you know is going to take a beating—like the one we keep near our tool kit that holds instructions—reinforce it on the sides and pockets with duct tape. It will last forever!

....

Worried about identity theft, but can't afford a proper paper shredder? This tip is not for the weak of heart, but it is for the thrifty: Use your washing machine instead! Put the papers in a stocking, tie the end, and throw them in for a wash. By the time the cycle is over, the ink will be bleeding, the papers a shredded mess, and your secrets safe from anyone picking through the trash.

....

Always store stamp pads upside down. This will ensure that they don't dry out in between uses.

....

Here's a trick used by office workers everywhere: When your printer's out of ink, remove the cartridge and shake it up for a bit. Stick it back into the printer, and you'll find it's got enough ink left for at least a few more print jobs.

....

Need to print out some helpful but not super-important pages (such as a grocery, chore, or to-do list)? You can conserve ink by changing the font color to gray rather than using the heavier black ink. Or simply choose a thinner font. Thinner fonts like Times and Century Gothic will use up to 30 percent less ink than Arial.

WORKSPACE

If your desk seems cluttered, make sure you're taking advantage of the space above it. Install a shelf or two for books and folders, and make sure to attach some hooks on their undersides. Hang small baskets on the hooks and now you have a hiding place for paperclips, pens, glue sticks, tape, and the hundred other things that are taking up room in your office space.

If you're getting rid of a computer, make sure to keep the speakers if they are detachable. Plug them into a portable CD or mp3 player, and you have an inexpensive stereo for your kitchen, bathroom, or workspace!

—*Christopher James*

A Rolodex is so old school, but not if you use it in a new way. How many gift cards or store credits expire before you use them? What about those self-multiplying rewards cards? They slide all over the place in your wallet, always out of sight when you make a purchase. Organize them into a Rolodex so you'll never leave home without the right one again.

Cereal boxes make great stacking trays for your home office. Carefully cut off the top and back of the box, and you have an inbox waiting to happen. If you don't like the Total, Wheaties, and Chex look, spray the boxes with silver spray paint and let dry before using.

—*David Dean, Fairbanks, AK*

» On-the-Go

ACCESSORIES

Old mittens make great glasses cases! You can also use them during their "off-season" to hold summer sunglasses.

Need a cover to store your wet umbrella while you're on the go? Look no further than the end of your driveway. The plastic bags newspapers come in are waterproof and the perfect size.

Looking for a container to store iPod earbud headphones where they won't get tangled? Coil the cord and then place it inside an old cassette case. Your headphones will be safe, and your friends can admire the *Flashdance* soundtrack decoration on the outside. So retro!

AUTO

Turn your car's visor into a handy place to store paper and other flat items by using rubber bands. Wrap several rubber bands snugly around the visor, then slip papers, CDs, or anything else under the rubber bands.

Sick of things rattling around your truck bed?
Divide it into several compartments for storage by using spring-loaded shower curtain rods. Brace the rods against the sides of your truck bed and each other. They'll keep larger items from shifting during flight.

....

When it comes to organizing your car, don't forget about all the paper that ends up in there—registration and insurance info as well as maps, scribbled directions, and more. We like to keep a small accordion file in our glove compartment to prevent those moments where we're on our hands and knees looking under the seats.

MAKE-UP

If your eyeliner or lip pencils are too long for your make-up case, break them in half to form two smaller pencils and sharpen them both. You'll not only save space, but you'll have a backup if one pencil goes missing.

....

You're headed out for a night on the town with that fantastic new clutch you found, but once you shove your cell phone, wallet, and keys in there you barely have room for your lipstick. So what do you do with the powder compact you were counting on for touch-ups? Simply take some of those pieces of pressed powder that inevitably break off of the mass and keep them in a tissue. When it's time to refresh, rub the tissue across your face.

PURSE AND WALLET

Who needs money clips when you have binder clips? They work just as well for keeping your money and cards together, and they cost a fraction of the price. You might even have some lying around the house already. They're also great for fastening your keys to your belt or waistband if you don't have pockets!

....

You'll never fumble with the wrong key again if you color-code them with a dot of nail polish. Just apply a thick coat of a different shade to the top of each key.

....

For the perfect container for keeping medicine with you in your purse or pocket, try a contact lens case. Since it comes with two handy sections, it's easy to store different pills in different compartments and label them, if necessary.

....

When you receive new checks in the mail, don't throw away the plastic cover that often comes with them. Instead, use it as an organizational tool to store receipts, itineraries, or other papers that find their way into your purse or wallet.

....

Don't have time to eat anything but a breakfast bar in the morning? Store it in a glasses case to make sure it doesn't get smashed in your purse or bag on the way to work.

Auto

Baking

Beauty

Cleaning

Clothing and Accessories

Cooking

Decorating

Entertaining and Holidays

Health and Wellness

Home Repair

Kids

Money

Organization

》》

Outdoors

Pest Control

Pets

Shopping

Utilities

Vacations and Family Activities

Websites

» Camping and Fishing

Looking for tips on Camping and Fishing? *See* **Vacations and Family Activities chapter, Camping and Fishing**

» Gardening

FERTILIZERS

If you've been putting off having a compost pile because of the hassle of always having to traipse to the other side of the yard, simply keep scraps in your freezer until you're ready to compost. Banana peels, apple cores, egg shells, coffee grinds, and other scraps can all go right into a plastic container.

....

Mix dried banana peels in with the soil next time you plant something new; you'll give it the potassium and phosphorous it needs to grow beautifully.

....

Fertilize your garden for free by planting clover; it will help repair the soil while also providing a nice green carpeting.

....

As you may know, bonemeal is an excellent source of nutrients for your plants. But instead of spending $8–$10 on a bag at your local gardening store, make your own! Bonemeal is just bones, after all. Save bones from chicken, turkey, steaks, and stews, then dry them out by roasting them in a 425°F oven for a half an hour or microwaving them on high for 1–6 minutes (depending on how many bones you have). Then place them in a plastic or paper bag and grind them up by hitting them with a hammer, then rolling them with a rolling pin. Mix the resulting powder into your soil for a life-producing treat for your plants. And you didn't spend a cent!

The best thing you can give your carrot seeds is also what keeps you going during the day—coffee! Mix carrot seeds with coffee grounds before you plant them. Having some extra bulk to plant will ensure they don't end up all lumped together, and the coffee will provide your growing plants with much-needed nutrients.

Banana skins and eggshells are excellent natural fertilizers, and the minerals they provide are not readily found in many synthetic fertilizers. Flat club soda is another great option for your garden: To perk up colors, give your plants an occasional sip or two.

Who knew geraniums love potatoes? They contain all the nutrients a growing geranium plant needs and can also make it easier for you to transplant these beautiful flowers. Simply carve out a hole in a raw potato using the end of a vegetable peeler, insert the stem of a geranium, and plant the entire thing in its new pot or in your garden.

Lilacs hate grass. More specifically, they must compete with grass and any other vegetation for food and water. To help your lilacs flower beautifully, keep a 16- to 24-inch circle around the base free from grass. Lime and manure are great fertilizers for lilacs.

If you've got pansies in your garden, take the time to pinch out the early buds. It encourages the flowers to grow, and you'll ultimately get more blossoms this way.

This advice definitely sounds like an urban legend, but it's such an easy way to grow fantastic sweet peppers that you have to try it. A matchbook buried with each pepper plant will transmit sulfur, a great fertilizer for them. In addition, to give these nutrient-seeking plants the magnesium they need, add 2 tablespoons Epsom salts to ½ gallon water and soak the plants with the mixture when you see the first blossoms of the year.

Want to give your roses an extra dose of fuel? A small amount of fat drippings placed at the base of a rose bush will keep it healthier and make it bloom more frequently.

Did you know that eggshells help rose bushes grow? The nutrients contained in the shells are a great benefit, especially if you crush up them up and deposit them under the surface of the soil, near the bush's roots. The same applies to water that you've used to boil eggs in—when you're finished cooking, just dump the cooled, nutrient-enriched water on your rosebush.

HOUSEPLANTS

Looking for Houseplant tips? *See* **Decorating chapter, Houseplants**

PESTS

Looking to Control Pests? *See* **Pest Control chapter, Outdoors**

PLANTING

If you've never had a vegetable garden, now is the time to start! Here's how: In the fall, decide where you'd like your garden to be and mow away the grass. Then cover the area with several layers of newspaper. Add as much mulch and leaves as you can to the top (aim for five inches), then get the entire area wet with a hose. By the time spring rolls around, the area will be grass-free and primed for planting.

At PlantNative.org, you can find lists of flowers, shrubs, trees, vines, and grasses that are native to your area. This means they'll not only be less expensive to buy, they'll also hold up well in your garden.

Be bold when planting flowers in sunny spots.
Pastel-colored flowers can look washed out in bright sunlight, so try red and orange flowers when planting in full sun.

What's black and white and warm all over?
If you're a seed, the answer is newspaper. Seeds need warmth, but not light, to germinate, so if you place newspaper (black and white only) over a newly sown area, it will keep the seeds warm and block out the light.

When you plant seeds, you want to make sure you bury them at the correct depth. Save time and energy by marking 1-inch measurements on the handles of your tools instead of using a ruler.

Not sure which seed you planted where? Write the name of the plant on a plastic knife and shove it into the ground nearby.

PLANT PROBLEMS

If your garden is infected with fungus, mix one piece of ground-up aspirin with a quart of water and use it to water your plants once a week. (Be careful, as too much aspirin can damage your plants.)

....

Here's an old treatment to prevent plants from suffering from mildew or black spots. Mix together ½ tablespoon baking soda with a drop of vegetable oil and 2 cups soapy water. Spray on both sides of the leaves of plants that are affected. Complete this treatment in the evening and never in full sunlight; otherwise the leaves may scorch. While the soap helps to spread the mixture and the vegetable oil causes it to stick, the baking soda makes the surfaces of the leaves alkaline, which will inhibit the fungal spores. The biggest advantage of this method is that there will be no adverse environmental impact, thanks to the all-natural ingredients.

....

This may sound like a cure from the Middle Ages, but garlic does a fine job of reviving diseased plants. Grate 2 cloves into 4 cups water and use as much as you need to quench the thirst of your struggling plants. Given the myriad health benefits garlic offers to humans, it's not surprising it can help the immobile organisms that share your home (and we don't mean your spouse and kids).

....

A broken stem doesn't have to mean the end of a flower. If you catch it in time, you can save the limb by making a little splint out of a toothpick and tape. It looks a little funny, but your kids will get a kick out of it, and it makes a great lesson in resilience.

....

If you have smaller outdoor plants, you don't necessarily need to bring them inside to keep them protected from frost. Simply cover them at night with small plastic garbage bags (the kind that have pull handles), and tie the handles snugly around the pots. Don't forget to remove the bags in the morning, though, so the plants can soak up the sun.

RIPENING

There's a frost predicted for tonight, and you have several unripened tomatoes on the vine. Don't risk them getting bitten by frost. Instead, pick them now and bring them inside. Wrap them inside a paper bag or in newspaper, place the bag in an airtight container, and put the container in a dark area like a cabinet or closet. Check back in a few days, and they'll be just-off-the-vine ripe.

....

If the end of the growing season is nigh, and you'd like your tomatoes to ripen on the vine more quickly, there are a few things you can try. Remove damaged, dead, or diseased leaves, and cut off all new flowers. Keep a daily eye on the tomatoes, and pick them as soon as they're ripe, so the plant can devote its effort to ripening the rest of the fruit. Harvest the tomatoes when they're red, but still firm. Believe it or not, watering the plant less will ripen the tomatoes more quickly!

SEEDS

Don't buy cardboard "seed starters" from your garden store. Instead, use a cardboard egg carton, or toilet paper and paper towel tubes. The tubes will need to be cut in halves or fourths, then placed on a tray, while the egg carton can be used as is. Put a little soil in each, place in a warm, moist area (it doesn't even need to get any light), and wait for your seeds to sprout with some regular watering.

....

If you have old seeds that may or may not be ripe for planting, test them out first: Pour a handful onto a moist napkin or paper towel, and cover with plastic wrap. Wait until the germination time has passed (check the wrapper for the correct time), and take a look at your seeds. If some are growing, the seeds are usable—just plant them deeply.

....

Save orange and grapefruit halves for use in your garden. They make great containers for starting seeds. Just fill them with soil and seeds, and plant them. After the seeds germinate, the holders will decompose, leaving nutrients in the ground.

....

Here's an inventive seed-starter: a sponge. Place a few seeds in the crevices of a wet sponge, and wait for them to sprout! Not only will it keep the seeds nice and moist, you can then plant the entire sponge in your garden.

....

Eggshells are a great fertilizer for seedlings. Get a head start on your garden by first sowing seeds indoors in clean eggshell halves. Let them grow in an egg container, and when it's time to transplant them outdoors, just dig a hole for the shells.

....

Got an unwearable pair of nylons? Don't trash 'em yet! Nylon stockings or panty hose make excellent storage containers for plant bulbs. Air is able to circulate, which helps prevent mold. Store in a cool, dry location.

TRANSPLANTING

When transplanting, always use lightly moistened soil and peat moss to help retain moisture in the roots. If the soil is dry, it won't hold together well during the transplant, which might result in a messy move at best and a plant casualty at worst.

WATERING

Good for you for remembering to water your garden! Just make sure you're not overdoing it. Here's a simple test. When you're finished with the hose, dig down half a foot or so and feel the soil. Moist is fine, but muddy means you should use a lighter hand.

....

If you live in a hard water area, add 1 cup vinegar to 1 gallon water, then use it to water plants that love acidic soil, such as rhododendrons, heather, and azaleas. The vinegar will release iron in the soil for the plants to use.

....

When watering your garden with a hose, take care not to drag the hose over your plants. Place a few short, heavy stakes in your garden to create an alleyway for the hose, restraining it from rolling around and distressing the delicate plants. If you don't have stakes, simply cut a wire hanger into six-inch pieces, bend them into arches, and use them to guide your hose.

....

Is your hose full of holes? If you have an old hose you're no longer able to use (or an extra one lying around) repurpose it as a soaker hose. It's easy: Just poke holes along its length with a straight pen, then place in your garden to slowly water your plants.

WEEDING

Weeding is easier when the plants are wet. Save this dull task for post-rain or watering. When you give a yank, it will be easier to get the whole plant out at the root.

Here's the most inventive weed-prevention technique we've heard: Wet newspapers and layer them around the plants (then cover with dirt and mulch so your yard doesn't look like a trash heap).

If you had a hammer, you wouldn't have so many weeds. Kneel down, turn the hammer backward, and bang it onto the soil to catch the weed between the claw. Now just pull. Yes it *is* okay to hammer when you're in a bad mood. As long as you can check something off your to-do list while you are at it.

When it comes to poison ivy, an ounce of prevention really is worth a pound of cure. So if you've got a patch of this pernicious vine on your property, kill it. Mix ½ gallon soapy water with a 1½ pounds salt, spray the plant, and run in the other direction.

In our family, we're never all ready to go at the same time. Since we love to garden, we keep a few pairs of garden gloves by the door so the early birds can pull out a few weeds. It prevents having to take the time to pull the weeds later!

You've just weeded your entire yard, put new edging along your flower beds, and trimmed your bushes. Now what do you do with all that garbage? Check with your town to see if they collect yard waste to turn into compost. Many municipalities will even come pick it up for you.

» Lawn

FERTILIZING

Did you know you can actually have a lazy lawn? If you feed your lawn too much, the roots won't need to reach down to find food. When it's hot, they'll dry out right away. The trick is to feed it once a year—in spring or fall. When roots aren't pampered, they'll grow deeper and become stronger. Just like people.

Epsom salts are one of the best natural lawn fertilizers around. They're composed of magnesium and sulfur, both of which are highly beneficial to grass. Magnesium kick-starts seed germination and is also a player in manufacturing chlorophyll, the substance that plants create from sunlight in order to feed themselves. Sulfur, meanwhile, also helps with chlorophyll, while simultaneously enhancing the effects of other fertilizer ingredients such as nitrogen, phosphorus, and potassium. It also deters certain pests such as ground worms. With all these benefits, it's no wonder that savvy lawn care specialists have been using Epsom salts for years. You can either sprinkle them on your lawn using a spreader or make a liquid solution out of them by adding some water and putting the mixture in a spray bottle.

You may not have time to build a compost bin (or the stomach for a bucket full of worms), but you can easily crush shells from last night's seafood dinner and scatter them over your lawn. The calcium helps the grass grow.

MOWING

The rain stopped just in time for your outdoor party, but not in enough time for the grass to dry before you want to mow it. To solve this problem, simply spray the blades of your lawnmower with vegetable oil or non-stick cooking spray, and the grass won't stick!

Try to keep your lawn about 3 inches high. The higher the grass, the less direct sunlight is available for pesky weeds to grow.

Don't worry about collecting clippings when you mow your lawn. It's a waste of landfill space, and you'll deprive your lawn of nutrients it can use through natural composting. Instead, take off the bag and leave the clippings in the grass. You'll be surprised how quickly they work their way between the blades and disappear.

If your grass turns brown after mowing, either you've cut it too short, or the lawn mower blades are dull. Dull blades tear up the grass instead of clipping it cleanly. It may be time for a new mower.

....

Save yourself the boring task of poking holes in your soil to aerate it. Instead multitask the easy way by wearing spiked golf shoes or soccer cleats to aerate while you mow your lawn.

....

Do you have a long extension cord you use with your electric mower, weed-whacker, or power washer? Keep it from getting tangled and running all over your garden's plants with a big bucket. Drill a hole in the bottom of the bucket and run the end of the cord through it. Then coil the rest of the cord inside. The cord will easily pull out and then coil back up when you're finished.

SEEDING

If a scarecrow doesn't work to keep birds from feasting on your grass seeds, try this modern-day equivalent before you resort to netting. Place stakes at the four corners of the area you want to protect. Now cut two pieces of string, long enough to reach diagonally in an X across the lawn. Every foot or two along the strings you'll want to tie one-inch strips of aluminum foil. The breeze will keep the aluminum pieces flapping about and scaring off would-be invaders.

....

Patches of dirt in your yard where grass refuses to sprout? Try planting morning glory, winter creeper, or lily of the valley. By forcing a perfectly green lawn, you waste water and miss out on a chance to do something a little more creative. These plants also work well in hard-to-mow areas.

TOOLS

To clean digging tools easily, invest in a barbecue brush with a scraper attachment. Use the scraper to remove layers of mud from the tool as you dig, and use the brush to brush off the dried dirt before you put the tool away.

....

Don't just toss your garden tools in a bin or bucket when you're done with them; they'll eventually rust. To prevent this, submerge the metal parts in a bucket of sand whenever the tools are not in use. (Better yet, add some mineral oil to the sand.) Make sure the sand is stored in a dry place where rainwater can't get into it, though. If you decide you don't want to store your tools in sand, then a good thing to do is to toss a handful of tea leaves in whatever container you keep them in. For whatever reason, the leaves will help keep the metal nice, new, and rust-free.

....

Use a solution of bleach and water to disinfect pruning sheers after you're done so you don't spread diseases between plants. Rinse with tepid water until the bleach is gone.

....

Care for wooden garden tools as you would your skin—moisturize! Over time, wood dries out and splinters. Apply a thin coat of linseed oil to wooden handles on rakes and shovels; it'll keep them safe and usable. A little goes a long way, so use the oil sparingly.

Take care when pruning your roses and other thorny plants in the garden—you don't want to prick your fingers. Try holding the branches with a pair of kitchen tongs while you snip.

Your garden hose will last twice as long if you store it coiled, rather than folded. Try coiling it around a bucket. Note that the hose will be easiest to work with when it's neither very cold nor very hot outside.

Our hose hook-up is on the side of our house, and unfortunately, we had our hose stolen twice! We were forced to keep rolling it up and putting it in our garage until a neighbor mentioned why she thought her hose had been spared—it was full of holes that had been repaired by duct tape. We slapped some duct tape on our hole-free hose, and it hasn't been stolen since.

—*Janice K. Smith, AZ*

When you're raking leaves, nothing is more frustrating than a plastic trash bag that slips down into the garbage can. Rest easy, friends: All you need to do is secure the bag with a bungee cord (or two) and get to work. Fold the open end of the bag over the rim of the trashcan and wrap the cord around the outside to hold it in place.

....

Extra mouse pads can do a lot more than take up space in a desk drawer. Repurposed pads are perfect to use for kneeling in the garden. Their knee-saving properties can also be put to good use by kids who are playing outside with sidewalk chalk!

....

Gardening after a heavy rain? Plastic bags are a must-have! If it's too muddy for even your beater sneakers, keep those shoes clean by sticking plastic bags over them. Secure them with rubber bands, and you're ready to go to work. The plastic bags you put your produce in at the grocery store are perfect for makeshift gloves. Slip your hands inside and fasten around your wrists with rubber bands.

TREES

If you need to attach a tree to a stake or two to give it support, make sure you're attaching the ties in the right spot. Run your hand up the trunk, holding it tightly, and the spot where the top of the tree no longer bends over is the spot to place the ties.

....

If you still have old, unused cassette tapes laying around, pull out the film and use it to tie up any trees or plants that need to be held to stakes. Better yet, old panty hose also makes an effective tie: Just cut the nylons into narrow strips. It works better than plastic ties because the panty hose expands as the plant grows.

Pruning will be less of a chore if you keep your eye on the goal of a strong and healthy tree. If it's more of a motivator, though, remember you don't want to get sued if a weak branch falls on a neighbor. On pruning day, follow a simple plan: first get rid of any branches that are clearly dead, dying, or infested. Then home in on the ones that are too long, crisscrossing each other, or growing weak. Step back and admire your work.

Treating your fruit trees like they're bad will yield a good crop. Smack the trunks with a rolled-up newspaper to get the sap moving more efficiently through the branches, which, in turn, helps the tree produce more fruit. Think of it like a massage to increase blood flow. And be prepared for strange looks from passersby.

Instead of disposing of brush or using it in your fireplace, consider leaving a pile or two around your yard to provide shelter for birds and other wildlife.

WATERING

Early morning is the best time to water your lawn or garden because you'll minimize evaporation. The absolute worst time to do it is during the bright sun of the afternoon.

....

In most areas, only 1 inch of water a week is needed to keep your lawn green and healthy. To find out how long you need to run the sprinkler, mark a jar with a piece of masking tape or permanent marker at one inch and place it on your lawn. Start the sprinkler and see how long it takes before the water reaches the mark. Next time, skip the jar and just set the timer.

» Outdoor Areas

BIRDBATHS

There's a chemical in lavender that inhibits the growth of algae. Make a bundle of lavender flowers and daylily leaves for your birdbath to keep it free and clear. Change every few weeks.

....

Your birdbath used to be a hot spot for the feathered folk, but ever since it became slimy with algae, they've stayed away! Make your birdbath as fresh as new by emptying the water, then covering it with bleach-soaked paper towels or newspaper. After letting the paper sit for 5–10 minutes, remove it and rinse the bath thoroughly. Then fill it with fresh water and watch the birds enjoy.

....

Want to make your birdbath a hotspot for your feathered friends? Simply add some colorful marbles or pebbles to attract neighborhood birds. The brighter the color, the better!

Keep bugs away from a birdbath! Just a few drops of canola or vegetable oil will keep mosquitoes from laying eggs in the water in your birdbath, won't hurt the intended residents, and will save you from lots of itchy bites.

CONCRETE

If you have stains on paving stones or a concrete patio, sometimes the solution is simple. Try pouring hot water from several feet above the stone onto the stain. Repeat several times, and your stain may just disappear. If this doesn't work, try rubbing some dishwashing liquid into the spot with a toothbrush, then rinsing off. For really tough stains, add a bit of ammonia to the water.

If your driveway or garage floor has become an easy place to do some Rorschach testing thanks to the grease, oil, and transmission fluid stains all over the place, take heart—clean concrete is only 10 minutes away. Spray any stained areas with oven cleaner, then let sit for 10 minutes. Rinse off with a hose, and the stains will disappear.

Unsightly marks on sidewalks and patios are often caused by tar, gum, and pet urine. These can usually be removed with vinegar, so if you're having trouble removing a stain from concrete, try dousing it with vinegar and letting it sit for a day.

Cleaning oil spots off the driveway is difficult, and the cleaners can be quite expensive. Instead, sprinkle baking soda over the stains, then rub with a wet scrub brush soaked with hot water. The baking soda breaks apart oil particles, so with a little elbow grease, you can have your driveway looking new in no time.

Another way to remove a grease stain from your concrete driveway is to rub kitty litter into the stain and let it stand for one to two hours before sweeping it up. The super-absorbent litter will soak up the stain.

You can keep paved areas looking spiffy with this trick. To remove unwanted grass or weeds from sidewalk and driveway cracks, squirt them with a solution of 1 gallon vinegar, 1 cup salt, and 8 drops liquid detergent.

Want to get rid of the grass growing in the cracks of your sidewalk or patio? Make a mixture of salt and baking soda, sprinkle it into the cracks, and the problem should be solved.

If you have rust stains on your concrete, pour on a little cola and let it sit. By the next time it rains, the stains will be gone.

—Jess Holman, Syracuse, NY

IMPROVEMENT PROJECTS

Looking for Outdoor Home Improvement tips? See Home Repair, Outdoor Projects

OUTDOOR FURNITURE

Make sure your wicker furniture is front-porch ready for the spring and summer months. Blow-dry off the loose dirt, then clean with white vinegar and warm salt water, and apply a coat of lemon oil.

> To keep wicker from yellowing in the sun, bathe it in salt water with a wet rag when it's new.

If your white wicker deck furniture has turned a grimy brown, you have some work to do. But take heart, it isn't hard! First, vacuum up the freestanding dirt on the seat and arms. Then cover the whole piece with a mixture of 1 gallon warm water and 3 tablespoons ammonia. Scrub it with a brush to get between the fibers, then let it set in a shady area to dry.

We'll admit, we're often guilty of doing things the lazy way. The laziest way to clean plastic or resin patio furniture? Just toss it in the swimming pool before going to bed, and in the morning it'll be good as new. Meanwhile, your pool's filter will clean up the dirt.

If your wicker seems to scream every time you sit in it, it's become too dry. Take off any cushions and spray the wicker with a hose. The water will give it enough moisture to silence the squeaks.

Your porch's doormat can be cleaned with a sprinkling of baking soda. Brush vigorously and then sweep away the dirt. The next time it rains, the job will be complete.

POOLS

When pool liners tear, it can be very costly to repair them. But duct tape can do the job. Simply cover the tear, and keep an eye on it to make sure it doesn't start to peel off. Believe it or not, a single piece of duct tape can usually last underwater for an entire summer.

If there is too much chlorine in your pool, don't buy expensive treatments that will just have you balancing and counter-balancing chemicals for the rest of the summer. Simply don't put the cover on your pool for several days. The sun will naturally lower the chlorine content, and after a bit of evaporation, you can add more fresh water.

When alkalinity needs to be increased in your swimming pool or hot tub, baking soda can be added to restore a balance if there is too much chlorine.

Save money and electricity by running your pool pump and filter for the minimum amount of time necessary. Experiment by decreasing the amount of time you run it until you find where that point is. You should also set it for off-peak electricity times (morning and evening).

» Winter Weather

PATIO

Before the first freeze arrives, bring all your wicker furniture inside to protect it from the cold. Freezing will cause the wicker to crack and split, which unfortunately, is impossible to repair.

No space to bring outdoor furniture inside in bad weather? Instead of buying pricey furniture covers, protect lawn chairs and tables by covering them with large plastic bags.

Before it gets too cold, consider applying a thin layer of petroleum jelly to the threads of all your outdoor light bulbs. It will prevent them from rusting and make them easier to replace when they blow out.

SNOW AND ICE

Here's a tip that you Northerners will appreciate. Before going out to shovel snow, coat the blade of your snow shovel with cooking spray. That way the snow and ice will slide right off the shovel instead of sticking to it. This works on both plastic and metal shovels.

—*Marty Owens, Portland, ME*

Make your winter season safer by salting icy ground in the most effective way possible. Use a lawn seeder or fertilizer spreader to distribute salt or sand in a thin, even layer. And don't forget to watch your step!

Icy sidewalk? Throw cat litter down instead of rock salt. It won't harm your grass, stain your clothes, or hurt the environment, but it will provide plenty of traction for safe walking and driving.

Auto

Baking

Beauty

Cleaning

Clothing and Accessories

Cooking

Decorating

Entertaining and Holidays

Health and Wellness

Home Repair

Kids

Money

Organization

Outdoors

>> **Pest Control**

Pets

Shopping

Utilities

Vacations and Family Activities

Websites

» Bites and Stings

BITES

Chigger bites? Aspirin helps—but not in the way you might think. Make a thick paste by crushing several aspirin tablets and then mixing in a bit of water. Rub the paste on any bites, and it will ease the pain and itching.

Getting lots of mosquito bites can turn a fun evening into a harrowing one. Alleviate itching after the fact by applying a mixture of rubbing alcohol and hand soap to the bites. It will make them practically disappear.

If you've just come back from a long weekend camping, you'll love this tip. Use meat tenderizer to treat insect bites! Moisten a teaspoon of tenderizer with a little water and rub it immediately into the skin. Commercial meat tenderizers contain papain, an enzyme from papaya. Papain's protein-digestive properties will help decompose the insect venom.

A great way to stop mosquito bites from itching is with a dab of diluted ammonia. In fact, ammonia is the main ingredient in many of the itch-relief products currently on the market. Just mix four parts water for every one part ammonia. You can also use rubbing alcohol in place of the ammonia.

STINGS

When you're stung by a bee, carefully grasp the stinger and pull it out as fast as you can. The less venom that enters your body, the smaller and less painful the resulting welt will be. Ice the area immediately to reduce the swelling. If it still hurts, try cutting an onion in half and applying the fleshy side to the sting. It should help ease the pain.

Been stung by an insect? It's lavender oil to the rescue! Rub a bit directly onto the sting to alleviate the pain. Or, mix a paste of baking soda and water and apply.

Stung by a wasp? Apply apple cider vinegar to the area with a cotton ball and the sting will subside.

If you're stung by a wasp, hornet, or bee, reach for a lemon. Make sure the stinger is gone, and quickly rub the area with some lemon juice. It will neutralize the venom.

If your kids get stung at the hotel pool, run upstairs and grab your toothpaste. Toothpaste is a great remedy for stings because it neutralizes their venom. Just dab a bit on the affected area to feel relief.

» Indoors

ANTS

If you can figure out where ants are entering your house, you can keep them out. Simply sprinkle salt, cinnamon, chalk dust, or ashes on the their path of entry, and they'll turn around and go elsewhere.

Ants hate oranges, so blend orange peels with water, and pour the concoction wherever the little guys are bothering you. Some people also swear by hot chili peppers. Use whichever smell you prefer to have permeating your living space!

Get rid of carpenter ants naturally with this formula: Mix one packet dry yeast with ½ cup molasses and ½ cup sugar, and spread on a piece of cardboard. Leave this sticky trap wherever you see the ants; they will come in droves to the sweet smell. Unfortunately for them, they'll also get stuck. Wait until your molasses mixture is covered with the creepy pests, then throw away.

BEES

Swatting at bees is unnecessary (and never leads to anything good). Just turn out the light and open a window. The light from outside will attract them even more than your nice, juicy arm.

If a bee or other stinging insect gets trapped in the car with you, do *not* swat at it! Instead, pull your car off to the side of the road, open all the windows or doors, and let the critter fly out.

If bees or moths have found their way into your home, don't panic. Fill a wide-mouthed jar with 1 cup sugar and 1½ cups water. The wasps will be attracted to the sugar and will drown in the water trying to get to it.

CENTIPEDES

Borax works for repelling centipedes and millipedes. Sprinkle around areas where you've spotted them making a run for it. (Also works for the less offensive crickets.) Borax is an inexpensive cleaner than can be found at larger supermarkets, home stores, and discount retailers. Unfortunately, it isn't pet- or kid-safe, so sprinkle wisely.

COCKROACHES

Nothing is more revolting than roaches, except perhaps the chemicals we use to kill them. Try using this natural pesticide: Make a mixture of equal parts cornstarch and plaster of Paris, and sprinkle it in the cracks where roaches appear. If you're lucky, they'll be a thing of the past.

To get rid of roaches, chop up cucumber skins and bay leaves, mix together, and spread around the areas that have been invaded. The hideous creatures will steer clear, meaning you don't have to do the dirty work of throwing the dead ones out as you do with traditional traps (one of our least-favorite chores).

To repel roaches, make a "tea" with catnip by submerging the leaves in hot water and straining them. Then spray the solution in your kitchen, bathroom, and other areas where roaches like to stray. Repeat every time you mop or vacuum to permanently keep cockroaches away.

—*Anna Boudinot, Los Angeles, CA*

Another great method for eliminating cockroaches is to fill a large bowl with cheap wine, then place it under the sink or wherever you see the revolting little bugs. The pests drink the wine, get drunk, and drown.

If you've tried every other solution, and those pesky roaches still want to call your house home, it's time to make roach balls. Here's how: Combine 2 cups borax, ½ cup sugar, ½ cup chopped onion, 2 tablespoons cornstarch, and 2 tablespoons water in a bowl, then roll into small balls. Place three balls into an unsealed sandwich bag and place the bags wherever your roach problem exists. Remember, though, that the roach balls are poisonous; be sure to place them where kids and pets can't reach them.

FLEAS

Fleas can be eliminated from upholstery and carpets by vacuuming with a high-powered vacuum cleaner (ideally with a canister) with a bag that seals well. Remove the bag and dispose of it outside as soon as you finish.

....

You can remove pesky fleas from your pet's coat without having to pay for expensive flea collars or medications. Simply bathe your pet in salt water, and the fleas will stay away. You can also try steeping rosemary in warm water and using that as bathwater. Better yet, use a combination of the two.

....

To ward off fleas from a pet's sleeping area, try sprinkling a few drops of lavender oil in the area. Fleas hate the smell of lavender oil and will find somewhere else to hide. Your pet, meanwhile, can enjoy a good night's sleep—and smell great in the morning.

FLIES

If you don't keep trashcans and compactors sealed tight, you can end up with a swarm of flies, pronto. Luckily, flies, like fleas, are repelled by lavender oil. Soak a few cotton balls with the oil and toss them into your garbage at the beginning of each week. The flies will stay away and your garbage won't smell as bad! Other natural repellents that will send flies in the other direction include clove oil and wintergreen mint sprigs.

....

If you prefer not to use chemicals to get rid of flies, and you're not the most accurate fly swatter, invest in a strong fan. Scientists say that flies' wings are unable to operate in a breeze above nine m.p.h, so open the windows, turn the fan to full power, and they'll soon buzz off. This is also a great trick for an outdoor party—just aim a few fans at the center of the action instead of spraying down your yard with awful-smelling repellent.

The easiest way to get rid of fruit flies is to limit their access to their favorite foods. Let your fresh fruit ripen in closed paper bags. Then, after they ripen, store them in the refrigerator.

Fruit flies are always a pain, because they usually hover around fruit baskets and other areas you don't want to spray poisonous bug spray. Instead, spray a little rubbing alcohol on them. They'll fall to the floor and you can scoop them up and throw them away.

To get rid of crickets or other critters, place packaging tape sticky-side-up along the wall in your basement or wherever else you find them. This inexpensive flypaper will snag them so you can stomp them out and throw them away.

MEALWORMS

Keep a few sticks of wrapped spearmint chewing gum near any open packages of pasta, and they'll never get infested with mealworms.

MICE

As cute as they are, you don't want a mouse in the house, and certainly not around the kitchen. Shake baking soda around their hiding spots, and they'll stay away. It's safe for pets and kids, and easy to clean up with a broom or vacuum.

If you're suffering from a mouse infestation and can see the mouse holes, smear a bit of mint toothpaste nearby and the smell will deter them. You can also rub toothpaste along the bottom of your baseboards and anywhere else mice may get into your home.

If you've seen a lot of Disney movies, you probably think mice live for cheese. But when you're baiting a mousetrap, a better bet is peanut butter. Since it's sticky, you can be sure the mouse won't grab it and run, and scientists say they love its sweet scent even more than your best piece of Cheddar.

If you're squeamish about having to pick up the remains of a rodent you've set a trap for, place the baited trap inside a brown paper lunch bag. Rodents like exploring small spaces, and once the trap has done its trick, you can scoop it right up and throw it away.

If you've got problems with mice getting into places they're not supposed to, fill in any openings or gaps with steel wool. This will kill the mice by causing internal bleeding after they eat it. If you'd rather not kill them, just put some caulk into the crevice, too, which will keep them out altogether.

—*Tayshaun Boyd, Chanute, KS*

MOTHS

Trap moths by mixing one part molasses with two parts white vinegar and placing the mixture in a bright yellow container. The moths will be attracted to the color and the smell, then drown inside.

Clothes moths are a pain in the neck to get rid of once they've invaded your closets. Since mothballs are toxic, pick up cedar chips at a craft or home store instead. Cedar is an effective, natural solution to fend off those pesky clothes moths—and it smells great, too. Stick the chips in cheesecloth or an old nylon sock, tie it closed, and store in closets or drawers to keep the pests away.

If your cedar chips or cedar chests have lost their aroma (along with those moth-repelling powers), restore them with this simple trick: Rub the wood lightly with fine sandpaper. Repeat every season to make sure your closets are moth-free.

When winter rolls around, do your sweaters smell like mothballs? Ick. Mothballs work great, but leave a nasty odor. When you're storing winter clothes next year, put a few leftover soap slivers in a vented plastic bag and add it to your closet or cedar chest instead of mothballs. The soap will keep moths from damaging your clothes, and it smells fresh, too.

Mothballs have that telltale old attic smell, and even worse, they contain a carcinogen. Use a pretty-smelling natural potpourri made of rosemary, mint, thyme, ginseng, and cloves for the same effect. You want about eight times as many cloves as the other ingredients, since they are what actually keeps the moths away. You can also add lemon peel and tansy. Store in little sachets, which you can buy in a craft store, or tie up in old rags. If you have moths on an item of clothing, put it in your freezer for two days and then clean as usual.

To eliminate moth damage or mildew from your wool sweaters and down jackets, wash the garments before storing, and never keep them in plastic bags or airtight containers. Your clothes need air, so consider a trunk made of wicker, cedar, or rattan, and avoid hot attics or damp basements.

Placing your woolen clothes in a well-sealed bag isn't always enough to keep moths away, as any eggs laid in them beforehand will hatch—and the new moths will have a field day. To make sure all the eggs die before you put your clothes in storage, place the airtight bag of clothes in the freezer for 24 hours.

REPELLING, GENERAL

If flies or bees have invaded your home and you want to get them away from you fast, squirt a little hairspray into the air. They hate the stuff and will go elsewhere.

To repair small holes in window screens, cover them with a few of layers of clear nail polish. It will keep the hole from becoming bigger and prevent insects from coming through.

A number of herbs will ward off crawling insects. The most potent are fresh or dried bay leaves, sage, and cloves. Place any of these herbs in locations where a problem exists, and critters like centipedes, silverfish, and spiders.

Here's a great way to use the gum you regularly confiscate from unruly offspring—leave the mint-flavored variety in the pantry to keep away insects. A few slices (even wrapped) can do wonders.

Basil is not just for pesto! If you have a problem with any type of flying insect, keep a basil plant or two around the house. Drying the basil leaves and hanging them in small muslin bags will also repel flying insects—they hate the sweet aroma.

Each summer we travel to our cabin, and when we arrive there are always droves of flying insects inside. We tape five to ten pieces of duct tape to themselves (making a ring with the sticky side out), then hang them from the rafters near the overhead lights. The bugs become stuck, we throw out the tape, and our problem is solved!

—*Frank R., Michigan City, IN*

SILVERFISH

Silverfish are disgusting, down to each and every one of their legs. An effective, natural way to repel them is with whole cloves. Just sprinkle a few in drawers and other areas where you see them.

Our boys are pretty tolerant of (read: obsessed with) creepy crawlies, but the delicately named silverfish are too gross even for them. Sliced up lemons are effective at keeping them at bay. Put lemons down where they like to appear, and replace with fresh lemons every few days.

» Outdoors

ANTS

To get rid of ants for good, sprinkle cornmeal near anthills. They'll eat it, but they can't digest it, and they'll begin to die out. Wait a couple of weeks and see if your ant problem improves.

Are ants overrunning your hummingbird feeder? Rub a bit of olive oil at the tip of the feeding tube, and they'll stay away. The ants can't get through the oil, but hummingbirds can.

APHIDS

Are aphids invading your garden? Here's another easy, organic way to keep them out. Chop up an onion, place it in a cup of water, and puree it until it's liquid. Pour the concoction into a plastic spray bottle and use it to mist the plants aphids are attracted to. For best results, try it at dawn before the sun starts blazing.

Want to repel aphids? Just plant mint and nasturtiums, which will aphids hate. These plants also repel whiteflies.

BEES AND WASPS

If you can't beat 'em, join 'em (kind of). At your next picnic party give stinging party crashers like bees and wasps a treat of their own—a few cans of open beer around the perimeter of your yard. They'll go for the beer and stay away from your guests. You can also try using sugar-covered grapefruit halves.

....

No one likes having to worry about a bee hijacking his soda while having a drink outside. So cover the top of the cup or can with foil, then poke a straw through. Now you can sip in peace!

....

Unlike bees, wasps can sting again and again. If you spot wasps flying to one spot, look for a nest, which can produce up to 30,000 wasps! Contact your local health authority to remove it without delay.

BEETLES

Keep your rosebush the pride of your garden by getting rid of those icky Japanese beetles. Pour a bowl of self-rising flour and go outside, sprinkling it over the whole bush like it's some kind of magic potion (which, in this case, it is).

....

Plant some garlic in your garden to help keep away beetles. Finding some garlic to plant is easy. If a head of garlic you have in your kitchen sprouts, simply plant it with the green part above ground.

BIRDS

If birds or other critters are nibbling at your fruit trees, try hanging long strips of aluminum foil from the branches. They'll be attracted to its shiny surface, but once they bite it, they'll fly away.

If pigeons or other birds won't leave your patio alone, try sprinkling baking soda anywhere they like to perch. They don't like the feeling of it under their toes! You can also try sticky-side-up tape.

If woodpeckers in the garden bother you, try hanging an aluminum pie plate to the tree where the pests reside. The reflection off the plate will scare the birds away.

CATS

If your neighbors' cats are causing havoc in your yard, don't even try to go talk to their owners—once the cats are let out there really is nothing they can do to keep them fenced in. Instead, sprinkle the edge of your yard with orange peels and coffee grounds. Cats don't like the smell, and the scraps will eventually create great compost for your lawn.

DEER

Buh-bye, Bambi! Hanging small pieces of a deodorant bar soap on trees will keep deer from munching on them. Or, try a piece of your clothing that you've worn for several days—deer don't like the smell of humans.

....

Keeping deer, antelope, elk, and other large animals away from your garden and trees is a breeze with eggs that have gone bad. Just break them open (outside of the house) and place them around the area that you want to keep the critters away from. The smell of hydrogen sulfide from the rotten eggs will keep them away long after you can no longer smell the offending odor.

....

If deer are getting to your flower garden, throw a few mothballs on the ground. Deer hate the smell of mothballs. (Who doesn't?)

FLIES

There's nothing more irritating than having flies and other bugs swarm around you while you're trying to take a dip in the pool. We've had some luck keeping bugs away by applying a liberal amount of vinegar around the perimeter of the pool with a sponge.

GNATS

If you suspect that one of your plants has a gnat problem, here's how to find out for sure. Slice off one-third of an uncooked potato and place it face down (peel side up) on top of the soil. Leave it for a week to 10 days, and if the potato is still clean, you've got no gnats to worry about. If gnats are present, however, there will be larvae on the underside of the potato slice. To rescue your plant, kill the gnats with vodka. (Yes, vodka.) Mix one part vodka to three parts water, pour it into a spray bottle, and spray away. Do this for a week, and the pests will be long gone.

MOLES

Moles are pretty cute, until they're wreaking havoc on your yard. Use this all-natural solution to get rid of them: Just soak some old rags in olive oil, then stuff them in all the holes you can find. Moles hate the smell and will stay away.

MOSQUITOES

Use this (almost) all-natural insect spray to repel mosquitoes as well as other insects like flies. Chop 1 small onion and 1 head of garlic. Mix together with 4 cups water, 4 teaspoons cayenne pepper, and 1 tablespoon liquid dish soap. Spray around your deck and in places where your children play (rather than on the children themselves). This mixture will last a week or so if stored in a jar with a tight-fitting lid and kept in a dark, cool place.

It's a little known fact that mosquitoes hate basil and tansy. Keep those plants in your yard and around your porch. If you're not familiar with it, tansy is a pretty yellow perennial, which has been harvested for its medicinal properties for several thousand years. In Colonial times it was used to preserve meat and keep insects away. It's a low maintenance flower, except for the odor, which irritates some people almost as much it does the bugs.

RACCOONS

Have the raccoons grown rather bold around your backyard and trashcans? Try this equivalent of a phony "Beware of Dog" sign by distributing dog hair around your property. You can also try planting cucumbers, which both skunks and raccoons avoid like the plague.

To keep raccoons and other critters out of your garbage, regularly spray the side of your cans with a mixture of one part ammonia and one part water.
—*Holly L., Wenham, MA*

REPELLING, GENERAL

If you keep plants in window boxes, paint them white first. The bright, reflective surface will deter insects and reduce the risk of dry rot. It looks great, too!

Mice, moles, squirrels, gophers, and even rats hate the aroma of peppermint. Try planting mint near your home—chances are you will never see one of these pests again! For a preexisting gopher problem, soak cotton balls in peppermint oil and then drop them down a gopher hole.

If you find a toad in your garden, tell it "thanks" and send it on its way. A single toad will feast on more than 100 slugs, cutworms, grubs, caterpillars, and assorted beetle larvae every night. If the toad is in top form, it can consume more than 10,000 invaders in just three months!

If you want to keep bugs off your plants, try spraying their leaves with a solution of 10 parts weak tea and one part ammonia. Try it first on a few leaves to test for damage, and make sure pets and children don't try to eat or lick the leaves (hey, they've done weirder things!).

Sometimes, getting rid of insects is as easy as making it hard for them to get where they're going. Smear petroleum jelly around the base of plant stems, and ants and other crawling insects will slide right off, protecting your plants.

When watering outdoor plants, place a few drops of dishwashing liquid into the water, and make sure it gets on your plants' leaves. The detergent will keep bugs away, making sure your plants remain healthy and beautiful.

French marigolds are not only beautiful, they're also the most practical plant you could have in your garden. Why? They have a strong odor that helps bewilder insects in search of their preferred eating plant. Plant some marigolds, and your other plants will thank you!

One way to keep unwanted pests out of your garden is to infuse it with a garlicky odor that will be unpleasant for insects. Take ¼ cup garlic and mix it with 2 cups water in a blender, strain it with an old nylon stocking, and scrape the paste into a jar. Add 2 teaspoons mineral oil and several squirts of dishwashing liquid. Carefully replace the lid on the jar and shake well. Transfer the solution to a spray bottle and use it on your garden in the early morning hours.

RODENTS

If squirrels are making a nuisance of themselves around your home, keep them away with a homemade pepper spray. Take a cup of your favorite hot sauce, add a spoonful of cayenne pepper and a capful of Murphy's Oil Soap, and mix together. Spray the mixture in whatever areas you want the squirrels to steer clear of.

—*Megan Rye, Washington, DC*

Make sure squirrels, mice, and other critters don't chew through the rubber pipeline that connects your propane tank with your grill—reinforce the entire thing with duct tape. This is a good idea for anything else in your yard made out of rubber, as this is a favorite chew toy of rodents!

If you've ever bitten into a shred of foil that had gotten stuck to a piece of candy, you know how unpleasant the sensation is. Rodents hate the feeling of foil between their teeth, too, so placing strips of foil in your garden mulch will help deter rodents and some bugs. If rodents are eating the bark of your tree, you can also wrap the trunk in foil.

SLUGS AND SNAILS

Need to get rid of snails or slugs in your garden? Find the cheapest beer you can, then pour it into several shallow containers (shoeboxes lined with aluminum foil work well). Dig a few shallow holes in your garden and place the containers inside so that they are at ground level. Leave overnight, and the next morning, you'll find dozens of dead (or drunk) snails and slugs inside. These critters are attracted to beer (who isn't?), but it has a diuretic effect on them, causing them to lose vital liquids and die.

If you're having problems with slugs eating your flowers, and nothing seems to work, your solution might be in the form of distraction. Slugs love cabbage, so planting a few in your garden will ensure they stay away from your flowers and go for the cabbage instead.

SPIDER MITES

Do you have trees that are infested with spider mites? You can make a mixture to get rid of them using ingredients already in your kitchen. Take a pound of flour, five gallons of water, and a cup of buttermilk, mix it all together in a large bucket, and put it in a plastic spray bottle. Use it on your trees once a week, and it should keep the mite population under control.

» Personal

CHIGGERS

There may be nothing more disgusting in this world than chiggers. You can pick them up in the woods, and they will lay eggs in the folds of your skin, causing a poison ivy–like rash. If you think you've been exposed to chiggers, take a hot bath. The heat will cause the larvae to die, making your pain (and disgust!) short-lived.

LICE

Looking for tips for treating Lice? *See* Kids chapter, Safety and First Aid

MOSQUITOES

Our favorite way to keep mosquitoes away? Simply keep a fabric softener sheet in each pocket. A chemical in dryer sheets is similar to citronella, which is used in expensive bug-repelling candles.

Mosquitoes are attracted to dark blue clothing. (It's true!) If you usually have trouble with mosquito bites, trying wearing light, pastel clothes when you're outdoors. Many flying insects also like colorful clothing. Believe it or not, bugs are fooled by bright colors and floral prints on fabric. They think the prints are real flowers and end up flying too close to you or your kids.

Don't spend money on bug sprays. Their main ingredient is usually alcohol, so save some money by simply making a mixture of one part rubbing alcohol and four parts water, then spraying it on as you would bug spray. Another natural (and great-smelling) alternative is equal parts water and pure vanilla extract.

For an effective personal insect repellent, rub fresh catnip leaves over exposed skin—just stay away from friendly cats!

Another ingenious way to keep mosquitoes from biting you? Rub any exposed skin with orange or lemon peels. Mosquitoes hate the smell and will find someone else to attack. Ants also don't like the smell of lemon and orange peels, so grind them in your blender with some water, then spread in areas you find ants to keep them away.

TICKS

Oh no, you've got a tick! If you're having trouble prying the little bugger off, apply a large glob of petroleum jelly to the area. Wait about 20 minutes, and you should be able to wipe him off with ease.

The most important thing is not to rush to pry off a tick, because you might leave some of its body parts behind. Ticks have to be feeding on you for about 24 hours to transmit Lyme disease.

You and your dog just enjoyed a fun romp through the forest, but you brought back a souvenir: ticks. To more easily remove them from you or your dog, first wet a Q-tip with rubbing alcohol. Dab it on the tick, and he'll loosen his grip. You should then be able to pull the tick straight off.

Auto

Baking

Beauty

Cleaning

Clothing and Accessories

Cooking

Decorating

Entertaining and Holidays

Health and Wellness

Home Repair

Kids

Money

Organization

Outdoors

Pest Control

>> Pets

Shopping

Utilities

Vacations and Family Activities

Websites

» Cats

BEHAVIOR

To keep your cats from scratching furniture or getting up where they don't belong, cover the area with double-sided tape or aluminum foil. They can't stand the feeling of the stuff under their paws.

Here's something you probably didn't know: Cats hate hot sauce. So if you can't get your cat stop clawing at your woodwork, just rub in a little hot sauce, buff it thoroughly, and your cat will stay clear.

If your pet always wakes you up precisely five minutes before your alarm goes off so she can be fed, you know that animals are creatures of routine. Changes in behavior could be a sign that something is wrong. Just to be sure, you should take her to the vet if you notice changes in appetite, thirst, frequency of urination, energy level, hiding behavior, or anything else that seems strange to you. Your pet will thank you!

One of the worst things you can discover in the backyard is that your cat has (once again) used your kids' sandbox as his litter box! Pour vinegar around the sandbox to keep cats away. Reapply about every two months just to be sure. Vinegar should also help if your cat likes to use your plant's pot as his litter box.

If your cat likes to eat your plants, get some potted wheatgrass from the grocery store and put it near the plants she's nibbling on. She'll prefer the wheatgrass, but be sure to put it near enough to distract her from eating the other plants, and far enough that she doesn't associate the joy of eating with the location of the forbidden plants.

—*Zachary Miller, Chicago, IL*

All cats will run and hide if they hear a loud noise, but some cats seem particularly flighty. If your overly anxious cat runs when she hears regularly occurring noises like shut doors, loud steps, or even sound effects from the TV, here's how to help. Begin by tapping a wooden spoon very gently against a pot or pan while he is eating. Make sure the sound is loud enough that he notices, but not so loud that he gets scared. After you've done this for a couple of days, you can begin slowly increasing how loudly you tap. Once your quiet tap is a loud bang and your cat is still calm, change the surface you're tapping to wood, or try to incorporate a sound that has easily spooked him in the past—just make sure to begin quietly and work your way up again. Finally, begin introducing these sounds into your cat's daily life. Eventually he won't even notice that clap of thunder from outside.

Unfortunately, cats rarely respond when you tell them "no." So to make sure they have a reason to not repeat bad behavior, spray them in the face with water from a spray bottle when you catch them being bad. If this doesn't work, try spraying them with air from a compressed air can (usually used to clean electronics and computer keyboards). Cats hate the feeling of air on their faces.

FEEDING

Cats tend to get upset stomachs from super-cold food. Prevent tummy aches (and, worse, vomiting) by letting the food warm to room temperature before feeding.

....

If you have a cat who frequently vomits, you should (of course) take her to the vet. Unfortunately, your vet might tell you that some cats just throw up a lot. (Why do we love them so much again?) If your cat frequently vomits, it could be because she's eating too fast. If she won't overdue to it with so much food available, try leaving dry food out all day, to let her eat at her own pace. But if she becomes overweight, this might not be an option. Another trick to try is pulverizing some mint with some fresh catnip and seeing if she'll eat it—mint is good for calming stomachs.

....

If you have trouble getting your cat to play with toys for exercise, make him or her work a little for food! First you'll need a cylindrical container—a yogurt container (with the yogurt and foil removed) that has a top for granola or candy works well. Cut a hole in one or both ends and re-enforce with masking or duct tape to make sure there are no sharp edges in the plastic. Then put some dry food inside and put it in front of your cat. Cats love the noise the food makes when rattling around inside, and will continue to bat at the toy to get the food to come out.

....

Add up to ¼ teaspoon olive oil to your cat's moist food once a week to stave off hairballs and make his coat extra-shiny.

HEALTH

If you have trouble getting your cat to swallow pills, try rubbing them in butter first. It will make them taste better to your cat, and they'll slide right down his throat.

Magnesium can cause urinary tract infections in some cats. Canned food should have a maximum magnesium content of around 0.025%.

If you accidentally cut your cat's claw too short, and it bleeds, fill a small bowl with cinnamon, and dip the paw in really quick. The cinnamon acts as a coagulant and the cat will clench its paw tighter and help stop the bleeding. Then go to the vet.

—*Beth Peters, Waltham, MA*

LITTER

Don't spend extra money on scented cat litter. To keep cat litter fresh-smelling, simply mix a bit of baby powder into clean litter.

—*Peter and Sarah Bailey, Fitchburg, MA*

If your cat's litter box smells like, well, a litter box, rinse it out and add a half-inch of white vinegar in the box. Let it stand for half an hour, then swish it around, rinse, and dry the box.

If your cat leaves trails of litter around the house, set a sisal mat just outside her litter box, where she enters and exits the box. The fibers and grooves in the mat will catch any flyaway litter before it hits your floor.

ODOR ELIMINATION

If the smell from your in-heat housecat's spray has more than nine lives, try mixing 1 cup hydrogen peroxide with ½ tablespoon baking soda and 2 squirts liquid dish soap. Pour into a spray bottle and use wherever Fluffy has left her trademark. (Be sure to spot-check as you run the risk of bleaching certain materials.)

PLAY

Cats love toys, and they aren't picky about where they come from! Don't spend money on expensive cat toys. Instead, use a balled up piece of paper, a cork, a jingle bell, or anything else they can bat around the house. To make the toy extra enticing, throw it in a Kleenex box that has the plastic part removed. Cats will love sticking their paws inside to try to fish out the toy.

....

A great way to keep your indoor cat mentally and physically fit is to keep a laser pointer next to your TV remote. Every time you watch TV you'll be reminded to shine a laser light for the cat to chase. This allows you to be a lot lazier than your cat, for once!

—*Justin Ott, Weehawken, NJ*

» Dogs

BEHAVIOR

If your dog simply won't come when called, it might be time to start from scratch. Once a dog has decided that a word doesn't mean anything to him, it's much harder to make him understand that "come" means "come to me," not "do whatever you want." Pick a different word like "here" or "move," and begin your dog's training over again by standing several feet away, saying your new word, and offering treats when he obeys. Your friends at the dog park might think it's weird when you shout, "Draw nigh, Rover!" but it's way better than having him run the other way.

If your new puppy isn't adorable enough to make up for all those chair and table legs he's been chewing, head to your local vitamin or health food store and ask for some clove oil. Oil of cloves smells great to us but terrible to dogs. Wipe it on the legs of anything wooden, and he'll stay away.

FEEDING

If you've bought a new brand of food and your dog doesn't want to eat it, put a piece of beef jerky in the bag and reseal it. By the next day, the smell will have worn off on the food, making it seem much more appetizing.

When getting a "treat" for being good, most dogs are just excited about a special snack, not that it's in the shape of a bone. The truth is, doggie treats have almost the exact same ingredients as dog food, and most dogs can't tell the difference. Instead of paying extra for dog treats, keep a separate container of dog food where you normally keep the treats, then give your dog a small handful when he's done something reward-worthy.

PLAY

If your dog is teething, you can create a cheap chew toy by soaking an old washcloth in water, twisting it into a fun shape, and leaving it in the freezer. Give it to your pup fully frozen, and when it thaws out, simply repeat the process. Be careful doing this with tiny dogs, though, as they can get too cold if they chew on frozen toys too often.

Dog toys are expensive and can be made from harmful materials. In the Colonial era, kids made their own dolls from rags. A canine version will make Fido just as happy as any designer plush toy. All you need to do is braid together three old dish towels. Before you start, cut two strips off the side of two of them. Then use these to tie the tops and bottoms of the braid together.

It seems like a silly habit of guilty "dog parents," but it's true: leaving the TV or radio on low in the room next to your pup will keep him calm while you're away.

....

Is your dog leaving brown spots on your lawn where he decides to pee? Put a few drops of vinegar into his water bowl every time you refill it and brown spots will be a thing of the past.

....

If you're training a new puppy, here's the best way to get accidental wet spots out of the carpet. First soak up as much of the urine as possible with paper towels. Then combine 2 cups warm water, 2/3 cup vinegar, and 2 teaspoons dishwashing detergent. Mix everything together, then blot the stain carefully with the solution, making sure not to apply excess liquid. Rinse it off with tap water and dry it with paper towels. When the carpet is completely dry—usually the next day—kill off the lingering smell by sprinkling a heavy dose of baking soda on the spot and letting it sit for one hour before vacuuming up.

....

House-breaking your new puppy is the hardest part about being a new dog parent, but you can make it a little easier with this tip. If your puppy has soiled newspaper, bury it just underneath the soil where you'd like him to relieve himself outside. The smell will tell him it's the right place to go.

WASHING

You've finally trained your dog how to be good while getting a bath in the tub, but his tiny hairs always slip through your drain's catcher and clog up your pipes. To keep this from happening, stuff some steel wool into the opening (but not too far down). It will catch every hair from even the furriest of creatures. When you're done bathing, make sure to fish the steel wool out immediately.

Forget about using soap and water on your dog's messy paws. It's faster and easier to simply wipe his paws with a baby wipe. It's a great way to remove dirt and mud—before he cuddles up with you on the couch.

If your dog tends to track mud into the house, you can confine that mess to one area by creating an outdoor walkway for him to use before entering. The best bet is filling a path with gravel, which helps keep mud off the pooch's paws and keeps the house cleaner.

Our niece's white dog was always getting stains under her runny eyes until we tried applying our miracle liquid: vinegar. Rub a little vinegar into white fur to remove yellow or brown spots.

» General

FLEAS

Looking for tips about Fleas? See Pest Control chapter, Indoors

FEEDING

If you're cooking a chicken or turkey and don't have a use for the giblets, go ahead and cook them up for your dogs or cats. (You can usually just zap them in the microwave for a few minutes.) It's less pet food you'll have to buy and even more love you'll receive from your furry friend.

Give cats and dogs yogurt to help their GI systems. Mix a few spoonfuls with their regular food once a day. Seek a veterinarian's attention if problems persist.

Sometimes, your pet is just plain stinky. If you're beginning to notice pet odor when you open your front door, it's time to take action. Add a bit of brewer's yeast (1 teaspoon for cats and small dogs and 1 tablespoon for bigger dogs) to your pet's food, and your pet will secrete fewer of those unpleasant odors.

When choosing a water and food dish for your pet, opt for stainless steel instead of ceramic. Ceramic provides a porous surface for bacteria to hide.

If your pet's food dish always ends up three feet from where it started by the time he's done eating, make it skid-proof. With a glue gun, make a thin strip of glue around the bottom rim. When dry, the hardened glue will prevent the bowl from slipping so much across the floor.

Never have to throw away an ant-infested bowl of pet food again. Simply sprinkle some ground cinnamon around the bowl, and the ants will stay away.

Petroleum jelly will keep ants out of a pet food dish. Simply rub a small amount on the rim around the bottom of bowl.

Do ants keep sneaking into your pet's food? Secret tip: Ants can't swim! Place the bowl of dog or cat food into a shallow bowl filled with water.

FUR REMOVAL

Even regular brushing can't get every last hair off your pet, but a dryer sheet can. Run a dryer sheet over your pet's coat and static will cause any loose hairs to be picked up.

If you don't have the heart to banish your pet from the couch, here's a solution for removing all that hair from your sofa. Just use a dry, unused dish sponge to wipe the hair into a pile with your hand. Discard the hair and then repeat the process. After you've gotten most of the hair, take a sheet of fabric softener from the laundry room and use it to pick up the rest—the hair will be naturally attracted to it. When that's done, use a vacuum cleaner to add the finishing touch.

Uh oh, guests are on their way and you've just realized that your beloved cat has made a cat-fur nest all over your couch. For a quick and easy way to remove pet hair from furniture, turn to your rubber dishwashing gloves. Just slip them on, then rub the offending furniture with them. The hair will stick to the gloves and you can quickly throw it away.

GROOMING

To make your short-haired pet's fur extra-shiny, rub it down with a piece of silk, velvet, or chamois cloth.

Pet owners know that matted hair can make brushing an animal a frustrating experience for you—and a painful one for them. To prevent this, rub your pet with baby powder prior to brushing. It'll be easier to remove the tangles, for which both you and your pet will be grateful.

Cleaning out your own hairbrush is bad enough, but cleaning out the one that belongs to your furry companion can be a half a day's work. Instead of getting angry next time you snag your pantyhose, give it a second life. Cut strips of hose and lay them over your pet's clean metal brush, poking the pins of the brush through. The next time your cat or dog looks like he just stepped out of a salon after a heavy brushing, all you'll have to do is remove the scraps of material, throw them out, and replace with new strips.

The busiest days at the pet groomer's are Friday, Saturday, Sunday, and Monday. Find a groomer who offers discounts on Tuesdays through Thursdays, or ask your groomer if she will offer you a discount for coming midweek.

HEALTH

Pet medications are often insanely expensive. Luckily, we've discovered Omaha Vaccine, which offers great deals on meds that cost more elsewhere. Visit OmahaVaccine.com to search for your pets' medications, and get free shipping for orders over $35.

We all love our pets and will go to any lengths to make sure they are happy and healthy, but this shouldn't mean taking out a second mortgage to pay vet bills. Look at your local shelter to see what services they provide. Many will spay/neuter and administer vaccinations and annual shots for less than half the price of your friendly neighborhood vet.

If you have both cats and dogs, you may be tempted to feed your cat dog food. Don't do it! Besides being highly insulted if he happens to see the can, your cat needs certain nutrients that are found only in food made specifically for cats.

If your poor pet's pads are cracked or dry, the solution is simple. Gently rub a little petroleum jelly into her pads while she's sleeping. It will moisturize the area and is completely safe if your pet decides she wants to lick it off later.

A great household remedy for ear mites is to dissolve 1 teaspoon baking soda in 1 cup warm water and rub a cotton ball soaked in that mixture on your pet's ears. Of course, if you see a pet scratching his ears, you should always take him to the vet first, just to be sure.

If your pet likes chewing on plants, beware: Some common house and garden plants are poisonous to animals. They include: tomato plants, rhododendron, daffodils, crocus, lilies, poinsettia, holly, mistletoe, lantana, laburnum, taro, yew, cyclamen, foxglove, hyacinth, hydrangea, rhubarb, narcissus, and the pits of many fruits like apricots, plums, and peaches. If you see your pet eat any of these, take him to the vet immediately! For more information about plants that may be toxic for your animals, visit ASPCA.org and go to their "Pet poison control" section.

SIMPLE SOLUTIONS

It's not actually fur that causes allergies, but dander, salvia, and urine particles. If you keep your cat's litter box inside, clean it out before allergic friends come over and they'll have a better time.

If your cat or dog has horrible breath, try adding some fresh chopped parsley to his food.

Did you know that light-colored animals can get sunburn, too? Guard against this by dabbing a bit of SPF 15 sunscreen on your pet's nose and the tips of his ears.

No need to buy a fancy nighttime collar for your furry friends. Simply cover a regular collar with reflector tape and watch Rover roam all over, even in the dark.

TRAVELING

If you're going to be unable to pay attention to your pet for a while—such as when she's in a carrier on a long trip—put an old, worn T-shirt (the best are ones you've recently exercised in) inside the pet carrier with her. Your scent will help ease your pet's worries.

You're taking your pet on the plane, but you're worried about her getting water while you travel. Instead of filling a water dish with water, which can splash out during transit, put a few ice cubes in the dish. Once your pet's cage is settled in cargo, the ice cubes will melt, giving her some much-needed refreshment.

—Art Gallagher, Burnside, CT

WASHING

Washing a pet can sure be a hassle—especially if it's a cat. Save yourself the trouble (and several scratches) by using cornstarch instead. Sprinkle cornstarch on your pet's coat, then work it into his hair. It will soak up grease and odors and even fluff up his fur.

Whether your dog is covered in sap or your cat's been hanging out under the car (or you have no idea *what* she's been up to!), use shampoo to remove that sticky substance from her fur. Dab on a little, rub it in a bit, and then rinse with water.

» Other Pets

BIRDS

If you have a parakeet or other bird, make sure you have perches in various diameters. Birds' talons don't get a proper workout unless they have different things to grasp. Use tree branches or store-bought perches, especially those with a rough feeling, to keep your bird exercised and happy.

It may seem silly, but not to your bird—put a mirror in his cage to make sure he doesn't get lonely. The bird will see the reflection of himself and think it's another bird to keep him company. Of course, the other solution is simply buying your bird a real feathered friend!

FISH

Even old water from your aquarium can be used again. Use it to water your houseplants—they'll love the extra "fertilizer" the fish provided.

If your fish tank is marked with hard-to-remove deposits, just rub the tank with a cloth dipped in vinegar, and rinse well. The spots should disappear. Just make sure you rinse the bowl thoroughly before putting your fish back in.

Having fish is fun, but not when you have to periodically replace the water. Make your job easy with the help of some old pantyhose and a wet/dry shop vac. Place two or three layers of pantyhose over the nozzle of the hose and secure it with a rubber band. Remove your fish to a safe location, then stick the hose in the tank and start sucking. The dirty water will find its way into the vacuum, but the rocks won't make it through the nylon.

....

Before you clean out your goldfish's bowl, first prepare a salt-water bath for him. Even though goldfish are freshwater fish, salt will help your fish absorb much-needed electrolytes and kill any parasites on his fins. To get the salt water ready, run tap water into a bowl and let it sit for a day to allow the chlorine to evaporate (you should do this when filling his freshwater bowl, too). Add a teaspoon of non-iodized salt and mix until it dissolves. Then let Goldy go for a swim in the salt water for approximately 15 minutes.

SMALL MAMMALS

If you have a rabbit, guinea pig, hamster, or other small pet who lives in a cage, try refilling his water dish by sticking a turkey baster through the bars. It will allow you to give him something fresh to drink without scaring him by opening the door and moving things around.

Auto

Baking

Beauty

Cleaning

Clothing and
Accessories

Cooking

Decorating

Entertaining
and Holidays

Health and
Wellness

Home Repair

Kids

Money

Organization

Outdoors

Pest Control

Pets

>> Shopping

Utilities

Vacations
and Family
Activities

Websites

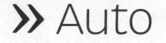

» Auto

AT THE DEALERSHIP

If you're buying a car, make sure you test-drive it at night. Driving in the dark will give you an opportunity to make sure the car's lights work and will draw your attention inward toward its dash, so that you take in all of its interior features and can decide whether or not you like them.

....

Ask your local dealerships if they're selling their program cars, and you can save big. Program cars are cars that are driven by people who work at a car dealership and are sold after they reach 100,000 miles. Since it's often car mechanics themselves who drive these cars, they're always kept in good shape.

BEFORE YOU GO

Before heading to the dealer, go to TrueCar.com first. TrueCar has great articles on buying cars, but better still, it has reader-compiled prices of what people across the country have paid for various makes and models. It's better than "Blue Book" pricing, because it doesn't just tell you what the vehicle is worth, it tells you what people have actually paid when buying the car new and used. Just enter the make of the car and your zip code, and you can find the cheapest place to buy a car near you.

....

After gas, one of the biggest costs associated with having a car is the interest you pay on the loan. Before you go buy a car, get a loan in place first—the financing the car dealership will offer most likely won't be as competitive. Know your credit rating, and check with your employer's credit union or look online for deals on car loans. A good place to begin is a page that lets you compare rates and find out information on car loans. One site we like is BankRate.com. Click on "Auto" from the homepage.

....

Go manual and save. If you're buying a new car and can't afford a hybrid, consider going with a stick shift rather than an automatic. Manually changing gears saves energy because your car is using only as much energy as it needs to—it's never in a higher gear than it should be. Being able to coast down hills also saves you tons.

WHERE TO SHOP

The internet can be a great resource for buying a car, particularly a new one. Instead of relying on a salesman's sketchy pitch, do your own online research on the pros and cons of each model. Go test-drive one to make sure you like it, but don't buy it right then. Instead, go home and hunt around for the best price among dealers in your region. Even if the dealership offering the best price is located far away, you may still come out ahead by having them deliver the car to you. We once paid $500 to have an out-of-state dealer ship a vehicle to us—and that was still $1,000 cheaper than buying the car locally.

—*Jerri Thompson Barry*

» Clothing

ALTERATIONS

Going to a tailor may seem like an expensive proposition, but it's often worth it if you unearth a good deal on a suit or other item of clothing that doesn't quite fit. Found some jeans for ten bucks that look great but are an inch too long? A jacket that's a steal, but a bit too baggy in the arms? For a small price, you can get these items custom-fitted at a tailor. And you'll still be saving a bundle from what the normal retail price would be.

Not happy with the color of a handbag or pair of fancy shoes? Instead of buying new accessories, turn that unbecoming chartreuse into an elegant black with a can of shoe color spray. You can pick up an inexpensive can of shoe color from a repair shop, then revamp those heels yourself instead of paying someone else to do it for you.

AT THE STORE

When you're buying clothes, always go for classic looks rather than modern, trendy ones. A blue V-neck T-shirt will be fashionable year after year, while something with more exotic colors or patterns will go out of style quickly. By choosing the basics, you won't have to buy as many new articles of clothing each season.

If you have a favorite shop you find yourself spending a lot of time in, make sure to get friendly with the sales staff! Clothing stores often have unannounced sales, or they regularly begin sales on certain days of the week. If you're down with the people who work there, they'll often you tip you off. And if they really like you, they may let you put an item on layaway until it goes on sale a few days later.

BEFORE YOU GO

Are you afraid you'll be buried in a fabric avalanche every time you open your closet? It's time to take control of your wardrobe. A great time to tackle this job is at the beginning of spring and fall. You'll have a better handle on what clothes you need for the season, cutting down on duplicates and making impulse buying less likely. If you tend to buy a lot of items that are similar to each other, try organizing your closet by color, so when you pause by that black polo shirt at the store, you'll remember just how many black short-sleeved shirts you already own.

For the best deals on clothes, shop in the off-season. Buy spring and summer clothing in July and August, and fall and winter clothing in January and February. (You can often find the best sales right after the holiday season.) It's sometimes a bummer to buy something you're not going to be able to wear for six months, but when the time comes to switch seasons, you'll be happy you already have some new clothes to wear—all of which were purchased on sale!

WHERE TO SHOP

How many times have you purchased an $80 sweater, only to find a nearly identical one for much less later? When you begin to look for clothes for the new season, always start at the least expensive store first. Since most clothing stores carry similar items each season, you'll make sure to get each piece for the best price. You should also try to buy most of your basics—solid-color T-shirts, socks, and so forth—at the cheaper stores. Save the expensive stores for the uniquely designed and patterned clothes, where you can see the difference in quality.

At ShopItToMe.com, you enter your favorite brands of clothes and they do all the online searching for you. When items come up for sale on a department store's site, they'll send you an email, alerting you to the discount. The best part is, you can specify your size, so you won't have to waste your time wading through links only to find that the store is all out of extra-large!

If you're trying to save money, obviously it's probably a good idea to try to stay away from designer fashion labels. But if you just can't help yourself, Bluefly.com is the best place to go for a bargain. You'll find discounted prices on men's and women's designer clothing, including such labels as Kenneth Cole, Burberry, Armani, Marc Jacobs, Calvin Klein, and Prada. Just try to keep it to a couple of outfits and a handbag!

....

At Zappos.com, you'll find more shoes than you ever imagined possible, including men's, women's, and kids' sneakers; dress shoes; boots; and sandals. Not only do they have free shipping, they also include a return shipping label with your order, so if you don't like the shoes once you try them on, you can easily return them for free. Another great site for shoes is 6pm.com, which carries lots of shoes that used to be on Zappos. You do have to pay shipping, but the savings can be worth it because the selection and prices are usually quite good.

....

If you need new glasses and aren't sure how you're going to afford them, check out 39Dollar-Glasses.com. For around $45 (with shipping), you can get attractive (though bare-bones) glasses, including the lenses! Walmart also offers good deals on frames and lenses. If you're looking for something more stylish, try WarbyParker.com, which offers good prices on brand name frames. Plus, you can try out their glasses online "virtually" by uploading a picture of yourself. Neat!

» Cosmetics and Beauty Services

AT THE STORE

When trying to compare a pricey cosmetic with a less-expensive one, you only have to look at one thing: the active ingredients list. Products that have the same active ingredients are going to do almost the exact same thing, even if the percentages are a bit off. (The only thing you might have to worry about is which smells better.) You'll be surprised how many expensive brands—especially hair products like shampoo—have the exact same ingredients in them for vastly higher prices.

....

If you're looking for a way to cut back on your cosmetics budget, the first place to start is with your moisturizer. Whether it's night cream, day cream, anti-aging lotion, or anti-wrinkle solution, it's all pretty much the same. Pick a moisturizer with an SPF of at least 15—other than that, go with a less expensive brand whose smell you like. Your wallet will know the difference, but your face never will.

....

You might be reassured that a "hypoallergenic" product won't cause problems for your sensitive skin, but the term actually doesn't mean much. Companies put this word on cosmetics that they think are less harsh than others, but there are no federal regulations guiding the use of the word. Most dermatologists agree than a product labeled as "hypoallergenic" is no different from a product without the label—if you can even find one.

....

When shopping for perfume, hair spray, nail polish, and other cosmetics, keep an eye out for phthalates on the ingredient list. Phthalates can be absorbed through the skin and have been found to damage the liver and reproductive system. They have been outlawed in Europe, but they're still legal in the US, so make sure you check the label before you buy.

BEFORE YOU GO

Most make-up is exactly the same, except for whether they call that shade of red you love "cherries jubilee" or "red crush." Make shopping for make-up easier by keeping an index card with your favorite colors on hand. Rub a bit of lipstick, blush, or eye shadow on the card, then mark down the brand and what the color is called. When it's time for more make-up, you can easily compare the colors of the sale brand with your card. Then write down what *that* color is called on your card. You'll soon have a list of all your favorite colors from each brand.

—*Arlene DeSantos*

HAIRCUTS

Get your haircut on the cheap by students who are studying to be beauticians. You may risk a less-than-professional 'do, but generally speaking, the students are supervised by trained instructors, who can fix any mis-snipping that might occur. Student haircuts are also great for kids, whose simple cuts are usually hard to screw up. To find a beauty school near you that offers cuts and styles at low prices, go to BeautySchoolDirectory.com.

If you're used to getting an expensive haircut, it's hard to switch to a bargain salon such as Supercuts. But what you can do to save yourself hundreds of dollars a year is to get a hairstyle that doesn't need a lot of upkeep. When you need a trim in between cuts, go to an inexpensive salon. While hair stylists at the bargain salons sometimes can't give you the fancy cut you want, they can usually handle a simple trim, following the path of your normal stylist. If you just need your bangs cut, ask at your usual salon if they offer free bang trims in between cuts.

If you want to save at the hair salon, ask if you can get a discount if you skip the blow dry at the end. Many salons will knock at least $5 off the price. Even if you don't want to walk out of the salon with a wet head of hair, this is a great tip for kids' cuts, since kids often don't like getting their hair dried anyway.

WHERE TO SHOP

When shopping for make-up and other cosmetics, never ever shop at department stores! Because of sales commissions and the cost to rent the space at the store, they're never a bargain. Instead, check out your local grocery store or discount store such as Walmart or Target—they almost always have the exact same brands for much less. If you can't find them there, try to find a cosmetics discount outlet such as Ulta, or search for "discount cosmetics" online. If you still can't find your brand, consider switching to another brand you *can* find. Choose one a good friend uses, and ask her if she'd be willing to buy it from you if you don't like it. It shouldn't be too hard to find one you like just as much that costs much less.

Good make-up doesn't have to be expensive! For a great deal on cosmetics on the web, head over to EyesLipsFace.com, where they have everything from lip gloss to nail polish for only a dollar apiece. They also have a great "Gifts" section, with cute box sets for unbelievable prices. For instance, eye shadow, mascara, eyeliner, a brush, and an eyelash curler for only $5!

Addicted to fancy shampoo? Find all the same brands you buy at your salon for much less at SalonSavings.com. Shampoos and hair-care products are 10–80 percent off, and skincare and fragrances are offered at much less as well. This site is also a great place to check if you have a favorite beauty product that has been discontinued.

» Coupons

FINDING COUPONS

Believe it or not, the best place to get coupons is still your Sunday paper. But what if you've starting clipping coupons, and even printed them out from the internet, but you still don't feel like you have enough to make a dent in your grocery bill? Make sure your co-workers, friends, relatives, and neighbors all know that you're a coupon-clipper, and ask them to save any coupon inserts they have. Perhaps it's their guilt at not taking advantage of coupons themselves, but you'll be surprised how many extra coupons you'll receive from others who don't mind lending a hand to help you save.

Do you shop at a store that features coupon machines in the aisles? Make sure to take advantage of these free coupons even if you don't need the product right away. Most expire in a month or more, so take one (or better yet, two!) and save it for a few weeks to see if the item goes on sale, doubling your savings.

If you get to the store and find that they are out of an item that they've advertised as on sale, ask the clerk for a rain check. Most stores will give you a piece of paper that allows you to buy the item at the sale price once it's back in stock.

In one of our favorite movies, *Mr. Mom*, Michael Keaton starts a poker game where coupons are used instead of money. While you don't necessarily have to gamble for them, trading coupons with friends is a great way to get rid of coupons you don't need and get some you do in return—even if Michael Keaton isn't involved.

Can't get enough coupons? How about making a "Take a Coupon, Leave a Coupon" box? Set it up at your office, or ask your library or a local cafe if you can place one there. Everyone leaves coupons they can't use, and takes what they can.

Save yourself the tedium of sifting through the Sunday coupons and circulars by finding your coupons on the web. There are literally dozens of websites that allow you to print out coupons and take them right to the store. Coupons.com is our favorite site, but Coupons.smartsource.com is also a great site that shows you the new coupons first, so if you visit frequently you won't have to wade through ones you've already seen. Another great site to visit is AllYou.com/Coupons.

Ever go to buy something online and see that little box to enter a promotional or coupon code? Well, now you never have to wish you had something to enter into that box again. At RetailMeNot.com, you can find hundreds of codes that will give you savings at a large variety of websites, including Kohls.com, Amazon.com, and JCPenney.com. If this site doesn't have a code for the store you're looking for, also try MomsView.com, Deal-Taker.com, or PocketDeal.com. Or simply type the name of the online store and the word "coupon code" into a search engine.

....

Looking for a coupon for a particular item? Try visiting the company's website directly. Most products list a website on their packaging, but if they don't, try typing the name of the product and the word "coupon" into a search engine. (This is also a good trick if you visit a site and it seems too confusing to find where the coupons are.) Many brands offer coupons on their site, including General Mills, Betty Crocker, Reynolds Wrap, Colgate, Seventh Generation, Charmin, and more. If the brand doesn't offer coupons on their website, try writing to the company directly by clicking on their "Contact" tab. Explain how much you enjoy their product, and ask if they have any coupons available. Many companies save coupons for promotional purposes and are happy to mail them out to their loyal customers.

....

At Cellfire.com, you can sign up to get coupons sent directly to your cell phone or your supermarket savings card! In addition to grocery coupons, you can find special offers for restaurants, entertainment, and major department stores. Browse the offers online or via your phone's web application. This is a perfect activity for when you're waiting around to pick up your kids!

ORGANIZING

Remember: when organizing your coupons, you need to have a place to store them. We use a store-bought coupon organizer with tabs, but you can also use a recipe box, a shoe box, file folders, clear business card or baseball card holders that can be put into a three-ring binder, individual letter-sized envelopes, or anything else that you feel will be easy to carry with you to the store.

To easily sort your coupons, create categories that make sense to you. We organize ours by sections of the store, such as snacks, frozen foods, and dairy. However, you may find that sorting them alphabetically or by store layout works better for you. Create separate categories for store coupons, meaning coupons that can only be used at your drugstore or a particular supermarket. You may also want to create a separate category for coupons that are about to expire.

STRATEGY

Coupons don't actually save you money if you're buying a product you wouldn't normally buy or are buying a higher quantity than you will ever use before the item expires. Also make sure to check generic and other brands to see if they are still cheaper than the product you are buying with a coupon! A coupon that saves you 30¢ isn't much good if the item is still 40¢ more expensive than the store brand.

You can save big (twice as much, in fact) if you shop at a grocery store that doubles coupons—that is, offers you $1 off for using a 50¢-off coupon. Unfortunately, these stores are few and far between in most states. Visit Couponing.about.com/od/groceryzone/a/doublecoupons.htm for a reader-generated list of stores that double. And if you find one, consider yourself lucky!

....

The most important thing to remember about couponing is that, unless the coupon states otherwise, you can use as many as you want for the same item. That means that if you have your own Sunday paper coupon insert and a friend's, you can clip both coupons for toothpaste and walk away with twice the savings.

....

Each week, compare your coupons with flyers you have received for in-store sales. See if any of the coupons match up, and put those in a special place (like the front of your organizer or box) so you make sure to use them while you're shopping. You may also want to indicate which items you have a coupon for on your grocery list. As for the rest of the coupons in your stash, make sure to bring them with you to the store every time. You never know what else is going to be on sale, and by matching up store sales with your coupons, you'll save even more—this was a key factor for us in feeling like cutting coupons was really worth it!

....

Here's a great tip if you find yourself balking at spending the time to clip coupons just to save 50¢ here or there. Cut out coupons from the Sunday paper, then let them sit for four weeks. Many food and cosmetic companies plan their promotions so that customers buy their products right when the coupons are released. Then, when they run out of the product, they go back to the store and find that the store has it on sale. (Then you're hooked!) If you wait to use your coupons, you'll find that they often sync up with an in-store promotion, so you'll save twice as much.

Now that most drugstores are offering cash-back offers, something called "the drugstore game" has sprung up among frugal shoppers. To "play," all you have to do is keep a careful watch on in-store promotions and the coupons you have on hand. Whether you're getting money back through a frequent buyer club card, or coupons are printed directly at the register, most drugstores are eager to promote these savings, and you can use them not only to save, but to *make* money at the store. This is possible because you may receive, for instance, a $2-off "cash back" coupon for buying a $2 item that you have a 50¢-off coupon for. In other words, you'd be making 50¢! Other drugstores offer deals for spending a certain amount alongside their normal offers. For instance, during a recent week at Walgreens, a shopper could receive $5 in "register rewards" (money-off coupons that print out at check-out) for spending $25. That's a $5-off coupon for free! The secret to being successful at the drugstore game (besides being intimately familiar with each store's reward program) is knowing what's on sale before you go. If you don't regularly receive store flyers, check the store's website. For everything else you need to know about the drugstore game, visit ChiefFamilyOfficer.com/2008/09/drugstore-game-primer.html.

» Deals, Finding

AT THE STORE

Before you're convinced to buy something just because it's on sale, make sure to carefully consider the discount offer. For example, when something is offered for 25 percent off, with an additional 25 percent taken at the register, you're usually not actually getting 50 percent off—you're getting 25 percent of 25 percent—or 43.75 percent off. Also, make sure to ask whether "buy one, get one free" promotions require you to purchase two items, or if you can simply get one for 50 percent off. Finally, be aware that many stores put quantity limits on sale items just to try to convince consumers that the product is in demand. Buying more than you regularly would doesn't save you money—it makes them more.

One of the best methods for negotiating at the store is the "good cop, bad cop" strategy, so make sure to bring your spouse or a friend. One of you acts really interested in the product, while the other continually points out the flaws and negative aspects. Because of the "good cop," the salesperson will remain hopeful that he can sell the product, but "bad cop" will make him work for it.

If you're buying a big-ticket item and several accessories for it, make sure to ask for a discount on your purchase, whether you're buying at a mom-and-pop store or at the mall. Most stores have a higher mark-up on accessories for top-selling items so that they can sell the main attraction at a discount.

You're shopping in your favorite store and notice that there are tons of markdowns. After you fill your arms with bargains, go home and mark the day on your calendar! Most stores receive shipments of new goods every 9–12 weeks and discount current merchandise to make room for the new stuff. Return to the store during that time frame to find more deals.

If you're lucky enough to own an iPhone, Android, or other smartphone, you're also lucky to have access to applications that make shopping easier. Once installed, you can use your phone's camera to take a snapshot of the barcode, or enter the UPC numbers underneath. Your phone will then give you a list of how much the item costs at locations near you and online. Search your phone's app store for Barcode Scanner on iPhone and Android, ScanLife on Blackberry, and Shop-Savvy for Windows phones. If you don't have a smartphone, you can still easily compare prices online. You don't get to use your phone as a scanner (which is half the fun), but you can enter the UPC code of any product to get prices from around the web by using Google's Product Search (Products.Google.com). Just type in the numbers found near the barcode and away you go!

Here's an online shopping secret that can save you hundreds. When you're visiting a company's online store, make sure to hit up the "sale" section first. Many sites will also keep sale items in their original locations—without the prices marked down. Look in the sale section first to make sure you're getting the best price.

BEFORE YOU GO

Sure, you've always been able to haggle at car dealerships and mom-and-pop stores. But did you know that "big box" stores such as Home Depot and Best Buy are getting in on the act, too? With sales slipping, the staffs of chain stores are now being told that bargaining is OK. Make sure you haggle to get the most bang for your buck!

Before you go to the store, do a little research at competing stores or on the internet beforehand. If you ask a salesperson to match the price at a nearby store, there's a good chance she will. Make sure you're aware of "extras" that the competing stores may be offering. Even if you're not interested in an extended warranty or free engraving at the other place, you can use the incentive to your advantage when bargaining.

WHERE TO SHOP

Every month, hundreds of cars and other items are confiscated by the police. And hey, just because a criminal used it doesn't make that $100 laptop any less useful. Look in the classifieds section of your newspaper to find local auctions, or check out PropertyRoom.com or PoliceAuctions.com to find unbelievable deals on tools, electronics, bicycles, video games, and more, not to mention some truly bizarre items like a Freon tank, "assorted copper tubing," night vision goggles, and an adorable cement frog. And if you're OK with not telling the recipient where it came from, you should know that auctions are also one of the least expensive places to buy beautiful jewelry and gemstones.

....

If you're like most people, you probably shy away from buying refurbished electronics, but you shouldn't. We go out of our way to buy refurbs, which not only save cash, but also provide more or less the same level of reliability as brand-new items. Whether it's a cell phone, laptop, gaming console, or television, a refurbished item is arguably less likely to be defective than a new one, because these items are tested at the factory before they're resold. And in the rare instance where a refurb does fail, all of the other refurbs you've bought will have saved you enough money to replace it. Contrary to popular opinion, most refurbished units aren't simply broken items that have been repaired. They may have been returned to the maker for any number of other reasons. A customer may have returned a gift he didn't want, the packaging (but not the actual item) may have been damaged in shipping, the item might have a cosmetic blemish, or the item may have been missing a nonessential accessory. If you can live with those things, then refurbished items are definitely for you. Many of them even come with the original manufacturer's warranty intact.

» Groceries

AT THE STORE

When shelving items, grocery stores customarily put the least expensive items on the bottom shelves. That's because most customers, when looking for a particular product, will just take the first item they see—at eye-level. When at the market, make sure to check the lower shelves for lower prices.

Remember the cardinal rule when it comes to saving money on food: If it's "convenient," it's probably costly. For example, pickles cut flat for sandwiches, juice in single-serving bottles, pre-shredded cheese, and "baby" carrots. Think carefully about what you're buying and decide if the convenience is worth the extra cost!

When shopping, know your terminology: Only the term "use by" means that you shouldn't eat the food after the date indicated. "Sell by" dates are only an indication for the store, and foods will usually keep one to two weeks after. "Best before" is only an indication of food quality, not of food safety, so again, your perishables may still be fine to eat.

If you find you're making a lot of impulse purchases at the store because your kids are begging for snack foods, keep them quiet by buying them a package of animal crackers or a similar snack right when you get to the store. Most stores don't even mind if your kids eat the crackers before you pay for them.

Beware of sneaky supermarkets! It's important to know that not *all* products are cheaper when you buy bigger sizes. Make sure to compare unit prices carefully at the store, because we have found that some items—like cereal and prepared frozen foods like French fries—are less expensive in smaller sizes. This is probably because the store knows these items are more likely to be purchased in bulk.

Want to save money every time you shop? A great site to visit is MyGroceryDeals.com, where you'll see what's on sale at your local grocery stores before you go. Just enter your zip code and start saving!

Buying lots of groceries in one trip rather than a few groceries in several trips is better for your wallet. Not only do you save on gas money, but according to a study by the Marketing Science Institute, shoppers who are only making a quick trip to the store purchase an average of 54 percent more than they had planned. In addition to visiting the store less frequently, make a grocery list before you go cut down on impulse buys.

Here's a supermarket tip to live by: Never go to the grocery store on an empty stomach. If you're hungry, you'll not only want to rush through shopping (taking less time to compare unit prices), but you'll make more impulse purchases because everything looks so tasty! Eat before you go and save money.

When you've been buying the same brand-name product for as long as you can remember, it's hard to make the switch to generics. However, you'll be surprised when you find many generic and store-brand products taste exactly the same (or better!) for less than half the cost. Always buy generic baking ingredients such as flour, oil, and sugar. These generics are indistinguishable from their more-expensive counterparts. Frozen and canned vegetables are also usually exactly the same. As for products such as cereals, cookies, and crackers, basic is better—we've had good luck with plain granola, potato chips, and wheat crackers. No matter what the product, it never hurts to try. If you end up having to throw away one can of soup, you've wasted a few dollars, but if you like it, you can save a lot over the course of a year.

> Save the boxes from name-brand products your kids are attached to, then empty the generic products into them. Your picky eaters won't know the difference if they can't see it on the outside.

DAIRY AND EGGS

Never buy milk in clear containers. When exposed to light, low fat or skim milk can lose up to 70 percent of its vitamin A. Tinted or opaque containers will protect the vitamin A.

When buying cheese at the supermarket, make sure to check both the cheese section (usually by the deli counter) and the dairy section for the best prices. The dairy section will have much less expensive processed cheeses, while you may find a deal on an equivalent cheese in the cheese section. Also check at the deli counter to see if they're having any sales on Cheddar, Munster, and other sandwich cheeses. You can always ask them to just cut you a slab if you are planning on cubing or shredding the cheese.

The truth about eggs? White and brown eggs are identical in nutritional value and taste. Believe it or not, the only difference is that white eggs come from white chickens, and brown eggs come from brown chickens! When at the store, simply buy whatever is cheaper.

DESSERTS

Never, ever let us catch you buying sundae toppings in the ice cream aisle! These nuts and mini candies are up to 50 percent cheaper in the baking aisle, which often even has sprinkles, too. Melt some chocolate chips in a double broiler, then let them cool a bit and add to the top of ice cream for your own "instant shell."

To save money, purchase solid chocolate candy (usually in bunny or Santa form) after major holidays when it's gone on sale. Store in the freezer, then shave off bits with a vegetable peeler to use on top of desserts.

MEAT

Supermarkets have started using their own wording on meat packages to make you think that the product you are buying is a better grade than it really is. Most of the major chains are buying more select-grade beef, but may call it by any number of fancy names such as "top premium beef," "prime quality cut," "select choice," "market choice," or "premium cut." Be aware that these titles don't actually mean anything!

Grocery stores make a lot of money on meat, so it's not surprising that they display the priciest cuts in the case! Experience dramatic savings by instead asking the butcher to slice different cuts for you from the same primal (or section) of the cow or pig. These cuts can be as little as one-fifth the cost of the expensive, pre-packaged cuts, and they'll be just as tender and tasty. Here are a few discounted (yet delicious) cuts you can ask for: Instead of buying ground beef, ask the butcher to grind up a bottom round roast for you. If you're looking for rib eye steak, request chuck eye. (You may need to ask the butcher to cut a 4-inch roast off the front of the boneless chuck, then to peel out the chuck eye and cut it into steaks.) Instead of pork tenderloin, buy an entire loin roast and ask the butcher to cut it up for you.

If you're going to buy a canned ham, purchase the largest one you can afford. Most smaller canned hams are made from bits and pieces glued together with gelatin. Cured hams are injected with a solution of brine salts, sugar, and nitrites. The weight of the ham will increase with the injection, and if the total weight goes up by 8 percent, the label will usually say "ham with natural juices." If the weight of the ham increases by more than 10 percent, the label must read "water added."

Never buy meat that's already been shaped into patties (unless it's on sale). Instead, buy your own and shape into patties yourself. Place a sheet of waxed paper between each, then place the entire stack in a resealable plastic bag and put in the freezer.

Even if you want to prepare low-fat meals, you don't always need to buy the leanest (and most expensive) ground beef. If you're preparing hamburgers on a grill or on a broiler rack, most of the fat will be lost during the cooking process, so stick with the moderately lean varieties.

PRODUCE

If you're buying produce that is priced by the item rather than by the pound (such as a head of lettuce, lemons, or avocados), take advantage of the store's scales and weigh them to find the heaviest one. This way, you'll be sure you're getting the most for your money.

The best way to save on produce is to buy fruits and veggies when they are in season. Any crop will be much cheaper when a farm near you is harvesting it, because the price won't include the transportation from another country. When a harvest has been particularly good, expect deep discounts as distributors try to get rid of a product before it goes bad. Visit Eat-TheSeasons.com to find out what produce is in season in the US and Canada.

When selecting limes or lemons at the market, go for the biggest you can find. They tend to be sweeter than their smaller counterparts.

When corn is piled high in supermarket bins, go for the ears that are on top. Why? Corn gets rapidly less sweet the warmer it gets, and even the heat generated by all the corn on the top of the pile can make the corn on the bottom start to lose its deliciously sweet taste.

When shopping in the freezer aisle, avoid packages of frozen vegetables that have frost on them. It's a sign that the food has thawed and refrozen, and a percentage of moisture has already been lost. You should also give bags of frozen food a quick squeeze before putting them in your cart. If the food is solid, it has thawed and refrozen, and should be avoided.

WHERE TO SHOP

It may be a pain, but the best way to save on groceries is to shop at more than one market. You'll soon find that one store will have cheaper produce, one will have cheaper meat, and so forth. Explore grocery stores you've never shopped at—perhaps one that is closer to your workplace or gym rather than by your home—and you may find even lower prices. We've even found cheaper products at stores that are the same chain, just a different location. Write down the prices of your most frequently purchased items, or bring a receipt from an average grocery trip with you. That way you can be sure to remember where the prices are the most reasonable.

Any time a new grocery store opens up in our area, we always stop by to take a look. It may be a pain to navigate differently laid-out aisles, but new supermarkets offer big sales and the lowest prices possible in their first few weeks and months of business, as an incentive to get shoppers to switch stores. Many stores also offer contests and giveaways to celebrate their grand openings, so visiting during the first week is a good idea.

Especially in cities, stores by and for immigrants abound. Whether it's a Mexican, Indian, Ethiopian, Chinese, or Korean grocery, you'll find cheap deals on foods that are native to that country. Bulk spices can be especially cheap, and you'll also find items such as inexpensive tortillas and avocados. We never buy rice unless it's from an ethnic market, as it's usually up to 80 percent cheaper than buying it at the grocery store.

Need a little help budgeting your trips to the supermarket? Many chains now offer prepaid gift cards. Buy one for yourself and think of it as a portable checking account: Put money on the card, then "withdraw" from it every time you shop. With a dedicated grocery "account," you'll find it's easier to keep a tighter rein on your spending.

Shop later in the day to take advantage of markdowns in your grocery store's bakery and meat departments. Also make sure to keep an eye on the prices at the salad bar. If you only need a few artichoke hearts or croutons, they may be cheaper to buy there by the pound than elsewhere in the store.

» Household Items

AT THE STORE

Let's be honest. If you have kids or pets, your furniture is going to get banged up. So why not get deep savings on furniture that already has a few dings on it? Almost all furniture stores sell floor samples of their merchandise. Ask a sales representative if the store is willing to sell the floor samples; often, stores have sales specifically for floor samples and the salesperson can tell you when that happens. Otherwise, they may only be willing to sell the floor sample if it's the last piece left. Ask if you can leave your phone number for when the rest run out, and don't be afraid to bargain on the price!

If you're shopping for accessories to match a color on a bedspread, couch, or piece of art, taking a photo often doesn't cut it. Especially if you print it out on your home printer, the variance in color from the photograph to the actual article can be dramatic. Instead, go to a paint store and pick up paint swatches that you think are similar in shade. Then go home and find the closest match. Mark that color, then bring the swatch to the store instead.

When you're shopping for towels in a superstore, skip housewares and go straight to the automotive section. You'll find packs of 12 white terrycloth towels, often for as little as $5. They're durable and can be used anywhere in the house.

When shopping for carpet, here's a strange-but-true rule of thumb: The carpet will seem a whole shade lighter once you get it home. Don't ask us why, but it holds true every time!

BEFORE YOU GO

When shopping for carpet, make sure you do more than just leave your swatches on the floor. When you've narrowed your decision down to a few different shades, take them outside and get them a little dirty! You may surprised how well dirt is hidden—or revealed—on each sample.

If you're in the market for a new TV, DVD player, portable music player, or other electronic device, the best time to buy is in the late spring and early summer. Prices will drop because new products are usually introduced in the late summer and early fall. New computers are also often released in February, so shop in January for savings.

If you're looking to buy large appliances or household furnishings like a washing machine, dryer, dishwasher, refrigerator, or sofa, the best time to buy is in October. At this time of year, businesses are busy making room for their holiday inventory, so you'll find tons of sales on last year's merchandise. Go ahead, celebrate a little early!

WHERE TO SHOP

Overstock.com has great prices on everything, but if you're looking for furniture, it should be your first stop. They carry furniture that has been discontinued, so you can get deep discounts on pieces for every room of your home.

....

It's nice to be able to look at furniture in person before you buy it, but the internet usually has the cheapest prices. The solution? While you're at the store, write down the piece of furniture's brand and model number (which can usually be found on the price tag). Then type that information into Google and see what prices come up.

....

Looking for inexpensive, quality building supplies? Check out one of Habitat for Humanities' Re-Stores, which sell used and surplus wood and other building materials for low prices. To find a location nearest you, visit Habitat.org/env/restores.

....

Instead of buying something you'll only rarely need, how about renting it? Zilok.com puts you in touch with local businesses and individuals who are renting cars, vacation homes, tools, TVs and video game consoles, and more. Better yet, you can list your own items to rent! (Unfortunately, you can't rent out your kids.)

Auto

Baking

Beauty

Cleaning

Clothing and Accessories

Cooking

Decorating

Entertaining and Holidays

Health and Wellness

Home Repair

Kids

Money

Organization

Outdoors

Pest Control

Pets

Shopping

»
Utilities, Saving Energy

Vacations and Family Activities

Websites

» Electricity

AROUND THE HOUSE

Even when you're not using appliances, they still continue to use energy. So pull the plug when you're done with the blender, toaster, food processor, even your television—everything except appliances that need constant power to preserve a special setting.

One of the easiest ways to save money on electricity is to turn off electronics when you're not using them. To make it easier, get a power strip like the SmartStrip, which powers down devices based on one device's usage. For example, when you switch off your computer, the SmartStrip will cut the power to your monitor, printer, and scanner as well.

If you're trying to decide between deep or baby blue for your walls, you should know that lighter colors of paint well help you use less energy. They reflect the light and heat in a room better than darker hues.

You may not realize that most electric companies charge more for power during the day than at night. Contact your local utility to find out whether this is the case in your area. If it is, make sure to do all your laundry, dishwashing, internet surfing, and other power-intensive tasks during off-peak hours. We noticed the difference on our electric bill, and you will, too.

DRYERS

Removing the lint from the screen in your dryer may not be enough to make sure it is running as efficiently as possible. The fabric softener used in dryer sheets can get caught in the mesh, even if you can't see it. To be sure you're completely cleaning the screen, remove it and clean it with warm, soapy water and a brush. Leave it out to dry completely before placing back in your dryer.

LIGHTS

If you know about going green, you've probably heard about compact florescent bulbs. If you haven't changed out your regular light bulbs yet, do it today! Not only will they last ten times longer, they use up to 75 percent less energy, bringing your electricity bill down.

....

One of the easiest ways to waste money is by leaving lights on that aren't being used. Save your hard-earned cash by buying motion-activated lights for your home, especially for bathrooms and hallways. It may seem expensive at first, but they'll pay for themselves soon enough. You'll love seeing a smaller electric bill each month!

—*Kitty Lubin Rosati, Crested Butte, CO*

REFRIGERATORS AND FREEZERS

Leaky fridge? If your refrigerator is more than a few years old, the rubber lining that runs around the door (also known as the gasket) could be loose. To find out, close the door on a piece of paper. If you can pull it out without it ripping, your gasket is loose. To figure out where, turn on a battery-powered lamp or flashlight and place it in your fridge. Turn the lights off in your kitchen and close the door. Wherever you see light peeking through, cold air is leaking! Try regluing your gasket or buying a new one from wherever you purchased your fridge.

Your freezer is more energy efficient when it's full of stuff, so don't be shy about stuffing it as much as possible. When you're running low on food items, just fill a few empty juice cartons or soda bottles with water and use them to fill up the space.

You can make your refrigerator more energy efficient by understanding how it works. Refrigerators use energy to reduce the humidity inside, which helps cool foods. Therefore, any time you leave an open container of liquid inside, you're wasting energy. Make sure all your pitchers have lids, and make sure dressings and moist leftovers are well covered. You should also let hot foods cool for up to an hour before placing them in the refrigerator, so the fridge doesn't have to use extra energy to bring them down to room temperature.

It may be time to rearrange your kitchen for energy-efficient savings. Keeping appliances that heat things up (like a stove, oven, or toaster) away from your refrigerator will make it easier for your fridge and freezer to stay cold, which can save you lots of money in the long-run.

....

A chest freezer will remain colder when its door is open than an upright freezer (even though its door is larger than an upright freezer's). This is because cold air is heavier than hot air, and tends to stay put when the door of a chest freezer opens up. Meanwhile, an upright freezer releases most of its cold air the minute the door is opened. Buying a chest freezer can save you money both in energy costs and by giving you a place to store food you've made ahead of time, which will (hopefully) cause you to order in and eat out less.

» Heating and Air Conditioning

AROUND THE HOUSE

Be smart when using your heating or air conditioning. When the heat's on, open the blinds on windows that are exposed to the sun, and use a little solar heat to help out your furnace! When you have the AC going, close as many blinds as possible, so that the sun won't get in and warm your house more than necessary.

....

Close the heating and air-conditioning vents in rooms in your home you don't frequently use, like a guest room or laundry room. If your vents don't have closures, simply seal them off with duct tape.

—Barbie Rodgers, Wilmington, NC

According to the Environmental Protection Agency, a well sealed home can be up to 20 percent more energy efficient. Most leaks occur in the basement or attic—look where you feel a draft or around wiring holes, plumbing vents, ducts, and basement rim joints. You'll be able to seal lots of leaks with a simple caulking gun, but for instructions on how to plug larger holes, go to EnergyStar.gov and search for "plug leaks."

For accurate temperature readings, make sure to place your thermostat away from sources of artificial heat, like ovens, appliances, computers, or direct sunlight. An inaccurately high temperature at the thermostat will cause the rest of the house to be colder than you want it to be. Similarly, make sure that cold air, such as that from windows or wiring holes, isn't making its way to the thermostat either. Also, ensure your thermostat is reading the inside room temperature and not the outside temperature.

If your furnace and AC don't seem to be paying attention to your thermostat, don't call the expensive repairman just yet. It could be a simple case of your thermostat's connectors being dirty. Take off the casing, and run the point of an index card through the connectors to remove any crud. Stand back and cross your fingers, and your thermostat may be as good as new.

UTILITIES, SAVING ENERGY: ELECTRICITY | HEATING AND AIR CONDITIONING | WATER

COOLING

It may feel like a waste to keep the fans on at the same time as the air-conditioner, but it's not. You'll actually save money, because you can keep the thermostat higher once you've created an internal breeze that will make you feel several degrees cooler (think of how much the wind outside affects how cool you feel, regardless of the actual temperature). Keep the fan on only while people are in the room, though, and remember to regularly vacuum both fan and air-conditioner vents for optimum efficiency.

In the summer months, make sure to keep your closet doors closed. Otherwise, you're paying to cool your closets, which will increase your energy bill.

The color of the White House isn't just tradition— it's energy-efficient! Painting your house (and especially your roof) a light color helps reflect light, which reduces the retention of heat and will keep your house cooler.

One way we save money on our electric bill is by providing our house with natural shade. Planting trees and shrubs so that they shade the sunny side of your home will help cut down on the amount of air conditioning needed.

HEATING

Brrr, it's cold in here! Wrap a very large piece of corrugated cardboard in aluminum foil (shiny side out), and place it behind your free-standing radiator. The foil will reflect the heat, and you won't have to keep telling your landlord to turn up the boiler.

When it's time to turn on the heat, be patient. Your house won't heat up any faster if you crank the thermostat way up, but you *are* likely to forget to turn it down, which can be a huge energy waster.

It's true that it's not the heat that makes you feel warm, it's the humidity. Humid air feels warmer than dry air, so in the winter, instead of cranking the heat, run a humidifier. This allows you to turn down the heat, save energy, and still feel comfortable. Live, leafy plants also help raise humidity levels.

Don't let your fan go to waste just because it's no longer warm outside. To stay toasty during the frigid days of winter, hit the reverse switch to push hot air down into your room.

In the winter, don't just keep windows closed, make sure they're locked for the tightest possible seal. This could greatly reduce drafts.

....

If you have a sliding glass door that's rarely used during the winter, seal the top, bottom, and sides with duct tape to keep cold air from coming in.

—*Belinda Duchin, Portland, ME*

» Water

DISHWASHERS

Much of the energy your dishwasher uses is during the dry cycle, when it heats up water to the point of steam. To save energy, turn off the dry cycle (or simply open your dishwasher after the rinse cycle is done). Leave the door open a crack and let your dishes drip-dry. You'll save a lot by avoiding the heat-drying cycle on your machine, and your glasses will streak less.

....

Having an Energy Star dishwasher is energy-efficient, but not when you are running it twice a day. Cut back on the amount of space you take up in your dishwasher by washing large pots and pans the old-fashioned way—in the sink. By using a little extra water to wash these items separately, you'll save a lot of water in fewer loads washed.

HOSES

If you've ever turned a sprinkler or soaker hose on and have forgotten about it, then the mechanical water timer is the gadget for you. Available at your local hardware store, these hose attachments work like egg timers and turn off the water supply after the amount of time you specify, usually between 10 minutes and two hours.

SHOWERS

If the showerheads in your home were installed before 1994, you should seriously consider replacing them with their modern, energy-saving equivalents. Check out your local hardware store for low-flow alternatives, and remember that just because it's low-flow doesn't mean it has to be weak!

Quit fiddling with the knobs on your shower when trying to get the water just right before you hop in. Find your favorite setting, then mark where the knob is pointing on the tile with a dab of nail polish. This water-preserving trick is great for kids, who often take a long time adjusting the water before they get in.

Does your teenager take 45-minute-long showers? If you have teenagers, try giving them an incentive to take shorter showers. A great one is five minutes added on to their curfew for every minute they shave off their showering time.

—*Salina Gonzalez, Minden, LA*

TOILETS

A great way to save water is to fill a plastic bottle or two with sand and put them in your toilet tank. You'll use a lot less water with each flush. Just make sure you place them away from the operating mechanism. Also, don't use bricks—they disintegrate and can damage your toilet.

—*Brad Elgart, Winters, TX*

Does your toilet have a leak? To find out, put a drop of food coloring in the tank and see if it shows up in the bowl. If it does, fix the leak to save up to 73,000 gallons of water per year!

WASHING MACHINES

The number one energy-sucker in everyone's home is usually heating hot water. Cut down on your bills by washing your clothes in cold water with a cold rinse. Due to advances in detergents and washing machines, the only time you really need to use warm or hot water is when you need to get a really bad stain, like red wine or oil, out of an article. Not only will you help the environment, you'll save money on heating the water, too.

WATER HEATERS

You never use your water on full-blast hot anyway, so it's worth it to lower how hot you keep your water heater. You can save up to $125 per year by simply lowering the thermostat on your hot water heater from 140° to 120° F.

....

A water heater insulation jacket (also called a blanket) costs $15–$35, but it can cut the cost to heat your water dramatically. By insulating your water heater, you'll cut down on the amount of energy it needs to use to heat standing water in half, also cutting down on the amount you need to pay. To find out if you need a water heater jacket, touch the side of it. If it's warm, it's leaking energy.

....

Make sure to drain your water heater once a year to get rid of sediment. Left too long, this grit can build up until you're using energy to heat sludge. To find out how to complete this simple home maintenance trick, type "how to drain a water heater" into Google or another search engine. And start to save!

Auto

Baking

Beauty

Cleaning

Clothing and Accessories

Cooking

Decorating

Entertaining and Holidays

Health and Wellness

Home Repair

Kids

Money

Organization

Outdoors

Pest Control

Pets

Shopping

Utilities

》》
Vacations and Family Activities

Websites

» Activities, Free and Discounted

DEALS, FINDING

If you find Ticketmaster and other ticket sites as annoying as we do, you'll love ZebraTickets.com. Zebra Tickets collects ticket prices from around the web for sporting events, concerts, and plays, so you'll be sure to know which site is offering the best deal.

....

If you are an educator, a member of the military, or a government employee, always ask if there is a discount available to you! You'll often find travel and admission discounts offered to these groups. If you're over 60, of course, never ever buy anything without asking if there's a senior discount! Some discounts even start for those 50 and over. Even if you don't look your age, you might as well take advantage of the savings available to you!

FREE FUN

For ideas on fun, free activities to do over the summer, try checking out your community center or park district. Most towns have tons of free summertime events, from sports clinics for kids to free concerts for adults. See if they have a website or pick up a calendar at your local branch.

....

If you live near a big city, especially Los Angeles or New York, one of the most fun free activities you can do is attend a TV taping. Talk shows, sitcoms, and game shows are always looking for studio audience members, and it's not only a blast to see a show live, but also to get a peek at what happens behind the scenes. To get tickets to shows, visit TVTickets.com for shows in LA, or NYC.com for events and shows in New York (just enter on "TV show tapings" in the search box). NYTix.com offers an even wider range of New York tapings, but requires you pay $3 to take advantage of their "special relationships" with the shows. If a show you know and like is being taped in your area, try looking it or its network up online or seeing if there is a phone number at the end of the show to call for audience tickets.

Even if they normally have high admission prices, most museums offer opportunities for you to visit for free. If a museum gets money from the government, it's usually required to either offer free admission one day a week or to charge admission as a "suggested donation"— that is, you only have to pay what you want. Other museums have late hours that are free to visitors once a week or month. If you like looking at art, also check out galleries, where you can find cool, local art displayed for free in the hopes that someone will buy it.

If you love going to see sports, but don't love the price tag of taking your whole family to a professional game, consider amateur sports instead. Colleges as well as intramural leagues have games every weekend for free or a couple of dollars. It's great to support local teams, and younger kids won't even know the difference in skill between a pro player and a Division Three league anyway.

All you need to know when you're searching for fun things to do at Goby.com is what you're interested in and where you are (and, if you want, when you're going). Whether it's getting coffee, going to a playground, hitting up a museum, or more adventurous activities like sailing and horseback riding, Goby will tell you what's out there, and even give you a map to see where it is. The best thing about Goby is its straightforward, user-friendly design: no huge ads, no "sponsored results," no long loading times or signing up. For those of us who have spent a lot of time searching for things online, it's a welcome respite.

Sometimes, vacation is all in your mind. If you can't afford to get away but you feel like you're ready to scream, consider taking a personal day off work, and convince your spouse or a friend to do it, too! Then enjoy an empty mall, a relaxing afternoon at the beach, or just a huge brunch (complete with mimosas). Whatever you do, get out of your house (which will just remind you of all your chores), and have fun! You'll be surprised how refreshed you feel after a day away.

MOVIES

See a movie for free! Many museums and colleges offer free screenings of films. Sure, they're not the latest big releases, but if you're in the mood for a classic or artsy flick, check and see if they are offered nearby. Many facilities even have full-sized screens in auditoriums. And they won't get angry if you sneak in your own candy!

....

These days, it costs a small fortune to take your family to the movies. But at FilmMetro.com, you can get free tickets to advanced screenings and movies that have just been released! Search by city, or browse current listings. The pickings here are often slim, but the site gives you a sneak peak at future offerings, so if you make it a habit to check back often, you may be able to snag free tickets to the latest blockbuster.

....

The easiest place to get free DVDs may be at the homes of your friends! Try starting a movie-lending circle with friends or neighbors who also watch a lot of movies. Each person has another person they give movies to, and someone they receive them from. When you get your own movie back, it's time to pick a new one! You may want to pick a timeframe to exchange the movie— for example, sometime before each weekend or at a weekly book club or school-related meeting. Movie-lending circles are a great way to discover movies you might not have picked out yourself, but really enjoy.

....

You've probably heard of Netflix.com, where you pay a low monthly fee and receive unlimited DVDs in the mail, then watch and return them in postage-paid envelopes. But did you realize you don't need a computer to use the service? The company's well-staffed call center will set you up for an account, add movies to your queue, and even make recommendations for movies you might like. Best of all, you get patched through directly to a person—no sifting through automated menus and then waiting for a half an hour. You can reach Netflix 24 hours a day at 1-866-716-0414.

SKIING

Like skiing? You'll love Liftopia.com. It offers discounts on lift tickets for more than 100 ski resorts across the United States and Canada. You can search by destination, or by categories like "good for beginners" and "nighttime skiing." You can also sign up for an email newsletter that will let you know about upcoming deals.

THEME PARKS

Before you get to the theme park, consider the real money-wasters: food and souvenirs. Bring lunches from home, and give each child a certain amount they are allowed to spend at gift shops. For more indecisive kids afraid of hitting their limit, make sure to offer them the chance to go back for an item in a store if they don't find anything they like more (they usually will).

Nothing's more fun than taking the kids to an amusement park, especially when they've been begging you to do it for two summers now. Whether you're going to a local Six Flags type of park, or going all out for that Disney World vacation, call the park and ask about deals and discounts. Most parks (or their automated representative) will tell you about current deals being offered, and may offer promotions of their own. Also check the website of the individual park you're visiting.

Looking for savings? Visit AmusementPark.com, which has great deals on tickets to amusement parks around the country. They also have savings on local tours, dinner cruises, museums, and tourist attractions.

Headed to Six Flags or another theme park or attraction? Go with a bigger group and you could get a discount. If you have at least 15 people in your party, you can usually get a good deal, depending on the time of year. Just call up the park or visit their website to see if they offer group discounts.

If you're headed to an amusement park over the summer, keep an eye out for merchandise tie-ins. Many products—especially soda and chips—offer easy discounts such as bringing the wrapper or can to the park to get several dollars off.

» Booking Travel and Lodging

AIRFARES

Flight days flexible? Try searching for trips that begin and end on a Tuesday or Wednesday, when we've found that flights throughout the US and Canada are cheaper.

....

Planning a trip to a far-away locale? Before buying plane tickets, check out booking sites such as Expedia. com, Kayak.com, or Orbitz.com, which show the cheapest deals from every airline. Once you've found the best prices, write down the flight times and/or numbers and check the airline's site directly. You may find a better fare.

....

If you're looking for the best deals in travel, head over to AirfareWatchdog.com, which catalogs the cheapest fares as they are listed on travel and airline sites. The nice thing about this site is that it polices all the different sites for you, rather than offering fares itself (like Expedia, Orbitz, and other sites). If you normally spend a lot of time trying different combinations of travel dates and nearby airports, this site will take a lot of the guesswork out of it for you.

....

If you've been to an airport lately, you've probably noticed that the ticket counters are staffed by fewer people than ever before. It's annoying on a regular travel day, but if there are lots of flight cancellations, this can mean a two-hour-plus wait in line. Save yourself a lot of time by skipping the line all together. Instead, call the customer service number for your airline and rebook your cancelled flight right over the phone.

CRUISES

If you're dying to get away on a cruise but don't want to spend a lot, check out CruiseDeals.com, which has packages to Alaska, the Bahamas, Hawaii, Mexico, and just about anywhere else you'd want to go on a boat. The company negotiates with some of the world's biggest lines to bring their customers the best rates on cruises. If you want to hit the water, this is the best place to start.

DEALS, FINDING

The best summer vacation you'll ever take might not be in the summer. As soon as Labor Day goes by, the rates go down drastically on hotels and airfare to most vacation destinations. Some of the most-discounted areas are the Caribbean, Hawaii, California, and anywhere else there's a beach. In a warm climate, it will still be as hot as ever on the sand. But the price will be much less, and you'll get the added benefit of having fewer crowds. Check out a travel site like Travelocity.com for good deals to your dream destinations.

When digging for discounts on rental cars and hotels, always call the hotel or rental company directly for the best deals. If the only phone number you have is a national, toll-free one, look up the local number for that particular location and speak to them directly instead. The closer you get to your travel date, the better—in fact, don't be afraid to call the day before to confirm your reservation and ask for a better rate.

Reward points getting out of hand? Check out Points.com, which lets you keep track of your airline miles at other rewards points, all in one place. Better yet, you can swap points from one reward program to another!

When searching for travel deals online, make sure to scroll through a few pages of results before making your pick. Many sites have "sponsored results," which means that companies have paid to be featured at the top of search results.

If you're headed to a large theme park such as Universal Studios and Disney World, your best bet for savings will probably be a package deal. Big attractions almost always offer package deals on—for example—a flight, hotel, and park tickets. These aren't usually significantly cheaper than buying tickets online through a site like Expedia.com or Orbitz.com, but they do often offer added incentives like free transportation or breakfasts.

....

If you're 26 or under, you have all the luck. Not only do your knees never get sore and people still try to flirt with you, but you can also get great deals when you're traveling in Europe. If you're aged 12–26, if you're a student of any age, or if you're a teacher or faculty member, you qualify for the International Student ID Card. Available at ISECard.com, the card costs $25, but with it you get discounts on trains, rental cards, tourist attractions, and more. Best of all, they'll provide medical travel insurance up to $2,000.

LODGING

When booking a hotel for your summer vacation, make sure to choose one that offers a free breakfast and an in-room refrigerator and microwave. Eating a couple of meals at the hotel is one of the easiest ways to save while you're away.

—*Rita Guerrero, Middlebury, VT*

....

If you're staying somewhere for a week or longer, you may be able to save money on your accommodations by renting a timeshare. Timeshares are pieces of property that are owned jointly by several different families, who split up their time at the property during vacation months. You'll often find people renting out their time, or landlords who rent out their properties on a week-to-week basis over the summer in tourist-filled areas. To find a cheap timeshare in your destination, search on Craigslist or Ebay. You can also try SellMyTimeshareNow.com and TimesharesOnly.com.

RENTAL CARS

Save money on car rental by not renting at the airport, which charges rental car companies concession fees. Instead, take a cab to a nearby location—even with the fare factored in, you'll be surprised how much you save.

—*Drey Luca, CA*

If you're renting a car for your vacation this year, try Rent-a-Wreck (RentAWreck.com), which offers older cars (that are far from being wrecks, by our standards!) at discounted prices. You can also try asking at local dealerships to see if they rent cars—many have begun to in an attempt to make extra cash!

When looking for great deals, Hotwire.com is a good place to turn. The downside to this site is that you don't know which airline you're flying or which hotel you're staying at until after you've booked. While we aren't always a fan of this format for flights or lodging, for cars, who cares what dealer it is, as long as it's at the airport?

» Camping and Fishing

CAMPING

Waking up to the sights, sounds, and smells of the forest can be one of the most peaceful things you'll ever experience—not to mention, the most inexpensive vacation you'll take in years. If you've never gone camping, it's time to start! If you don't have any equipment, ask friends if you can borrow theirs in exchange for lending them something of yours. You and your kids will enjoy working together while roughing it (and don't worry, "roughing it" can involve bathrooms and showers, electricity hook-ups, and even wireless internet). Best of all, with all that hard work each day, plus all the room in the world to run around in, your kids will get exhausted fast! To find campsites across the United States and Canada, visit ReserveAmerica.com, and for a great article for first-time campers, go to RoadAndTravel.com/adventuretravel/campingforfirsttimers.htm.

....

When going camping, mark your campsite by tying brightly colored helium balloons to a few trees nearby. Your tents will be easy to find even from far away.

—*John T., Murfreesboro, TN*

....

If you have a propane lantern, soak the wick in vinegar for several hours before you use it. This will prolong the life of your wick, helping you get more for your money.

Always, always pack duct tape when you're going camping. It's a must-have to repair rips or holes in tents and air mattresses and can be used to string up food out of bears' reach. You can even use it while you're hiking. Tape your pant legs to your boots with duct tape to avoid bites from ticks, flies, and mosquitoes.

Rain on a camping trip is enough of a bummer; it doesn't have to ruin your campfire as well. Melt paraffin wax (available from the supermarket) in a coffee can inside a pot of water on the stove. Remove the can and begin to mix in sawdust until you have about 3 parts sawdust to 2 parts paraffin. Pour into paper cups and let cool. Then all you need to do is pop them out of the cups and store them in a Ziploc bag. They'll light up easily when the time comes. Now all you need is a spark.

Before your camping trip, smear petroleum jelly on some cotton balls and keep them in a Ziploc bag. Even if you find yourself camping in the middle of a rainstorm, these bits of kindling will definitely get your fire roaring.

This trick is an old family favorite. Wrap rocks in foil and place them in your campfire. When it's time for bed, take them out and let cool until comfortably warm, then place them at the bottom of your sleeping bagfor toasty toes.

—*Greg Schoenfeld, Dawson, MN*

....

Whether you're on a big camping trip or your kids are just sleeping in the backyard for fun, place a long sheet of aluminum foil underneath each sleeping bag to keep moisture from sinking into the fabric.

FISHING

If you're getting ready for a big fishing trip by looking for bait in your backyard, begin by soaking an entire newspaper with water, then spreading it out in one hunk in your garden or on your lawn. Lift it up in the early morning, and loads of worms will be underneath. To keep your worms alive until it's time to use them, store them in a can with soil and coffee grounds.

....

Did you know that fish have a sweet tooth? It's true! To make some scrumptious bait, mix 2 cups flour, 2 cups cornmeal, and 2 tablespoons molasses into a thick dough. Roll it into balls and boil in water for 20 minutes. Place the balls directly in an ice water bath after removing them from the boiling water, and now you're ready to catch some fish.

....

If you use a hollow plastic tub jig on your fishing line, slip a small piece of Alka-Seltzer or denture cleaner inside before tossing it into the water. It will release a string of bubbles that will attract fish.

If you're caught without a lure and have a fishing trip ahead, use aluminum foil instead. Cover your hook with foil, then rip it away in small sections so that it will dance in the water. Fish will be attracted to the movement and reflected light.

» Eating Out

AT THE RESTAURANT

As if you needed another excuse to sit at the bar, here's one more: many restaurants offer the same food at the bar as in the main restaurant, but for cheaper prices. You may have to order a few dishes to share since the portions may be smaller, but your savings will still be substantial. And since most restaurants also have table service in the bar area, you can take the kids.

The easiest way to make a dinner out an expensive one is to order a bottle of wine—but who can resist a little pinot with their pasta? Get rid of this extra expense by going to a BYO (Bring Your Own) restaurant, which doesn't serve alcohol but will happy uncork (or de-cap) yours for you and pour it into a glass. Restaurants that serve alcohol also often allow guests to bring their own anyway—call ahead and ask. Some will charge you a "corkage fee," but it's usually a smidgen of what you would pay ordering off the menu. If you'd only like one glass on wine, try asking if there's a "house wine" available. Many restaurants will pour you whatever is left in a bottle from behind the bar for as little as $3.

DEALS, FINDING

At Restaurant.com, you can purchase gift certificates for local restaurants—for less than a third of the price! Enter your zip code or city, and you'll be taken to a list of restaurants in your area that are offering $25 gift cards for only $10. Most of the big chains are absent, but if you've been looking for an excuse to try out a local joint, this is a great one.

Love a particular chain restaurant? Make sure to visit their website and find out what deals they offer. Many sites offer a mailing list that will email you coupons, and other restaurants have a frequent diner program that will earn you free meals over time. Lots of chains have certain days each week in which they offer deals on particular entrees (especially for seniors). Ask your waiter or a hostess what the web address is (if it isn't written all over the menu!), or type the name of the restaurant into a search engine.

Almost all big cities offer a "restaurant week" once or twice per year. During this week, you can dine at some of the nicest restaurants in town for the cost of eating at Applebee's! Most restaurants will offer a three-course fixed price, or "prix fixe," menu that allows you to choose from several different options for your lunch or dinner. This is an excellent opportunity to try that fancy restaurant you've read about or seen on TV, but could never afford. Just make sure you don't order off-menu! That cup of coffee could cost you half of what you just paid for your entire meal!

No matter how hard we try, we always end up eating out way more than we'd like. It's easier to not feel bad about it when we go to a restaurant where the kids eat free. To find a bunch in your area, visit KidsMealDeals.com. Enter your zip code, and you'll find deals from chain restaurants and local joints alike, and they even have apps for iPhones and Blackberrys in case you need it on-the-go. Remember, a restaurant that offers deals for kids also usually offers frugal prices for adult entrees, so this site could potentially save you hundreds (or if you're as bad as us, thousands) per year. Bon appetit!

TAKE-OUT

If you're considering take-out for dinner, think first of your grocery store. Supermarkets often offer pre-made foods at a low cost to attract shoppers, and you'll often find low prices on rotisserie chickens, French fries, coleslaw, pasta salad, and more. Just make sure you don't make any impulse purchases once you're in the store!

How much do you spend each week eating out? To cut costs, find out if your favorite restaurants offer take-out, which is sometimes cheaper and will at least save you the tip. Pick it up on your way home from work, and you'll have a restaurant-caliber meal without the temptation of impulse purchases like another drink or dessert. You'll just have to supply the silverware.

If you often order take-out food, consider visiting your favorite restaurants at lunchtime. Most take-out joints offer lunch specials that are the same food as dinner for less. They'll usually come in smaller sizes, but we've found that we usually don't need what the restaurant considers dinner-sized portions. Buy in the afternoon, stash in the fridge, and then reheat at dinner for savings!

If you're a coffee fiend, you know how costly those delicious coffee-shop lattes can be. If there's a college or university near your home, check out the campus coffee shop for your caffeine fix—it's less expensive and just as good as the local Starbucks.

» Preparation

PACKING

Especially when you have to pack tons of presents, it's usually more frugal to pay to ship the contents of your suitcase to your destination ahead of time. Most airlines charge between $15 and $30 for the first checked bag and much more for the second, while it only costs around $14 to mail up to 70 pounds via the post office.

Packing for vacation? Consider packing clothes that are in the same color family, and pants that can go with a lot of different shirts. You can more easily mix and match them, so you'll have to pack less. This trick will also come in handy when you spill something on yourself—if your blue shirt soiled, you still have another in your suitcase.

> When packing a suitcase for a trip, put at least one outfit in the suitcase of your spouse (or other travel buddy). If your suitcase gets lost, you'll have at least a few clothes to tide you over until it's found.

When packing for vacation, place your pants in the bottom of the suitcase, with half of them hanging over the side. Place the rest of your clothes on top, then fold the pants back over on top of the clothes. When you unpack, your pants won't need to be pressed.

When packing a camera, place it in a plastic container for bar soap—usually the perfect size for your digital point-and-shoot.

Before you travel internationally, pack a spare passport photo and write down your passport number and the date it was issued. If you lose your passport while abroad, you'll have all the materials you need to get a new one. Bring your photo and passport info to a nearby US embassy: It'll take much less time to process your request if you come prepared.

Is your suitcase is a bit musty? The night before packing, pour a cup of baking soda in it, close it and shake. In the morning, vacuum up the baking soda and the smell should be gone.

When you return home from your summer vacation, throw a few dryer sheets in your suitcases before you put them away. The sheets will prevent any musty odors from festering while the bags are stored.

WHILE YOU'RE AWAY

If you are going on a long vacation and are unable to find someone to care for your plants, place a large container of water near your plant (if you have several, gather them into one spot to make it easy). Then place one end of a long piece of yarn into the water, and stick the other end into the plant's soil, near the roots. Lay the strand across the stalks of the plant. This will keep it moist until you return.

Now there's one less thing to worry about when you're on vacation. Water your plants yourself *in absentia* with this handy trick. Poke a small hole in the side of a plastic soda or water bottle, fill it with water, and place it hole-side-down in the soil next to your plant. The slow drip will keep your plant watered slowly but continuously. Now go enjoy your trip and know you won't come home to a bunch of withered geraniums!

....

If you're concerned about your house being broken into while you're away, don't stop at automatic light switches. Ask your neighbor to park his car in your driveway, so robbers will think someone's at home.

....

Many newspapers and magazines will allow you to suspend your home delivery or subscription. If you're going on a long vacation, make sure to call them up and stop service while you're away. You can also often do this for online movie rental and other services. You won't miss them while you're gone, and then you'll get an extra week or two when your subscription would normally be up.

....

The perfect time to take your car to the mechanic is while you're on vacation! The mechanic can take all the time he needs to fix any recurring problems and give it a tune-up, so you know it will get special care. Most mechanics don't mind keeping your car until you get back from your trip so that they can get more time to work on it!

Auto

Baking

Beauty

Cleaning

Clothing and
Accessories

Cooking

Decorating

Entertaining
and Holidays

Health and
Wellness

Home Repair

Kids

Money

Organization

Outdoors

Pest Control

Pets

Shopping

Utilities

》
Websites

Vacations
and Family
Activities

» Careers

CREATIVE SERVICES

If you have a gift for taking beautiful photographs, there may be a side career for you in photography. Advertise your services to become a wedding and special events photographer, and make some extra dough on the weekends—just make sure you have a sophisticated website where people can view your work. You can also make money selling your images to publishers and creative professionals who are looking for stock photography. Go to Shutterpoint.com, Dreamstime.com, or iStockPhoto.com to find out more about selling your images online.

If you're a good writer and have a love for your local community, why not share your knowledge with others for a little cash? Examiner.com regularly hires writers to write about events and community interest articles from around town. Just go to Examiner.com and click on "Write for us." DemandStudios.com (which supplies articles to eHow.com) also hires writers, as well as copyeditors and videographers. The base pay isn't much, but you'll get more money as you get more hits to your page.

INVENTORS

Do you have an idea for a great invention, but not enough money to get it off the ground? Then you'll love Quirky.com. Submit an idea for a new product on the site, and get feedback from the Quirky community on how to make it better. Then put it up for a vote on the site and if your product wins, it will be manufactured and sold to companies like Target, Toys "R" Us, Barnes & Noble, and more—and you'll get a portion of the proceeds! To find out more information, go to Quirky.com/learn.

MYSTERY SHOPPING

Mystery shopping can get you free products and a bit of money on the side, but most of all it's downright fun. Visit a store, then fill out an online survey about your experience. The pay isn't much—usually not more than $15—but you'll be reimbursed for products as varied as designer sunglasses to lunch and a beer at a restaurant. Check out one of our favorite mystery shopping services at GAPbuster.com/mysteryshop.

....

If you're interested in mystery shopping, it can be hard recognize the scams from the reputable offers! (One tip you should know: You should never have to pay to be a mystery shopper.) Search for mystery shopping and focus group opportunities near you at MysteryShop.org/shoppers, which is run by the Mystery Shopping Providers Association.

RESEARCHERS

If you're between jobs and have a laptop and typing skills, court researching can be a perfect way to earn money. Companies pay you to visit your local courthouse with a laptop and find the information they're looking for in public court records. Check out Jellybean Services at Work4jbs.com/jbs/cr.htm or Sunlark Research at SunlarkResearch.com/Work-for-Us.php.

SELLING ITEMS

If you've ever been interested in selling cosmetics, kitchen items, candles, toys, books, or more, find out everything you need to know at DirectSelling411. com. It contains a directory of legitimate home-selling opportunities and everything you need to know about joining up with various companies (including how to claim it on your taxes).

....

Are you a crafter? A knitter? A genius with paper mache? Etsy.com will give you a worldwide venue to sell your item. Sign up for free and get your very own virtual shop, then pay 20¢ for every item you list. You can set the price at whatever you want, and when it sells, you pay Etsy 3.5 percent of the price to handle the credit card transaction. You can also pay extra fees to be featured on the Etsy home page, which is visited by thousands of people looking to buy handmade items.

TRANSLATION SERVICES

Do you know more than one language well enough to translate written words? If so, you can make between $10 and $50 an hour working from home. Visit TranslatorBase.com to find people needing free-lance translators for material in many languages, including English, Spanish, Chinese, French, German, Japanese, Portuguese, Italian, Greek, Russian, Arabic, Korean, and many more. Projects range from large websites to a single marriage document.

TUTORS

If you know how to play an instrument or have a background in math, science, or English, tutoring may be a good way to make some extra cash. If you have a bachelor's degree and a fast internet connection, sign up to be a tutor at EduWizards.com.

Do you have something you teach? Join SkillShare.com and connect with people across America who want to learn your skill, which could be anything from cooking to origami to selling real estate. SkillShare gives you a unique forum to list your class and your price per student, and will even help you find a place to hold your class. In return, it takes 15 percent of the fee you collect. A similar site is Limu.com.

WORKING FROM HOME

There are many opportunities available for becoming a customer service representative right in your own home. Sign up with Alpine Access (AlpineAccess.com) or (Arise.com/work-at-home) and you'll receive calls from customers needing help from major organizations like Sears, Office Depot, and the IRS. You usually need to provide your own computer with a high speed internet connection, and sometimes an extra phone line, but you'll make up to $14 an hour and won't even have to change out of your pajamas.

....

Did you know that Google occasionally offers telecommuting jobs? Though open positions are not always easy to come by, it's worth it to check out Google.com/about/jobs/locations/multiple to see if they have any openings. Some jobs, like reading their ads to make sure they make sense, don't have many requisite skills, and you still get to work for one of the top-rated companies in the world!

....

Make that typing class you took way back when pay off! If you're quick and accurate when it comes to typing things up on the computer, you may want to try out KeyForCash.com. Register with the site and take an evaluation test, and you'll be on their list of people willing to type for cash! You'll get paid per 1,000 (accurate) characters/keystrokes, and the amount changes depending on their demand and supply of typists. Workload also varies, but some people have reported getting a lot of work around tax time. In any case, if you're quick at a keyboard it's worth checking out!

» Deals and Freebies

BABY SUPPLIES

There are a plethora of websites featuring free stuff for newborns, but one of the best is BabiesOnline.com/offers. There, you'll find loads of free offers and discount coupons for mothers-to-be. They have free magazines, formula samples, coupons for baby food, contests to win free diapers for a year, and more. All you have to do is check off the offers you want, then fill out your name, address, and due date.

If you are feeding your baby formula, make sure to sign up at Enfamil.com/Join to get free samples and coupons for Enfamil formula.

Get BabyCenter's free email newsletter, which allows you to track your baby's development week by week and includes articles on important topics hand-picked for your particular stage of pregnancy. You'll also receive valuable coupons, sale notices, and free offers from BabyCenter and their partners. It's available at MySavings.com/offer/baby-center.asp.

BOOKS AND STORIES

For free books, we love PaperbackSwap.com.
Featured on the Today Show and in Real Simple and
Good Housekeeping, the site allows you list books (not
just paperbacks) you don't want any more. Once you send
them to other users, you'll get credits you can use toward
a new (to you) book of your own.

....

**Head over to RavenousRomance.com for a free,
steamy short story each and every day!** Then
check out their great deals on full-length online novels.
Another great place to find free online romance novels
is PublicBookShelf.com. (Warning: Some of the stories
are explicit!)

CLASSES

**Did you know that, in addition to selling craft
supplies at great prices,** Michaels also offers free
classes on making crafts? Free classes often center around
a holiday (such as Mother's Day, Fourth of July, or Thanksgiving), and will teach you how to make something you
can bring home as a present or decoration. Michael's also
offers more general classes on beading, painting, and
other crafts for a small fee or free with purchase. To find
out what your local Michael's is offering, go to Michaels.
com and click on "Find a store." Once you've located your
nearest Michael's, click on "This store's events" to see what
kind of crafts you can learn for free.

....

Love to cook or wish you knew more? Take free cooking classes at your local Williams-Sonoma store. They offer technique classes and product demonstrations that range from making your own soda to cooking steak to dinner-worthy sandwiches. To locate your nearest Williams-Sonoma and to see their events calendar, go to Williams-Sonoma.com and click on "Store locator." Then keep an eye out for the "Store events" section.

....

At The Home Depot's Kids Workshops, you and your child can build fun projects like toolboxes, fire trucks, mail organizers, birdhouses, and bug containers. The workshops are free, designed for kids 5–12, and occur the first Saturday of each month in all Home Depot stores. These fantastic classes not only give you a fun activity to share with your kid (adult participation is required), they teach safety and skills. In addition to the newly constructed project, each child receives a kid-sized Home Depot apron and an achievement pin. Details can be found at HomeDepot.com. Once there, just enter "Kids workshops" in their search bar.

....

Lowe's is another good source for DIY kids' projects. Bring the entire brood into any Lowe's store and build a free wooden project. Each participant also receives a free apron, goggles, a project-themed patch, and a certification of merit upon completion of the project. Clinics are offered every other Saturday from 10 a.m. to 11 a.m., and all building materials and tools are provided. Get the details at LowesBuildAndGrow.com.

FOOD

OpenTable.com is not only convenient for making reservations at thousands of restaurants nationwide, they also give you freebies! Earn points each time you make a reservation, then redeem them for a free meal at any of their partner restaurants. Another great site for getting money back on meals out is RewardsNetwork.com. They give you points and money back on your tab at restaurants nationwide.

Thank God for Fridays! Go to TGIFridays.com and click on "Give me more stripes" to sign up for their rewards program, which gives you a coupon for a free appetizer or dessert immediately! You'll also get points toward free food every time you dine there.

You can get a free birthday dinner at Houlihan's! Just join their email club at Houlihans.com/EmailClub.aspx.

Want a free burrito? Receive a free birthday burrito at Moe's Southwest Grill by signing up for "Moe's e-World" at Moes.com.

Get a free chips and salsa and more by joining "Qdoba Rewards" at Qdoba.com.

Donut-lovers, rejoice! Dunkin' Donuts now has a reward program in many areas, and you earn a free cup of coffee just for signing up! Go to DDPerks.com and register for a rewards card that allows you to get free food and drinks when you use money that you've loaded on your card.

Join the "OJ Quench Club" at OrangeJulius.com/ Quench-Club. You'll receive a free drink or smoothie at an Orange Julius location.

How about some free ice cream? Get a free sundae from Friendly's by joining their BFF program at Friendlys.com.

Get a free sandwich at Schlotzsky's! You can join their "Bun & Fun e-club" at Schlotzskys.com.

Pancakes your pleasure? Sign up at IHOP.com for the "Pancake Revolution," their email list. Receive a free meal on your birthday and a freebie for signing up, along with other perks.

Want to know where the Burger King free sample truck is going to stop, which fast food joints are giving away free food on Tax Day, how to get free coupons to Olive Garden, and when new deals are being released at chain restaurants? Look no further than

EatDrinkDeals.com. They're a great all-in-one source for restaurant coupons, sales, and other promotions. You'll never have to eat out at full price again!

If you love making desserts, check out the site for coupons, contests, and freebies from Betty Crocker brands: BettyCrocker.com/coupons-promotions. In addition to their delicious cake and brownie mixes, you'll find deals from Bisquick, Green Giant, and Hamburger Helper. They even have a free iPhone application!

MONEY BACK

Even if trolling the internet for coupons isn't your bag, there is still one site you definitely need to sign up at: FatWallet.com. Signing up at FatWallet is one of the best ways to start saving money online immediately and easily. All you have to do is log on to the site before making purchases at such websites as Babies-RUs.com, Payless shoes, Nordstrom.com, Buy.com, and Walmart. They'll give you money back on everything you buy—usually 2–8 percent, and let you know if there are any coupon codes for sales on the site. You can even earn cash back for using travel sites like Hotels.com, Expedia.com, and JetBlue.com, and if you use an online dating site, you can save a huge portion on your membership (Match.com gives you 30 percent back and Chemistry.com 50 percent!). You'll usually have to wait several months for your money, but when it's as simple as clicking through, why not? (For more details on how it all works, check out their FAQ page.) And if you do enjoy coupon clipping, they also offer printable coupons and one of the best user forums about recent deals on the web. A similar site to FatWallet is Ebates.com, so check there if you don't find your store.

Have unused gift cards? Head over to PlasticJungle.com or GiftCardRescue.com to get cash from unused gift cards! They'll pay you a portion of the total cost of your card (around 80–90%) and resell it on their site. If you've purchased a deal from a site like Groupon or Living Social that you now realize you're not going to use before it expires, check out CoupRecoup.com, where you can sell your purchased deals to someone who will use them.

REBATES

Find loads of items on sale near you that are free after a mail-in rebate. Just visit PriceGrabber.com/home_rebates.php. This fantastic site lists hundreds of manufacturers' rebates and gives you everything you need to take advantage of them, including links to the rebate form online.

» Government Sites to Know

GRANTS AND FINANCIAL ASSISTANCE

The government has myriad programs offering financial assistance, awards, loan repayment and other benefits. If you own your own business, are paying for college, are or were in the military, are part of a minority group, or live in a rural area, check it out to see what you can get. The best way to see what is available is to go to GovBenefits.gov and fill out their simple questionnaire, which will give you a complete list of the programs for which you're eligible. You'll be amazed at what is available.

....

These days, college can cost $15,000–$35,000 for one year! And that's just for a bachelor's degree. The good news is that there is a lot of free money out there. FedMoney.org is the most comprehensive online resource on all US government grants and student financial aid programs. Here, you will find detailed information about who can apply and how for more than 130 government grants and loans related to education. You can also check the US Department of Education's site at StudentAid.ed.gov.

LOST MONEY, FINDING

If you've ever had a mortgage insured by the department of Housing and Urban Development, you might be due a refund! Take a look at your paperwork or contact your mortgage company to find out whether you paid an upfront premium; then visit HUD.gov, search for "Refunds" in the keyword search bar, and click on the article entitled "Does HUD owe you a refund?" Then type your name and case number.

Did you know that more than 25,000 mature savings bonds aren't cashed each year? To find out if there is a bond in your name that you didn't know or have forgotten about, check out TreasuryHunt.gov or call 1-800-722-2678.

There is over $24 billion worth of unclaimed property in the United States, and Unclaimed.org is the official government site to find out if any of it is yours. Search by name and state, and be connected to federal and state databases to see if there is any money, land, or possessions that have been left to you and are in government custody.

RESOURCES

Whether you homeschool your children or one of them has expressed interest in a particular subject, it's hard to know where to turn online for accurate information. At Free.Ed.gov, you can find free, professional learning resources—including online videos, audio lectures, interactive features, and printable lessons—from government agencies. They list information by subject, including math, famous people, the arts, state history, and more.

....

The Health Resources and Services Administration (HRSA.gov) can direct you to a health center that provides health and dental care to people of all ages, whether or not they have health insurance or a lot of money. Just go to their site, enter your zip code, and click on "Find Centers."

....

According to the National Highway Traffic Safety Administration, approximately 175 car parts are recalled each year. If you're having a problem with your car, make sure to check out SaferCar.gov before you take it into the shop. The site allows you to search for recalls by part (just select "Vehicle owners" and then "Safety recalls"), which you should be able to get from a dealership for free. You can also sign up to receive email alerts about recalls for your car, and for child safety seats.

» Index

grease, 121, 122,
  145, 148, 175,
  389, 512
ink, 78, 175–176
ketchup, 176
laundry, 171–180
on leather, 170
on leather furni-
  ture, 144–145
lipstick, 104
mold, 103
mustard, 176
nail polish, 80
oil, 169, 170
paint, 177
perspiration, 171,
  173, 177
rust, 178, 513
setting, 171, 172
shoe polish, 178
on shoes, 191–192
on suede, 170
sun tan lotion, 178
tar, 179
tobacco, 179
tomato, 176
tomato sauce, 112
tub, 95
undiluted fabric
  softener, 169
unknown origin,
  177
vegetable oil, 176
on wallpaper, 148
wine, 121, 180, 296
on wood, 154
Stairs
  painting, 384
Stamp pads, 486
Stamps, postage, 336
Static cling, 195

Steam
  for cold relief, 366
Steel wool, 110–111
  for mice, 526
  sharpening scis-
    sors, 406
  tire cleaning, 15
Stews, 241
Stomach aches, 374
Storage, 477–479
  accessories, 466
  bathroom, 464–465
  batteries, 479
  candles, 300
  charcoal, 330
  cords, 472–473
  egg cartons for,
    473, 478
  under furniture, 476
  hanging shoe orga-
    nizers for, 478
  hydrogen peroxide,
    465
  linens, 474, 476
  marshmallows, 30
  medications, 465
  nail polish, 465
  pantyhose, 467
  paper towel tubes
    for, 479
  plastic boxes for,
    478
  shoeboxes for, 474
  shoes, 470
  skates, 470
  stamp pads, 486
Storage containers,
  111–112
  odors in, 111, 112
Stoves
  cleaning, 134–136

containing splat-
  ters, 134
Strawberries
  hulling, 216
  tooth whitening, 62
Stress relief, 375–376
Strollers, balancing,
  430
Studs, wall, 402–403
Style
  clothing, 192–195
Suede, 170
  storage, 182
Sugar
  attracting bees, 521
  in baking, 33
  brown, 33
  for browning pan-
    cakes, 203
  cheese mold and,
    219
  confectioners, 40
  decorations, 33
  for hiccups, 372
  "lemon," 34
  prolonging flower
    life, 308
  softening, 33
Sugar, brown
  chapped lips, 61
  exfoliant, 59
  facial masks, 59
  storage, 232
Sunburn, 363
  yogurt/oatmeal for,
    60
Sunscreen, 89
Sweaters
  laundering,
    180–181
  shrunken, 181

who knew?™
online

VISIT US ON THE WEB AT
WhoKnewTips.com!

- Money-saving tips
- Quick 'n' easy recipes
- Who Knew? books and ebooks
- And much more!

 Facebook.com/WhoKnewTips
Daily tips, giveaways, and more fun!

 Twitter.com/WhoKnewTips
Get a free daily tip and ask us your questions

 YouTube.com/WhoKnewTips
Watch demos of your favorite tips

 Pinterest.com/WhoKnewTips
Hot tips from around the web!